Globalization, the State, and Violence

Globalization, the State, and Violence

EDITED BY JONATHAN FRIEDMAN

ALTAMIRA
PRESS

A Division of
ROWMAN & LITTLEFIELD PUBLISHERS, INC.
Walnut Creek • *Lanham* • *New York* • *Oxford*

ALTAMIRA PRESS
A Division of Rowman & Littlefield Publishers, Inc.
1630 North Main Street, #367
Walnut Creek, CA 94596
www.altamirapress.com

Rowman & Littlefield Publishers, Inc.
A Member of the Rowman & Littlefield Publishing Group
4720 Boston Way,
Lanham, MD 20706

12 Hid's Copse Road
Cumnor Hill, Oxford OX2 9JJ, England

British Library Cataloguing in Publication Information Available

Library of Congress Cataloging-in-Publication Data

Globalization, the state and violence / edited by Jonathan Friedman.
p. cm.
Includes bibliographical references and index.
ISBN 0-7591-0280-5 (cloth : alk. paper)—ISBN 0-7591-0281-3 (pbk. : alk. paper)
1. Political violence—Case studies. 2. Globalization. 3. Citizenship. I. Friedman, Jonathan.
JC328.6 .G56 2002
909.83—dc21   2002002634

Printed in the United States of America

∞™ The paper used in this publication meets the minimum requirements of American National Standard for Information Sciences—Permanence of Paper for Printed Library Materials, ANSI/NISO Z39.48-1992.

Contents

v

Introduction

JONATHAN FRIEDMAN

The purpose of this collection is twofold. First it seeks to develop an approach to the understanding of the increasing violence that has occurred on a global scale over the past couple of decades. This is an endeavor that has crossed disciplinary boundaries and we have in a series of seminars had the help of urbanists, anthropologists, sociologists, and political scientists. As violence involves the structuring of local lives; of collective projects, and individual intentionality, we have made a concerted attempt to gain a purchase on the relations between global processes and local lives. This has led to our second purpose, which is to rethink and offer an alternative understanding of the global conditions that have been the source of so much contemporary talk, writing, interpretation, and media hype. This second purpose arises from an attempt to construct a more adequate comprehension of the global processes than has been provided in the language of globalization.

There has been a virtual flood of literature on globalization over the past ten years. A great deal of it has been of a celebratory nature and much of it has even taken on a self-conscious millennial pose. The latter is expressed in a dichotomization of world history or at least recent history into a past defined with an array of terms linking what appears as the bunker mentality of nation-state thinking—homogeneity, ethnic absolutism, racism, indigenism, essentialism—all of which express closure and can in themselves be understood as the source of the evils of the modern world. This is opposed to a future characterized by globalization, transnationalism, a

postnational world of hybridity, mixture, global flows of practically everything, and that evince openness and, as some would put it, a new cultural
liberty, the liberty of cosmopolitan existence. Thus, before we were local,
national, and hopelessly closed, but now we can finally be open, postnational, and creole. The language of this categorization is itself worthy of
analysis. The announcing of a new era began in numerous quarters, led by
business economists, and mostly clearly advocated in the work of Kenneth
Ohmae, who heralded the demise of the nation–state and its replacement by
a more efficient globalized capitalism. This position is today associated with
what many call neoliberalism, since the freeing of capital accumulation
from the bounds of national interests and controls is understood as the cornerstone of the increase in the welfare of the entire world. While postcolonial and cultural studies "theorists" would certainly deny the connection,
much of their language is extraordinarily similar. I have argued previously
that this is related to the transformation of Western ideology over the past
couple of decades, a shift that has promoted liberalism to the core of what
it means to be progressive while much of what was previously thought of as
progressive has become relegated to conservatism and even to reactionism.
This is also the discourse of many dominant global elites both political and
cultural who are associated with media, with international organizations,
and with information technology and its global consultancies.

Not all of the literature on the subject has been so completely positive
vis-à-vis the liberating force of globalization. There are the works of political-
economy-oriented researchers that have taken up much of the globalization process in terms of the restructuring of capitalism, increasing rates of
circulation, time–space compression, increasing levels of exploitation, dislocation, poverty, exclusion, and cultural and ethnic fragmentation. But
this research has been acceptable to the global elites referred to above only
to the extent that it is ambivalent, stressing the basically positive aspects of
the new era that we are headed for and interpreting the negative aspects as
spin-off or simply as inevitable, the unfortunate costs of the brave new
globalized world. The recent reactions against globalization have even resulted in some attempts by former celebratory advocates to backtrack in
admitting the underside of globalization. But the latter is still understood
as a phenomenon of nature that requires structural adjustment and elicits
the basic hope that things will work out in the end. Hutton and Giddens
(2000), intellectual representative of this self-defined progressive and cau-
tious globalizing elite, has recently gathered a collection of representatives
from the academic and world capitalist community to present a politically
correct perspective on the current trend. The book is appropriately titled

On the Edge and it might be taken as an official elite view of where we are headed and what the elite can do to make our voyage a success. In his defense of the Third Way, he goes to some lengths to redefine a progressive identity that is simultaneously that of the establishment

> "Radicalism" cannot any longer be equated with "being on the left." On the contrary, it often means breaking with established leftist doctrines where they have lost their purchase on the world. (Giddens 2000:39)

This statement is crucial in understanding the formation of a new elite, a new center, and it is significant that the equivalent of the Third Way in German is the *Neue Mitte*, neither right nor left, but in between, that is, just right. For champions of *la voie unique*, both left and right, there is only one way to do things, only one viable road to the future, one that is truly adapted to changes that are understood as natural and to which, as good naturalists, we must adapt. Here is the secret of successful evolution.

Now this position is not absurd, of course, and I do not wish to belittle it. On the contrary, it is worth a good argument, and most of the chapters in this book are concerned with making a good argument, starting from the empirical description of a world that is clearly not evolving toward an ecumene of sharing and understanding but one in which polarization, both vertical and horizontal, both class and ethnic, has become rampant, and where violence has become more globalized and fragmented at the same time, and is no longer a question of wars between states but of substate conflicts, globally networked and financed, in which states have become one actor, increasingly privatized, among others. This is not chaos by any reckoning, and one of our purposes here is to discover the systematic nature of the global as it configures what might appear as chaotic, at most, and disjunctive, at least, on the surface. It is precisely this surface understanding that is the source of much of the naturalistic, evolutionist, and millenarian jargon that many of the contributors to this book oppose. In the following chapters there are suggestions as to a way of framing the current situation, one that accounts for both the globalization discourse itself, and the simultaneous real fragmentation on the ground that has been the source of much of the nationalist and ethnic violence that is today condemned by global elites as a sign of barbarism, a barbarism that is the true essence of localism.

The contributions to this book present a contrasting approach to the global than has been current in the past few years. For some of them, such as my own, this approach is rooted in a global systemic frame of reference that owes more to the Braudelian tradition than to that which became established in cultural sociology and is, in its anthropological trappings, closer to an older diffusionism, a relation that is often made explicit by its practitioners (Hannerz 1999; Appadurai 2000). This has led to a focus on a limited number of topics such as transnational migration, the movement of images, TV programs, films, brand names, commodities, all reduced to flows of cultural substance. The metaphors are of the trans-x variety and they stress often in quasi-evolutionary terms the need to go beyond all that is contained within any kind of borders. Now this is not a metaphorization that is the product of empirical research. On the contrary it is already being spontaneously generated in other domains of current economic and political activity, in the media, among consultancies, among diplomats, and among top politicians where globalization has become naturalized. Anthropologists (including Friedman 1999a, 1999b, 2000; Tsing 2000) have often criticized this tendency. Tsing, who is less critical than I am of this discourse suggests that globalization is a definite project, like modernization, and that it contains a great deal of pretension concerning the newness of the intensification of global flows. But in her recommendations she remains faithful to the idea that global analysis should be primarily concerned with issues of concrete interconnections among places as ethnographically describable. While this is clearly a component of the approach adopted here, there is much more to global process than transnational connections. In fact the latter are very much conditioned and even preconditioned by those systemic processes that distribute social conditions of existence, of differential power, of control over resources and people in the world arena. The cultural globalization approach is founded on a cultural diffusionism that itself is seriously essentialist in its tendencies. The very idea that it is culture that flows around the world is a seriously essentialized assumption in which the human practice of meaning is simply erased. This transforms the study of society into an all-consuming concern with identifying who people and objects are, that is, how they can be identified, rather than accounting for their lives. And identifying people is simply a question of ascertaining where they really come from. Thus, instead of explanation, we are offered genealogy. By elevating the cosmopolitan to the highest form of identity, much elite discourse consists in morally ranking people and societies with respect to their degree of their worldliness.

I mentioned above that there are plenty of dissenters from the celebration of globalization. Even those who once wrote of the "cultural freedom" to be gained by our entry into the new global age, have become critical. There is globalization and "globalization"—the kind that produces hybridity and felicitous cosmopolitan ecumenism, and the nasty kind that produces poverty and causes ethnic and other kinds of conflict and that subscribes to neoliberal ideology. This has led some to try to reformulate their position as explicitly normative, not the cosmopolitanism of the capitalists, but a "new and post-universalist cosmopolitanism" (Pollock et al. 2000:585), a "situated universalism" (585), which seems embodied in a yet-to-be-created "cosmofeminism" (584). This contorted and tortured language conveys a certain anxiety among those who may have thought that the world was moving in a different direction. But it is still totally grounded in the issue of culture and identity from which this kind of globalism first arose. Appadurai who has played a central role in this development that is so obsessed with the critique of closure bears witness to what must appear to him to be the paradoxical qualities of globalization, which in contemporary Bombay have, as he clearly argues, produced violent ethnic conflict and Hindu nationalism (Appadurai 2000). There even seems to be a touch of nostalgia for the cosmopolitan past of the nineteenth and early twentieth century, when the city was truly ordered and truly cosmopolitan, where Parsees (an expression of diaspora)[1] were famous philanthropists and where everyone had his place in the hierarchy.

> The truly destitute were always there, but even they fit into a complex subeconomy of pavement dwelling, rag picking, petty crime, and charity. (Appadurai 2000:629)

How edifying to know that everyone fit in so nicely in this cosmopolitan splendor! And why does it go without saying that cosmopolitanism is the solution, or that it is even the issue for those who live in Bombay? As suggested above, the genealogical mode of thought, via its unreflexive rewrite of reality, totally distorts the latter and asks questions that may be totally irrelevant in the lives of those we are trying to understand.

THE CHAPTERS

In chapters 1 and 2 the global framework is made explicit. Chapter 1 is an attempt to introduce, in a panoramic way, how the issues of this book are linked to one another, claiming that there is indeed a systematic relation between ethnic conflicts on chicken farms in Virginia, the privatization of states in Eastern Europe and Africa, ethnic war, flexibilized informal economies, global cities and globalizing discourses, and the global system in which they occur. Chapter 2 is a political economic analysis of the rise and demise of the nation–state and its cultural productions. Turner argues, as do other contributors, that the state is alive and well and that it is merely the nation that is dying or at least sulkily contracting. It also argues that much of the current discourse of "lemon" nationalism, just as the neoliberal discourse that seems to have penetrated cultural studies and anthropology, is part of the same transmuting world of capital accumulation.

In chapter 3 Sassen argues even more strongly that it is the nation–states themselves that have rewritten the rules of the game that has allowed multinational or as they are now called, global firms, to demand new citizens' rights in relation to national governments. The issue of globalization cannot be understood without its locally grounded preconditions in the regulatory practices of states. Ghezzi and Mingione focus on the transformation of the labor market, arguing that the distinction between formal and informal is no longer applicable in a system of increasing flexibility, which at once presses wage levels by escaping social controls and combines numerous forms of transitional employment in ways that are adaptable to conditions of market instability and increasing global competition. Wieviorka offers a panorama of the transformations of the conditions and structures of violence that have accompanied the contemporary social changes that correlate with economic globalization. He argues for a model of the decline of "modernity" as a class-based formation with strong nation–states and imperial orders where the conflicts were clearly organized around such structures, and a transition to a fragmentation of such units and the emergence of new culturally based identities, social movements, and higher levels of social disorder that are the basis of new forms of violence.

The second part of the book concentrates on specific cases illuminated by a broader global perspective, one that is less oriented to "connections" and "movement," as such, as to global forces and their effects on life conditions. Wikan introduces an issue that has become problematic in the connection between migration and the structure of the modern welfare state. It is related to the control exercised by Muslim families over their daughters, the use of diasporic relations to maintain them within the separate community, and the confrontation with a Norwegian state in which other values and laws prevail, not least in relation to children's rights. Chapter 7 by Nonini details the parallel, if variable, effects of neoliberal globalization in three local situations taken from the South in the United States, Japan, and Indonesia where downward pressure caused by flexibilization and liberalization led to ethnic conflict between local nationals and immigrant workers. While the local situations and conditions are different, their relation to global process generates comparable results.

In chapter 8 Glick Schiller and Fouron provide a longer-term analysis of the way in which global capitalism has led to the social devastation of Haiti, from the collapse of its subsistence agriculture to its increasingly urban criminalized and drug-dependent economy in which remittances from the emi-

gration of one-seventh of its population are essential to the survival of the island population. Here global forces and globalized relations interact in the
production of local disaster. Kapferer's analysis of the transfigurations of sorcery in relation to global transformations demonstrates in a powerful way the
structural continuities and changes of form in several kinds of sorcery up to
the present postcolonial context. He argues as well against the currently popular discussions that simply equate sorcery with the modern, denying all historical process in order to discover something "new." Reyna's historical analysis of the decentralization of violence in Chad supplemented by a broad
comparison is the basis of an argument that the early centuries of capitalist
growth were about the formation of a predatory military-capitalist complex
that took on the form of increasing territorial centralization, both within
nation–states in the construction of colonial systems, arriving at a state structure
that provided Weber with his famous definition. The post–World War II era is
characterized by the abandonment of this centralizing tendency in the colonial world, first decolonization and then a more recent concomitant increase
in decentralized violence that has become fragmentary to the point of institu-
tionalizing a state of anarchic warfare, an anarchy that is thoroughly financed
by the great powers themselves. In chapter 11 Sampson focuses on the ways in
which global structures of funding, project personnel, and capital goods interact with processes of internal fragmentation, especially in the former East
bloc. He argues that the state is not a mere reactive locus to larger global
movements and projects. On the contrary, the state, understood not as a homogeneous object, but of congeries of actors and relations to resources, is actively engaged in constituting and reconstituting various forms of political
power in interaction with such projects and their personnel. Chapter 12 is an
analysis of the articulation of the global and the local in the disintegration of
Congolese political and social organizations. Ekholm Friedman argues that
the emergence of state classes in large parts of Africa in the 1970s and 1980s
organized in part in terms of the logic of kingship became independent of
their peoples, in the Congo case reproducing themselves on global flows of aid
funds and kickbacks from oil companies and appropriating all sources of internal revenue resulting in the internal disintegration of Congolese society.
The pullout of the West and the East from Africa after the fall of the Berlin
Wall led to a total collapse of these polities that took the immediate form of
"democratization" but in reality was a political, territorial, and ethnic fragmentation that has led to the violent destruction of the country.

    In all of these chapters there is a certain unity of focus. They all concern the
contemporary situation from a global perspective. This a situation in which there
is increasing violence of various kinds, in which the character of the violence is

increasingly based on processes of fragmentation of former political units and on the intensive incorporation of the new fragments into regional and global circuits of control and finance by both state and nonstate actors. In order to understand the processes involved it is necessary to take seriously the systemic changes occurring in the global political economy that have produced major shifts in forms of control over resources, the relation between capital and states (Sassen) and in the transformation of the conditions of livelihood and labor (Ghezzi and Mingione). The global transformation of capital accumulation is articulated to major reconfigurations of political power in the world, to major dislocations of population, to the disintegration of microsocial forms of life for many, and to the intensification of both everyday domestic, local, and regional violence. The analyses suggest that the global is about the relation between world processes, the distribution of conditions of social existence, and the way people in such conditions create and configure their worlds, whether they are the worlds of investment bankers or of the marginalized and "flexible."

NOTES

1. Parsees, who formed and form a true caste, one of the wealthiest in India, are identified by their Persian origins. But to treat their existence as evidence of cosmopolitanism conflates genealogy with cultural and social praxis. This seems to be a hallmark of much transnational thinking, a perfect exemplar of that so hated phenomenon, *essentialism.*

REFERENCES

Appadurai, Arjun. 2000. "Spectral Housing and Urban Cleansing." *Public Culture* 12, no. 3:627–51.

Friedman, Jonathan. 1999a. "The Hybridization of Roots and the Abhorrence of the Bush." In *Spaces of Culture: City, Nation, World.* Edited by M. Featherstone and S. Lash. London: Sage.

———. 1999b. "Indigenous Movements and the Discreet Charm of the Bourgoisie." *Taja: Australian Journal of Anthropology* 10:1.

———. 1999c. "Class Formation, Hybridity and Ethnification in Declining Global Hegemonies." In *Globalization and the Asia Pacific: Contested Territories.* Edited by K. Olds, O. Dicken, P. Kelly, L. Kong, and H. Yeung. London: Routledge.

———. 2000. "Des racines et (dé) routes" in L'Homme, no. 157:187–206.

Giddens, A. 2000. *The Third Way and Its Critics.* Oxford, U.K.: Polity.

Hannerz, U. 1999. "Epilogue: On Some Reports From a Free Space." In *Globalization and Identity.* Edited by B. Meyer and P. Geschiere. Oxford, U.K.: Blackwell.

Hutton, W., and A. Giddens, eds. 2000. *On the Edge: Living with Global Capitalism.* London: Random House.

Pollock, S., H. K. Bhabha, C. Breckenridge, and D. Chakrabarti. 2000. "Cosmopolitanisms." *Public Culture* 12, no. 3:577–89.

Tsing, A. 2000. "The Global Situation." *Cultural Anthropology* 15, no. 3:327–60.

Acknowledgments

This volume has been a long time in the making. It began some years ago with a project financed by the Harry Frank Guggenheim Foundation dealing with globalization, multiculturalism, and the nation–state. It has dealt with the way in which the dynamic reconfiguration of the world arena has led to a multiplication of forms of conflict and violence. The project involved me, Kajsa Ekholm Friedman, as well as a number of doctoral students. It was meant as part of a long-term effort to research the contemporary situation in global systemic terms. "Global systemic" is a term that we have used since the mid-1970s and cannot be reduced to the notion of "globalization" that has become so popular since the late 1980s. The kind of approach that we have engaged in is shared by our colleagues and is clearly in evidence in the current volume. The project led to the idea, even the necessity, of organizing a series of multidisciplinary workshops in order to expand on our original work. The present book is the result of three separate workshops sponsored by the same Foundation from 1996 to 1998. The workshops provided the basis for assembling and reworking the chapters into their present form.

I wish here to express my deepest gratitude to the Guggenheim foundation for its endorsement of our research through these years. I wish more specifically to thank Karen Colvard, program director, for her unfailing support throughout the entire period, for her wonderful hospitality, and stunningly successful efforts to make our meetings a success. I daresay that this endeavor would have been impossible without her support and engagement. I would also like to thank the participants in the workshops for making the series a fruitful and exciting venue for interdisciplinary discussion and cooperation. Special thanks go to Kristin Couper, the translator of chapter 5. The political as well as intellectual engagement required to understand the relation between global process and violence has been a source of inspiration for my own development and, I hope, for the other participants as well. I would like to express my gratitude to all of the authors who patiently waited out the long and sometimes painful process of production.

Globalization, Dis-integration, Re-organization

The Transformations of Violence

Jonathan Friedman

GLOBALIZATION AND THE GLOBAL SYSTEM

There is no doubt that the current period of world history is one of globalization. Capital accumulation has decentralized geographically at an accelerating rate since the 1970s. There is no need to repeat the well-known statistics of this phenomenon. Capital has not, however, flowed equally to all corners of the globe. East Asia has been the major recipient along with a number of other regions, including India, Brazil, Chile, and Mexico, albeit to a significantly lesser degree. Thus a view once common in international circles in the 1960s and 1970s that equated development with increasing underdevelopment in the Third World has been largely abandoned, although the world's poorest regions are still in the South. The world has indeed changed, and I recall an interesting debate that we were engaged in at the time of this preglobalization era. We had written a number of articles that attempted to understand the world system today in terms of a long historical process of civilizational expansions and contractions regulated by similar dynamics for the past 3,000 years. We suggested that the scenario was one in which the rise of centers of accumulation was not a static phenomenon but was followed by a decentering via a decentralization of the accumulation process itself. This, we said, could occur within a global system and take on the form of shifting hegemony within a larger central region. It was followed by a more general decline of the central region as a whole and a large-scale geographical shift. This kind of cycle occurred in the past and can be described for the rise and fall of previous centers of wealth accumulation and even of civilizations. The rise of Europe itself was a process that can best be understood as in counterpoint with the decline of the Middle East at the end of the Middle Ages. Thus European capitalism did not simply evolve from feudalism. It was a product of the shift of accumulation from one world region to another. Europe was, in this argument, largely a dependent area in the previous Arab empires, a relation that was gradually reversed in the centuries following the Renaissance. The foremost mechanism in this process was and is the decentralization of capital within the larger system, a phenomenon that we refer to today as *globalization*. So the entire history of Europe understood in global terms can be seen in terms of a series of pulsations, expansions, and contractions, from the growth of the Mediterranean and Flanders as the Middle East entered into its terminal economic crisis to the shifts from the Italian city–states to Portugal and Spain, followed by Holland and then England. Each of these cycles was characterized by periods of centralized accumulation and expansive trade followed by decentralization (capital export or globalization) and a longer-term shift in hegemony. In this century, England became the world's banker after being the world's workshop, and the United States took over the leading productive role. Periods of shift are also periods of increasing competition and conflict, even warfare. After World War II the United States was truly the workshop of the world but this changed rapidly throughout the 1950s. The Marshall Plan and a generalized and massive export of capital from the United States led to the rise of postwar Europe as well as Japan. By the 1970s the entire West had become a major exporter of capital to much of the rest of the world and this might be seen as a major shift of accumulation from West to East. The formation of the Pacific Rim economy from the 1970s until the late 1990s represents a substantial redistribution of economic power in the world system. This phase corresponds to the rise of the globalization idea and its institutionalization in the West. In fact it was a rather selective operation in geographical terms even if it changed the terms of competition in the world as a whole.

We have been hinting here at a cyclical perspective on the current phenomenon of globalization, calling it a phase rather than an era, an issue to which we shall return shortly. Before doing so it might be worth recalling that one of the most explosive developments in the world economy that has often been signaled as a novelty is the enormous expansion of financial markets. Their massive development is, of course, an important phenomenon to understand. Since the beginning of the 1980s, financial assets have been increasing 250 percent faster than the "aggregate GDP of all the rich industrial economies" (Sassen 1996:40). The current global financial markets are estimated to be worth about $75 trillion and the statistic has risen to $83 trillion in 1999, that is, three and a half times the OECD's aggregate Gross Domestic Product (GDP) (Sassen 1996:41; Sassen 2000:3). In contrast with world cross-border trade, $6 trillion and foreign direct investment, $5.1 trillion is truly astonishing. While it is debatable to what extent this is the product of the successful struggle of capital against the nation–state, it is not debatable that technological changes have made the movement of capital an instantaneous process in which sensitivity to conditions of accumulation has increased logarithmically. If this increase is related to the general trend in the growth of fictitious capital in periods of declining profitability of industrial production, it might be suggested that the current growth of finance capital (generated in the West) combines such tendencies with a new information technology that raises the rate of speculative turnover exponentially, thus accounting for the appearance of "global glut."

Globalization need not be an evolutionary stage of world history. There may indeed be tendencies to the establishment of worldwide institutional arrangements, of which the United Nations is but one example. But such tendencies have occurred in the past only to be replaced by opposite tendencies.

THE RECENT HISTORY OF GLOBALIZATION IN THE WORLD SYSTEM

We have suggested that globalization is a phase within the pulsation of the global system. We need only to return to the turn of this century to get an idea of the salience of this phenomenon as historical rather than world evolutionary. Globalization is not new at all, according to many who have actually researched the question. While there is much debate, there is also an emergent consensus that the world is no more globalized today than it was at the turn of the century. Harvey (1981), who has done much to analyze the material bases of globalization, puts the information revolution in a continuum that includes a whole series of other technological time–space compressions. Hirst and Thompson (1996) go much further in trying to despectacularize the phenomenon.

> Submarine telegraphy cables from the 1860's onwards connected inter-continental markets. They made possible day-to-day trading and price-making across thousands of miles, a far greater innovation than the advent of electronic trading today. Chicago and London, Melbourne and Manchester were linked in close to real time. Bond markets also became closely interconnected and large-scale international lending—both portfolio and direct investment—grew rapidly during this period. (Hirst and Thompson 1996:3)

Foreign direct investment, which was a minor phenomenon relevant to portfolio investment, reached 9 percent of world output in 1913, a proportion that was not surpassed until the early 1990s (Bairoch and Kozul-Wright 1996:10). Openness to foreign trade was not markedly different in 1993 than in 1913. In the 1890s the British were very taken with all the new world products that were inundating their markets (Briggs and Snowman 1996), cars, films, radio, X-rays, and light bulbs.

By the late twentieth century trade was booming, driven upward by falling transport costs and by a flood of overseas investment. There was also migration on a vast scale from the Old World to the New.

Indeed, in some respects the world economy was more integrated in the late nineteenth century than it is today. The most important force in the convergence of the nineteenth century economies was mass migration, mainly to America. In the 1890s, which in fact was not the busiest decade, emigration rates from Ireland, Italy, Spain, and Scandinavia were all above forty per thousand. "The flow of people out of Europe, 300,000 people a year in mid-century, reached 1 million a year after 1900. On top of that, many people moved within Europe. True, there are large migrations today, but not on this scale" (*Economist* 1997–1998).

This was a period of instability, to be sure, of enormous capital flows, like today. It was also a period of declining British hegemony and increasing British cultural expansion. Britain had no enemies as such, except those that it was helping to create by its own export of capital. Arrighi (1997) argues on the basis of historical research that massive financial expansions have accompanied all the major hegemonic declines in the history of the European world system.

To borrow an expression from Fernand Braudel (1984:246)—the inspirer of the idea of systemic cycles of accumulation—these periods of intensifying competition, financial expansion, and structural instability are nothing but the "autumn" of a major capitalist development. It is the time when the leader of the preceding expansion of world trade reaps the fruits of its leadership by virtue of its commanding position over world-scale processes of capital accumulation. But it is also the time when that same leader is gradually displaced at the commanding heights of world capitalism by an emerging new leadership (Arrighi 1997:2).

The period from 1880 to World War I was followed by a period of deglobalization and regionalization in the global system, one that was not reversed until the 1950s, a reversal that has accelerated in the 1970s until the present. There is already evidence today that the world is again beginning to regionalize strongly into three major zones, APEC, NAFTA, and EU. Of course the system has historically increased in size. Of course there is technological speedup and increasing capacities for movement. But it is not at all clear that such changes have led us to the threshold of a new era in human history, even if it might well be argued that "time–space" compression in itself may ultimately transform the very conditions of operation of the global system. Instead of either celebrating or castigating globalization, we would do better to try and grasp the potential trajectories and tendencies in contemporary historical change.

THE REGIONAL SHIFT

Whether or not one conceives global process in terms of shifting accumulation or the formation of a new globalized economy, there is a de facto emergence of a new powerful economic region. And in spite of the current crisis, there is no doubt that there has been a redistribution of shares in the world economy in favor of the Asian Pacific.

The fact is that as nation–states exist, the level of welfare is still a national phenomenon, that is, the degree to which capital investment tends to concentrate in one place or another. It is this clustering that makes it possible for Porter (1990) to argue for a comparative advantage of nations in an era of globalization. In 1956 the United States had forty-two of the top fifty corporations, a clear sign of hegemony over world production. In 1989 that number had dropped to seventeen. Europe as a whole has a larger number (twenty-one) of the fifty top firms today than the United States.

This would imply that the globalization of capital is a temporally delimited phenomenon or phase within a larger system rather than a general evolutionary phenomenon. It would in this case be related to the breakup of hegemonies, a process of fragmentation and decentralization of accumulation of wealth in the larger system. Now in the contemporary situation there are clear markers of this process. While production and export have increased unabated since the 1960s, the developed market economies decreased their share of total world production from 72 to 64 percent while developing countries more than doubled. Between 1963 and 1987 the United States saw a decrease in its share of world manufacturing from 40.3 percent to 24 percent. Japan increased its portion from 5.5 percent to 19 percent in the same period. West Germany was stable around 9 percent to 10 percent, but the United Kingdom declined from 6 percent to 5 percent to 3.3 percent. France, Italy, and Canada also declined somewhat in this period (Dicken 1992:27), and while there were quite significant increases in Spain, Brazil, and India, the Asian NIC countries have been the major benefactors of the decentralization of capital accumulation and especially of manufacturing (Dicken 1992:27).

Countries such as Hong Kong, Taiwan, Korea, and China have moved up rapidly in rank on the list of manufacturing export nations at the same time as the leading advanced economies have lost ground in this arena, some such as the United Kingdom and the United States, by significant amounts.

And it is the center that is the target market for this new production. Between 1978 and 1989 manufacturing exports to the United States increased from 17.4 percent to 31.8 percent. The process is one where exported capital produces products that are reimported to the center. The trend here is toward increasing competition, decentralization, and a clear shift of capital accumulation to the East (Bergesen and Fernandez 1995:24). The model for this argument is that rapid multinationalization of capital is a general process in periods of hegemonic decline.

That we are heading toward an increasingly integrated world, a globalized economy, is certainly a tendency in economic terms, but it does not necessarily mean that we are entering a new kind of world. The world of transnational capital and accompanying transnational institutions, clubs, classes, and elites is certainly a part of the globalization process, but this does not account for the changes in regional distribution of accumulation and power in the world. Globalization, in other words, does not mean unification or even integration in any other way than coordination of world markets. TNCs are, in important respects, the agents of decentralization of wealth rather than its geographical concentration.

The redistribution of manufacturing in the world system has led to a more or less three-way division of the world, with the developed Asian countries increasingly becoming the leading region while the United States and Europe have declined. So while there is clearly the emergence of a global structure of capital accumulation, the very rationality of the accumulation process is predicated on geographical shifts of capital. While transnational capital represents a truly global force, the geographical decentralization of accumulation still leads to declining hegemony in some areas and increasing hegemony, however short lived, in others. The ultimate question, suggested earlier, is to what degree a threshold of qualitative change is achieved in which entirely new structures establish themselves, in this case an institutionalization of global order via political reorganization. The emergence of global cities may be a sign of this kind of restructuring, but it is far from complete.

On the other hand there is clearly an increase in the regionalization of capital, the formation of three great blocks of investment. The major investors in China have been Japan, Hong Kong, Taiwan, Singapore, and the Chinese overseas communities. According to some estimates the Chinese diaspora, which constitutes only 4 percent of the total population, is an enormous economy in its own right (equivalent to two-thirds of China's GDP and is an important investor in China (three-fourths of China's 28,000 firms) (Camilleri 1997:22).

Another process that should be noted is the internal differentiation within the region itself. There are countries like Japan that have quickly moved from exporters of goods to exporters of capital and importers of goods, often of their own exported capital, a pattern linked to the decline of other major economic powers. Hong Kong has become a major investor in Shanghai real estate and in Guangdong industries, displacing a significant portion of its own home investment to the mainland.

PARAMETERS OF GLOBALIZATION I: HORIZONTAL FRAGMENTATION

The decline of hegemony of the advanced industrial centers has led to a process that I have previously described in terms of fragmentation. It relates the decline of modernist identification to an increase in "rooted" forms of identity, whether regional, indigenous, immigrant-ethnic or national. If the modernist nation–state is based on the identification of a subject population with a national project that defines its members, in principle, in terms of equality and political representativity, and which is future oriented and developmentalistic, when this project loses its power of attraction, its subjects must look elsewhere. The modern nation–state is founded upon a massive transformation of the world system in which a homogenizing, individualizing, and democratizing process in the center is combined with and dependent upon a hegemonic expansion in the rest of the world, the formation of a center–periphery organization. The modernist state is one in which the ethnic content of the nation is usually secondary to its function as a citizenry-based development project, in which cultural assimilation is a necessary by-product of the homogenization of regional and ethnic differences that might weaken the unity of the national project. The decline of hegemony is also the decline in the unifying force of its mechanisms of identification. Those who were partly integrated and stigmatized move to establish themselves and those who were totally assimilated must search for new forms of collective belonging. This leads to a range of cultural identifications that fragment and ethnify the former political units, from ethnic to religious to sexual, all in the vacuum left by a vanishing future.

Indigenous populations have increased in size since the mid-1970s, not as a matter of biology but of identity choice. It is estimated that there are 350 million indigenous people and they have become increasingly organized as well as winning a series of battles over land and cultural autonomy.

Subnational regionalism is also on the increase and forms, for example, a powerful lobby in Europe today, aiming for a combination of a strong centralized Europe and a decentralized nation–state. This has, like indigenous movements, been developing since the mid-1970s.

Migration is again a massive phenomenon in a destabilized world. But immigrants no longer come to their new countries simply to become good citizens.

On the contrary, the ethnification of such groups has led to a strong tendency to diasporization and to a cultural politics claiming recognition in the public sphere. In some cases this has led to a fragmenting of a former national unity. That is, rather than becoming assimilated to declining nation–states such groups maintain and develop transnational identities, cultures, and social existences.

National identity has become increasingly ethnified in this period as well in parallel with the ethnification of immigrants. This is expressed in the emergence of nationalist movements, and xenophobic ideologies that are themselves partially generated by economic crisis and downward mobility (see next section).

This process cannot be understood without placing it in the context of a weakened nation–state structure as a specific form of relation between people and their representative governmental bodies. The decline of modernism is very much a product of the weakening of the nationalizing component of the state machine, its tendency in the 1970s toward bankruptcy and general insecurity largely a result of the accelerating mobility of capital and taxable income. The transformation of the state is an issue in itself to which we must return. What is crucial here is that the focality of the state in identity formation is giving way to competing identities from indigenous, regional, and migratory populations. The latter has also entailed a decentralization of resources within the state, along broadly ethnic lines, and an increasing division of powers, between the state as representative of the nation and the subgroups that tend to displace it. This might be understood as a temporary phenomenon. Certainly with respect to immigration earlier periods of our history are filled with debates concerning assimilation versus weaker forms of integration or even the formation of more loosely federal structures (Kallen 1924). On the other hand situations in which the subgroups themselves were so organized are rare, and there was nothing like the strong multiethnic tendency that predominates today. From quite early on in the century, assimilation became the absolutely dominant policy in the United States, just as it was simply taken for granted in Europe. Assimilation was not only about the absorption of newcomers, but of the continuous homogenization of all sorts of cultural differences. Wieviorka (chapter 5 in this book) has reminded us that contemporary ethnic fragmentation is merely an aspect of a much broader cultural fragmentation including gender, age, religion, and most of the other cultural categories that constitute modern society.[1]

It is worth noting the difference between previous tendencies to multiethnicity at the turn of the century and the current situation. In the earlier period, while there were, as we said, debates on the reconstitution of society in multicultural terms, the same kind of debate was not present in Europe where assimilation was simply taken for granted.[2] Europe was still or-ganized around the combination of a strongly mono-ethnic/civil state and a colonial world structure in which coming to the metropolis was inter-preted as social mobility, an increase in status implying a will to assimilate to the superior. This was structured strongly enough to be more or less ob-vious to nationals as well as immigrants, regionals, and indigenous peoples. While there were clearly differences in the constitution of nation–states, such as the jus sanguinis of Germany and the jus soli of France, the process of assimilation was powerful in all cases. The high proportion of Polish la-borers in German industrial development did not deter their eventual ab-sorption into German national identity. The legal processes and cultural processes were not, of course, equivalent, and there was clearly both phys-ical and psychological violence involved. While the conditions of assimila-tion are difficult to ascertain, I would argue that the ideological situation in earlier parts of the century was strongly nationalist while this situation has become reversed in the past decades. This reversal or ideological inversion is an important aspect of the general situation. Gitlin (1995) has argued for the same identity shift in the United States. Earlier in the century, immi-grants came to become part of the country whereas today they come to re-main part of their countries of origin. Immigration in the current situation harbors strong tendencies to diasporization. The latter must be understood in terms of a set of practices in which identification with a homeland is the basis for the organization of cultural, economic, and social activities that transgress national borders.

GLOBALIZATION, INVERSION, AND HORIZONTAL POLARIZATION

It is important to note that it is not immigration itself that is the basis of ethni-fication but of the articulation of migration and social integration. In a period of declining hegemony, then, migration leads to ethnification, enclavization, and diaspora formation. The two arenas where ethnification is evident is in the public political discourses and struggles for recognition of such groups and in the ethnic formation of underclasses in the different national states. In virtually all western countries of Europe, there has been a significant increase in crimi-nalization within marginalized ethnic groups. In Europe such groups are pri-marily immigrants. In Canada, the United States, and Australia they are prima-rily black and indigenous populations. The parallels, however, are noteworthy.

There is a change in the view and also the activities of minority popula-tions. West Indians in the late 1960s and 1970s were not associated with crime in the United Kingdom.

A widely shared official view of the early 1970's that people originating from West Indies were a law-abiding community changed within three or four years to an equally widespread official view that black crime was a particular threat. (Smith 1997:173)

Similarly, in other parts of Europe, immigrants tended to integrate into the larger national arena. This does not imply that there were no conflicts, but that in the process of accommodation, the cultural hierarchy between national versus immigrant was clearly established. This situation began to be reversed from the late 1970s. The same people have now become ethnically stronger, and opposed to integration.

In Germany this is expressed in the shift to diasporic rather than national minority identity.

Although approximately half of eighteen-to-twenty-four-year-old immigrants express the desire to live permanently in Germany, the vast majority (73 percent) felt strong bonds to the home culture and denied a "German identity." (Siefert 1991:40 in Albrecht 1997:56)

The above examples are not so much expressions of migration but of changing minority identity in general. This accounts for the structural parallels between certain immigrant populations in Europe and more well-established minorities, not least indigenous populations in Canada, the United States, and Australia, all of which are settler societies. The tendencies for certain minorities to become parts of underclass or marginalized zones in a period of increasing cultural identification creates a highly ambivalent and cathected situation for those involved. Marginalized zones are increasingly integrated into nonnational sodalities. The latter provide conditions of reproduction in economic and cultural terms that the nation–state has not been able to afford. The result is the formation of oppositional identities that become increasingly transnational.

PARAMETERS OF GLOBALIZATION II: VERTICAL POLARIZATION

While cultural and social fragmentation is occurring with various degrees of confrontation and violence in the former hegemonic regions of the world system, there is another process that has been discussed widely. Class stratification in the old centers is on the increase and often in quite astounding proportions, not least in the old centers of the world system. This is not, of course, a simple process and is definitely not limited to a combination of impoverishment and the enrichment of a capitalist class. The stratification process includes significant elites connected to public institutions, international bureaucracies, and professional classes all of whom depend in varying degrees on tax funds, their speculative growth, and other sources of income that have been in one way or another transferred to the public sphere. I have referred to this earlier in my work as the global pork barrel phenomenon (Friedman 1997), which plays an important role in consolidating global class identities and novel cultural discourses. The economic parameters of this process in the old centers of the world system are well known through variations on a number of common themes. Countries like Sweden with a low level of class differentiation and countries like the United States with much higher levels, have experienced the same transformational vectors in the past decade, vectors that are common properties of a global dynamic. While the wealth ratio of richest to poorest in Sweden is 2.7 as opposed to 5.9 for the United States, the same kinds of changes have occurred. These are the economic vectors discussed in the first part of the chapter; the combination of global shift, speedup, and the changing composition of capital. The United States has experienced the clearest example of this kind of change where downward mobility since the 1970s has been a constant. Flexible labor regimes have expanded, leading to a larger proportion of working poor. Incomes have stagnated or declined and mobility has become increasingly limited. In Europe unemployment has reached alarming proportions. In Sweden it was above 12 percent in the mid- to late 1990s and has now declined, primarily due to public sector spending and make-work programs. While there is current evidence of a slight reversal of these trends they in no way match the economic growth rates of 2 to 4 percent that are their basis. In other words there appears to have been a structural shrinkage of the work force that is only offset in countries like the United States where there are large-scale low-wage service sectors.

The actual situations of populations vary significantly according to the degree of welfare. And the latter are very much products of the way in which the national arenas are constituted. At one extreme there is a cultural minimal state, which is approximated in the United States, where individualism and a sacred private sphere have entailed a certain disinterested tolerance for cultural difference as long as it is not politicized. In continental Europe, on the other hand, the nation–state has a much stronger cultural character and multiculturalism there appears as a serious threat to a former social contract that has always been considerably weaker in the United States. Public economics are clearly expressive of the different natures of the nation–state. In Europe the percentage of the population below the poverty line that is raised above that threshold by government transfers is between 40 percent and 60 percent with the Scandinavian countries approaching 100 percent. The equivalent figure for the United States is 0.5 percent. The United States sports an official poverty rate of more than 15 percent for the nation as a whole, jumping to considerably more than 20 percent in some states. If one calculates in terms of families and raises the income to $25,000, which might be a more adequate definition of the threshold of subsistence adequacy, then the figure rises to 28 percent (Hacker 1997:229). More important, with an unemployment rate below 5 percent, there's a considerable population of working poor. In both Europe and the United States the rate of ghettoization has been extreme and the formation of underclasses has been the formation of marginalized minorities as well, whose unemployment rates are often several times higher than those of the native born or more often those identified as "real nationals." Here of course there is a significant difference between polar extremes such as Sweden where in the relatively well-off welfare supported ghettos, unemployment reaches 90 percent or more, and states like California where entire industries are dependent on the influx of undocumented immigrants.

Downward mobility and deindustrialization have been accompanied by an upward mobility in the upper echelons of society. It is reflected in reports of enormous incomes among the capitalist elite as well as increasing incomes among political and cultural elites. The spate of scandals concerning credit cards, double salaries, long vacationlike "official" trips, and nightclub visits by politicians has led to a generalized crisis of confidence in the political elites. This crisis of accountability expresses an increasing rift between elites and the "people." The former along with capitalists, who were always in such a position, have been assimilated into a global circuit of relations with similarly placed people, so that elite interests have become forged into a class for itself in many ways. The European Union has become a kind of supernational and weakly accountable political organ that makes increasing numbers of decisions that affect national-level political situations. The real salaries of Union officials are considerably higher than those at the national level. And as there is no clearly defined social project, careers in themselves have become the modus vivendi of this massive reorganization of European political elites.

This kind of development at the regional and international level has produced new kinds of experiences for those involved. A person with such a career is very bound to his or her peers in the system. Representativity becomes less important than position itself. And the position may be imbued with a new moral posture. The cosmopolitan is promoted to a new kind of legitimacy. It is increasingly associated with a series of agendas that may contradict those of the nation–state itself. Sweden is interesting in this respect since it has been known for its strongly taken-for-granted welfare nationalism and stress on demotic power. Recent political discourse in Sweden has stressed a combination of multiculturalism, democratization, and globalization as the new agenda of society. The very notion of having control over one's social existence has begun to take on a negative connotation. In recent interviews on the concept of peoplehood, or *folk*, in Sweden I discovered a certain inversion in values. While it is, in fact, the case that the notion of folk in *folkhem* or people's home was taken over from the conservatives by the social democrats in the 1930s, it became associated with the notion of the people's will, with plebiscite, with concepts and symbols that expressed the notion of a "captured state" or a "captured elite," a dominant class that had been domesticated by ordinary working-class people. Such words, just as nationalism, were associated with the progressives in the 1950s through the 1970s. Today, however, there is an inversion of values. The notion of "people" is associated with reaction, nationalism with essentialism and racism. In my interviews, "plebiscite" was understood as dangerous, the concept of *folkhem* was highly suspect, and the expression "people's will" "smelled" of the 1930s. Opposed to this was the view of the nation–state as an obsolete object ready for the junk heap or for a serious face-lift. The New Age is the age of democracy, multiculturalism, and globalization. It is interesting to consider the reversal of perspectives in which a formerly nationalist elite, which may have seen "the people" as a motley foreign mixture, today identifies itself as hybrid/multicultural and views "the people" as dangerous purists.

COSMOPOLITAN DISCOURSES AND IDEOLOGICAL HEGEMONY

The formation of new globalizing elites is the social foundation of the increasing hegemony of celebratory globalization. Vertical polarization has characterized most of the societies of the West. It unites a number of political and cultural elites and links them to an economic project of transnational solidarity among such elites that sometimes mistake themselves for the "international community." This is the much-flaunted "revolt of the elites" discussed by Lasch (1995). The former implicit relation of representativity that united national elites with the "people" began to fracture as early as the 1970s in some countries, that is, during the same period as the nation–state began to weaken financially and multiculturalism began its contemporary career.

Le constat de l'épuisement du modèle social-démocrate a transformé les militants de la révolution, puis de la réforme, en militants du libéralisme culturel. (Julliard 1997:201)

And the notion of *classes dangereuses* was reborn (Julliard 1997:204). If the elite could be said to have been "captured" in the earlier phase of the welfare state, it has now been liberated. The product of this freedom is the production of a new set of discourses. Chief among these is multiculturalism and hybridity. The latter is a logical product of a real experience of the world from the top. A "We Are the World" encompassment of humanity is not a new perspective. It can be found in the proclamations of the Freemasons, various representatives of the British Empire, as well as in the more recent discourses of the Mount Pelerin Society and the World Economic Forum. The logic of this discourse is one that reduces the national population to an ethnic group among many and that seeks to replace national identity by pluralism. It is significant that pluralism was the core of colonial rule. J. S. Furnivall, one of the foremost analysts of colonial society, stated the case as follows:

> In tropical dependencies there was no common social will to set a bar to immigration, which has been left to the play of the economic forces. The plural society arises where economic forces are exempt from control by social will. (Furnivall 1948:306)

Cosmopolitanism in this sense implies the capacity to distance oneself from one's place of origin and to occupy a higher position above a world in which indigenous, national, and migrant populations all inhabit an enriched cultural territory. Cultural difference is consumed in the form of cultural products, from cuisine to art, and is, of course, the stuff for innumerable festivals and dinner parties. Difference is appropriated into the lives of the elites and becomes a kind of furnishing of their existences. The embodiment of the world's diversity becomes a new kind of self-representation. This is not merely the way the world is represented by postcolonial intellectuals, by the international media, and by other cultural elites; the language of this New Age is firmly anchored in the international business community and its own cultural producers. The New Age is also, of course, the age of New Age and the discourse of the latter, like related elite discourses of the British Empire's Freemasons, are excellent expressions of a structural position within the global system. The self-definition of contemporary managerial elites is strongly resonant and often configured by the kind of cosmopolitan encompassment befitting a journal like *Public Culture*.

> Now a new kind of human is developing on planet Earth. A Universal Human. A co-creator. Emerging from every faith, culture. You come from the traditions that nurtured you. . . . You express a unique being connected to the whole, mo-

tivated from within, leading you to creativity. Once you step into that you are no longer an American, a Buddhist, a Jew and so on. . . . We are part of cosmogenesis. We are the Universe in Person. (Salamon 2000:27)

In multinational consultancy firms, it is important to be "connected" to be part of a larger world in order to truly realize oneself,

J'avais 30 ans et j'aspirais à m'ouvrir sur le monde. . . . Je suis pour l'évolution: le décloisonnement est très enrichissant. On s'apporte mutuellement beaucoup. (Chemin 2001:22)

The metaphors of opening, of *décloisonnement*, of being unique and yet connected to the whole, carry the message of a new leadership, one that belongs not to the local but to the global. In the words of a well-known business consultant,

Awareness of global interconnectedness is the key. Most globally aware individuals can tell you about the gradual process they experienced or the "ah-ha" moment when they suddenly realized "its all one world". From Earth Day to the Amazonian rainforest, it may have been their interest in ecology and the environment; for others it may have been actual travels, or exposure to international organizations like the United Nations or humanitarian relief agencies, even the Peace Corps. Space exploration has also contributed to the "one world" realization. Whatever the source, being able to think and feel interconnected on a global level is what's causing the paradigm shift here. The world is borderless when seen from a high enough perspective, and this has all kinds of implications: socially, politically, economically, and even spiritually. . . . Regardless of how the awareness began, it generally culminates in a sense of global citizenship. . . . The best approach is to develop a sense that "I belong anywhere I am, no matter who I am." (Barnum 1992:142)

The same logic of this social distancing generates an embodiment of democracy as an inherent attribute of the new elites. Thus both Haider and "Red" Ken Livingstone are accused of being somehow basically undemocratic in spite of the fact that they have large constituencies. Recently the same reaction occurred in Scandinavia with respect to both the increasing popularity of Hagen in Norway and the vote against the EMU in Denmark. One Norwegian social democratic politician exclaimed that it was time to find a new population for the government since Norwegians were no longer democratic. Politicians and members of the cultural elite, journalists, and intellectuals, have become increasingly explicit concerning the undemocratic nature of the people. Populism has come to mean racism, Nazism, and communism in this discourse. The prime minister of Sweden stated that he would not allow a plebiscite on the EMU in his country for several years following an educational campaign (more than 60 percent of the population was, most recently, against the unitary currency). Alas, only the elites really understand what is best for everyone. Only they, by definition, are true democrats. Sweden has today got itself a minister of democracy, an entirely new position that has gone almost entirely without comment. The woman occupying this position has said in an interview that she obtained the job via her mother, a former minister of justice in the government. Politicians, who vote their own wages, have had the fastest growing incomes in the country in the past few years, a country in which the Gini index, the measure of economic stratification, has increased by a record 25 percent mostly since start of the 1990s (only the United Kingdom has experienced a greater increase).

To the extent that these representations resonate with a significant proportion of the populations of the West, they become naturalized and self-evident. This has been the case for many of those for whom they make immediate sense. Academics, artists, media "intellectuals," and others who identify themselves as the new "travelers," have been instrumental in the production of discourses of transnationalism and hybridity, border crossing, and a number of "antiessentialist" representations of reality. These have been employed extensively, sometimes in political projects, such as those of self-proclaimed multicultural states. In Australia, perhaps the most immigrant-dense country in the world, the government some years ago launched a multicultural policy program and a book called *Creative Nation* that was meant to recreate unity out of increasing diversity. An apocryphal story is that on one occasion a representative literary scholar went to talk to a group of Aboriginal artists and intellectuals, presumably to entice them into the new multicultural project. He went on for some time about how *mixed* the Aborigines were as a population and that any other view of themselves was tantamount to *essentialism*, that favorite word of cultural studies. When he was through, an older man rose and looked the hybridist straight in the eyes and said, "Listen, mate! I'm an essentialist and if you don't like it you can bugger off!"

There is clearly a conflict between hybridizing elites and those who identify as indigenous. Canada, another state that has declared itself multicultural, has faced similar opposition from Indians who refuse to be classified as just another ethnic minority. They are the First Peoples, and this, of course, is more than cultural distinctiveness. It is about rights to land and political autonomy.

There is little evidence that hybridity works on the ground. Attempts to establish "biracial" identity in the United States have had an interesting development. The biracial movement is primarily a middle-class activity and it contains a strong strategy of distinction making in which class mobility leads to attempts to separate oneself from a preceding, in this case, lower-status identity. The polarizing attractor in this is "whiteness." The logical contradiction in this kind of identification lies in the interstice between individual and collective identity. Every individual has a specific genealogy and is thus a very particular mixture. Collective creole identities in the past have always and continue to be closed ethnic identities, indistinguishable, in this sense, from nonmixed identities. The biracial movement split some years ago when Asian biracials protested the dominance of African Americans. The new group took on the title, *Hapa* Forum, *hapa* being the Hawaiian word for "half." This is a normal product of the above contradiction. Any attempt to form a collectivity must also create boundaries and raise issues concerning the particular constituents of that identity. Hybrid identity only works as a discourse, as an individual identity or in situations where the specificity of the hybridity can be ignored. It is thus most suitable for elites where the only commonality of the identity is that it is positioned above the fragmenting multiethnic world below.

PARADOXES OF GLOBALIZATION

What is often summarized by the term globalization is, in this analysis, a complex process of double polarization, of cultural fragmentation, and of the formation of transnational networks: economic, social, and cultural. These flows interact with the fragmentation process, often splitting it by creating microclasses. The example of the Maori is of importance here. The Maori indigenous movement made important inroads into New Zealand politics in the 1970s and 1980s. This led to numerous concessions, both cultural and economic. The restoration of tribal lands led ultimately to the establishment of "tribal capitalism" (Rata 1997) in which the tribal units were able to run fisheries while maintaining their conical clan structures. This created a new hierarchy of control within the tribal units since those closest to the central lineages were those who controlled the capital. The Maori today control a third of New Zealand's fisheries, but in an unequal way. More seriously, those Maori who do not have genealogical access to tribal land remain in their urban slums. They make up between 40 and 50 percent of the Maori population. Thus the Maori success story has created a class division within the group that did not exist previously. Throughout the world NGOs are helping to create similar kinds of divisions. The same kind of class division occurred historically among the Sami, between the small minority of reindeer owners and those who had been cut off from this livelihood and lost their territorial rights. There is also a considerable skim-off within the Fourth World that has created a traveling class of tribal representatives based largely around UN organs as opposed to those who stay home. Now this new class does not partake of a hybrid ideology as such, but they might be seen as minor actors in the multiculturalization of the world in which the hybrid encompassers occupy the apex. The interaction of globalization and fragmentation consists in driving a class wedge through the ethnic groups themselves, leading to a whole new set of internal conflicts. My own material from the Hawaiian movement contains instances of increasing divisions between central actors and the grassroots, which in some cases has led to the withdrawal of support for new "chiefs." There are international consultant firms today that specialize in what they call the "sovereignty business," specialized, that is, in milking the funds that are destined for indigenous groups.

At the same time indigenization has been a powerful factor of identification among the marginalized populations and underclasses of the declining hegemons. The ideologies of the New Rights in Europe, and militia groups in the United States are evidence of this. Many of these groups have strongly indigenous ideologies, invoking antiuniversalism, local autonomy, nationhood over citizenship, "tribal" religion, and antimodernist holism. There are African American Indian tribes such as the Washitaw who are allied with the Republic of Texas, and there are even examples of cooperation between Black Power organizations and the Ku Klux Klan, primarily under the common banner of antistatism, anticosmopolitanism, anti-Semitism, and separatism.

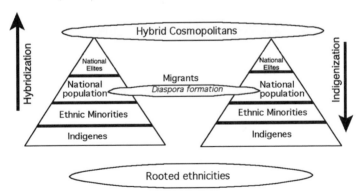

FIGURE 1.1
The dialectic of hybridization and indigenization.

These tendencies, summarized in figure 1.1, are not isolated from one another. They all interact on the Internet and are thoroughly embedded in the world systemic processes that we have discussed, the combined and seemingly contradictory phenomena of increasing cultural fragmentation in substantial parts of the world at the same time as there is an apparent increase in global unity in the form of communication, capital flows, and global elite formation. These simultaneities are organized by a single nexus of global political economic processes and form the basis for the differential identity politics that are sometimes referred to in terms of "globalization," the globalization of the local and the localization of the global. The latter metaphors, however, are not expressions of cultural processes in themselves but aspects of more powerful forces of local/global articulation. Class and ethnicity, vertical and horizontal polarization, are the two contradictory patterns that emerge from the dynamics of globalization.

But even class is constituted in the language of cultural identity, which, of course, is nothing new and surely adequate to a situation in which cultural production is increasingly stratified by the internal colonialization of the social order.

GLOBAL PROCESS AND THE STRUCTURING OF VIOLENCE

The process referred to by the term globalization results in a double polarization of the kind sketched above. In social terms it implies massive dislocation in the lower reaches of the global arena, not least in those zones that are party to hegemonic decline either directly or as peripheries. As the Western state relinquishes its national responsibilities, welfare declines seriously and perilous zones appear in the large urban areas. These zones are constituted by downwardly mobile nationals, second- and third-generation immigrant workers and newly arrived immigrants, products of the larger disorder in the weak links of the system. These weak links are the areas in which imperial orders such as the Soviet Union have collapsed or where peripheral postcolonial states have disintegrated, phenomena that are systematically connected to the transformation of the West as these areas were related via the import of funds and capital and now via the export of people. These are zones of ethnification, the privatization of the state, of warfare and banditry. The process of fragmentation has not been a particularly peaceful one. In 1993, for example, there were fifty-two major violent conflicts in the world in forty-two countries, the most severe conflicts being in Eastern Europe, Central Asia, and Africa. Half of these conflicts had been under way for more than a decade (UNRISD 1995:15). This is very different than the previous decades of the Cold War when there was a simpler division and a much stronger degree of control in the world system.

All but five of the twenty-three wars being fought in 1994 are based on communal rivalries and ethnic challenges to states. About three-quarters of the
world's refugees, estimated at nearly 27 million people, are in flight from or have
been displaced by these and other ethnic conflicts. (Gurr 1993:350)[3]

The fragmentation of these larger units is not merely a process of disintegration since the fragments themselves are integrated into larger networks of
trade in drugs, arms, and people. And the fragmentation does not apply only
to political, ethnic, or regional units. It penetrates into the basic social fabric,
dissolving kinship and even nuclear family sodalities, producing, as in parts of
Africa, a population of youths who are expelled from a larger context of sociality, of social integration, and of life cycle expectations. The capital circulating in such networks reinforces the fragmentation insofar as the fragments
are linked to raw materials or other sources of wealth, including the funds to
acquire weapons. For example, the liberation of young men from family structures combines with the political and economic projects of petty bosses in the
form of the proliferation of private militias supplied with arms from international networks, drug sales, and the control of local resources such as diamonds or oil. In terms of the organization/disorganization of social worlds
there is much to be asked and to be learned. The kinds of violence that are
most salient are located in the arenas produced by the process of disintegration of larger unities. There is a violence of lumpenproletarianization in many
of the word's urban zones. There is the ethnic violence that is related to soci-
ocultural fragmentation and there is the violence related to both of these that
consists in the formation of transnational criminal networks. The role of state
violence should not be underplayed here, but it should be noted that this violence, for example in Africa, is not part of a project of national integration
but of control over resources by privatized elites. The state has become an actor with its own special interests that are not related to the function of representing a larger population.

   The national spheres have got to be understood here in both historical and
spatial terms. Levels of violent crime are not well understood in relation to
their larger social contexts. In the material on ethnicity and crime there are
clear trends that relate ethnic dominance and racial discrimination as structures of society to the formation and reproduction of criminal habitus. That
blacks and aborigines are predominant among those overrepresented in crime
statistics in Canada, Australia, and the United States says a great deal about the
way in which the history and class structuration of such countries has created
such zones. The mirror image to be found in Europe is also quite interesting
where it is certain immigrant groups that are most overrepresented in criminal

activities: in France, Maghrebians; in Germany, more variations with a large percentage of Eastern Europeans such as Romanians; in Holland, Moroccans and Surinamians; and in Sweden, Arabs and Chileans. This is complex and the question of discrimination certainly plays a role in creating criminal subjects, but it is not sufficient. Middle-class blacks in the United States have substantially lower rates of crime and many minority groups of immigrants, such as East Asians are well known for being underrepresented in police statistics.

In Europe there is a clear parallel tendency among those groups that are overrepresented to becoming increasingly so over the past decade. This overrepresentation is also quite extreme. Ratios of five or six times the national rates are common for such ethnic categories (tables). The other side of this equation is the image/imagination of such groups where xenophobia is very much on the rise, in most of Europe reaching beyond 50 percent. "Fear of crime" runs parallel with other crime statistics.

This is the violence related to the fragmentation of larger homogeneous social worlds. The political violence of the past has proliferated into smaller operations. Wieviorka (1997; chapter 5 in this book) has referred to this as a "new paradigm" of violence, one in which broad ideological struggles are increasingly replaced by local identity struggles or simply fragmented interests of an economic or political nature. This, he claims, is an indicator of the failure of the modern project. The notion can be systematically extended in terms of the model of globalization suggested here.

The gamut of conflict harboring potential violence occurs primarily on the fault lines of larger social fields of which there are several kinds today. There are fault lines caused by fragmentation, lines that are discussed by Wieviorka and his coresearchers. But there are also the fault lines of transnational organizations themselves. These can be summarized by transnational associations such as politically and economically organized diasporas and organizations that have specialized in living off the larger disorder in the system. Diasporas create new fault lines at local levels to the extent that they represent fragmentation within larger state societies. They have and are accused of activities that are incompatible with the maintenance of the nation–state. This is true no matter what the activities involved. Ahiwa Ong details middle- and upper-class conflicts in residential areas of California that have been "infiltrated" by wealthy Chinese transnationals. Yen (1997) describes a conflict that arose in an Orange County California town where Vietnamese immigrants transformed the social space of an urban area into an Asian center, growing from 8 to 22 percent of the population. Conflicts arose between long-term residents, mainly elderly, in this mobile home capital of the United States before the establishment of Little Saigon, whose problems ranged from youth gangs to the noise of the nightclubs across the street from the mobile homes. The latter, afraid of "losing their homes and way of life" (56) protested and the city council had to intervene. In the end the elderly had to move their homes, but at substantial potential profits, with council help, since Little Saigon was all too important as a source of income to be forced to move or change its ways. Diasporic populations that have not fared as well have also become more seriously affected by underclass formation and entered into the international circuits of arms, drugs, and people that have plunged many of their members into seriously violent crime. In Europe, there are clearly established transnational networks for cocaine, heroin, arms, and refugees. These are targets of discrimination, but also sources of violence related to criminal activities in host countries or in turf wars and related conflicts.

There is an important difference between identity-based conflict and the violent activities of global networks, but both represent the violence that comes of disintegration of larger territorial homogeneities and/or hierarchical orders.

TRANSNATIONALISM AND VIOLENCE

The relation between transnational ideology and the interpretation of violence is wonderfully exemplified in Appadurai's "Dead Certainty: Ethnic Violence in the Era of Globalization" (1998). This elegant discussion reveals a clear underlying frame of reference that is largely taken for given. His argument concerns boundaries and matter out of place. He suggests that violence is about the reestablishment of the purity of once recognizable categories mixed (hybridized) by globalization. This depends on the notion that globalization causes matter to be out of place, categories to become ambivalent. Violence is a means of restoring the order of fixed categories against the process of globalization that creates havoc with such categories. There are two different kinds of havoc involved here. First is the territorial havoc of the existence of the wrong people in the space of the host. The second is the genealogical or ethnic content of the body itself and its ambivalence. Ethnic cleansing is about territories and not about bodies. The identification of bodies is merely a means for he cleansing of space. In our interviews with Swedish nationalists the motif of matter out of place is quite obvious. The leader of one of the nationalist groups in southern Sweden, himself a former communist intellectual, is concerned with the problem of space itself, the recognition of others within a social space of interaction and the problem of penetration of that space by the foreign. The leader in question is not against foreign cultures. He spends a great deal of time in Italy, and his girlfriend is from there. He recounts one of his visits to Rome, "If I were to wake up one morning and look out the window and see a Swedish hotdog stand in the piazza I would be disgusted. In the same sense I feel that other cultural forms have no place here in Sweden." I appreciate all cultures but they should be located in the places that produced them." In Appadurai's essay it is precisely this attitude that is seen as the problem. Globalization is producing hybrid, category mixtures and boundary crossings that should be celebrated as the core of the "postnational." Nationalists, reactionary by definition, would eliminate them by violence. There is, however, a great difference between matter out of place and matter mixed up, a difference between occupied space and the body itself. Appadurai conflates the two, presumably on the grounds that they both represent a certain kind of border crossing. The problem is that ethnic violence has not been concentrated to ambivalent subjects. On the contrary it has been primarily directed to known enemies. And, of course, the boundary crossings are not the result of a recent globalization but a commonplace of world history, not least in the areas pinpointed by Appadurai, ex-Yugoslavia, Burundi, Northern Ireland. To clarify the field of analysis I would suggest the following:

1. Violence is directed at an Other who is in conflict with the Self and that resurfaces or exaggerates identity.
2. Territorial violence is about control over spaces and, as a consequence, over the identity of persons who occupy such spaces.
3. The result of boundary making is that boundaries themselves become the zones of ambivalence. These are the zones of contact and therefore of a special kind of conflict. The conflict based on fear of elimination, of treachery, of ambivalence. These are the hybrid zones (see below), but they are products of the larger categories that establish the boundaries.
   A. It is not the boundary zones that establish the categories but the reverse.
   B. In Feldman's analysis of violence in Northern Ireland it is not the identity of Catholics and Protestants that is at issue, but the fact that their interaction is dense in the contact zones.
      1. The Irish case is exemplary insofar as there is a minimum of bodily signs that can be used to identify the other. The identification is instead based on knowledge of families and networks.
   C. The issue in Belfast border zones is not about ambivalence of identity but simply about matter out of place and about the contest over space.
   D. The fact that most violence occurs in this zone is related directly to the intensity of contact and interaction, to the ambivalence of the situation, not to the ambivalence of the identities of the participants.

That all violence against people out of place is an act of identification is in this approach a mere fantasy. Death is not a means of identification, but, as it always has been, a means of elimination. Certainty is not about disambiguating the other; it is about the elimination of the already identified. This totally reverses Appaduarai's argument. Rape is important in this respect. It would be quite insane to rape the ambivalent other if there were a risk that the other were in fact part of one's own group. Rape, on the contrary, produces a new ambivalence in destroying the purity of the other. It might in fact be argued that it is an act of defilement in the sense of impurification. All of this may be less interesting for those involved with the realities of the wars in Jugoslavia where imported mercenaries were among the major perpetrators of sexual offences. Kapferer's work on sorcery (chapter 9) proposes a more interesting frame where the destruction of the other is simultaneously the production of self. The defilement of the already identified enemy, by rape, which destroys the identity of the offspring, may be a powerful device of empowerment, or at least disempowerment of one's enemies. The penetration of the other is the destruction of the integrity of the other, the fragmentation of the other, and it is not senseless that the fantasy of dismemberment of the body is often related to the same complex of violent practices.

HYBRID ZONES

Following this argument we might argue that hybridity might also be used to refer to the dangerous ambivalence of contact zones. This would be closer to Feldman's description of the border areas of Belfast and to other similar border zones where instead of merger and accommodation there is seething ambivalence and potentially explosive contact. Arantes (1996) depicts the liminal spaces in Sao Paulo, Brazil, behind the cathedral, as zones of in-betweenness in which fear and compassion for the street youth who are assembled there produce a certain kind of interstitial space. The liminality of the zone is related to the lack of social control. It is here that there are often riots, that the police kill youths, where there is a "high incidence of robbery, drug dealing and open consumption of marijuana and 'glue', the construction of 'invisible' houses along with a general underemployment, begging and the peddlers of the illusion of a better life through lotteries, magic medicines and religious preaching" (82).

The trajectories, effectively and affectively encountered on the ground, are very different from an overview, such as that which can be seen from the top of some safe place. The steps of the attentive walker do not simply articulate disconnected and aleatory points of the landscape. The pedestrian takes risks, crosses thresholds and, in so doing sees differences, builds meanings and takes a stand (86).

It is precisely the view from the "top of some safe place" that seems to inform the celebratory discourse of hybridity, the view of the fabulous mixture of difference down there which is so common in many of the depictions of the urban as a "swirl," as a cosmopolitan wonderland. Hybridity unplugged, that is, minus the conflict, becomes an ideal image of the unity of mankind. This difference is, itself, a token of the vertical polarization that characterizes the contemporary globalized world.

VIOLENCE AND STRUCTURE

It might be argued that two kinds of potential violence are generated by the process of double polarization. Both are produced around the fault lines generated by that process. There is the violence of fragmentation that is a violence of differential identities in competition for economic resources and social space. This includes the ambivalence that is both the satisfaction and danger of cultural identification in disintegrating worlds. The practice of identity reintegrates the subject into a larger collectivity and is the core of the latter's constitution. But such identities can only exist in opposition to both larger and equally opposed identities in formation. The dialectic of integration and differentiation accounts for the volatility of the contemporary world arena where violence has become increasingly intrastate and fragmentary. The other form of violence is that produced by vertical polarization in the state units of the world system. It is based on the very destruction of larger identities. Within national states it consists in the separation of the elites from the people, in the cosmopolitanization of the former and the indigenization of the latter. The historical irony of this process is that the violence of nation–state formation in which lower order sodalities were pulverized in order to create individual citizens whose only identity was the state's nationally constituted "self" are now left behind with their nations to fend for themselves. This situation drives former nationals to seek roots, to become increasingly indigenous. In Europe it has led to a plethora of ultranationalist movements, some, like the New French Right, quite sophisticated, others like many nationalist and pro-racist movements, less so. Their common denominator is their communitarianism, a reinstatement of the value of the collective. This tendency creates strange overlaps since strong fundamentalist trends are also essentially communitarian. It might be argued that fundamentalism is itself a product of such communitarian tendencies. These are the tendencies that produce homogeneities confronted with the threat of social and cultural disintegration. This "rooting," as we have suggested, produces strange bedfellows as when black nationalists find common cause with the Ku Klux Klan. When mountain dwellers of various backgrounds, Christian fundamentalists, hippies and militia folk find common cause against the forces of the state and cosmopolitanism. The links go so far as to connect many Fourth World movements to elements of the New Right that are also antiuniversalist, anti-American, antiimperialist, against the Church and pro-Islamic fundamentalist. While the disintegrating peripheries of the former Soviet block were never nationalized as such, ethnification has been a simpler struggle for exit or for control over key political and economic positions and resources. Similarly, in Africa, the collapse of state power has led to an ethnopolitical struggle for power. Interestingly, however, in the central arenas of a more nationalized Russian sphere, the same representations have appeared in the form of extreme nationalism structured in ways that perfectly mirror developments in the West. Japan as well has undergone a similar process of nationalist reaction.

Two kinds of potential violence are generated by the process of double polarization described above. They are often combined and the separate categorization suggested here is primarily analytical, highlighting the point of origin of violence rather than its particular expression. Both are produced in and around the fault lines generated by the polarization process. There is a horizontal violence of fragmentation that takes the form of differential identities in competition for economic resources and/or social space. Agonistic identification is strongly ambivalent, being the source of both the satisfaction and danger of such cultural identity in disintegrating worlds. The practice of identity reintegrates the subject into a larger collectivity and is the core of the latter's constitution. But such identities can only prevail in opposition to either larger or to equally opposed identities in formation. The dialectic of integration and differentiation accounts for the volatility of the contemporary world arena where violence has become increasingly intrastate and fragmentary. Vertical polarization is characteristic of state units and is expressed in fracture of such units, the separation of elites from "peoples." In nation–states it takes the cultural form of cosmopolitanization of the former and the indigenization of the latter. The historical irony of this process is that the original violence of nation–state formation in which lower-order sodalities and communities were pulverized in order to create individual citizens whose only identity was that of the state's nationally constituted "self," are now left behind with their nationhood to fend for themselves. In Europe this has led to a plethora of ultranationalist movements. Some, like the New Right in France are quite sophisticated, while others, like the French *Front National*, more of an immediate nationalist reaction, are less so. A strong common denominator is a tendency to communitarianism, a reinstatement of the value of the collective. This is, in structural terms, a general tendency that might be seen to create strange bedfellows. The New Right, as well as certain American militia groups are quite supportive of Islamic fundamentalism and even Islamist violence against the international order. It might even be argued that what is called fundamentalism is a product of strongly communitarian tendencies, tendencies that produce localized homogeneity as a resistance to cultural and social disintegration. This "rooting" has enabled certain black nationalists to find common cause with the Ku Klux Klan in St. Petersburg, Florida, where the local Klan leader was a former official in SDS who sports a poster of Che Guevara in his office. The Washitaw Indian movement whose members are black and allied with the militia-based Republic of Texas and are openly fascist is a clear expression of tendencies to a certain fusion of horizons. It should not be overlooked that many of the proposals of Fourth World movements dovetail with those of the New Right. They are all localist, antiglobal, anticosmopolitan, anti-Catholic, anti-American, anti-imperialist. The editor of the left-wing journal *Telos*, aware of this conflation wrote some years ago:

> Three principles: self-determination, radical democracy (direct), federalism unite the new right with the left . . . a proposal for a more tribal structure . . . and all of this is in opposition to the "Universalizing New Class seeking to impose an abstract liberal agenda on everyone." (Piccone 1993:21)

It is difficult here to locate the precise difference between this indigenizing identity and that described above as ethnification. The source of the identification is, however, different in that it grows out of a situation of downward mobility and is directly expressive of an opposition to global elites even as it harbors strongly ethnic tendencies. For example, the anti-Semitism of such movements is directly related to the identification of Jews as representatives of cosmopolitan power, but the same is true of the Vatican, Washington, and transnational capital.

In the disintegration of the Soviet Empire there are similar tendencies to violent reidentification. As the former peripheries of Moscow were never integrated in fully national terms, ethnification or ethnopolitical renaissance has been a straightforward struggle for exit or for control by local elites of key political and economic resources. It is significant, however, that in Russia itself, which was more "nationalized," there is today an emergent virulent nationalism that is clearly reminiscent of other areas of the West. Even a declining and crisis-ridden Japan has recently begun to witness the return of extreme nationalist movements. In Africa, the economic and political decline of states has led to a rapid ethnification or, for some, tribalization of the political arena. Here the issue is not exit, but competition for control of the state itself since the latter is the major source of wealth and power.

At the upper end of this process is a nervous elite that has become increasingly identified with the cosmopolitan as a collector of cultural differences, champion of globalization and "democracy."[4] The insecurity of this newly acquired position has led to a virtual war against all forms of indigeneity, especially including demands for sovereignty. And since the transformation is quite rapid there is often fear of contact with the recent more national past, a fear of contagion. There is a growing tendency to conflate all forms of antiglobal or even anti–European Union sentiment with reactionary ideology, racism, nationalism, and populism. An editor of one of Sweden's major newspapers referred to the demonstrations against globalization in no uncertain terms.

> In anti-globalism, left and right can become unified in a new nationalism—against American, EU, EMU, NATO, free trade, migration, market economy and finally democracy.
>
> For younger generations who have grown up with disdain for politicians, encouraged by populist leaders on the left and right, the struggle against globalization a new front has appeared." (*Svenska Dagbladet*, Denmark, 14 August 2000:2)

The prime minister of Sweden confronting the Danish plebiscite decision not to join the European Monetary Union voiced his concern that this was a dangerous nationalist and right-wing tendency that needed to be countered. Elites understand that the people are a "dangerous" bunch in need of socialization into the correct norms of the modern world, the postnational world, run by state elites no longer representatives of the people but their masters. Democracy is no longer the description of a particular kind of political arena. It is a substance, a personal attribute, that is increasingly the exclusive possession of respectable political elites in contrast to the "people" who are conceived as essentially "populist." This enables them to single-handedly ostracize and marginalize dangerous misfits who express ideas unbefitting "democracy," whether on the "left" or the "right." The formation of this elite has been one in which executive functions have taken increasing precedence over parliamentary functions, as in the European Union but also in its member states, in which a new center has been defined as the only possibility of rule, the Third Way, *Neue Mitte, la voie unique*. This produces some nasty paradoxes, like humanist intervention, to bomb a country to democracy and tolerance; the witch hunt syndrome propagated by politically correct elites who today represent something that might simply be called "the respectable" as opposed to the riffraff, the rednecks, both left and right, and all in the name of progress. It is understandable that the political elites who have assumed the responsibility of representatives of democracy and not simply of their constituencies are increasingly worried that the people have no respect for them and that their lack of interest is directly observable in the polls. Fear of the demise of popular support has led to violent attacks on those who appear to be populist and thus popular. As Zizek has put it,

The *Neue Mitte* manipulates the Rightist scare the better to hegemonize the "democratic" field, i.e. to define the terrain and discipline its real adversary, the radical Left. Therein resides the ultimate rationale of the Third Way: that is, a social democracy purged of its minimal subversivesting [sic], extinguishing even the faintest memory of anti-capitalism and class struggle. The result is what one would expect. The populist Right moves to occupy the terrain evacuated by the Left, as the only "serious" political force that still employs an anti-capitalist rhetoric—if thickly coated with a nationalist/racist/religious veneer (international corporations are "betraying" the decent working people of our nation). At the congress of the Front National a couple of years ago, Jean-Marie Le Pen brought on stage an Algerian, an African and a Jew, embraced them all and told his audience: "They are no less French than I am—it is the representatives of big multinational capital, ignoring their duty to France, who are the true danger to our identity!" In New York, Pat Buchanan and Black activist Leonora Fulani can proclaim a common hostility to unrestricted free trade, and both (pretend to) speak on behalf of the legendary *desaparecidos* of our time, the proverbially vanished proletariat. While multicultural tolerance becomes the motto of the new and privileged "symbolic" classes, the Far Right seeks to address and to mobilize whatever remains of the mainstream "working class" in our Western societies. The consensual form of politics in our time is a bi-polar system that offers the appearance of a choice where essentially there is none, since today poles converge on a single economic stance—the "tight fiscal policy" that Clinton and Blair declare to be the key tenet of the modern Left, that sustains economic growth, that allows us to improve social security, education and health. In this uniform spectrum, political differences are more and more reduced to merely cultural attitudes: multicultural/sexual (etc.) "openness" versus traditional/natural (etc.) "family values." (Zizek 2000:37–38)

The recent violence (2001) in Gothenburg and in Genoa where thousands of demonstrators and violent gangs protesting upscale political meetings to formulate the agenda of globalization were met by police armed with live ammunition is evidence that vertical polarization is taking on more immediate and open forms. The potential crack in the official representation of the events is clearly expressed in the words of a policeman in Gothenburg where the violence got very much out of control leading to many wounded on all sides.

I think it is disgusting that we police are out here guarding the politicians against mass demonstrations while they are all inside drinking champagne.

In the centers of the globalizing world system there are significant zones where violence is latent, poised to be triggered by escalating conflicts. The new transformed elites have had a great deal of difficulty in understanding their own position in all of this. Not only the politicians, but the cultural elites and many academics, including anthropologists, consciously producing what they see as a new anthropology that thinks itself beyond the nation–state into a fantasy world of multicultural and hybrid delight. But down below in the fragmented and marginalized and increasingly lumpenized zones of the system there is a different perspective emerging.

St. Johns is most notorious for its high white-trash quotient. Yet more blacks and Mexicans live here than in most parts of the city. For economic reasons, the trash—be it black, brown, or white—have always lived side by side in America. It's the Gold Card whites who've always paid to segregate themselves, leaving the rednecks, niggers and spics to fight over day-old cookies. (Goad 1997:135)

NOTES

1. This generalized fragmentation is clearly expressed in the deconstruction of gender identities, both in intellectual discourse and in much middle-class experimentation. Here roles are reversed and varied in the extreme and identities are reduced to acts. Judith Butler has gone so far as to suggest that there are no gender identities other than those that are imposed externally by the state or a related Foucauldian power structure.

2. As Noiriel as noted, "It is somewhat surprising that Halbwachs [a noted French sociologist] attributed the appearance of the Chicago school to the specificity of the immigrant experience in Chicago itself (Halbwachs 1932). At the same time there were as many immigrants in France as there are today. . . . What was missing, then, was the sociologist, not the object." (Noiriel 1996:13)

3. These statistics, of course, vary substantially and cannot be simply understood as the expression of global processes. Thus, while from the mid-1970s through the mid-1990s there were two waves of increase in substate conflict, this has now begun

to decline (Gurr 2000). This is partly because the conflicts have often led to the formation of new independent or quasi-independent units, or multiethnic regimes have replaced more strongly integrative states. On the other hand, the general level of substate political conflict has increased substantially since the end of World War II and it has remained at a higher threshold since the end of the 1970s.

4. The word elite is of course broader than its cosmopolitan component. While there may be a strong tendency toward cosmopolitanization, there is also a nationalist component that can become resurgent in precise periods of polarization.

REFERENCES

Albrecht, H-J. 1997. "Ethnic Minorities, Crime and Criminal Justice in Germany." In *Ethnicity, Crime and Immigration: Comparative and Cross-National Perspectives.* Edited by M. Tonry, 31–99. Chicago: University of Chicago Press.

Appadurai, A. Winter 1998. "Dead Certainty: Ethnic Violence in the Era of Globalization." *Public Culture* 10, no. 2:225–247.

Arantes, A. 1996. "The War of Places: Symbolic Boundaries and Liminalities in Urban Space." *Theory Culture and Society* 13, no. 4:81–92.

Arrighi, G. 1997. "Globalisation, State Sovereignty, and the 'Endless' Accumulation of Capital." Revised version of a paper presented at the conference on States and Sovereignty in the World Economy, University of California, Irvine, Feb. 21–23.

Bairoch, P., and R. Kozul-Wright. 1996. "Globalization Myths: Some Historical Reflections on Integration, Industrialization and Growth in the World Economy." UNCTAD Discussion Paper no.113.

Barnum, C. 1992. "Effective Membership in the Global Business Community." In *New Traditions in Business: Spirit and Leadership in the 21st Century.* Edited by J. Renesch, 141–58. San Fransisco: Aerrett-Koechler.

Bergesen, A. and R. Fernandez. 1995. "Who Has the Most Fortune 500 Firms?: A Network Analysis of Global Economic Competition, 1956–1989." *Journal of World Systems Research* 1, no. 12. http://csf.colorado.edu/wsystems/jwsr.html.

Braudel, F. 1984. *The Perspective of the World.* New York: Harper and Row.

Briggs, A., and D. Snowman. 1996. *Fins de Siecle: How Centuries End, 1400–2000.* New Haven, Conn.: Yale University Press.

Butler, J. 1990. *Gender Trouble.* London: Routledge.

Camilleri, J. 1997. "Regionalism and Globalism in Asia-Pacific." Paper presented at the conference, Human Security and Global Governance in the Asia-Pacific, at the Toda Institute for Global Peace and Policy Research, Honolulu, Hawaii.

Chemin, C. 2001. "Rhétoriques modialisantes, rhétoriques de la mondialisation et production des champs sociaux en entreprise." In *Mémoire DEA en Anthropology Sociale.* Paris: EHESS.

Dicken, P. 1992. *Global Shift: The Internationalisation of Economic Activity.* London: Chapman.

Economist. 1998. "The Century the Earth Stood Still," December 20, 1997–January 2, 1998, 71–73.

Friedman, J. 1997. "Global Crises, the Struggle for Cultural Identity and Intellectual Pork-Barreling: Cosmopolitans, Nationals and Locals in an Era of De-hegemonisation." In *The Dialectics of Hybridity.* Edited by P. Werbner, 70–89. London: Zed Press.

———. 1998. "The Hybridisation of Roots and the Abhorrence of the Bush." In *Spaces of Culture: City, Nation, World.* Edited by M. Featherstone and S. Lash, 230–55. London: Sage.

Furnivall, J. S. 1948. *Colonial Practice and Policy.* Cambridge, U.K.: Cambridge University Press.

Gitlin, T. 1995. *The Twilight of Common Dreams: Why America Is Wracked by Culture Wars.* New York: Holt.

Goad, J. 1998. *The Redneck Manifesto: How Hilbillies, Hicks and White Trash Became America's Scapegoats.* New York: Simon & Schuster

Gurr, T. 1993. *Minorities at Risk: A Global View of Ethnopolitical Conflicts.* Washington, D.C.: U. S. Institute of Peace Press

———. 2000. *Peoples versus States: Minorities at Risk in the New Century.* Washington, D.C.: U. S. Institute of Peace Press

Hacker, A. 1997. *Money: Who Has How Much and Why.* New York: Scribner.

Halbwachs, M. 1932. "Chicago expérience ethnique." *Annales d' Histoire Economique et Sociale.* January.

Harvey, D. 1981. The Postmodern Condition. Oxford: Blackwell.

Hirst. P., and Thompson, G. 1996. *Globalization in Question.* Cambridge: Polity.

Juillard, J. 1997. *La faute des élites.* Paris: Gallimard.

Kallen, H. 1924. *Culture and Democracy in the United States.* New York: Arno.

Kapferer, B. 1997. *The Feast of the Sorcerer: Practices of Consciousness and Power.* Chicago: University of Chicago Press.

Lasch, C. 1995. *The Revolt of the Elites.* New York: Norton.

Noiriel, G. 1996. *The French Melting Pot: Immigration, Citizenship, and National Identity.* Minneapolis: University of Minnesota Press.

Piccone, Paul. 1993. "Confronting the French New Right: Old Prejudices or a New Political Paradigm?" *Telos.* Nos. 98–99:3–22.

Porter, M. 1990. *The Competitive Advantage of Nations.* New York: Macmillan.

Rata, M. 1997. "Global Capitalism and the Revival of Ethnic Traditionalism in New Zealand: The Emergence of Tribal Capitalism." Ph.D. diss., University of Auckland.

Salamon, K. L. 2000. "Faith Brought to Work: A Spiritual Movement in Business Management." Journal for Applied Anthropology in Policy and Practice 3, no. 1:24–29.

———. 2001. "Going Global from the Inside Out: Spiritual Globalism in the Workplace." In *New Age Religion and Globalization.* Edited by M. Rothstein, 150–72. Aarhus, Denmark: Aarhus University Press.

Sassen, S. 1996. *Losing Control? Sovereignty in an Age of Globalisation.* New York: Columbia University Press.

———. 2000. "Economic Globalization and the Redrawing of Citizenship." Chapter 3 in this book.

Siefert, W. 1991. *Ausländer in der Bundesrepublik–Soziale und ökonomische Mobilität.* Berlin: Wissenschaftszentrum.

Smith, D. J. 1997. "Ethnic Origins, Crime and Criminal Justice in England and Wales." In *Ethnicity, Crime and Immigration: Comparative and Cross-National Perspectives.* Edited by M. Tonry, 101–82. Chicago: University of Chicago Press.

UNRISD Report. 1995. *States of Disarray: The Social Effects of Globalization.* London: Banson.

Wieviorka, M. 1977. "Un nouveau paradigme de la violence." In *Un nouveau paradigme de la violence.* Edited by M. Wieviorka. Paris: Harmattan.

————. 2001. *La Différence*. Paris: Balland.

Yen, Maria. 1997. "From Eima Bean Fields to Little Saigon: Coping with Diversity in an American Suburb." In *The Multicultural Neighborhood: Our Multi-ethnic Society of Today and Tomorrow*. Copenhagen: Naevnet for Etnisk Ligestilling, Indengrigesministerium (Board for Ethnic Equality, Ministry of the Interior).

Zizek, S. 2000. "Why We All Love to Hate Haider." *New Left Review* 2:37–38.

2

Class Projects, Social Consciousness, and the Contradictions of "Globalization"

TERENCE TURNER

Over the past three decades, national economies have become increasingly integrated into, and subordinated to global markets for money and commodities, under the aegis of transnational corporations, monetarist policies, and neoliberal ideology. "Globalization," as this process has come to be called, has been driven by the quest by private corporate and financial capital to escape effective regulation and taxation by states, to exploit cheaper, often unwaged forms of labor, and to realize greater efficiency and cost-effectiveness from transnational forms of corporate organizations such as sourcing networks and vertical integration of productive and distributive operations.

The strategic focus of globalization, however, has been the development of world financial markets through which money is traded as a commodity, under conditions of instantaneous communication made possible by the new informational technologies. In this way, enormous volumes of financial and monetary transactions are made in virtual or "real" time and space, abstracted from material time flows and the political-geographical space of national boundaries. The ability of contemporary financial markets to trade national currencies, financial assets, and debts through this virtual network of instantaneous electronic communication has caused states to lose control over their national currencies and obliged them to reorient their economic (and less directly, social) policies to support the value of commodity money and the stability (and profitability) of the global financial market, which now determines the value of their currencies. (The United States is a possible exception to this generalization, but the ability of the Federal Reserve to withstand a concentrated assault on the dollar has not been tested.) The result has been to undermine the autonomy of states as economic and in some respects political units, although it has also given states new economic and political functions as supporters and enforcers of policies that contribute to the stabilization and protection of the global market economy. As McMichael has summed up these developments,

> The market de-nationalizes, or produces a "destatization of the political system" (Jessop 1997:574). Arguably, this is the intent, or consequence, of structural adjustment, where indebted states are bailed out by the IMF under conditions that "open" their economies and implement social austerity measures to privilege powerful global economic actors. Viewing the market as a de-nationalizing movement does not imply a borderless [or stateless] world, rather it implies transformed states. . . . this transformation involves a shift from states managing national economies, to states managing the global economy—in two senses: facilitating global circuits of money and commodities, and resolving the contradictions of global capitalism. (McMichael n.d.:21)

It is commonly recognized that globalization in this sense has been, and continues to be, a major factor in many changes in social, political, and cultural patterns, as well as in new forms of social conflict stemming from these changes. There is much disagreement, however, as to the nature of its relation to these changes, and in important respects, the nature of the changes themselves.

There is a striking difference, for example, between the perspectives on globalization of analysts who take as their standpoint the market itself (whether as global reality or programmatic abstraction), and those for whom the market must be understood as a historic product of political, ideological, and social processes. The market, taken on its own terms, is a self-regulating system that renders historical time, and increasingly, in the case of the new financial markets that operate in virtual space and "real" time, space as well, irrelevant. As the sphere of circulation and exchange par excellence, it also renders production—its social and political conditions and spatiotemporal organization—irrelevant, along with all other social, political, and cultural relations not directly implicated in circulation, exchange, and consumption. Taking the market, in its globalized form, as the theoretical vantage point for understanding globalization tends to produce uncritically one-sided representations of globalization as a "new age" dissociated from previous historical time and social space, a synchronic phenomenon that either inevitably will, or already has, succeeded earlier forms of economic, political, social, and cultural life (some commentators have gone so far as to suggest that capitalism itself should be included among these outmoded forms). As one critical observer has commented, "One of the distinguishing features at the turn of the century is the powerful apparatus of communication dedicated to the image of a world unified by global technologies and their universal appeal. One could say that this discursive agenda is geared to persuading people that there is no alternative" (Rist 1997:226, cited in McMichael n.d.:1).

Academic compartmentalization has also contributed to obfuscating the interrelated economic, political, ideological, and cultural character of globalization as a historical process. The main bodies of literature on globalization thus deal respectively with aspects associated with the disciplinary divisions of the academy: 1) political economy (including production and markets, money and money markets, the development of transnational corporations and financial circuits, and the intensified commodification of all aspects of life; 2) the political prerequisites and effects of globalization (including the shifting fortunes of the nation–state, problems of governance and control at both state and transnational levels, and tensions between old and new forms of sovereignty); 3) sociological and ideological changes in class relations, including the fragmentation of the middle class, the emergence of new elites, the crisis of the class compromise and the welfare state, and the ideology and politics of neoliberalism as it both represents and promotes these phenomena; 4) changes in social consciousness and their material correlates such as transformations in categories of space and time, new material forms of spatial and temporal organization, the role of the new media, communication and transportation technologies; and 5) the new politics of cultural difference, including the rise of ethnic nationalisms, multiculturalism, identity politics, xenophobic movements, the florescence of subcultures, new social movements (NSMs) and issue-oriented voluntary nongovernmental organizations (NGOs), human rights activism, and indigenous peoples' struggles. The result is reminiscent of the old fable of the blind men and the elephant: each theorist contributes an account of a part of the total phenomenon as it appears from the perspective of his or her own discipline, while the shape and direction of the whole remains elusive.

The effect of the diffraction of the common object, globalization, through the multiple disciplinary lenses of the specialists who have studied it has been to obfuscate the central issue of whether and to what extent the "process" of globalization should be understood as the project of an identifiable class or social group, as opposed to a spontaneous result of technological, cultural, or other impersonal forces without social agents. Another crucial issue that has been obscured more than clarified by the same process of refraction is that of the relation between the inner contradictions of globalization and the rise of political and ideological movements directly or indirectly opposed to global

capital and the neoliberal ideology and policies that have served as its ideological and political auxiliaries.

THEORETICAL AND METHODOLOGICAL ISSUES

I propose to focus on this last issue in this chapter. I will attempt to identify
specific connections between the political-economic and social aspects of
globalization and its correlated contemporary political, cultural, and ideological manifestations. To this end, I will make extensive use of two critical theoretical and analytical categories, class and social consciousness, that have frequently been ignored in the voluminous literature on globalization and the
associated crisis of the nation–state. As I have mentioned, much of this literature has tended to focus either on the political-economic and/or social aspects
of globalization or on the cultural forms of categories such as identity, space,
and time, without paying much attention to the nature and importance of the
relations between them. Discussions of the cultural forms of globalized social
consciousness, for instance, rarely attempt to specify that they deal with the
perspective of a particular class (as they generally do, often quite un-self-
consciously: typically, that of the "professional-managerial" fraction of the
middle class or the new upper-middle-class elites that have formed as a new
service class attached to global capital) (Ehrenreich and Ehrenreich 1979; Pfeil
1990; Gill 1994). Most of the authors who have attempted to deal with cultural
aspects of globalization, who have come primarily from anthropology and
cultural studies, appear in fact to operate with a notion of culture in which
class perspective plays no conscious part. This blind spot has obstructed understanding of the social and political-economic roots of the forms of social
consciousness they have attempted to describe, as well as their pragmatic role
in orienting members of the classes in question toward conflict as well as accommodation with aspects and effects of the system as a whole.

These are issues that can only be dealt with in historical perspective, in contrast to the ahistorical models of market-oriented neoliberal and rational-
choice theorists. I shall therefore begin my discussion with some historical observations on the development of the political-economic framework of the
nation–state and its associated political and ideological forms, with special attention to the changing roles and perspectives of classes and status groups. My
particular focus will be the relationship between what may broadly be called
the cultural and ideological aspects of these shifting relations, on the one
hand, and their social and political-economic aspects on the other. The primary aim of the exercise will be to identify the historical roots of structural
tensions and contradictory tendencies inherent in contemporary global capi-

talism and the nation–state system that underlie current transformations in political and ideological formations, social movements, and conflicts.

In this attempt, the concept of social consciousness plays an essential role. I use the term "social consciousness" rather than "culture" to emphasize that the collectively shared forms of consciousness with which I shall be concerned are directly rooted in patterns of social activity. They are, in other words, formed as schemas guiding and mediating the orientations, interactive relations, and projects of social actors, as conditioned by their membership in classes, class fractions, and status groups. General categories, symbols, and representations may be abstracted from such schemas and become reified as elements of cultural systems (or of anthropological descriptions of such systems). At the level of material social activity, however, these notional elements have their being not as ideal abstractions, but as aspects of less differentiated, more concrete patterns (schemas) of material action and transformation. A culture, for example, may be said to possess abstract notions or categories of space and time. At the level of material social activity, where they form aspects of schemas, however, "space" and "time" may have no consequential existence as distinct abstractions, but appear rather as complementary aspects of relatively undifferentiated pragmatic schemas of action: that is, as space–time. Schemas in this sense comprise the level at which consciousness and social action directly interpenetrate and affect each other. As such they were the forms of social consciousness par excellence.

Social activity, of course, is organized at various levels. The level at which classes and class perspectives are formed is that of the processes of production and reproduction of the society as a whole. Processes of social production are organized through a collective division of labor in which different social categories or groupings have different roles to play in the relations of production. Such groups are classes. In complex organizations of productive activities, a class may become differentiated into subclasses or class fractions according to the specific roles assumed by each fraction in the overall organization of production. As the term "role" implies, each class or class fraction has a specific form of activity, oriented toward specific goals and values within this overall organization, which constitutes its collective project. As members of the class act in accord with this project, they define themselves as actors with specific identities, and by the same token as agents with specific powers and intentions. Their class-specific roles or activities, meanwhile, constitute particular schemas of space–time. As collective categories of actors, in sum, classes and class fractions produce, as an intrinsic aspect of their characteristic activities, forms of social consciousness that comprise schemas of space–time, types of agency or powers to act, and specific social identities. Such composite forms approximate to Bakhtin's concept of the "chronotope" (Bakhtin 1981).

The kinds of social activity proper to a class (its role in the overall organization of social production) embody its relations to other classes and the social system as a whole: in other words, its class perspective on the rest of society and thus, reflexively, its own identity. Such a perspective must be, by its nature, partial; while bringing some aspects of the social formation and its own role within it into clear focus, it will tend to obscure others or distort their real social character (for instance by making them appear natural and thus immutable by social agency). These conscious aspects of collective activity and perspective become the basic constituents of the social consciousness specific to the class: in other words, its social (class) consciousness.

An example is the way the members of middle class segments involved with mediating processes of exchange, communication, and consumption, but not directly with production, tend to conceive the social world in terms of market relations and forms of circulation, while ignoring the role of processes of production and thus of class. Much current theorizing about globalization bears the stamp of this class perspective.

The interpenetration of economic class with the political organization of society, through which the performance of specific roles and functions becomes a basis for the distribution of differing proportions and qualitative forms of social value, defines social status. Groups such as classes or class segments, occupational groups, or politically distinct ethnic or regional groupings may be able to identify themselves with, or be obliged to assume, a status and its associated social values: they thus become what Max Weber called status groups. What have come to be called "identity" groups, "ethnic" groups, and "subcultures," in recent literature are essentially status groups in this sense.

The total assemblage of classes, groups, and individuals that make up a social formation possesses an overall organization that corresponds to a specific ordering of the process(es) of social production; this organization, in other words, constitutes a political order. The state is one form of such a political ordering. The social group or element that succeeds in imposing such an overall ordering on the classes and individuals of a social formation, and whose leadership, perspective, and project are acknowledged and accepted by the latter, may be called the hegemonic element of the society composed of all the classes and elements of the formation. Hegemony in this specific sense of class or group leadership and domination are sustained by specific forms of social consciousness that embody the social values and perspectives of the hegemonic group and are also accepted to varying degrees by other classes and groups. This may lead them to view the leadership of the hegemonic group and the social and political order with which it is identified as natural, necessary, and desirable. Forms of social consciousness that contribute to hegemony in this sense constitute ideology, but may come to be accepted as "culture."

Hegemony in this sense may be associated with sovereignty, or the authoritative exercise of power and leadership within a territorial social unit. Status groups with their associated cultural identities and values may or may not be "hegemonic." Hegemony does not necessarily imply sovereignty, and sovereigns, as in the limiting case of popular sovereignty, may not be hegemons. In this definition of hegemony I follow Gramsci's original conception in terms of class leadership rather than Williams's depoliticized reformulation of the concept as "culture."

The hegemonic order identified with the dominant class or element of a social formation inevitably tends to generate opposition from other groups, which produce their own counterhegemonic ideologies, giving rise to conflict and eventual structural change. The transformations of social consciousness that form part of such processes of conflict and change, including the emergence of new hegemonic ideologies, must be understood as rooted in the dynamics of orders of social domination among the classes, groups, and categories of the social formations of which they form integral parts. Attempts to explain them by appeal to ostensibly asocial factors, such as cultural forms of "tradition" or "imagination," technological change or naturally self-unfolding historical processes, tend to obscure the interplay of social, ideological, and political-economic relations involved in such changes, and in particular their relation to the projects of hegemonic classes or groups. They may thus constitute de facto ideological supports for such political-economic orderings and hegemonic relations.

NATION–STATE, POPULAR SOVEREIGNTY, CAPITALISM MARKET ECONOMY, MIDDLE-CLASS HEGEMONY: THE SHIFTING PARAMETERS OF THE MODERN WORLD SYSTEM

The social, political, and economic dynamics of contemporary globalization, and the cultural and ideological forms that have developed along with it, can only be understood in the context of a historical analysis of the changing relations of interdependence among the main constituents of the modern world system: state, "nation" and nationalism, political sovereignty, class relations, and capitalism.

In the development of modern capitalist society, state and market economy have played interdependent roles; neither, however, can be reduced to a simple effect or product of the other. The modern nation–state took form in the seventeenth and eighteenth centuries, as the outcome of a historical struggle between absolute monarchies, the feudal aristocracy, and the rising bourgeoisie, in which the latter served as indispensable allies of absolute monarchs in developing centralized bureaucratic governance and uniform sovereignty and destroying the decentralized feudal powers of the aristocracy. The bourgeoisie then turned against the monarchs, chopped off their heads, and installed themselves as the hegemonic class within the state. This scenario was repeated in its essential outlines, if without the overtly regicidal details, in the settler colonies of the Americas and Australasia. In Germany, Central Europe, prerevolutionary Russia, and Japan, where aristocracies, allied with military establishments, held more power and bourgeoisies were weaker, relatively partial, and more socially conservative versions of this scenario were enacted, with the central government playing a more direct role in fostering and coordinating economic development. In all cases, however, the eighteenth-, nineteenth-, and early twentieth-century state took form in interdependence with the mercantile and industrial bourgeoisie and the expansion of the market economy both domestically and internationally. The market, and the capitalist system in its industrial, corporate, and financial aspects, took form pari passu with the centralized modern state.

The early modern states of Europe in the age of absolutist monarchies were not nation–states. Their greatest achievement—the exclusive concentration of sovereignty in centralized state regimes and its uniform extension to the whole state population—was based on the dynastic legitimacy of the monarch as head of state. The bourgeoisie, in seizing state power from the monarchy, sought to legitimize its struggle for dominance and hegemony within the state by claiming to act on behalf of the nation—that is, the people as a whole (meaning the male, propertied, freeborn part of it). To supplant the sovereignty of dynastic monarchs, they proclaimed the doctrine of popular sovereignty: the people as a whole, as a nation of equal citizens, was recognized as the sole legitimate sovereign. The uniform extension of sovereignty under the absolute monarchies thus became transformed as the uniform distribution of sovereignty among an ideologically homogeneous citizenry. But who are the "people"? Or, as the Abbé Sieyès famously asked and answered in one of the most influential pamphlets on the eve of the French Revolution, "What is the Third Estate?" Sieyès answered his own question: It is the nation (that is, the people as sovereign community of citizens). (Sieyès 1972) The Third Estate, the bourgeoisie, in other words, as the most progressive, responsible, industrious, politically and economically competent element of the populace, was thus identified ideologically with the people as a whole, and thus simultaneously as the effective custodians of sovereignty in a state founded upon popular sovereignty, and the hegemonic leaders of the "nation" composed of themselves and the other classes and "estates" (status groups) thus subsumed under their domination.

Nationalism as a form of social consciousness—the idea of the nation as "imagined community" of sovereign citizens—was thus born out of the struggle of the middle class for hegemony and sovereignty at the birth of the modern state. Class struggle, in other words, was the decisive element in the formation of modern nationalism, which arose as the ideological vehicle of bourgeois class hegemony. The fact that many people read the same newspapers no doubt helped, but nationalism as a political and ideological phenomenon cannot be attributed to technological factors like "print capitalism" or socially dissociated cultural faculties like "imagination" (cf. Anderson 1983).

The abstract notion of the nation as a homogeneous community of citizens sharing a common identity and a uniform loyalty to the state that constituted its political form was derived from the notions of uniform sovereignty and governance that had developed in the struggles for the centralization and bureaucratization of state power under the absolute monarchs, in alliance with the bourgeoisie, against the aristocracy, in the context of the exigencies of military rivalries with other states in the polycentric European state system. It was only the subsequent struggle of the bourgeoisie as a class to appropriate the sovereignty of the monarchs with the support or acquiescence of the other estates, however, that the received notion of the community of subjects of the sovereign was transmuted into the nation as a sovereign community of citizens in its own right. This synthesis was accomplished through the bourgeois conquest of hegemony, as the class whose social identity and status values most directly corresponded to the principles of rationality and uniformity intrinsic to the forms of common citizenship, social equality, the rights of private property, and uniform sovereignty. The spread of modern nationalism is coextensive with the hegemony of these essentially bourgeois values, even in cases like Germany where the bourgeoisie failed to gain outright sovereignty. These values, of course, are also associated with capitalism, at least in its early competitive forms, and the rise of bourgeois hegemony was everywhere powered by the political-economic dominance of capitalism.

From the time of the early modern absolute monarchies, state governments supported the mercantilist projects of their national bourgeoisies as a source of national wealth and potential financing for state projects and military operations against other states. This support included legal and administrative measures for the development and regulation of markets. As industrial production developed from the end of the eighteenth century through the nineteenth century, and the exploitation of wage labor replaced commerce as the principal source of capitalist wealth, the state intervened to guarantee cheap food prices (and thus lower wage costs), promote the creation of national labor markets, regulate working conditions, and to give the working class a measure of representation in legislative assemblies. The state, markets, and capitalist relations of production thus developed in interaction with one another, as modern social and political systems took form in the nineteenth and early twentieth centuries. Throughout this period, the state remained the essential unit of economic organization and regulation, as well as the unit of political sovereignty. Class relations developed along broadly parallel lines within each state. The middle class tended to divide into segments respectively identified with capital and business activities, on the one hand, and segments consisting of professionals, administrators, and intellectuals, on the other. Electoral politics was developed to allow all segments enough participation in the state to forestall undue polarization. Working-class movements were largely co-opted through participation in socialist politics with representation in state institutions and the provision of government programs of social benefits. For both the middle and the working classes and their respective segments, the overriding fact that the nation–state remained the dominant unit of economic, political, social, and ideological structure thus made possible the development of national political and ideological forms that served to prevent internal class divisions from becoming destablizing conflicts. The leading states developed colonial empires as guaranteed sources of raw materials and labor and as markets for their industrial products. On this social and political-economic foundation, international trade developed to an unprecedented degree, but nation–states and their respective colonies remained the primary structural units of the system.

Despite the shocks of the Great Depression of the 1930s and World War I, this nation–state–based global system remained essentially intact until the aftermath of World War II. The Allied victory over Germany and Japan and the ensuing peace arrangements, including the Bretton Woods accords, the North Atlantic alliance, the Marshall Plan, and the economic rehabilitation and reintegration of the Axis powers created a historically unprecedented situation among the major capitalist countries. For the first time in their history as modern states, it became unthinkable that any of them could advance their national interests by going to war with any of the others. A peaceful capitalist *oikumene* was thus established. The removal of military rivalries among the Western powers and Japan thus eroded one of the main historical supports of state-level nationalism: military rivalry between states. The Bretton Woods international economic accords among the capitalist allies, worked out before the end of the war, established the economic framework for the reintegration of the defeated powers into the international political and economic system, maintaining the nation–state as the primary unit of economic organization and currency regulation while making possible a rapid expansion of international trade.

Following the war, the U.S. government, with broad support from private capital, continued to follow three broad social and economic policies that had been initiated in the previous interwar period: 1) to continue to foster the shift of national economic production away from heavy capital goods to the production of consumer commodities (a policy first introduced in the 1920s); 2) to guarantee the rights of labor to organize and engage in collective bargaining as well as to provide public assistance to unemployed working-class and lower income groups of the population (i.e., the "class compromise," institutionalized in the "welfare state"); and 3) to stimulate the development of a greatly expanded professional-managerial class, to be trained and recruited largely through a vastly enlarged system of publicly supported higher education. Analogous policies were undertaken by other First World countries.

Finally, the Cold War, as it developed after 1948, provided the pretext for a fourth major policy that was to shape the political-economic reality of the United States and the other major capitalist countries in a variety of ways: the reinitiation of massive armaments production and the development of "military Keynesianism" in the national security state.

In the United States, and to varying degrees in the other major capitalist nations, these policies largely achieved their primary objectives of promoting individualized consumerist consciousness, oriented to the self-production of personal identity and lifestyle, as a substitute for antagonistic class politics and consciousness among the middle and upper echelons of the middle class and also among the lower-middle and working classes (severe and sustained political repression of radical unions and working class organizations contributed to this effect among the latter). By the mid-1950s, the state's ability to guarantee access to the market for consumption goods at sufficient income levels, and thus ensure a comfortable "standard of living" (enabling a satisfactory "lifestyle" and "quality of life") had thus become established as a major, if not the primary basis of the legitimacy of the state for many members of American society.

In the ideological formulations of official state discourses in the United States and other leading capitalist countries, it was inextricably identified with "democracy" and "private enterprise" (i.e., capitalism) as the basis of the good life.

For the time, the political and business establishments as well as critics from the left consumerism were seen as a fundamentally depoliticized form of individualistic hedonism. The elevation of personal self-production through consumption, education, and income to the status of a fundamental political value, however, had potentially political implications of a different kind than those originally envisioned by the initiators of the turn to consumerism. Commodity consumption on a sufficient scale can become a significant mode of self-production, and as such a form of social empowerment (as emphasized in Miller 1998). In the face of state policies or economic developments that might threaten that power, it might thus be expected to give rise to political protest and social movements intended to defend the consumers' standard of living, personal identity, and/or social power. As we shall see below, this potential political effect began to be realized in the last three decades of the century.

The optimistic class-compromise policies of the postwar period were sustained by the long economic boom of the 1950s and early 1960s heavily subsidized by "military Keynesianism," through which the private economy was supported by continued massive infusions of public funds. That this huge public investment was directed into essentially unproductive investment had, among other unfortunate social consequences, the creation of large amounts of financial capital in the hands of a growing rentier group that drew its income largely from military production. This mass of mobile financial capital was to become the principal basis of the globalized financial market of the 1970s.

By the end of the 1960s, however, an economic contraction set in that lasted six years, culminating in the OPEC-precipitated energy crisis of 1973. The failure of the economy to continue to expand precipitated a tightening of the competition for resources among the main sectors of society (workers and salaried middle class, capitalists, and government), which O'Connor (2002) has called "the fiscal crisis of the state." The fiscal crisis occurs because the state must bear a large share of the research and development and infrastructural costs required by private industry to remain competitive. Competition drives private industry to raise productivity and thereby cut labor costs. As the private economy lays off workers, the state must devote more resources to sustain the unemployed as well as other groups of the population that lack the resources to support themselves (O'Connor calls these social subsidies "legitimation payments"). To meet the rising levels of legitimation payments, as well as its growing responsibilities for infrastructure, and so on, to private business, the state must sustain and increase its own bureaucratic apparatus. To do this, it must raise taxes; but after a point the tax burden begins to erode the profitability, and thus the competitiveness of industry, as well as the ability of the mass of the population to consume the goods and services it produces. Taxes cannot be raised further without becoming counterproductive, but the demands on the state continue to increase. The result is fiscal crisis. As long as the national economy can continue to expand at a satisfactory rate, the fiscal crisis can be held at bay, even if (as was the case) state costs for infrastructure, research and development, state administration, and social welfare proportionally increase. When a relatively sharp downturn arrives, however, these costs are likely to rise even higher as the sources of revenue available to the state from taxation decline. The fiscal crisis would then be at hand.

GLOBALIZATION AFTER 1973: FROM THE FISCAL CRISIS OF THE STATE TO THE FINANCIAL CRISIS OF THE WORLD

The fiscal chickens came home to roost at the end of the long postwar boom in the late 1960s and early 1970s. The huge increase in the volume of mobile finance capital in circulation in the globally integrated financial markets by the end of the 1960s, much of it coming from U.S. military spending, had become a major destabilizing force in the global economy. The United States had begun running a trade deficit, largely because of its bloated military expenses, exacerbating economic tensions with its main trading partners, but the value of the dollar could no longer be sustained without European and Japanese support. One result was to force the United States to go off the gold standard in 1971, a major blow to the Bretton Woods system. International credit and currency transactions were increasingly destabilized, threatening trade in commodities, capital goods, and flows of productive capital. The OPEC-produced energy crisis of 1973 was another heavy economic blow. The U.S. Federal Reserve and the central banks of the other major capitalist countries became unable to prevent destabilizing trading in their national currencies on international financial markets. The Bretton Woods system of regulation of international financial capital by the governments and central banks of nation–states thus effectively collapsed. Meanwhile, private corporate capital, taking advantage of the peaceful international order created by state political and economic policies, during and since the war, moved rapidly into transnational operations and forms of corporate organization, thus escaping the pressures and responsibilities of the fiscal crisis (notably taxation and the state budgetary constraints imposed by the costs of social policies associated with the class compromise) and the restraints of state policies protective of the rights of labor. At the same time, transnational financial transactions, freed from the restraints of the Bretton Woods system, and fueled by large amounts of speculative dollars generated by the U.S. military economy, rapidly increased in volume. New communications technology made possible virtually instantaneous transactions of enormous scope, with the potential (soon realized) for destabilizing effects on national currencies and economies. "Globalization," in the contemporary sense of a transnational system of trade and financial transactions in which the nation–state is no longer the primary organizational framework of the economy, was at hand.

The contemporary globalized economic system, in other words, is to a large extent the result of deliberate efforts of private capitalists, both corporate and financial, to realize the higher profits to be made through evasion of state regulation and social responsibility as well as by taking advantage of the inequalities and differences in the global division of labor among state economies.

The dynamic expansion of the transnational sector in recent decades, in other words, has been the result of deliberate efforts of corporate and financial capitalists to develop and exploit it as a space beyond the power of states or international bodies to regulate or control, and to use their ability to operate in this unregulated transnational sphere as a powerful source of leverage to undermine regulation of their activities by the states within which they operate.

Globalization, in sum, constitutes an essentially unregulated intensification of the capitalist dynamic of competition, accumulation, exploitation, and class conflict, as realized through the deliberate actions and policies of political and corporate leaders, rather than a spontaneous or natural result of new informational or other technologies.

THE PERSISTENCE OF THE STATE
IN THE GLOBALIZED ECONOMIC ORDER

The development of the global capitalist system over the past three or four decades has not led to any withering away of the state itself. On the contrary, while the state has lost much of its power to regulate its own internal economy, it has acquired a new importance as a support of the transnational financial, commodity, labor, and capital markets. Nor has the heightened importance of transnational commerce, financial transactions, labor migration, and media communications led to any general weakening of the state as a political organization or as a territorial entity. On the contrary, it has if anything heightened rather than undermined the importance of state boundaries. The frontiers dividing state territories, especially those separating the economically successful state economies from the relatively unsuccessful ones, have more than ever become dialectically identified with the internal class divisions of the social systems that are at once separated and connected by interstate frontiers. The ways states attempt to regulate, encourage, or obstruct flows of workers, capital, and commodities across their borders are directly related to their explicit or implicit social policies with respect to mitigating or exacerbating their internal class divisions.

THE NEW ELITES, CLASS REPOLARIZATION,
AND THE CRISIS OF SOVEREIGNTY

As corporate and financial elites, armed with neoliberal ideology, have gained political control and ideological hegemony within states, the result has been to narrow the ideological basis of popular identification with and loyalty to the state and its institutions of political participation (representative democracy). The narrowing of the class base of state control to the new transnationally oriented elites, in other words, has tended to undermine the political basis of nationalist ideology at the state level. At the same time, new multilateral institutions like the World Bank, IMF, WTO, and credit-rating agencies acting directly at the transnational level now exercise considerable sovereignty beyond the borders of any state. Sovereignty, in other words, has become distributed among states and an array of transnational institutions: it is no longer the monopoly of states.

The specialized rentier, industrial, and financial elites that have developed within First World and other states in the period of globalization have become increasingly oriented toward strengthening the viability, profitability, and competitivess of the transnationally oriented sectors of their national economies. The unproductive state expenditures from which the financial and rentier elites draw much of their wealth are themselves in considerable part the results of state policies designed to maintain transnational economic and political hegemony at regional or global levels. These elites tend to be politically, socially, and economically indifferent to those sectors of the state population with little to contribute to the competitive performance of the national economy in relation to the global system (Gill 1994).

The sustained attack on the welfare-state class compromise with labor mounted over the past two decades by the advocates of neoliberal policies who speak for the interests of globalizing capital has had the cumulative result of leaving both the working class and the salaried middle class increasingly insecure, frustrated, and resentful and mistrustful of the political systems and governments of their nation–states.

The result of these policies, coupled with the social and economic effects of the development of transnational corporate operations and financial markets, has been the polarization of an extremely wealthy elite of cadres and managers of global corporations and rentier financial speculators from the majority of the professional-managerial class, which remains engaged in the national economy and civil society. It has likewise led to the relative erosion of the economic security and relative income levels of the salaried middle class and the working class. Wage levels and employment of the industrial workforce in the more developed capitalist economies have also been adversely affected by the reallocation of production to less-developed countries with lower wage levels and weaker labor legislation, and by the practice of job substitution whereby wage labor in developed countries is replaced by unwaged forms of labor, including forced labor and slavery, in poorer regions. There has thus developed a "global crisis of wage labor" (McMichael 1999).

A corollary effect of the hegemony of neoliberal policy and capitalist elites and their "cadres" (Gill 1994, 1996) has been the implicit weakening of the principle of popular sovereignty on which the modern state has been based since the eighteenth century. The result has been a crisis of sovereignty in the contemporary state. This crisis is directly related to the weakening of nationalism at the state level in the more economically successful capitalist states, and the rise of substate (ethnic) nationalisms among the more economically disadvantaged and politically disempowered groups of their populations. Success at the game of competitive free-market capitalism, with its winner-take-all and devil-take-the-hindmost mentality, is a mean and narrow basis for a national community, that excludes many and threatens to exclude any who fail to contribute to national economic competitiveness. The narrowing of the ideological basis of citizenship—or in other words, of the nature of the social community represented by the state—while the state as such increases its political-economic power as a participant in the global economy, is a political and ideological counterpart of the crisis of overproduction, in which the expansion of wealth through production for the market coincides with a narrowing of the proportion of the world population that can be integrated into the workforce and is thus able to earn the wherewithal to consume the commodities that are produced.

THE DECLINE OF NATIONALISM AND
THE DEHYPHENATION OF THE NATION-STATE

The corollary of the crisis of sovereignty is widespread and increasing alienation from the political system, as reflected in the low levels of political participation in many Western states. One casualty of this appears to be a decline in nationalism as an expression of solidarity or "community" among all the citizens of the state, at least in those states, like the United States and the United Kingdom that have adopted neoliberal market-oriented policies. As state governments are forced or induced to reorient themselves to the management of global economic processes as a prerequisite of fiscal survival, at the cost of discontinuing social programs for the aid of relatively disadvantaged elements of the population, the latter have less and less reason to identify with the state as the political form of a "community" of which they can feel themselves full and equal parts. Nationalism, under these circumstances, reciprocally has little power to induce political loyalty to the state among the relatively disfranchised masses.

The globally oriented elites who direct or strongly influence the policies of many contemporary states, and who act as mediators between the global economic system and the internal economy of the state, meanwhile, have little stake in an identity as citizens of their states of origin. In their new class role, they are not wholly or unambiguously based in the internal economic and political processes of their nations, unlike their former fellow members of national bourgeoisies. They thus have little basis of identification or sense of national community with economically unproductive or uncompetitive elements of the national population such as the unemployed or unemployable underclass and other marginal groups it comprises. They no longer depend for the legitimation of their power within the state on the ideological claim to represent all the citizens of the nation, even the nationally oriented members of the bourgeoisie, in the way Sieyès claimed for the Third Estate at the time of the French Revolution. They thus have little need for nationalist ideology, to throw a veil of imaginary community, political equality, and collective solidarity over the stark social inequalities being exacerbated by the global processes they serve. Nationalism at the state level, at least in the more neoliberal-influenced states, has thus increasingly tended to become moot, both in the economically successful countries of the First World, and for complementary reasons also in those of other regions.

The efforts of the alienated citizenry to create new vehicles for the unemployed portions of its civic and social values outside the formal political structure, meanwhile, have led to a great multiplication of New Social Movements (NSMs). These include not only ethnic nationalist movements and those oriented to "identity" issues but also those committed to universalistic values and "quality of life" issues, like human rights and environmentalism. These movements, I suggest, stem directly from the quest by alienated citizens for forms of civic and political action commensurate with their social values, which they feel can no longer be realized through the constituted political institutions of nation–states. NSMs provide bases for critically opposing and resisting political and economic policies of states and global capital alike. They have increasingly learned to cooperate on a global scale, typically through the formation of temporary alliances that Keck has called "issue-oriented networks" (Keck and Sikkink 1998). To this extent, they represent a kind of transnational nemesis that the global capitalist system and its participating state regimes and corporations have raised up against themselves.

EMERGENT CONTRADICTORY TENDENCIES

Two distinctive sets of contradictory tendencies (potential if not yet full-fledged contradictions) characterize the present age of "globalization" to a degree that sets it off, quantitatively if not qualitatively, from previous eras in the history of capitalism. One of these involves the conflicting political and economic demands on the state by the national societies contained within state borders and their constituent classes on the one side, and the global system of financial and corporate capital and multilateral regulatory institutions on the other. The second is centered in the tension between the empowering and disempowering aspects of the consumer economy as mediated by the market, as they bear on the class that until very recently has been the hegemonic class of the modern state and economic system. This is, broadly speaking, the middle class, and more specifically the professional-managerial subclass in the advanced capitalist countries, that has been its most dynamic and influential segment, economically, socially, culturally, and politically speaking, for the past century.

These two tendencies are interdependent. Taken together, they signal the end of the hegemony of the nation–state, the national economy as the primary unit of economic structure, and the hegemony of the national bourgeoisie as a class, as well as their associated forms of social consciousness including nation–state–level nationalism, the notion of history as progress along a linear time dimension, and its corollary, the conviction that cultural and social differences within state populations are destined to be assimilated into homogeneous national communities. In so far as these interrelated phenomena can be taken to define "modernity," the contradictions in question signal the end of modernity as a historical era. The main constituents of the modern world system, however, including the state, capitalism, commodity consumerism, and forms of social consciousness such as liberal individualism (with its related concepts of democracy, equality, and rights), and the importance of collective status groups defined in terms of "identity" or "culture" (as substitutes for state-level nationalisms), continue, in altered forms, in the emerging world system that is replacing it. To grasp the shifting lines of conflict and potential change (for better or worse) of the new system, it is essential to understand clearly the nature of these contradictory tendencies.

The first potential contradiction arises from the way that, at the level of the global system as a whole, the extension of corporate capital, and above all finance capital, into the transnational domain has destabilized national monetary systems and financial markets to the extent that states have been obliged to reorient their political and administrative systems away from the internal social, political, and economic concerns of their populations toward the stabilization and support of the global financial and money markets, and to a lesser degree the global flows of commodities, workers, and compartmentalized manufacturing processes. States have thus been obliged to remain very much a part of the transnational economy, in both its financial and corporate aspects, and play indispensable roles in maintaining its conditions of equilibrium and growth. They have no alternative, for to fail to do so would threaten the viability of their own internal economies. To fulfill their functions at the global level, however, they have been obliged to attenuate or abandon many domestic functions, above all, those associated with social services and support of the relatively poor and unproductive segments of the population: the usual constituents of the welfare state or social democratic "class compromise" regimes. This tends to weaken their legitimacy among these groups of the population, disempowering them both socially and politically, and thus undermining the principle of popular sovereignty on which the political cohesion of the nation is based. This in turn threatens to erode the political ability of states to continue to sustain the transnational market economy, and increases the pressures on them to make further inroads into their domestic social base of legitimacy and political support.

The second contradictory tendency is on a different level: not that of the system as a whole, seen as it were from the outside, but that of the perspective of a specific class, the middle class, which now finds itself divided against itself as never before, as part of it transforms itself to form the new globally oriented elites directly engaged in servicing transnational corporate capital, while the rest remains anchored within national economies and suffers the relative insecurity and diminution of expectations that are among the local effects of global economic pressures. In this respect their situation increasingly resembles that of the stably employed working-class wage-labor force. These two national classes or class segments account for the great majority of the 600 million relatively affluent consumers in Europe, Japan, and North America identified by Ohmae (1990) as the most important bloc of purchasing power in the present world economy. For the members of this bloc, the huge accession of purchasing power they have received through the growth of the market for consumer commodities and the expansion of salaried and professional employment since World War II has been an important form of social empowerment. Consumerism on an unprecedented scale has meant a great expansion of the power of self-production: in other words, the capacity to produce personal identity, create individual and group lifestyles, and achieve personal and social values. This increase in the power of self-production, however, has come at the price of a diminution of their political and social power to influence the relations and conditions of production, including not only working conditions, job stability, and benefits but also environmental and social effects of corporate policies and the increasing impotence of electoral and other institutional political mechanisms to affect globally influenced economic conditions. Private capital, for instance, retains virtually unlimited control over decisions to reallocate production, engage in job substitution at the expense of wage workers and salaried employees, close or reorganize productive and marketing processes, and centralize and amalgamate corporate operations. These effects are amplified by the decline of the regulative powers of states resulting from the first contradictory tendency, so the middle and working classes have been less and less able to look to the state as an ally in restraining the behavior of private capital in ways that affect their well-being.

One result of this contradictory combination of empowerment and disempowerment has been the huge increase in the number, size, and variety of NSMs and NGOs, staffed overwhelmingly by members of the national middle class, with increasing support from organized labor. These movements typically appeal beyond the state to universal principles of ecology, philanthropy, or human rights to sanction their efforts to challenge and resist abuses by corporations, governments, and multilateral development agencies working in collaboration with private capital. The new movements draw upon the power of the professional-managerial class as a repository of purchasing power, professional skills, and access to communication networks to challenge the disempowering and lifestyle-disrupting effects of capital and state policies created to satisfy its needs.

A third contradictory tendency, the chronic crisis of overproduction, is of course not new but, as an intrinsic feature of unregulated competitive mass production, acts to reinforce the other two in new ways. As the transnational economic system has grown and complexified to the point where it has become an effective basis for corporate leverage on state economic and regulatory policies, it has also taken on some of the besetting contradictions of state-level capitalist economies. The chronic crisis of overproduction has emerged as a structural limit of the global system as a whole. As labor becomes ever more productive under the pressure of global competition, relatively fewer workers are required to produce ever greater quantities of commodities, with the result that an ever-increasing proportion of the world's population is effectively excluded from the opportunity to consume the constantly increasing amounts of goods and services. The market for commodities thus tends to shrink as the supply continues to expand. Greider (1997) has stressed that tendencies toward overproduction are inherent in the dynamic of globalization.

This limiting contradiction acts as a feedback loop, reinforcing its own effects at different levels of the system: that of the transnational system as a whole and that of the internal political-economic systems of its component state-level economies. The need for national economies to remain competitive under global conditions becomes an effective lever for the dismantling of welfare-state class compromises at the state level, while relatively more highly paid workers from the original state populations of successful states are increasingly replaced by cheaper migrant labor from poorer states, and exportable productive operations are moved out of the territories of successful states to areas of cheaper labor. The result is a polarization of class incomes and social conditions, increasingly unmediated by social welfare policies at the state level. The result is intensifying pressure for class conflict. At the level of transnational relations the same pattern is replicated by the widening gulf between the more successful capitalist economies, net exporters of capital, and those relatively unsuccessful state economies that cannot meet the economic needs of their populations and thus become net exporters of labor, feeding the competitive demands of the more competitive economies for ever cheaper laborers.

These nascent contradictions are really manifestations at different levels of the fundamental capitalist contradiction between the increasing power of private capital, derived from private corporate control of production, marketing, and finance, and the growing power of the forces of production of social life, as embodied in self-producing persons, social groups, and political institutions.

The relatively new specific forms this contradiction has taken under the conditions of globalization result more than anything else from their mediation by the market, in its increasingly unregulated ("free") forms brought on by transnational economic activities and neoliberal policies at the national level. The market generates contradictory political and economic effects. At the level of the global system as a whole, it is the institutional matrix for limiting the regulatory powers of states to tax and to make social policy, at the same time that it has become the source of pressures for the assumption by states of new or transformed powers, as they are forced to internalize the functional needs of unregulated markets for averting monetary and financial crises and dealing with the social consequences of labor migration, job substitution, and production reallocation, as well as creating and maintaining the infrastructure for market access and expansion. At the level of the national middle class, whose empowerment as a category of economic agents derives directly from its capacity to participate in the market for consumer commodities, the market is thus at once the source and limit of the power of the middle class as a bloc of consumers.

SOCIAL CONSCIOUSNESS: NEW CHRONOTOPES FOR OLD

These contradictory tendencies form the basis of the contrasting formations of social consciousness that have emerged in the period of unregulated globalization from the 1970s to the present. As mentioned above, the collapse of the Bretton Woods system for regulating the global movements of finance capital and transnational corporations at the end of the 1960s, also constituted a decisive step in the uncoupling of the nation from the state. The development of unregulated global markets has compelled states to reorient

their political and bureaucratic apparatus, as well as the ideological basis of
their legitimacy, away from the national community of all citizens, conceived
as exercising equal and mutual "popular sovereignty," toward the globalized
market and the new sovereignty embodied in its new multilateral regulatory
institutions. The effect is to substitute the market for the nation as the hegemonic political and ideological principle ordering the relation of the state to
society. The supremacy of the globalized market has also led to the polarization of the middle class into an elite directly associated with transnational
capital and those segments of the national middle class, including the large
majority of the professional-managerial class and lower middle class, which
remain predominantly identified with the internal economies of their respective states. As sovereignty has become redistributed between states and
transnational corporate and multilateral institutions, the original class basis of
nationalism has thus become divided against itself. The new globally oriented
elites that now constitute the hegemonic segment of the middle class have no
ideological need for identification with the state much less the rest of the nation, for the legitimation of its political and economic dominance. Nationalism, under these changed historic circumstances, has increasingly become an
idiom of last resort for social losers and marginal groups to make claims upon
the state for amelioration of their marginal or otherwise disadvantaged situations (Turner 1999).

These developments have led to substantial transformations in the structures of social consciousness. In the ideological perspective of classic bourgeois nationalism, differences of class, region, and/or culture were regarded as
stigmata of incomplete assimilation into the national community. The bourgeois project of national state formation thus assumed the temporal form of
a linear process of progressive assimilation of difference within the spatial
limits of the state territory. With the substitution of market hegemony for the
hegemony of nationalism, however, the assimilation of difference as a linear
diachronic process has given way to a vision of synchronic pluralism, in which
culturally marked differences of identity are positively valued. The spatial frontiers of states thus tend to lose their cultural and ideological significance as
boundaries of the relevant units of identity, although they retain economic and
political functions within the global order. This shift of chronotopes or categories of space–time, with its social and political-economic causes, leaves the
national middle class without a hegemonic project, or indeed any class project
other than the production of its own multifarious identities through commodity consumption and the symbolic politics of multiculturalism (Turner 1993).
The transnational elite segment of the old professional-managerial class, by
contrast, has become the champion of the hegemonic project of neoliberalism,

the promotion of the free market on a global scale. In the ideological vision that goes with this project, the uniform market mechanism, conceived in abstraction from nations, states, and cultural identities, is substituted for the ostensibly egalitarian project of uniform national community, the fundamental value of nationalism as championed by the older national middle classes.

Nationalism, as an assertion of the unity of the population of a state, has thus lost much of its ideological force, along with national middle-class hegemony under the assault of free market neoliberalism. As a corollary, difference, rather than homogeneity as vested in unified national identity, has become the ideological touchstone of the new social consciousness ("identity politics," "multiculturalism," etc.). Under the aegis of the new hegemony of the market, "identity" pluralism has accordingly become positively valued as an end in itself in consumerist societies committed to the realization of personal identity and collective difference. With the eclipse of "assimilation" (or at least, the repression of difference) as the essential character and mission of the nation, "progress" and the conception of historical time as a linear process of social consolidation within the spatial framework of state boundaries lost their dominant status as formative categories of social consciousness in the more fully developed capitalist societies.

The vision of society as a pluralism of equal differences is a static vision, with no room for the directed assimilation or transformation of any identity, collective or individual, into any other. "Synchronic pluralism" thus replaces the diachronic assimilationism (i.e., "progress") of the modern nation–state as the new form of social consciousness of the consumerist middle class. In the synchronic pluralist society of equal differences, there can be no "center," nor any consequential boundary or periphery, in the sense of a point where difference begins to be devalued as alien or "underdeveloped." Where all identities and cultural styles are equally valid and synchronically self-existing, there can be no "deeper" systemic dynamics or infrastructure, no underlying causes or constraints, but only a surface pattern of contrasting signs of difference. Synchrony as "pluralism" does not imply a motionless world of fixed spatial enclaves, but rather a world of aleatory movements and freely circulating discourses, where "flows" do not amount to structurally consequential changes but are reversible, and thus lack a constant temporal direction. Carried to an extreme, the perspective of "flows," understood as randomized spatial movement, converges, in the thinking of some analysis, with the notion of "time–space compression" put forward by the geographer David Harvey (1989). According to this notion, a kind of synchronicity has been created by the development of new media of communication, information transfer, and means of rapid transportation, which have neutralized the significance of space and time as material obstacles to instantaneous social interaction and communication. In place of "material" space and time, the new technologies have made possible the emergence of virtual or "real" time and space as the privileged dimension of economic and ideological interchange, superceding such archaic features of social space–time as boundaries, specific places, and the distinct cultural and social identities associated with them.

Without discounting the importance of the new technologies of instantaneous information transfer and monetary transactions in constructing the financial circuits of transnational capitalism, however, I would insist that the technological achievement of near simultaneity of individual transactions does not commute, logically or pragmatically, to the foreshortening of historical time or the overthrow of the linear temporal conception of progress embodied in the nationalist notion of the assimilative mission of the nation–state. At this level of social consciousness, explanations for changes in concepts of space–time must be sought in macrosocial phenomena: specifically, in shifts in the hegemonic status and political relations of social classes, such as those involved in the contemporary transformation of the nation–state. In this connection, I have suggested that the fundamental changes in social consciousness I have described may be understood as integral parts of the development of new schemas of hegemony, unity, and opposition among polarized segments of the middle class and elements of the working class and marginal social groups.

The loss of its historic hegemonic project has left the national middle class with no project other than individual commodity consumption as the instrument of production of personal social identity. This, together with the individual character of professional and managerial work, the defining activity of the professional-managerial segment of the middle class, accounts for the individualistic character of the social consciousness of most members of this class. This in turn, together with the severance of professional and managerial work from direct involvement in economic production, accounts for the focus of the professional-managerial class perspective on processes of circulation and consumption in the market, in abstraction from production and a fortiori the exploitative relations of production (Ehrenreich and Ehrenreich 1979; Pfeil 1990). The combination of these features of class perspective leaves the middle class in general and the professional-managerial class in particular with no coherent political or ideological relation to society as a whole. The social vision of synchronic pluralism offers no depth, no center, no boundaries, no basis for a relation to any form of social reality beyond the shifting identities constructed by consumption, and thus no structure. It offers, in short, postmodernism.

FROM CONTRADICTIONS TO CONSCIOUSNESS TO POLITICAL ACTION

At this point, however, the fundamental contradictions of the contemporary global political economy identified at the beginning of this section come to bear. Under the pressure of these contradictions, some members of the middle class, especially its professional-managerial cadre, have begun to transcend the limitations of their default class perspective as a consumption-oriented service class, as they encounter the limits imposed by global capitalism and the political order of states subservient to its needs and interests on their ability to realize the increased individual and collective empowerment for personal self-production they supposedly derive from consumption. The rise of new social movements and the formation of thousands of voluntary nongovernmental organizations dedicated to ostensibly extrapolitical causes and universal principles (the defense of nature, human rights, indigenous peoples, consumer protection, health and food relief), all of which focus in different ways on issues arising from the pressure of private capital and state-sponsored development on the quality of life, or the limitation of human freedoms by state regimes seeking to offset their lack of popular support and resulting inability to pursue unpopular policies of "modernization" often linked with the requirements of global markets and multilateral regulatory institutions and development banks. These issues arise at points where the empowerment of the person for self-production through access to consumption through the market for commodities and the possession of valued professional skills comes into conflict with the self-empowerment of capital, whether private or public, deployed in the service of expanded capital accumulation and centralization. If production is defined as transformative activity oriented to social values and needs, the production of human social life and consciousness, including personal identity and lifestyle, family and kinship relations, qualify as forms of "production" as much as the production of commodities for exchange on the market. The production of social personhood and identity at both individual and collective levels consist of transformative activities undertaken by social actors acting not merely as consumers but as producers, exercising considerable freedom of choice of means and ends. They thus entail a measure of empowerment. The cumulative growth of the massive purchasing power represented by the six million essentially middle-class consumers (with the postmodern culture class segment accounting for a disproportionate share) identified by Ohmae (1990) thus represents a massive accumulation of social power for the production of personal and social existence. Despite its atomization as the property of individual persons, this accumulation of power for personal consumption and production may now be reaching a critical mass where it can begin to support challenges to the power of economic commodity and financial capital in the form of new social movements.

In the United States, for instance, opposition to globalization and its effects among different sectors of the population is growing, becoming more organized, and the different social movements and groups engaged in this opposition are beginning to unite in common protests and demonstrations. Salaried middle-class and industrial workers, whose jobs are threatened by downsizing, job substitution, and the export of production to less-developed countries, have been joined by salaried service workers, threatened by developments in information processing and the spread of part-time and temporary jobs. These middle-class white-collar workers, basically concerned about their jobs within the national economy, until recently seemed to have little in common with protesters against globalization primarily concerned with its effects on the working conditions of workers outside the United States (represented by the campus-based organization United Students against Sweatshops), or with those protesting the environmental damage caused by unregulated capitalism in other parts of the world. In the protests against the WTO in Seattle in November 1999, these distinct groupings of protestors were all present, but demonstrated separately. Six months later, in Washington, D.C., they united for the first time to protest what they jointly called "the corporate globalization agenda." As they combined their forces to present a united front against corporate and financial globalization, they also expanded their range of institutional targets. From a specific focus on the WTO in Seattle, the April demonstrators in Washington, in three successive actions, blocked a meeting of international directors of the IMF, picketed the spring meeting of World Bank directors calling for the total annulment of Third World debt, and denounced the U.S. administration's project to get China admitted to the WTO. In sum, the interorganizational demonstrations in Washington confronted the whole global capitalist apparatus of multilateral political, financial, and economic institutions, while bringing a new unity among themselves (Delattre 2000).

In a further portentous development, American labor unions and organizations have also begun to collaborate with these essentially middle-class–based protests, recognizing their overlapping concerns with the effects of globalization on jobs and working conditions within the United States and abroad. Some labor spokesmen made statements in support of the Washington actions. For all their concern with jobs and employment conditions, however, observers have reported more general concerns about the economic, social, and political effects of totally unregulated free markets among all these categories of protesters. Large numbers of Americans, it appears, doubt that

globalization without any governmental regulation will promote either political democracy or general economic well-being (Delattre 2000). The
widespread malaise was recently expressed in an influential article by an ex-
economist of the World Bank, Joseph Stiglitz, that appeared in an April issue
of the *New Republic.*

> Economic policy is without a doubt the most important element in the interac-
> tion of the US with the rest of the world. However, the culture of the people who
> make international economic policy in this country—notwithstanding its sta-
> tus as the greatest democracy in the world—is not democratic (Stiglitz 2000:60,
> my translation from the French translation of Stiglitz's original English text).

If one begins, as one should, from a recognition that the market and the state
are historically interdependent institutions and not mutually distinct and unrelated entities, it becomes possible to see the globalization project for what it
is: not an attempt to do away with the state or render it irrelevant, but rather
an attempt to shift the terms of the political interdependence of the two so
that states are increasingly forced to shift their policies from regulating the national economy to managing the global economy to maintain its stability, in
cooperation with other states while giving up the power to protect the national economy from the effects and requirements of the global economy
(McMichael at press). The question thus is not whether the state either should
or should not be brought into some form of interaction with the market, as
the issue is frequently framed by proponents of state regulation of the economy and neoliberal proponents of the global "free market," respectively. State
and market are already interpenetrating and interdependent: the only question, as Humpty-Dumpty expressed it, is which is to be master (Carroll
1896:chapter 6).

As of yet, the tensions and conflicts between NSMs and NGOs on the one
hand and private and public development capital on the other have given rise
to a relatively unconnected series of skirmishes. Even so, these confrontations
have resulted in some significant reverses for capital, in the form of blocked
dam projects, the defeat of the MAI (Multilateral Agreement on Investments),
and the rejection of the American bid to give the president "fast-track" power
to negotiate international trade agreements without consulting Congress, and
the disruption of IMF and World Economic Forum meetings by coalitions of
opposing organizations at Seattle, Davos, and elsewhere.

What lends these microconflicts the force of symptoms of a more serious
structural crisis is their resonance with the crisis of state sovereignty brought
on by the first of the contradictory tendencies identified at the beginning of

this section. To some degree, the multifarious projects of the NSMs substitute for the collective class project of the historic modern middle class, as its political and ideological hegemony passes to the new neoliberal elites oriented to global capital. These new hegemonic elites and the neoliberal ideologues that swell their ranks have also produced a form of social consciousness specific to their own project and perspective as agents of global capital. Neoliberalism is founded upon the substitution of the market for the nation–state as the hegemonic ideological and political-economic framework for political society at both state and transnational levels. The global market, in neoliberal ideology, is conceived not so much as a product of history as a manifestation of the transhistorical essence of social existence, whose material epiphany as the governing structure of political and economic relations thus marks the end of history. It is, in this sense, also a "synchronic" ideological vision. It is also "pluralist," both in the positive sense of its emphasis on the individualistic activities of consumption and accumulation in abstraction from governmental interference and in the negative sense that it is indifferent to assimilative notions of homogeneous national community. The neoliberal view is thus compatible with the "synchronic pluralism" of the emergent chronotope of national middle-class social consciousness. It too presupposes the dehyphenation of the nation–state, the elimination of the nation and national sovereignty, and with it the project of middle class hegemony of which state-level nationalism was the vehicle. It too wishes to reduce the state to the role of referee, manager, and enforcer of relations among mutually discrete and autonomous entities—in its case, private capitals, rather than the different identities and cultural groups of the pluralist vision of the national middle class. It, too, is unconcerned with any totalizing vision of "society." Unlike the synchronic pluralism of the national middle class, with its notion of random and reversible flows, however, the neoliberal vision allows for an unidirectional flow of capital and wealth to the private corporate owners of capital, creating an ever-increasing vertical polarization of society between rich and poor, empowered and disempowered. This vision of quantitative change within the limits of qualitative structural stasis defines the class project (and current ideological hegemony) of the elite class segments identified with global capital.

Ironically, until and unless some transnational movement can succeed in forging a viable global political framework capable of regulating transnational capital, the pivotal element in this conflict of class perspectives and projects remains the state. Just as the state, acting in concert with other states, created the institutional basis of the global market and financial system, and remains the most practicable source of the powers of international regulatory agencies and crisis intervention by central banks to avert periodic threats of monetary and financial collapse, so concerted action by states remains the most likely basis for the imposition of a new global order capable of regulating financial and corporate capital for social and political ends. This would take a concerted political movement that could retake control of state policy making from the current neoliberal hegemony; this in turn would require a more coherent social and political vision than the current array of NSMs and fragmented oppositional movements (including working-class organizations) have thus far been able to produce.

Can anthropology contribute to such a unifying vision? I have argued that the implicit common denominator of the new social movements for human rights, environmental protection, consumer protection, support of indigenous peoples, and numerous other causes is the defense of the power of production in the widest human sense of the term, including the production of personal identity and empowerment for the realization of cultural values as well as the production of material commodities and means of subsistence. The issue of the production of human personhood and social being in this sense lies at the heart of the contradictory empowerment of the middle class for self-production through consumption and its disempowerment through the consolidation of control by capital over conditions of work, commodity production, and marketing.

The struggle of the predominantly middle-class NSMs against the multiple ramifications of this contradiction is thus, in the most fundamental sense, a struggle over the meaning and control of production. This struggle has so far been carried on in isolation from working-class resistance to the intensified global exploitation of labor through such devices as job substitution and the reallocation of productive work to areas where more brutal forms of exploitation than are socially possible in advanced capitalist countries, including slavery, child labor, and various other forms of unwaged labor, can be practiced. Traditional working-class organizations, such as trade unions organized at the nation–state level, have lacked the resources to confront these global strategies at the transnational level (McMichael 1999:34). The communicational and organizational skills and access to political power and transnational media of the professional-managerial segment of the middle class could make an important contribution to the struggle to organize transnational working-class resistance in this context. Collaboration between working-class organizations and middle-class social movements might be catalyzed if both could recognize the other as engaged in a struggle for a measure of social control over production, in its complementary aspects as the production of commodities and the production of persons. The anthropological conception of production as a human and social totality could contribute a unifying ideological basis for such a collaborative struggle.

ACKNOWLEDGMENTS
Research for this paper was supported by the Harry Frank Guggenheim Foundation. I have benefitted from critical discussions of previous versions and drafts at the VIII Congreso de Antropología, Federación Asociaciones de Antropología del Estado Español at Santiago de Compostela, the Spanish National Research Council in Madrid, the Department of Anthropology of the Universidad Autonoma of Barcelona, the École des Hautes Etudes en Sciences Sociales in Paris, and the Departments of Anthropology of Cambridge University, the University of Edinburgh, and Goldsmiths' College in the United Kingdom.

REFERENCES

Anderson, Benedict. 1983. *Imagined Communities: Reflections on the Origin and Spread of Nationalism.* London: Verso.

Bakhtin, Mikhail. 1981. *The Dialogical Imagination: Four Essays.* Edited by Michael Holquist. Austin: University of Texas.

Carroll, L. C. 1872. *Through the Looking Glass.* London: MacMillan.

Delattre, Lucas. 2000. Ces Américains contre la mondialisation, *Le Monde,* April 19, 1, 17.

Ehrenreich, B., and P. Ehrenreich. 1979. "The Professional-Managerial Class." In *Between Labor and Capital.* Edited by P. Walker. Boston: South End Press.

Gill, Stephen. 1994. "Structural Changes in the Global Economy: Globalizing Elites and the Emerging World Order." In *Global Transformation: Challenges to the State System.* Edited by Yoshikazu Sakamoto, 169–99. Tokyo: U.N. University Press.

———. 1996. "Globalization, Democratization and the Politics of Indifference." In *Globalization: Critical Reflections.* Edited by James M. Mittelman, 205–27. Boulder, Colo.: Lynn Rienner.

Greider, William. 1997. *One World, Ready or Not: The Manic Logic of Global Capitalism.* New York: Simon & Schuster.

Harvey, David. 1989. *The Condition of Postmodernity: An Enquiry into the Origins of Cultural Change.* Oxford, U.K.: Basil Blackwell.

Keck, Margaret, and Kathryn Sikkink. 1998. *Activists Beyond Borders: Advocacy Networks in International Politics.* Ithaca, N.Y., Cornell University Press.

Laraña, Enrique, Hank Johnston, and Joseph R. Gusfield, eds. 1994. *New Social Movements: From Ideology to Identity.* Philadelphia: Temple University Press.

McMichael, Philip. In press. "Globalisation: Trend or Project?" In *Contemporary Theories of Global Political Economy.* Edited by R. Palan. New York: Routledge.

———. 1999. "The Global Crisis of Wage-Labour." *Studies in Political Economy* 58 (Spring 1999): 11–40.

Miller, Daniel. 1998. *A Theory of Shopping.* Ithaca, N.Y.: Cornell University Press.

Nagengast, C., and T. Turner. 1997. "Introduction: Universal Human Rights versus Cultural Relativity." Special Issue. Edited by C. Nagengast and T. Turner. *Journal of Anthropological Research* 53:269–72.

O'Connor, James. 2002. *The Fiscal Crisis of the State.* New Brunswick, N.J.: Transaction.

Offe, C. 1985. New Social Movements: Challenging the Boundaries of Institutional Politics. *Social Research* 52:817–68.

Ohmae, K. 1990. *The End of the Nation–State: The Rise of Regional Economies.* New York: Free Press.

Pfeil, Fred. 1990. "Makin' Flippy-Floppy: Postmodernism and the Baby-Boom PMC." In *Another Tale to Tell: Politics and Narrative in Postmodern Culture.* Edited by Fred Pfeil. New York: Verso.

Rist, Gilbert. 1997. *The History of Development: From Western Origins to Global Faith.* London: Zed Books.

Sieyès, Emmanuel Joseph Abbé. 1972. *Qu'est-ce que le tiers etat?* Critique avec une introduction et notes par Roberto Zapperi. Genève: Drosz.

Stiglitz, Joseph. 2000. "The Insider." *New Republic* 222, no. 16–17:56–60.

Turner, T. 1993. "Anthropology and Multiculturalism: What Is Anthropology That Multiculturalists Should Be Mindful of It?" *Cultural Anthropology* 8:4.

———. 1997. "Human Rights, Human Difference: Anthropology's Contribution to an Emancipatory Cultural Politics." In *Universal Human Rights versus Cultural Relativity.* Special Issue. Edited by C. Nagengast and T. Turner. *Journal of Anthropological Research* 53, no. 3:273–92.

————. 1999. "Indigenous and Culturalist Movements in the Contemporary Global Conjuncture." in Francisco Fernández Del Riego et al., *Las identidades y las tensiones culturales de la modernidad*, VIII Congreso de Antropología, Federación de Asociaciones de Antropología del Estado Español. Santiago de Compostela.

————. At press. "Anthropological Activism, Indigenous Peoples and Globalization." In *The Scholar as Activist*. Edited by C. Nagengast and C. Velez-Ibañez. Society for Applied Anthropology.

3

Economic Globalization and the Redrawing of Citizenship

SASKIA SASSEN

This chapter examines the impact of a strengthening global economy on the continuity and formation of rights we associate with citizenship, particularly rights that grant the power to extract accountability from governments. Together with sovereignty and exclusive territoriality, citizenship marks the specificity of the modern state. In view of the transformations in the territoriality and sovereignty of the nation–state resulting from economic globalization, we can posit that there may also be an impact on citizenship. The logic framing this chapter is that the embeddedness of the institution of citizenship suggests the possibility that these transformations may also have had an impact on some of the features of citizenship.[1] The history of the institution shows the importance of the underlying conditions in the shaping of modern citizenship.[2] Insofar as the global economy has created new conditions we might be seeing yet another phase in the evolution of the institution of citizenship.[3]

EXPANDING THE ANALYTIC TERRAIN FOR EXAMINING RIGHTS

In a world where the sovereignty of the nation–state and civil solidarity are possibly challenged by globalization, what is the analytic terrain within which we need to examine the question of rights in the social sciences? Do we need to expand this terrain? Said differently, do we need to introduce new elements in the discourse on rights in the social sciences?

This is a broad agenda and one I cannot do justice to in a short chapter. Elsewhere I deal with some of these issues[4] (see, for instance, Holston 1999; Basch,

Blanc-Szanton, and Schiller 1994).[5] In this chapter my focus is on the impact of economic globalization on citizenship. Here I use the notion of economic citizenship as a construct that destabilizes the linearity of the history of the institution. I want to take that history seriously—and that means underlining the particular combinations of conditions that had to crystallize for citizenship as we know it to emerge. My question is, have the specific conditions brought on by economic globalization, especially in highly developed countries, contributed to yet another major transformation/evolution in the institution of citizenship? My answer is yes. But with a twist.[6]

Historicizing the institution means not stopping at the latest bundle of rights that came with the welfare state. It means recognizing the possible erosion of some of the conditions presupposed by citizenship. Today's welfare state crisis, growing unemployment in many of the European economies and growing numbers of employed poor in the United States, and growing earnings inequality in all highly developed countries certainly can be read as signaling a change in the conditions of citizens.[7] If we take the history of the institution of citizenship seriously then these changing conditions have to be read as having, at least potentially, an impact.[8] To what extent they are connected to economic globalization will vary from country to country and is difficult to establish with precision. But overall, there is now a growing consensus that the race to the bottom in the highly developed countries and the world at large is a function of global competition; further, disinvestment or insufficient investment in industries that contribute middle-income jobs is also partly a function of hypermobile capital in search of the most profitable short-term opportunities around the globe. Finally, the increased liquidity of capital through securitization and the ascendance of finance generally has further stimulated the global circulation of capital and the search for investment opportunities worldwide rather than promoting long-term economic and social development.[9] These are typically investment decisions that do not necessarily favor the growth of a large middle class. One of the most disturbing trends today is the vast expansion in the numbers of unemployed and never-employed people in all the highly developed countries (Longworth 1998; Sassen 2001, chapters 8 and 9). Beyond these conditions in the highly developed countries are the growing masses of poor in the developing countries who lack access to the most basic means for survival (UNCTAD 1999).

Thus, while no precise measure is available, there is a growing body of evidence that signals that economic globalization has hit at some of the major conditions, including in the highly developed countries, that have hitherto supported the evolution of citizenship, and particularly the formation of social rights.

It could be argued that if there is one type of citizenship that is badly needed it is the right to a job, the right to work for a living, the right to economic survival.[10] This would be a new bundle of rights representing economic citizenship alongside the social rights corresponding to the welfare state.

There is an emerging body of scholarship and political analysis that posits the need for rights to economic well-being, to economic survival. These studies argue for the legitimacy of the claim. Some of them place this claim at the heart of democratic theory, arguing that employment and economic well-being are essential conditions for democratic politics. And I would agree with this. I consider it extremely important, it needs to be pursued.

But my question here is not about the claim to economic citizenship and its legitimacy. My question is rather, is there a reality today that represents an aggregation of economic rights that one could describe as a form of economic citizenship in that it empowers and can demand accountability from governments in economic matters?

My reading of the evidence suggests that, yes, there is. But this economic citizenship does not belong to citizens. It belongs to firms and markets, specifically, the global financial markets, and it is located not in individuals, not in citizens, but in global economic actors. The fact of being global gives these actors power over individual governments. Much of this is deeply bound up with some of the fundamental changes brought about by economic globalization.[11] This granting of rights and powers to global actors is in some ways a continuation of an older history whereby legal systems were inflected with the structures of privilege specific to a spatiohistorical period. In the case of Anglo-American law, the freedoms granted the sphere of the market reflect the particular conditions of the capitalist systems in formation (Biersteker et al., forthcoming). My concern here is with the specifics of this current phase.

It is this particular instantiation of the notion of economic citizenship that I want to address next. This use of the concept has the status, one could say, of a theoretical provocation; it is not a use that fits in the lineage of the concept. My beginning point is a set of practices: specifically the practices that firms and markets can engage in that amount to a bundle of rights, some of them formally specified and others de facto permissions that are a consequence of those practices and formal rights. Multinationals and the global financial markets are the most powerful of these actors.

It is the case of the global financial markets I want to address here, as they represent one of the most astounding aggregations of new "rights" and legitimacy we have seen over the last ten years. When I think of new locations for the aggregation of power and legitimacy that we have historically associated with the nation–state, two new institutions come to the fore for me over the last decades:

the global financial markets and the covenants on human rights. They are the two new contestants, alongside the authority of the national state, for redistributing power and legitimacy. They are quite different from each other. And they have different constituencies. Here I will confine myself to the global financial markets.[12]

THE GLOBAL CAPITAL MARKET: POWER AND NORM MAKING

The formation of a global capital market represents a concentration of power that is capable of influencing national government economic policy and, by extension, other policies. These markets can now exercise the accountability functions associated with citizenship: they can vote governments' economic policies in or out, they can force governments to take certain measures and not others. As deregulation and the new types of reregulation are instituted in a growing number of financial markets in countries around the world, investors worldwide can bring in massive amounts of capital on short notice and they can take it out equally fast. While the power of these markets is quite different from that of the political electorate, they have emerged as a sort of global, cross-border economic electorate, where the right to vote is predicated on the possibility of registering capital.

The deregulation of domestic financial markets, the liberalization of international capital flows, computers, and telecommunications have all contributed to an explosive growth in financial markets.[13] Since 1980, the total stock of financial assets has increased three times faster than the aggregate GDP of the twenty-three highly developed countries that form the OECD. And the volume of trading in currencies, bonds, and equities has increased about five times faster and now surpasses it by far. For instance, aggregate GDP stood at U.S. $30 trillion at the end of the 1990s while the value in the global trade of derivatives was U.S. $83 trillion for 1999, and had risen to U.S. $168 trillion by 2001. This is a figure that dwarfs the value of cross-border trade (ca. $6 trillion in 1999), foreign directment investment stock ($5.1 trillion in 1999), and the aggregate foreign currency reserves of the twenty-three OECD members, the so-called rich countries in the world.

As a consequence of this enormous capital that is highly liquid, the global capital market now has the power to discipline national governments. This became evident with the 1994–95 financial crisis in Mexico and the 1997–98 Southeast Asian financial crisis. In all the countries involved investors were capable of leaving en masse: in the Southeast Asian case they took out well over $100 billion over a short period of time. The foreign currency markets had the orders of magnitude to alter exchange rates radically for some of these currencies and overwhelm each and all of the central banks involved and their futile attempts to defend their currencies against the onslaught.

The foreign exchange market was the first one to globalize, in the mid-1970s. Today it is the biggest and in many ways the only truly global market. It has gone from a daily turnover rate of about $15 billion in the 1970s, to $60 billion in the early 1980s, and an estimated $1.3 trillion in 1999. In contrast, the total foreign currency reserves of the rich industrial countries amounted to less than $1 trillion in that same year. Just to make it more concrete, foreign exchange transactions were ten times as large as world trade in 1983; only ten years later, in 1992, they were sixty times larger, and by 1999, seventy times larger. And world trade has itself grown sharply over this period.

According to some estimates, we have reached only the midpoint of a fifty-year process in terms of the full integration of these markets. The financial markets are expected to expand even further in relation to the size of the real economy. Today the total stock of financial assets traded in the global capital markets[14] is equivalent to almost three times the GDP of OECD countries. Much more integration and power may lie ahead for capital markets. What really counts is how much capital can be moved across borders in how short a period of time. It is clearly an immense amount.

In addition to the direct impact on the economy via the market, we need to ask how this massive growth of financial flows and assets and the fact of an integrated global capital market affect states in their economic policy making. Conceivably a global capital market could just be a vast pool of money for investors to shop in without conferring power over governments. The fact that it can discipline governments' economic policy making is a distinct power, one that is not ipso facto inherent in the existence of a large global capital market.

The differences between today's global capital market and the period of the gold standard before World War I are illuminating in this regard. The first set of differences concerns today's growing concentration of market power in institutions such as pension funds and insurance companies. A second major difference is the explosion in financial innovations. Innovations have raised the supply of financial instruments that are tradable, sold on the open market. There are significant differences by country. Securitization is well advanced in the United States, but just beginning in most of Europe and Japan.[15] The proliferation of derivatives has furthered the linking of national markets by making it easier to exploit price differences between different financial instruments, that is, to arbitrage.[16] A third difference is the impact of digital networks on the functioning and growth possibilities of financial markets. The crucial difference here is the combination of the speed of circulation made possible by digital networks and the innovations that raise the level of liquidity and liquefy what was hitherto considered nonliquid. The properties the new information technologies bring to the financial markets are instantaneous transmission, interconnectivity, and speed. The speed of transactions has brought its own consequences. Trading in currencies and securities is instant thanks to vast computer networks. And the high degree of interconnectivity in combination with instantaneous transmission signals the potential for exponential growth. For certain matters, the increase in volumes per se may be secondary. But when these volumes can be deployed to overwhelm national central banks, the fact itself of the volume becomes a significant variable explaining the influence these markets can exercise over government policy making.[17]

The key features of the current global capital market affect the power of governments over their economies in market-centered systems that has been based on the ability to tax, to print money, and to borrow. Before deregulation, governments could (to some extent) directly control the amount of bank lending through credit controls and impose ceilings on interest rates contributing to make monetary policy more effective than it is today. For instance, to cite a well-known case in the United States, Regulation Q imposed interest rate ceilings and thereby protected the holdings of savings and loan associations by preventing their flight to higher-interest-bearing alternatives (Cooper and Fraser 1984). This in turn kept mortgages and home construction going. In 1985 Regulation Q was lifted. The absence of interest rate ceilings meant that money left the savings and loan association in hordes for higher-interest yields, creating a massive slump in mortgages and housing construction.[18]

There are now a series of mechanisms through which the global capital market actually exercises its disciplining function on national governments and pressures them to become accountable to the logic of these markets. The financial crises of recent years bring some of this to the fore in a brutal fashion. But there are others, often difficult to trace. Elsewhere, I have examined how key policies being instituted today in countries that become integrated into the global capital market reflect the operational logic of this market (Sassen 1996). The emphasis placed on anti-inflationary monetary policies by the central banks of these countries often entails a reversal of prior policies that prioritized employment growth and allowed for far higher levels of inflation than are feasible for the functioning of a global capital market. A second set of policies concerns the aim of making the state "competitive" by cutting down on social costs of a variety of sorts.

The global capital market is a mechanism for pricing capital and allocating it to its most profitable opportunity.[19] One of the problems today is that the most profitable opportunity is increasingly being seen as also the most productive. This signals the weight of the logic of the financial markets on economic policy. The search for the most profitable opportunities, and the speedup in all transactions, including profit taking, contributes potentially to massive distortions in the flow of capital. The global capital market has a logic in its operation, but it is not one that will lead inevitably to the desirable larger social and economic investments. The issue here is not so much that this market has emerged as a powerful mechanism in which those with capital can influence government policy—in many ways an old story.[20] It is rather that the overall operation of this market has an embedded logic that calls for certain types of economic policy objectives. Given the properties of the systems through which this market operates—speed, simultaneity, and interconnectivity—and the orders of magnitude it can produce, it can exercise undue pressure to get the right types of policies instituted, which is precisely what is happening. And this weight can be exercised on any country integrated into the financial markets, of which there are a rapidly growing number.[21]

A NEW ZONE OF LEGITIMACY?

Is the power of the global capital market a threat to democracy and to the notion that the electoral system is one way of extracting accountability and ensuring some control over governments by its citizens? Where does that leave this, an essential mechanism for citizens to exercise influence? One way of thinking about this is as a partial privatization of key components of monetary policy and of fiscal policy.

Roepke (1954), trying to understand the relation between international law and the international economy before World War I under the Pax Britannica, refers to that particular form of international realm as a res publica non christiana, seeing in it a secular version of the res publica christiana of the Middle Ages. Is the transnational web of rights and protections that multinational firms and global markets enjoy today the next step in this evolution—a privatizing of an international zone that was once a res publica? This is particularly so when we consider some of the debates around the matter of international public law. Some legal scholars are positing that we are headed into a situation in which international law will predominantly be international private law, largely international economic law.[22] While in principle that includes the individual citizen, in practice such private economic law addresses largely the needs and claims of firms and markets.

There is much to be said about this new zone of legitimacy. Let me begin with two observations. One is that national states have participated in its formation and implementation and thereby have reconstituted some of their own features, a subject I return to below. The second concerns the matter of what have been called the implicit ground rules of our legal system—a matter that has not been formalized into rules of prohibition or permission and constitutes a de facto set of rules of permission.[23] This type of analytical elaboration is helpful in the effort to conceptualize the bundle of rights that has accrued to firms and markets over the last decade of economic globalization. The ground rules on which economic globalization is proceeding contain far more permissions than have been formalized in explicit rules of permission and prohibition.

De-Nationalized State Agendas

At the level of theorization, these conditions signal that we need to capture and conceptualize a specific set of operations that take place within national institutional settings but are geared to nonnational or transnational agendas where once they were geared to national agendas.[24] I conceptualize this as denationalization—denationalization of specific, typically highly specialized, state institutional orders and of state agendas.[25] From the perspective of research I have argued that this entails the need to decode what is "national" (as historically constructed) about the particular set of activities and authorities of central banks or ministries of finance briefly described above.[26]

There is a set of strategic dynamics and institutional transformations at work here. They may incorporate a small number of state agencies and units within departments, a small number of legislative initiatives and of executive orders, and yet have the power to institute a new normativity at the heart of the state; this is especially so because these strategic sectors are operating in complex interactions with private, transnational, powerful, actors. The particular types of actors of interest to the argument in this chapter are global markets and firms. It is their agendas that get partly institutionalized in key aspects of government policy. This takes place even as much of the institutional apparatus of the state remains basically unchanged. The inertia of bureaucratic organizations, which creates its own version of path dependence, makes an enormous contribution to continuity.

Further, the new types of cross-border collaborations among specialized government agencies concerned with a growing range of issues emerging from the globalization of capital markets and the new trade order are yet another aspect of this participation by the state in the implementation of a global economic system. A good example is the heightened interaction in the last three or four years among antitrust regulators from a large number of countries.[27] This is a period of reinvigorated antitrust activities because economic globalization puts pressure on governments to work toward convergence in antitrust regulations in a situation where countries tend to have often very diverse competition laws or enforcement practices (Portnoy 1999). This convergence around specific antitrust issues frequently exists in an ocean of enormous differences among these countries in all kinds of laws and regulations about components of the economy that do not intersect with globalization. It is then a very partial and specialized type of convergence among regulators of different countries who often begin to share more with each other than they do with colleagues back home in the larger bureaucracies within which they work. There are multiple other instances of this highly specialized type of convergence: regulatory issues concerning telecommunications, finance, the Internet, and so forth. In some of these sectors there has long been an often elementary convergence, or at least coordination of standards. What we see today is a sharp increase in the work of establishing convergence, well illustrated by the intensified transactions among central bankers necessary in the context of the global capital market. While central bankers have long interacted with each other across borders, we can clearly identify a new phase in the last ten years. The world of cross-border trade has brought with it a sharpened need for convergence in standards, as is evident in the vast proliferation of ISO items. One outcome of these various trends is the emergence of a strategic field of operations that represents a partial disembedding of specific state operations from the broader institutional world of the state geared exclusively to national agendas.[28] It is a fairly rarified field of cross-border transactions among government agencies and business sectors aimed at addressing the new conditions produced and demanded by economic globalization. It is in many ways a new increasingly institutionalized framework for producing legitimacy around various objectives that lie largely in the domain of global markets and firms. This framework allows firms and markets to exercise enormous influence in shaping what ought to be "proper" government policy. The power of these firms and markets, discussed in the first half of this chapter, allows these actors to pressure governments into designing and adopting such policies.[29]

Making the Global Economy Work

Private firms in international finance, accounting, and law, the new private standards for international accounting and financial reporting, and supranational organizations such as WTO, all play strategic nongovernment-centered governance functions. The events following the Mexico crisis provide us with some interesting insights about these firms' role in changing the conditions for financial operation, about the ways in which national states participated, and the formation of the new institutionalized space described above.

J. P. Morgan worked with Goldman Sachs and Chemical Bank to develop several innovative deals that brought back investors to Mexico's markets.[30] Further, in July 1996, an enormous $6-billion, five-year deal that offered investors a Mexican floating rate note or syndicated loan—backed by oil receivables from the state oil monopoly PEMEX—was twice oversubscribed. It became somewhat of a model for asset-backed deals from Latin America, especially oil-rich Venezuela and Ecuador. Key to the high demand was that the structure had been designed to capture investment grade ratings from S&P and Moody's. This was the first Mexican deal with an investment grade. The intermediaries worked with the Mexican government, but on their terms—this was not a government-to-government deal. This secured acceptability in the new institutionalized privatized intermediary space for cross-border transactions—evidenced by the high level of oversubscription and the high ratings. And it allowed the financial markets to grow on what had been a crisis.

After the Mexico crisis and before the first signs of the Asian crisis, we see a large number of very innovative deals that contribute to further expand the volumes in the financial markets and to incorporate new sources of profit, that is, debts for sale. Typically these deals involved novel concepts of how to sell debt and what could be a saleable debt. Often the financial services firms structuring these deals also implemented minor changes in depository systems to bring them more in line with international standards. The aggressive innovating and selling on the world market of what had hitherto been thought to be too illiquid and too risky for such a sale further contributed to expand and strengthen the institutionalization of a private intermediary space for cross-border transactions operating partly outside the interstate system. The new intermediaries have done the strategic work, a kind of "activism" toward ensuring growth in their industry and to overcome the potentially devastating effects of financial crises on the industry as a whole and on the whole notion of integrated global financial markets.

These developments raise a question about the condition of international public law. Do the new private systems for governance and accountability and the acceptance by many states, even if under great pressure, of policies that further the agendas of powerful global economic actors indicate a decline of international public law and the capacities for democratic governance that is part of its aspiration?

COUNTERVAILING FORCES

Are there countervailing trends that can strengthen what is now being weakened, tools for a different kind of governance of the global economy? We can find a countervailing force in the fact that the state does contain agencies and interests that go against the ascendance of the global financial markets. The international role of the state in the global economic arena has to a large extent meant furthering deregulation, strengthening markets, and pushing for privatization. But does it have to be this way? The participation of national states in the global environmental arena has frequently led to the signing of multilateral agreements that aim at supporting measures to protect the environment. That is not to say that they are effective; but they do create a framework that legitimates both the international pursuit of a common good and the role of national states in that pursuit.[31] In the international economic arena, on the other hand, the role of the state seems to have been largely confined to pursuing the goal of maximizing the profitability of certain economic sectors and actors, not even all economic sectors and actors.

Can national states pursue a broader international economic agenda, one that addresses questions of equity and mechanisms for accountability vis-à-vis the major global economic actors? International cooperation and multinational agreements are on the rise: about one hundred major treaties and agreements on the environment have gone into effect since 1972, though not all remain in force. Aman (1998) notes that it is in the interest of the state to play an increasingly active role at the global level. In the longer term it is more likely that stronger legal regimes will develop on a global basis if the global issues involved have a national regulatory counterpart. Even when such regulatory approaches use the market as a tool for compliance, they can strengthen the rule of law (nationally and globally) and they can strengthen accountability. The participation of national states in new international legal regimes of this sort may contribute to the development of transnational frameworks aiming at promoting greater equity.

Another category of forces that represent a countervailing power are the active movements and ideologies that resist the erosion of citizenship. Most important is the spread of the institution of citizenship itself. Even though its specific cultural-political meaning may vary across the world, it has emerged as an aspiration held, it seems, by even extremely disadvantaged people who may not have had the benefit of an education introducing them to the history of the institution. It has now been formalized as a condition for the legitimacy of governments in the community of states. A new trend in international legal discourse conditions the international status of the state on the particular political rights central to classical liberal democracy; democratic government becomes a criterion for recognition of the state, for protection of its territorial integrity, or for its full participation in the relations between states. This is reflected, for instance, in the recent American and European Community guidelines on recognition of new states in Eastern Europe and in the territory of the former Soviet Union. There is also a recent international legal literature that seeks to establish a basis in international law for a right to democratic governance, and conditions statehood on this right. There are two related schools of thought. One is part of an older literature emerging with postcolonial government formation, especially in

Africa. It is part of a larger debate on the meaning of self-determination in post-colonial international law. It associates a state's right to self-determination with the right to representative democracy for its people. A second, newer school of thought, perhaps most prominently represented by Thomas Franck (1992) seeks to craft a right to democratic governance from existing rights of different lineages. Franck anticipates that the legitimacy of each government someday will be measured definitively by international rules and processes.

The major implications for those who are in a disadvantaged position in the current system—whether women, unemployed workers, poor, discriminated minorities, and so on—is that these new schools of thought reject the statist model in the international system, a model still prevalent today, which is indifferent to the type of domestic regime and the relation between state and society. They involve a reevaluation of the notion that the sovereign state is the exclusive representative of its population in the international sphere. And they contain a revision of the notion that the state is the only actor in international law that really matters. As I discussed in the prior sections of this chapter, there is already a growing role for nonstate actors, but it is disproportionately going to individuals and entities with power, whether arbitrators or global markets in finance. We need to redress that balance. The emergence of these nonstate actors signals the formation of an international civil society. But it does not mean excluding the institutional domain of the national state for the enactment of alternative projects. In my reading these can be enacted also inside that domain.[32]

CONCLUSION

The theoretical/political question running through this chapter has to do with what actors gain legitimacy for governance of the global economy and emerge as legitimate claimants to take over rules and authorities hitherto encased in the national state and hence subject, in principle, to citizens' approval. More specifically, the concern was to understand in what ways global economic actors, such as markets and firms, have not only amassed the raw power of their orders of magnitude, which can overwhelm those of the richest states in the world, but also established policy channels that have made it possible to institute inside national states, measures that further their interests. In the spirit of theoretical provocation aimed at destabilizing somewhat rigid conceptions of the institution of citizenship, I posited that global economic actors have now gained "rights" that allow them to make governments accountable to the operational logic of the global capital market. I interpret this outcome as signaling the emergence of a type of "economic citizenship" that becomes an entitlement of global firms and markets rather than citizens. This is an ironic turn on the notion of economic citizenship. And it is a deeply troubling turn in the longer history of the institution of citizenship. It has the effect of blurring the edges of the institution of citizenship as we have come to construct and represent it and signals the possibility of a relocation of authorities we have associated with individual citizens to strategic institutional domains of the increasingly globalized economy.

The particular development focused on in this chapter is part of a larger dynamic that contains countervailing tendencies that also emerge from the conditions produced by economic globalization. The territorial and institutional transformation of state power and authority associated with economic globalization has produced operational, conceptual, and rhetorical openings for subjects other than the national state to emerge as legitimate actors in international/global arenas. These actors include not only the global economic actors focused on here, but also institutional actors emerging out of the world of NGOs, the international human rights regime, first nation people's effort to get direct representation in international fora, particular types of feminist struggles, the global environmental agenda, and the struggle for global labor justice.

NOTES

This is based on the author's research project "Governance and Accountability in the Global Economy." Portions have been published in the author's *Losing Control? Sovereignty in an Age of Globalization* (Columbia University Press 1996). The author thanks Columbia University Press and the Schoff Fund for their support.

1. A key issue for this essay is the fact that citizenship is a crucial institution in addressing governing and accountability in national states. We might then consider that it may and should also play a role when it comes to governing the global economy. What forms this accountability might take, and to what constituencies it would respond, is not clear at all.

2. See, for instance, the analysis in Kalberg (1993) showing the extent to which a certain combination of conditions had to be secured for the institution of modern citizenship to emerge. In using a rather confined definition the author succeeds brilliantly in showing the rarity of this combination of conditions. See also Turner (1993), Isin (2000), and the new journal *Citizenship Studies.*

3. See, for example, the new scholarship on the erosion of citizenship as an institution embedded in nation–states, notably the work by Baubock (1994),

Jacobson (1996), Soysal (1995), Torres et al. (1999). See also "Symposium on Citizenship," *Indiana Journal of Global Legal Studies* (spring 2000).

4. The social changes in the role of the nation–state, the globalization of political issues, and the relationship between dominant and subordinate groups have major implications for questions of membership and personal identity (Sassen 1999a).

5. They call for a critical examination of the limits of nation-based citizenship as a concept for exploring the problems of belonging in the modern world. For good discussions of the issues and the literature, see Soysal 1995; Jacobson 1996; "Symposium on Citizenship"; Sikkink and Keck 1998.

6. There are other issues that are part of the larger inquiry on the issue of citizenship and rights that I cannot focus on here. It has to do with my thesis that we are seeing processes of incipient denationalization inside state institutions (Sassen 1996, ch. 1; 1999b). This would mean that citizenship, even if situated in institutional settings that are "national," is a possibly changed institution if the meaning of *national* itself has changed. One empirical question, then, is whether the transformations we associate with globalization that have changed certain features of the territorial and institutional organization of the political power and authority of the state, may entail changes in the institution of citizenship—its formal rights, its practices, its psychological dimension. I juxtapose this notion to those of postnational citizenship, which is centered on locations for citizenship outside the national state and cosmopolitan citizenship. See "Symposium on Citizenship." On the transformation of citizenship as it intersects with transformations in the authority of the state, see Franck (1992).

7. For a discussion and summary presentation of the evidence on the growing earnings inequality in all the major developed economies, see Sassen (2000, chs. 8 and 9).

8. Elsewhere I have examined other instantiations of this dynamic, especially as they involve immigrants and human rights (Sassen 1996, ch. 3; 1999a). The impact of globalization on sovereignty has been significant in creating operational and conceptual openings also for actors other than the global firms and markets that are the focus of this chapter. NGOs, first nation people, and agendas centered in the human rights regime are all increasingly emerging as subjects of international law that can make claims on national states. (For various treatments of these issues, see Hall 1999a; Castro 1999.)

9. Securitization describes a series of procedures that make various types of debts (and savings) more liquid, i.e., they can be bought and sold. This has meant that

various forms of debt and savings that used to be in fairly fixed accounts (e.g., a thirty-year mortgage, a long-term postal savings account) can now circulate in various types of markets.

10. See, for instance, Rosen 1993.

11. For a fuller discussion, see Sassen 1996, ch. 2.

12. Elsewhere I have addressed the subject of human rights and the normativity it introduces. In the larger research project one of the focuses is on human rights in terms of the challenges posed by immigration to states under the rule of law.

13. For extensive evidence of these issues, see Sassen 2000, chs. 3, 4, and 7. See also, for a different perspective on some issues concerning global finance, Garrett 1998; Eichengreen and Fishlow 1996.

14. Figures show that countries with high savings have high domestic investment. Most savings are still invested in the domestic economy. Only 10% of the assets of the world's 500 largest institutional portfolios are invested in foreign assets. Some argue that a more integrated capital market would raise this level significantly and hence raise the vulnerability to and dependence on the capital markets. It should be noted that extrapolating the potential for growth from the current level of 10% may be somewhat dubious; it may not reflect the potential for capital mobility across borders of a variety of other factors which may be keeping managers from using the option of cross-borders investments.

15. It is estimated that the value of securitization could reach well over US$10 trillion in the Eurozone. In Japan, deregulation is expected to free up about US$13 trillion in fairly immobile and highly regulated assets such as postal savings accounts.

16. It is well known that while currency and interest-rates derivatives did not exist until the early 1980s and represent two of the major innovations of the current period, derivatives on commodities, so-called futures, have existed in some version in earlier periods. Amsterdam's stock exchange in the 17th century—when it was the financial capital of the world—was based almost entirely on trading in commodity futures.

17. I have explored how the basic features of digital networks—instantaneous transmission, interconnectivity and speed—which in the case of the Internet, or "public-access" digital space, produces distributed power, and in the case of private digital networks such as those in wholesale finance produces concentrated power (see "Digital Networks and State Authority" paper prepared for the Bi-National

Expert Group, jointly sponsored by the National Academy of Sciences [US] and the Max Planck Institute for International Law [Germany]; a revised copy was published in *Theory, Culture, Society* Special Issue on Sovereignty (summer 2000).

18. We now know that the particular organizational structure of savings and loans associations made possible unusually high levels of fraud and that this was a major factor contributing to their financial crisis rather than interest rate ceilings. We also know from historians that the possibilities for fraud have long been high in these types of organizations.

19. An argument could be made that the financial markets are the result of multiple decisions by multiple investors, and therewith gain a certain democratic quality. Yet a key condition for participation is ownership of capital, which in itself is likely to produce a particular set of interests and to exclude a vast majority of a country's citizens. Further, small investors, including many households in the case of the U.S., typically operate through institutional investors, and the interests of these may not always coincide with those of small investors. The overall effect is to leave the vast majority of a country's people without any say.

20. See, for instance, Arrighi 1994. See also the "Debates" section in Davies 1999.

21. The global capital market consists of a variety of specialized financial markets. These markets discipline governments in a somewhat erratic way even under the premises of market operation: they fail to react to an obvious imbalance for a long time and then suddenly punish with a vengeance, as was the case with the Mexico crisis. The speculative character of so many markets means that they will stretch the profit-making opportunities for as long as possible, no matter what the underlying damage to the national economy might be. Investors threw money into Mexico even though its current account deficit was growing fast and reached an enormous 8% of GDP in 1994.

22. See the work by David Kennedy (1992). See also *Chicago Journal of International Law* Special Issue, *What's Wrong with International Law Scholarship?* vol. 1, no. 1 (spring 2000).

23. I am using work developed for another type of context to the case of the global capital market and multinaltional firms. In its original formulation, Duncan Kennedy (1993) argued that the ground rules in the case of the U.S. contain rules of permission that strengthen the power of employers over workers, or that allow for a level in the concentration of wealth under the aegis of the protection of property rights that is not necessary to that extent in order to ensure the protection of property rights.

24. For elaboration, see my research project "Governance and Accountability in the Global Economy." On questions of the national state and the global system, and the possibilities for the former to be more active and effective participants in the latter, see Aman, Jr. 1998.

25. When I first conceptualized a specific set of dynamics as denationalization in the 1995 Schoff Lectures (Sassen 1996), I meant to capture processes that take place inside the national state. Incipient and partial are two qualifiers I usually attach to my use of denationalization. For me, then, the key issue distinguishing the novel condition was not necessarily that it took place outside, beyond the confines of the national state as is the case with current theses about postnationalism and transnationalism. Specifically, my concern was to specify the particular ways in which the development of a global economy necessitated a variety of policies that had to be implemented in national economies through national institutions. Further, I argued that denationalization captured processes that were to be distinguished from older notions of extraterritoriality. Particular cases I focused on were a variety of national state agencies and committees that have emerged as the institutional "home" inside the national state for the implementation of various new rules of the game necessary for the development and maintenance of a global economic system. (For a full development, see Sassen in progress; for a short discussion see "The State and Economic Globalization: Any Implications for International Law?" [109–16]).

26. The question for research becomes: What is actually "national" in some of the institutional components of states linked to the implementation and regulation of economic globalization? The hypothesis here would be that some components of national institutions, even though formally national, are not national in the sense in which we have constructed the meaning of that term over the last hundred years (Sassen 1999b). For further discussion, see Walker (1993).

27. Known as competition policy in most of the world.

28. In positing this I am rejecting the prevalent notion in much of the literature on globalization that the realm of the national and the realm of the global are two mutually exclusive zones. My argument is rather that globalization is partly endogenous to the national and is in this regard produced through a dynamic of denationalizing what had been constructed as the national. Also, it is partly embedded in the national, e.g., global cities, and in this regard requires that the state re-regulate specific aspects of its role in the national.

29. The ascendance of a large variety of nonstate actors in the international arena signals the expansion of an international civil society. It represents a space where other actors can gain visibility as individuals and as collective actors, and come out

of the invisibility of aggregate membership in a nation-state exclusively represented by the sovereign (see, e.g., Franck 1992; Sikkink and Keck 1998; Hall 1999a).

30. The US$40 billion emergency loan package from the IMF and the US government and the hiring of Wall Street's top firms to refurbish its image and find ways to reenter the market, helped Mexico "solve" its financial crisis. With J.P. Morgan as its financial advisor, the Mexican government worked with Goldman Sachs and Chemical Bank to come up with several innovative deals. Goldman organized a US$1.75 billion Mexican sovereign deal in which the firm was able to persuade investors in May 1996 to swap Mexican Brady bonds collateralized with US Treasury bonds (Mexican Bradys were a component of almost any emerging market portfolio until the 1994 crisis) for a 30 year naked Mexican risk. This seems quite a testimony to the aggressive innovations that characterize the financial markets and to the importance of a whole new subculture in international finance that facilitates the circulation, i.e., sale, of these instruments.

31. Cf. Ruggie's work on multilateral agreements regarding the environment.

32. See my larger project (in progress) for development of this point.

REFERENCES

Aman, Alfred C., Jr. 1998. "The Globalizing State: A Future-Oriented Perspective on the Public/Private Distinction, Federalism, and Democracy." *Vanderbilt Journal of Transnational Law* 31, no. 4:769–870.

Arrighi, Giovanni. 1994. *The Long Twentieth Century: Money, Power, and the Origins of Our Times*. London: Verso.

Basch, L.N., Blanc-Szanton, C., Schiller, Glick. 1994. Nations Unbound: Transnational Projects, Postcolonial Predicaments, and Deterritorialized Nation-States. Amsterdam: Gordon and Breach.

Baubock, Rainer. 1994. *Transnational Citizenship: Memberships and Rights, in International Migration*. Aldershot, U.K.: Edward Elgar.

Biersteker, Thomas J., Rodney Bruce Hall, and Craig N. Murphy, eds. 2002. *Private Authority and Global Governance*. Cambridge, U.K.: Cambridge University Press.

Castro, Max, ed. 1999. *Free Markets, Open Societies, Closed Borders?* Berkeley: University of California Press.

Cooper, K., and D. Fraser. 1984. *Banking Deregulation and the New Competition in Financial Services*. Cambridge, Mass.: Ballinger.

Chicago Journal of International Law. 2000. "What's Wrong with International Law Scholarship?" *Chicago Journal of International Law* 1, no. 1 (spring).

Davis, Diana. 1999. "Chaos and Governance." In *Political Power and Social Theory*. Vol. 13 (Annual). Part IV: Scholarly Controversy. Edited by Diana Davis. Stanford, Conn.: JAI.

Eichengreen, Barry, and Fishlow, Albert. 1966. *Contending with Capital Flows*. New York: Council on Foreign Relations.

Franck, Thomas M. 1992. "The Emerging Right to Democratic Governance." *American Journal of International Law* 86, no. 1:46–91.

Garrett, Geoffrey. 1998. "Global Markets and National Politics: Collision Course or Virtuous Circle." *International Organization* 52, no. 4:787–824.

Hall, Rodney Bruce. 1999. *National Collective Identity*. New York: Columbia University Press.

Holston, James (ed). 1999. *Cities and Citizenship*. Durham, N.C.: Duke University Press.

Indiana Journal of Global Legal Studies. 2000. "Symposium on Citizenship." Special issue. Spring.

Isin, Engin and Byron Turner (eds). 2002. *Handbook of Citizenship Studies*. London: Sage.

Jacobson, David. 1996. *Rights across Borders: Immigration and the Decline of Citizenship*. Baltimore: Johns Hopkins University Press.

Kennedy, David. 1992. "Some Reflections on 'The Role of Sovereignty in the New International Order.'" In *State Sovereignty: The Challenge of a Changing World: New Approaches and Thinking on International Law*. 237 Proceedings of the twenty-first annual conference of the Canadian Council on International Law, Ottawa. October.

Kennedy, Duncan. 1993. "The Stakes of Law, or Hale and Foucault." In *Sexy Dressing Etc.: Essays on the Power and Politics of Cultural Identity*, 83–125. Cambridge, Mass.: Harvard University Press.

Longworth, R. C. 1998. *Global Squeeze: The Coming Crisis for First World Nations*. Chicago: Contemporary.

Olds, Kris, Peter Dicken, Philip F. Kelly, Lilly Kong, and Henry Wai-Chung Yeung, eds. 1999. *Globalization and the Asian Pacific: Contested Territories*. London: Routledge.

Portnoy, Brian. 1999. "Constructing Competition: The Political Foundations of Alliance Capitalism." Ph.D. diss., Department of Political Science, University of Chicago.

Roepke, W. 1954. "Economic Order and International Law. *Recueil des cours* 86, no. 2:203–50.

Sassen, Saskia. 1996. *Losing Control? Sovereignty in an Age of Globalization: The 1995 Columbia University Leonard Hastings Schoff Memorial Lectures.* New York: Columbia University Press.

———. 1999a. *Guests and Aliens.* New York: New Press.

———. 2001. *The Global City: New York, London, Tokyo.* Princeton, N.J.: Princeton University Press.

Sassen, S. 2002. "The Repositioning of Citizenship: Toward New Types of Subjects and Spaces for Politics." *Berkeley Journal of Sociology,* 46:4–26.

Soysal, Yasmin. 1994. *Limits of Citizenship.* Chicago: University of Chicago Press.

Torres, Rodolfo D., Jonathan Xavier Inda, and Louis F. Miron, eds. 1999a. *Theory, Culture, Society.* Special issue on Sovereignty 17, no. 4. (summer 2000).

———. 1999b. *Race, Identity, and Citizenship.* Oxford, U.K.: Blackwell.

UNCTAD (United Nations Conference on Trade and Development). 1999. *Report: Foreign Direct Investment and the Challenge of Development.* New York: UNCTAD.

Walker, R. B. J. 1993. *Inside/Outside: International Relations as Political Theory.* Cambridge, U.K.: Cambridge University Press.

4

Beyond the Informal Economy

New Trends in Post-Fordist Transition

SIMONE GHEZZI AND ENZO MINGIONE

FROM THE INFORMAL SECTOR TO FLEXIBLE WORK PRACTICES

When Keith Hart (1973) coined the expression "informal sector" at the beginning of the 1970s, he was trying to analyze the complexities of the economy of the streets in a large African city, Accra in Ghana. Populated by urban poor, who had migrated to the city in search of better income opportunities, the city slums had become arenas of multifarious working activities, an intricate web combining wage and self-employment incomes for subsistence. Certainly, the phenomenon he was describing was not unknown to anthropologists and students of development, yet it was this term, "informal economy," in his seminal article for the International Labor Organization that became popular in the following years. In fact it turned out to be a useful concept when Ferman (1978) a few years later brought to scholarly attention within Western countries, and the United States in particular, the issue of forms of occupational activities—overlooked by formal economic theory and concealed in official statistics—which were being "rediscovered" in Western capitalism. With the benefit of hindsight we may say that the term Ferman borrowed from Hart created a certain degree of confusion, as the two phenomena were to some extent conceptually different. While the industrially advanced countries of the West and the socialist countries of Eastern Europe were highly regulated contexts, Accra as well as many other cities of postcolonial Africa were much less regulated contexts, not amenable to the structural features of welfare capitalism and of the command economy.

The debate that followed raised and stimulated an increasing interest among scholars from different quarters, especially in the 1980s (Mattera 1985; Pahl 1984, 1988; Weiss 1987; Lomnitz 1988; Mingione 1987, 1991; Portes, Castells, and Benton 1989; Harding and Jenkins 1989, Benton 1990; Blim 1990, to name but a few). Despite the differences of these approaches, the debates underscored the idea that the informal economy was a growing and inescapable phenomenon throughout the world, but every time students tried to grasp its characteristics they had to come to grips with a number of difficulties, both conceptual and empirical. For one thing, data collection and field research are notoriously difficult tasks to carry out, as in most cases informal activities are performed without complying with existing labor legislation or other regulations; for another, it is conceptually difficult to set the boundaries of the phenomenon, due to its heterogeneity and ambiguity. The extraordinary variety of activities that may be included under the same encompassing category of "informal" made it arduous to construct a theoretical matrix from which to explain such an assortment of phenomena. They were assessed in different and opposite ways, depending on which interpretation one chose to adopt. Were they innovative responses to the regulation of the market and the state bureaucracy? Or, rather, did they represent the persistence of traditional (not to say backward) patterns of behavior rooted in petty commodity production, which formal theory had always considered noneconomic or antieconomic? Were they the result of individual and autonomous choices? Or, rather, did they constitute an entrenched part of the urban poverty system, and an exploitative mechanism in the social relations of production? By the same token, the social consequences of informal activities were also viewed in different ways: on the one hand, they could be seen as the basis for productive accumulation and, consequently, a mechanism generating processes of social polarization (Pahl 1988); on the other, they could be seen merely as a redistributive mechanism to resolve potential social conflicts (Portes and Castells 1989; Hart 1992).

At present that debate is still open, indeed, and it has been fueled by the remarkable contemporary transformations that have occurred in the industrial world. There are at least two issues that currently dominate the present debate: the first concerns the passage from the regulatory systems of "Fordist" society to flexible production. The second explores the consequences of the transition from the command economy to a free-market economy in Eastern Europe and, partially, in China. These recent developments provide further insight to the question of informal economy. By investigating the emergence of new economic regimes both in the West and in the East—essentially different from those that characterized welfare capitalism and the command economy—it appears that the occupational transformations that are currently taking place in such new regimes make occupational careers increasingly unstable and heterogeneous.

As we mentioned above, the informal economy in industrial societies was regarded as a sphere of activities in contrast to the standardized economic practices and regulations of "organized capitalism" (Offe 1985; Lash and Urry 1987) and to those of a command economy. Such a contrast retained several different meanings due to the fact that many practices remained outside the normative system as either innovative economic strategies or defensive forms of adaptation, but overall the informal economy was viewed as a phenomenon emerging from overregulated economic systems. However, as we will argue in the following pages, in the current trend toward flexibility, indisputable signs of different forms of activities are emerging: the so-called atypical jobs that have destandardized the regulatory processes of working practices and have created elements of discontinuity in the individual biographies.[1] Atypical jobs may be formal or informal, but above all they are the direct result of—and not indirect forms in opposition to—post-Fordist regimes of regulation.

The early problems with informal economic activity, framed in terms of unregulated activities within organized capitalism or centrally planned economies, still share with the current trends in global capitalism similar conceptual and methodological difficulties, due to the complexities of the forms of work practices. Being highly dynamic and escaping rigid regulations, such practices are not always adequately captured by official labor statistics.

In the following sections we shall dwell mainly on the characterization of the informal economy as it emerged in the context of welfare and organized capitalism and then we will show how such a characterization contrasts with the heterogeneity and diversification of flexible work practices of the post-Fordist transition. In the brief concluding section we shall draw from the discussion some indicators that can be used to interpret the current trends in the new regulatory processes.

INFORMAL ACTIVITIES IN DIFFERENT MODELS OF WELFARE CAPITALISM

There is a general consensus concerning the fact that the informal economy does not constitute a phenomenon disjointed or separable from a unitary vision of the economic system as a whole: that is to say that a clear-cut and absolute distinction between which activities are formal and which are not, simply does not exist. The identification of informal activities can only be made in relation to the regulatory and normative processes that developed through the institutionalization of nation–states and their bureaucratic apparatuses in the nineteenth and twentieth centuries. As an example, we may consider at those employment practices that in the last century, for a certain period of time, were considered ordinary and regular, such as child labor employed in factories. More or less gradually, they became informal (and indeed illegal) as labor regulations and normative restrictions were institutionalized. However, the regulative waves implemented by the nation–states to regulate social and economic relations did not have the same effect everywhere. Work, as we know, is the product of distinct historical forces bearing their own specificity in each society; therefore, the social context remains particularly crucial for understanding work differences across time and space (Tilly and Tilly 1998). This helps us understand why same work practices remained beyond the limits of institutionalization in certain contexts, while regulated in others. If the historical differences in the organization of work took shape within the differentiated regulatory systems of welfare capitalism (Esping-Andersen 1990, 1999), it follows that the problem of the informal economy may be better understood as a multifaceted phenomenon emerging from the different local configurations of the capitalist system. As we will show later, since such configurations are changing, the whole issue of informal activities becomes more complicated.

However blurred the borders between formal and informal, such a distinction emerged and evolved more clearly in Western industrial societies during the period—commonly known as Fordism—that stretches from the development of mass industrial production industry to the oil crises in the 1970s (Arrighi 1994; Mingione 1997). In general, the regulatory process that characterized this epoch of strong economic growth was accompanied by a democratic ideal that culminated in the consolidation of social citizenship principles and in the adoption of various models of welfare capitalism. Centered on the convergence of state bureaucracy and corporate industrial capitalism, this process became pervasive in the nation–states. It consolidated the transformations that had already begun at the end of the previous century by developing welfare programs, implementing policies for job security, and providing the labor market with an ideological basis for the reinforcement of the sexual division of labor—upon which hinged the male breadwinner role and the nuclear family with dependent children.

In most countries the regulatory framework of the labor market, including social benefits, wage structure, and job security, was completed in the 1960s and early 1970s at a time in which the trade union movement wielded a strong bargaining power and worker militancy was at its peak (Esping-Andersen 1999). This general process of construction of highly regulated industrial economies took place along different lines of development in the various models of postwar welfare capitalism. These models present differences not only in terms of welfare policies and their implementation, but also in terms of degrees of compliance with institutional regulation. We cannot dwell on the various processes of welfare regime formation, whose analysis would go beyond the aim of this chapter. However, a brief description of the characteristics of these models is necessary to show how the phenomenon of the informal economy, both in qualitative and quantitative terms, is connected to regulatory processes.

The American model was shaped by a marked dualism between a core and a periphery. The former was dominated by large vertically integrated firms that implemented forms of private welfare, whereas the latter was based on social and economic strategies set up by ethnic minorities and migrants. Great Britain, Canada, and Oceania pursued less liberal policies, as they had to compensate with public welfare programs for the weakness of large corporate industries and the insignificant potential of ethnic immigration. Scandinavian states, relatively homogeneous from a social point of view and economically peripheral, developed an encompassing public welfare system that incorporated a universalistic rights-based institution of citizenship. The remaining Western countries started with heterogeneous social conditions and a variety of local particularisms characterized by a rural-based economy, small family businesses, petty traders, petty commodity producers, artisans, and so forth. Differentiation among these countries took place mainly in the process of industrial development and welfare-state building after World War II. Those of central Europe went through a process of vigorous industrial development that created two kinds of economic models: the first was made up of large corporate industries that triggered a high demand for immigrants (mainly guest workers in German-speaking countries, and naturalized ethnic groups in the others); whereas the second was made up of a high number of small and midsized firms. In the "Latin rim," instead, the articulation between modern forms of production and traditional activities generated local patterns of development with stark contrasts among regions within the same country. Alongside the rise of large-scale factory complexes and the growth of a dense network of both traditional and highly dynamic small firms in some regions, there were conditions of marginality and stagnation in others. This situation gave rise to the formation of chaotic regulative systems whose functioning relied mostly on survival strategies and resources of the family, and where those were limited welfare policies that reproduced forms of dependency on public resources, as in the case of southern Italy and Spain.

Turning to the boundaries between formal and informal, if we had applied such conceptual dualism in the early seventies, we might have noticed a neat division between, on the one side, the Scandinavian model, highly regulated and almost entirely lacking in irregular activities other than the domestic economy and a small amount of occasional labor, and on the other, the Mediterranean model, characterized by a dualistic regulation and, therefore, an expanding "tolerated" informal sector alongside a core of regulated forms of employment. In between there might have been the other two models of regulation, that of central Europe, closer to the Scandinavian model, and the liberal regime, more similar to the Mediterranean model, due to the presence of poor ethnic groups that, although variously assimilated into the locally dominant industrial culture, were able in their ethnically homogeneous neighborhoods to provide highly conducive settings for networks of survival strategies based on informal activities.

However, by the time the importance of the informal sector was discovered and brought to scholarly attention, a potent process of transformation within these foregoing regulative systems was already taking place. The long-term trends of the Fordist system were halted, the welfare-state regimes faced a growing crisis, and the Keynesian views that inspired earlier social policies were superseded by neoliberal policies that paved the way to the dismantling of the welfare-state consensus (Mishra 1990). Indeed, the erosion of the synergy between economic growth and Fordist regimes had already begun in the 1970s with the emergence of the fiscal crisis of the state (O'Connor 1973); the incipient process of industrial restructuring (Piore and Sabel 1984); the diffusion of new practices of self-provisioning, individualized consumption, and informational technologies (Gershuny 1983; Castells 1989); and demographic changes (Lesthaeghe 1991), but it was in the mid-1980s that such erosion was accentuated. As a result of these trends, we are currently involved, at the turn of the century, in a transition toward a model of global capitalism dominated by new and heterogeneous practices of capital accumulation, and more flexible forms of labor as well as new structures of power and labor control (Sennett 1999).

The debate about the nature of these new trends in industrial capitalism has tended to converge on concepts such as "flexible specialization," "flexible accumulation," and "globalization." They have become omnipresent and, indeed, powerful concepts both in the literature and in policy circles; however, rather than suggesting a linear transition from Fordism to new models of capitalist organization, we prefer to speak of complex processes of transformation and adaptation, whereby the earlier forms of regulation of economic and social life are at odds with emerging practices and identities (Mingione 1997).

It is exactly the articulation of these different ideal types of regulatory systems that makes the picture of informal economy quite complicated. In attempting to delineate these new configurations, two points should be clearly noted. First, what we are trying to suggest is that in order to have a better understanding of the informal economy in light of the current and ongoing changes in employment and work organization, we need to incorporate these very changes into our analytical typologies. Second, what is required is an attempt to assess such activities in such a way that the formal-informal dualism can be reexamined and revised. The analytical elaboration of these points might open up new research perspectives and yield alternative interpretations of the characteristics of the informal sector.

BEYOND A TYPOLOGY: A FOCUS ON THE TRANSFORMATIONS

The elaboration of a single analytical definition of the informal economy in advanced industrial countries is not a simple thing to accomplish. A shortcut to reach a satisfactory definition is to include in a typological list all those aspects that are usually referred to in the various definitions of informal economy. In general there are five aspects or, rather, spheres that cover the definition of informal economy:

1. The sphere of unregulated labor. This may include irregular wage labor relationships, such as multiple employment, moonlighting, and irregular employment.
2. The sphere of irregular self-employment (practiced both on recurrent and occasional bases) that implies the nonregistration of the enterprise and its employees in contradiction with specific forms of national legislation.
3. The sphere of tax evasion sustained through the economic transactions of regular working activities.
4. The sphere of criminal economy; such as organized crime, prostitution, smuggling, illegal trading, and so on. What distinguishes this sphere from the rest is that it encompasses a whole series of goods and services whose production and marketing are strictly illegal and persecuted as crimes.
5. The sphere of nonmonetary activities such as the domestic arena, self-help, self-provisioning, volunteerism, and communal activities. Generally speaking these activities do not directly involve cash transactions; they constitute forms of unpaid labor whose impact on the whole economic system is hard to quantify, but it would be a gross miscalculation to dismiss them and assume that they are not important in economic terms. In particular the expansion of the nonprofit "third sector" (Laville 1994) is transforming this sphere into a very large, heterogeneous and complex field of economic and social experimentation.

As we cannot examine all these spheres, we would rather draw attention to a few "ideal typical" examples in order to show how the transformations of the regulatory systems result in the blurring of the distinction between formal and informal.

Before looking in more detail at the transformation of wage labor and self-employment, we may begin briefly with the last mentioned sphere. In fact there is evidence that the activities included in this group are becoming increasingly relevant in the light of the changes occurring within welfare policies of the capitalist system. A vast feminist literature (Sacks 1975; Hartmann 1981; Barrett and McIntosh 1980; Walby 1986) has already explored this issue by showing how such activities, subsumed in the realm of reproduction, were obscured within the general structure of the organization of production. Based on generalized reciprocity—and for this reason superficially considered as a collection of nonconflictual relationships—and in opposition to market values, this sphere often attributes roles that simulate and reproduce gendered divisions of labor within the household. But along with gender issues, there are also other new and extremely interesting elements that are worthy of mention. Volunteer work is an excellent example to illustrate what is occurring with the gradual disengagement of the state as welfare provider. Volunteer work, traditionally performed within structures governed by norms of reciprocity (Laville 1994), is being transformed in a process whereby its practice and symbolic construction are increasingly dominated by the norms governing commodified labor so as to blur the distinction between paid and unpaid labor. An increasing number of institutions (especially those providing health care) adopt an instrumental view of their volunteer organizations shaping the work of volunteers along the lines of commodified labor and using volunteers as a flexible source of paid labor replacement in times of budget cuts and welfare restructuring. There are obvious differences among the various models of welfare regime that must be taken into consideration: In liberal welfare regimes, for example, where the voluntary sector (mainly run by nonprofit social organizations) plays a significant role in many domains of society, an increasing number of students, who represent the majority of the new young volunteers are engaged in unpaid labor, as their attainment of future paid labor is conditional on their performance of volunteer work (Esteves 1999). Even if this phenomenon is not generally included in the informal sector of the labor market, since there is nothing "irregular" about it, it nonetheless borrows several features from the informal sector.

In this context we deal primarily with the importance of the changes that are taking place in the spheres of wage labor and self-employment. It would be impossible here to include an exhaustive list of the dimensions of change, but we may draw attention to a few of these and suggest a new focus of analysis.

Previous studies on the informal economy have shown how multiple or double jobholders needed to engage in irregular and nonregistered activities in order to counterbalance the erosion of income due to inflation and unemployment. Qualitative research revealed that the ways and the times in which cash money was raised depended on the needs and the requirements of the family life cycle, as well as on the resources of its members and the larger social environment (Mingione 1991:164). Both those with guaranteed employment and farmers—usually small landowners and worker-peasants—seeking supplementary income was the most common form of double employment. From a quantitative point of view, the major concern of the surveys of the informal economy in industrial countries was to provide an estimate of the importance of second jobs or irregular occupations within that part of the active population that already had one regular full-time job: these inevitably led national accountants to reevaluate the yearly GDP. Nowadays, it is exactly in these spheres that we can observe important transformations of work that coexist with "traditional" informal patterns. What we are experiencing is a transition from moonlighter activities developed and practiced within welfare capitalism to a variety of occupational activities that escape and challenge the "traditional" notion of work. We are referring in particular to those multiple and fragmented experiences of work that, for lack of a better name, have been called "atypical jobs"—including in this term various forms of self-employment, located at the frontier between jobholding and entrepreneurship, and forms of wage labor relationships that have emerged from new sectors of production and from the extensive privatization of public services following the crisis of Fordism. This somewhat vague term purports to capture the emergence of heterogeneous forms of work that in regulatory systems prior to post-Fordism were considered informal or irregular but nowadays in a deregulating labor market are becoming perfectly legal and formal, as they are the outcome of deregulation processes endorsed by the state and by supranational *power* structures (EU, NAFTA, WTO, etc.). In other words, the dominant element of such transformation is not the informalization of economic activities in the legal sense. On the contrary there may be less violation of the rules simply because there is a different regulation of work that is more tolerant of the spread of new forms of of flexible employment, like temporary or consultant contracts or new forms of subcontracting and network agreements.

Obviously, the impact of this phenomenon on individuals and households varies according to the already noted national differences. For example, in liberal countries such as the United States these forms of employment are more widespread than anywhere else in the West, while in the other four countries the policies that favored them have been hindered for some time by trade unions and left-wing parties, even though now the situation is rapidly changing. In any case, at the risk of overgeneralizing we might suggest that it is mainly in urban areas of advanced tertiarization that the combination of formal and informal activities seems to be superseded by a plurality of atypical, but *regular* low-wage jobs held by individuals with nonguaranteed occupations, working part-time or having part-time and temporary jobs. This is not to suggest that informal jobs and atypical activities are mutually exclusive. They may coexist as deregulation and flexibility in the labor market does not necessarily constitute a solution to rigidity. Besides that, off-the-books activities are still an effective way of beating the tax system. What we are trying to suggest is that we should at least be careful about assessing the social consequences of informal activities vis-à-vis formal occupations. The diffusion of flexible practices of labor brings about consequences that are different from those of the Fordist divide between formal and informal activities. First, flexible workers are all poorly tenured and have to face frequent shifts from one occupation to another. In such situations the need for new forms of protection concerns the transitions rather than the enforcing of tenure. Second, there is an increasing division between flexible workers who are protected by their updated and high levels of skill and, consequently, high income and freedom of choice, and others who have low or outdated skills, therefore fewer choices, fewer opportunities, and consequently lower incomes and extremely vulnerable conditions of employment.

EXAMPLES OF THE TRANSFORMATIONS
FROM INFORMAL TO FLEXIBLE ARRANGEMENTS

In most respects informal activities appear to share a few similar characteristics with atypical jobs: in general, other than being flexible, both lack union protection and social security; but this does not result in a similar weakness in the individual's position in the workplace, as the former are generally more stable and embedded in routine strategies, whereas the latter are the outcome of new flexible regulations. In the first case, for example, the relations of production are the result of a convergent interest between employer and employee. This situation might be effectively illustrated by the employment strategies of moonlighters who, in many cases, already hold a formal and steady occupation; by retired workers who may continue their previous occupation or related activities in virtue of their skill and experience; or by students who, on the one hand, may seek summer or temporary jobs to cope with the rising costs of education sustained by their families, and on the other, may pursue a strategy of employment in order to achieve better job opportunities in the future. On the contrary, the wage relationship of atypical jobs illustrates well how the scenario of formal employment has become more precarious and unpredictable: employees have to depend more on income from activities whose fragmentation and flexibility might not be compatible with households' strategies and needs, particularly when the family life cycle requires stable and/or additional revenue. However, it is not the question of low-income resources that constitutes the main issue here, but more broadly the long-term problem of social integration through these forms of work. If we maintain a conceptual separation between these forms of work we do little to enhance our understanding of how, as patterns of work change, people's strategies change as well. However refined it may be, research that continues to be promoted from within the "old" framework of analysis cannot entirely account for the social dimensions of new emerging profiles of labor and laborers nor is it able to assess the impact of new forms of social polarization.

Another example of how regulatory systems are changing is represented by the case of the northern Italian industrial districts. As we know, in this country a widespread system of small factories constitutes the main form of the Italian industrial structure; however, other fast-growing regions of southern Europe are also experiencing a similar kind of industrial development. Studies of the informal economy of industrial countries have always found a fertile terrain in the Italian context and particularly in the regions of the so-called third Italy where one finds a form of organization of production— the industrial districts—quite distinct from Fordist production in which large vertically integrated firms are dominant. Here, an industrial district is a flexible system of clusters of connected firms located in small areas featuring territorial specialization of production and practicing intensive subcontracting. The origin of the term *third Italy* is well known. To describe the Italian situation, Arnaldo Bagnasco (1977) coined the famous term *the Three Italies*, meaning that there is the "first" Italy of the industrial triangle (Milan-Turin-Genoa), the "second" Italy of the less-developed south, and the "third Italy" made up of previously rural areas of northeastern and central Italy that experienced social and economic development around the mushrooming of small family-based firms. This development was favored by local government intervention (Trigilia 1991): by creating industrial estates and providing special financing tools and institutions for supplying information on technology and markets, local governments of the third Italy promoted and forged small businesses (Brusco and Righi 1989). All this was made possible in a local milieu characterized by work practices that have been regarded—perhaps overhastily—as informal (Mingione 1999; Paci 1999). Actually, the cultural homogeneity of the local milieu shared by workers and entrepreneurs, and the existence of strong family networks, favored the consolidation of small factory organizations outside trade union regulations that came into force extensively in the large factories.[2] For this very reason industrial districts have been viewed as the "breeding grounds" for irregular wage work, self-employment, tax evasion, and so forth. In fact there is much more local variability than previously suggested. Therefore, what we may consider peculiar to one area may not be such in another, because of the various processes of historical variability and cultural variations at work in each local context (Ghezzi 1999).

In general, though, the most innovative systems of small- and medium-size firms, not exclusively in the third Italy and southern Europe, have followed a particular trajectory of transformation. Most of them started as unregistered firms—to avoid taxation and labor regulations—embedded in a local culture where the structure of exploitation was mainly based on kinship and other informal social networks. However, the high level of capital accumulation and profit reached during a rapid expansion between the 1970s and 1980s induced a process of "idiosyncratic" formalization. In order to protect themselves from high taxation and, at the same time, have complete access to public financial instruments, international funds, import/export companies, and so forth, eventually such firms had to formalize completely their production costs. In the 1990s the most dynamic small- and medium-size firms were involved in further changes of reorganization that caused a significant transformation in the way they functioned. First, by taking part in global financial circuits, some have become international corporations,[3] while others have been taken over by multinationals, but in any case most have begun to open new branches (divisions) abroad, especially in Eastern Europe. In other words, in the industrial districts many small factories are enjoying a remarkable growth not only in terms of productivity and profits but also in terms of employment and size, so that we can hardly still define them as "small," even when the family network, reproducing the family metaphor in the firm, continues to act as a management resource and labor recruiter. Second, to cope with the scarcity of a labor force due to the negative impact that the fall in the birth rate has had on local labor demand, they have started to hire foreign workers. As a result, the firms of the industrial districts are nowadays the most important employers of non-EU regular immigrants. In just one generation the image of a homogeneous local context promoting local forms of informal activities has been subverted, as we will show below.

In all southern Europe the concentration of small firms is no longer easy to localize in a clear-cut area since there is an increasing number of industrial regions where the presence of networks of small factories is a lively and widespread phenomenon. With the dismantling of numerous large factories in the last two decades, a great number of industrial plants have been supplanted by new small factories that have drastically changed the industrial structure of these areas. In other words we could say that, in general terms, a process of convergence between northern Italy and other areas (both of earlier and later industrialization) has already started, not only because of the structural changes that have occurred at the economic level, but also because of the consequences of state intervention that, on the one hand, has become less accommodating toward tax evasion, and on the other, has been trying to introduce more flexible labor regulations—which, incidentally, explains the increasing number of atypical jobs produced in these areas.

If all that we have said is true, as appears to be the case, one may argue whether it is still conceptually valid to regard, on the one hand, northern Italy as an area with a long-standing informal sector reproduced at the institutional level and practiced at the level of microenterprises; and, on the other hand, other regional contexts as areas associated with the informal subcontracting by large firms (Warren 1994), which in absolute numbers no longer dominate these regions. It is also questionable whether the local milieu of social consensus and communitarian integration still exists in the northern Italian regions. In fact there is growing evidence of indicators displaying the following shift: the collapse of the Christian Democratic Party and the emergence of regional parties in the "white" regions (northeast); the weakening of the left-wing parties in the "red" regions (center); the emerging conflictual relationship with the state at the regional and national level, seen by many entrepreneurs as an oppressive and overregulative political institution (in spite of its encouragement of general entrepreneurial expansion); and finally, the recent social protests against immigration that show the tension between the need for a regular foreign workforce and the intolerance for clandestine immigrants and illegal ethnic entrepreneurship.

As we said above, we should then argue whether it is still meaningful or helpful to maintain an interpretative model that, in the light of what we have just presented, does not seem to be able to incorporate new elements of social and economic change, nor take into account the incipient cracks in a social environment that has always been understood as a reference model of social integration.

The last issue we wish to raise, as we have anticipated above, is the consequences of the post-Fordist transition on the informal occupation of immigrant workers in the industrialized countries who constitute a significant part of the recent new waves of migration across the world. Compared with earlier migrant generations, recent patterns of migration appear to be more disorganized and unregulated. This is not due to blanks and gaps in the legislation of the host countries, for governments are producing more restrictive barriers to deal with immigration. If anything, the policy implemented by some countries of periodically formalizing a fixed number of illegal immigrants as guest workers demonstrates the complexity of the problem and the impossibility of closing off countries' borders or coping with highly successful smuggling networks

(Sassen 1998). The difficulty lies in the fact that immigrants—whether they are undocumented Mexican workers coming to the United States, or North Africans to southern Europe, to give only a couple of examples—appear more highly dispersed, individualized, and isolated in small groups. These immigrants, exploited as cheap labor, even if they sometimes possess some skills in their countries of birth, already embody the required attitudinal features for the low-skilled, highly flexible, and unprotected work they will be undertaking. The exploitation of newcomers has always taken place, but in today's deregulated labor market, such newcomers are unable to make formal claims for a general improvement of their—now fragmented and unstable—conditions in the workplace. This disadvantage is not only related to their particular situation: lack of union protection and social security is experienced by the young native workforce, as well. There are two other problems: first, immigrants are not always able to build protective social networks that allow them to compensate for the uncertainty of their work careers; second, creeping social discrimination excludes them from welfare rights, housing, and community integration, in general. As unprotected and "docile" outsiders, they inevitably become particularly vulnerable to management demands for higher flexibility and productivity. For those with the legal status of immigrant the situation does not change: their inherent characteristic as outsiders and their willingness to work at lower costs by necessity makes them a low-income social group. The situation produced by this new form of labor organization would seem to destabilize, rather than to favor, the reproduction of network strategies based on ethnic solidarities typical of those large immigration flows in an earlier period in which Fordist regimes offered more permanent and protected jobs (Sennett 1999). Alongside low-income employed immigrants there are also groups of immigrants incapable of being absorbed by the labor market. They are commonly found in the well-developed enclaves of urban areas where their own survival strategies are based on self-employment. From a more optimistic perspective they may start by providing the ethnic community with informal services. Soon afterward they may gradually move toward more formal ventures, if they are successful; otherwise, they may remain locked into informal work paid at the subsistence level (Portes 1995).

CONCLUSION

There is not one single line of interpretation of the informal economy, and informal work in particular. However, despite the heterogeneity of assessments, interpretations, and definitions, which, incidentally, show the vitality of the debate, there are further themes that can be developed to illustrate the question of informal work in light of the relevant transformation of employment systems in the post-Fordist age. That dichotomous typologies adopted in the past, such as market/nonmarket, monetary/nonmonetary, formal/informal activities are becoming inadequate to account for variability in contemporary Western capitalism has been clear for a while, yet such dichotomies have not been completely demolished. As the regulatory systems are changing, there are new phenomena and structures in contemporary Western capitalism that are raising new theoretical dilemmas and that, for this reason, need to be taken into consideration in outlining new research perspectives on the informal economy. The processes of industrial restructuring and tertiarization that are taking place within the post-Fordist regulation are producing a rapid and constant transformation of the patterns of work organization. The decline of "full-time full-life" wage work for adult males in large concerns and the rise of various forms of temporary, precarious, and atypical jobs are a case in point. As we have argued, workers are increasingly affected not by informal models of employment, but by these new forms of labor organizations that are gradually causing a qualitative erosion of the various formal/informal stable balances that were typical of organized capitalism in Western industrial societies. However, we are not suggesting that there is a direct causal link—more correctly an inverse relation—between irregular forms of occupation and flexible or atypical jobs. In only a few cases are informal activities sought in order to achieve flexibility in a rigid labor market. This might be the case of multiple jobs that are more frequently practiced in lieu of part-time or short-term jobs when these are not regarded as convenient in specific situations. In fact the deregulation and flexibility of the labor market do not necessarily provide a solution to rigidity. As we have said above, in the case of the Italian industrial districts—and also in the case of ethnic business—kinship ties and various forms of local familism resulting from the interpolation between work and family ethics may shape labor organization in a way that favors the informal work of family members and other people within the local network, while fiscal evasion, a major component of informal economy, remains a phenomenon independent of flexibility. What we are experiencing is a coexistence of different forms of work that are making the distinction between formal and informal become increasingly blurred and, to a certain extent, conceptually useless as it obscures the impact that those forms are having on people's livelihood and the role they are playing in generating social polarization.

It is of pivotal importance to pay closer attention to the changes in the regulatory systems expressed in terms of regional and local variability, and not simply in terms of adaptation to economic and political forces. In order to understand the implications of this point it is necessary to develop a more nuanced view of the dominant element of the transformations and their trajectories.

These new forms of occupation, which tend to blur the distinction between formal and informal activities, are continuously created within heterogeneous deregulatory processes arising from already fragmented and mixed forms of capitalism. This does not mean, though, that we cannot single out a few common elements of the transition. Local and regional systems, enmeshed in wider economic and political structures, may respond to general hegemonic trends of the global economy in a variety of ways, but there are always social and institutional costs behind such changes. The widespread diffusion of occupations such as atypical and flexible jobs, self-employment, immigrant work, subcontracting arrangements, and so on—favored by antiunion and deregulatory policies—shows to what extent the standard regulatory capacity of the wage contract is fading away. On the one hand, these new forms of occupation may offer an immediate advantage in terms of economic utility, but on the other, they may potentially cause growing disadvantages from a social point of view. This is the case when low-paid and fragmented occupations weaken older collective solidarities, or do not allow the reproduction of family welfare and social mobility. Yet, new flexible patterns of labor also bring to the fore a highly skilled and privileged labor force with the capability of protecting itself from the uncertainties of the labor market. Such individuals, to some degree empowered by their skills in the flexible organization of labor, do not face critical situations when moving from one occupation to another, for occupational mobility becomes a vehicle for further accumulation. It is clear, therefore, that the inequality takes on the form of social polarization between those who have high skills and better job opportunities, and those with low or outdated skills, who are extremely vulnerable to the discontinuities and fragmentations of their occupational careers. That is to say that the main concern now is to explore how more heterogeneous and unstable forms of employment (regardless whether they are formal or informal) are connected to and compatible with social life.

In light of the transformations we have illustrated, the discourse of the informal economy has to move toward a different set of problems concerning the complex configurations of social relations that we have sketched in this chapter. The emergence of new forms of work practices within networks and complex forms of subcontracting and, at the same time, the new forms of ethnic economies and survival strategies of diverse social groups have brought to the fore new and as yet unresolved tensions and contradictions. At the core of the discussions regarding the need for welfare and social regulation reform there is now increasingly the problem of new forms of polarization, social exclusion, and downward mobility generated by the limited social adaptability of the emergent precarious forms of labor.

NOTES

1. For various examples of fragmented biographies in post-Fordist regimes see the recent original contribution of Richard Sennett (1999).

2. An important characteristic of many regions of southern Europe is that in general capitalist enterprises and labor relations have been developed within various forms of familism and paternalism (Ghezzi 1999) reproducing highly dynamic and sophisticated regional models of development. Therefore their transition to flexible capitalism must be analyzed keeping these specificities in mind.

3. Well-known examples are the cases of Benetton in the fashion industry, and Delvecchio (Luxottica) in the design and production of optical frames.

REFERENCES

Arrighi, G. 1994. *The Long Twentieth Century: Money, Power and Origins of Our Time.* London: Verso.

Bagnasco, A. 1977. *Tre Italie: La problematica territoriale dello sviluppo italiano.* Bologna: II Mulino.

Barrett, M. and M. McIntosh 1980. "The 'Family Wage': Some Problems for Socialists and Feminists." *Capital and Class* 11:51–72.

Benton, L. 1990. *Invisible Factories: The Informal Economy and Industrial Development in Spain.* New York: SUNY Press.

Blim, M. L. 1990. *Made in Italy: Small-Scale Industrialization and Its Consequences.* New York: Praeger.

Brusco, S., and E. Righi. 1989. "Local Government, Industrial Policy and Social Consensus: The Case of Modena (Italy)." *Economy and Society* 18, no. 4:405–23.

Castells, M. 1989. *The Informational City: Information Technology, Economic Restructuring, and the Urban-Regional Process.* Oxford, U.K.: Basil Blackwell.

Esping-Andersen, G. 1990. *The Three Worlds of Welfare Capitalism.* Cambridge, U.K.: Polity.

———. 1999. *Social Foundation of Post-Industrial Economies.* Oxford, U.K.: Oxford University Press.

Esteves, E. 1999. "The New Wageless Worker: Volunteering and Market-Guided Health Care Reform." In *Care and Consequences: Health Care Reform and Its Impact on Canadian Women.* Edited by D. L. Gustafson, Halifax, N.S.: Fernwood.

Ferman, L. A. 1978. "Analysis of the Irregular Economy: Cash Flow in the Informal Sector." Report presented at the Bureau of Training, Michigan Department of Labor and Industrial Relations, Wayne State University, Ann Arbor, Mich.

Gershuny, J. 1983. *Social Innovation and the Division of Labour*. Oxford, U.K.: Oxford University Press.

Ghezzi, S. 1999. "Family-Run Factories in Lombardy: Familism and Flexible Specialization." Paper presented at American Anthropological Association, "The Making of Wealth and Poverty in a 'Europe of the Regions.'" Society for the Anthropology of Europe, Chicago.

Harding, P., and R. Jenkins. 1989. *The Myth of the Hidden Economy*. Milton Keynes, U.K.: Open University Press.

Hart, K. 1973. "Informal Income Opportunities and Urban Employment in Ghana." *Journal of Modern African Studies* 11:66–89.

———. 1992. "Market and State after the Cold War. The Informal Economy Reconsidered." In *Contesting Markets: Analyses of Ideology, Discourse and Practice*. Edited by Roy Dilley. Edinburgh, U.K.: Edinburgh University Press.

Hartmann, Heidi I. 1981. "The Family as the Locus of Gender, Class, and Political Struggle: The Example of Housework." *Signs* 6, no. 3:366–94.

Lash, S., and J. Urry. 1987. *The End of Organized Capitalism*. Cambridge, U.K.: Polity.

Laville, J. L. 1994. *L'Economie solidaire*. Paris: Desclée de Brouwer.

Lesthaeghe, R. 1991. *The Second Demographic Transition in Western Countries: An Interpretation*. PD Working Paper, no. 2, Vrjie Universiteit. Bruxelles.

Lomnitz, L. 1988. "Informal Exchange Networks in Formal Systems: A Theoretical Model." *American Anthropologist* 90, no.1:41–55.

Mattera, P. 1985. *Off the Books: The Rise of the Underground Economy*. London: Pluto.

Mingione, E. 1987. "Urban Survival Strategies, Family Structure, and Informal Practices." In *The Capitalist City: Global Restructuring and Community Politics*. Edited by M. Smith and J. R. Feagin. Oxford: Blackwell.

———. 1991. *Fragmented Societies: Sociology of Economic Life beyond the Market Paradigm*. Oxford, U.K.: Basil Blackwell.

———. 1997. *Sociologia della vita economica*. Roma: Nuova Italia Scientifica.

———. 1999. "Gli itinerari della sociologia economica in una prospettiva europea." *Sociologia del lavoro* 73:15–47.

Mishra, R. 1990. *The Welfare State in Capitalist Society: Policy of Retrenchment and Maintenance in Europe, North America and Australia.* Toronto: University of Toronto Press.

O'Connor, J. 1973. *The Fiscal Crisis of the State.* New York: St. Martin's.

Offe, C. 1985. *Disorganized Capitalism: Contemporary Transformations of Work and Politics.* Cambridge, U.K.: Polity.

Paci, M. 1999. "Alle origini della imprenditorialità e della fiducia interpersonale nelle aree ad economia diffusa." *Sociologia del Lavoro* 73:144–66.

Pahl, R. 1984. *Divisions of Labour.* Oxford, U.K.: Basil Blackwell.

———, ed. 1988. *On Work: Historical Comparative and Theoretical Approaches.* Oxford, U.K.: Basil Blackwell.

Portes, A., and M. Castells. 1989. "World Underneath: The Origins, Dynamics, and Effects of the Informal Economy." In *The Informal Economy: Studies in Advanced and Less Developed Countries.* Edited by A. Portes, M. Castells, and L. Bendon, 11–37. Baltimore: Johns Hopkins University Press.

Portes, A., M. Castells, and L. Benton. 1989. *The Informal Economy: Studies in Advanced and Less Developed Countries.* Baltimore: Johns Hopkins University Press.

Portes, A., ed. 1995. *The Economic Sociology of Immigration.* New York: Russell Sage Foundation.

Piore, M. J., and C. Sabel. 1984. *The Second Industrial Divide: Possibilities for Prosperity.* New York: Basic.

Sacks, K. 1975. "Engels Revisited Women, the Organization of Production, and Private Property." In *Toward an Anthropology of Women.* Edited by Rayna R. Reiter, 211–34. New York: Monthly Review Press.

Sassen, S. 1998. *Globalization and Its Discontents.* New York: New Press.

Sennett, R. 1999. *The Corrosion of Character.* New York: Norton.

Tilly C., and C. Tilly. 1998. *Work under Capitalism.* Boulder, Colo.: Westview.

Trigilia, C. 1991. *Grandi partiti e piccole imprese.* Bologna: Il Mulino.

Walby, S. 1986. *Patriarchy at Work: Patriarchal and Capitalist Relations in Employment.* Cambridge, U.K.: Polity.

Warren, M. R. 1994. "Exploitation or Co-operation? The Political Basis of Regional Variation in the Italian Informal Economy." *Politics and Society* 22, no. 1:89–115.

Weiss, L. 1987. "Explaining Underground Economy: State and Social Structure." *British Journal of Sociology* 28:216–34.

The New
Paradigm of Violence

MICHEL WIEVIORKA

Violence changes with the times. In this sense the historian Charles Tilly (1986) has made a useful contribution by suggesting that each of the major historical periods he studies is characterized by its specific "repertory" of forms of action, and more particularly of violence. Now, it happens that the changes that have taken place since the 1960s and 1970s, are so considerable that they justify exploring the idea of entry into a new era and, following on from there, the idea of a new paradigm of violence, characteristic of the contemporary world. Whether it be a question of the tangible expressions of the phenomenon, the way in which it is represented at the moment, or the approach adopted by the social sciences, such in-depth changes are at play that it is legitimate to stress the inflexions and ruptures in violence rather than the continuities that, however, should in no way be underestimated. We should add that by leaving aside the question of technological and scientific innovations in the sphere of armaments, as we shall do here, we are depriving ourselves of elements that undoubtedly go in the direction of a new paradigm of violence (Michaud 1996).

CHANGES
New Meanings

Today, there has been a considerable renewal in the meaning of violence and in its most concrete manifestations and we shall primarily insist here on the changes that have occurred since the end of the 1960s. If we were to adopt

107

a more long-term view taking the whole century as period of reference this would probably not invalidate the hypothesis of a new paradigm that we are going to examine; it would merely perhaps suggest that among the most decisive meanings today, some are comparable with those that characterized the entry into the age of industry, when the emerging protesting classes were primarily seen as dangerous or when, in a country like France, the phenomena of gangs and the juvenile violence attributed to the "Apaches"[1] made the headlines and were dealt with by the press in terms that are not unlike contemporary descriptions of angry young people in deprived peripheral urban areas.

The political violence and the extreme left terrorism, which was widespread in the 1970s and into the 1980s, linked with the long destructuring of ideologies, regimes, and Marxist-Leninist-type parties, as well as with an increasingly artificial refusal to recognize the historical decline of the working-class movement has decreased everywhere; organizations like *Action Directe*, the Red Brigades, Revolutionary Cells, the Red Army Fraction, and so on, have come to an end almost all over the world—in historical terms they have been practically liquidated. This does not mean that we should exclude the possibility in the future of a return of Marxist-Leninist ideologies as we see today in Mexico where the orientation of the EPR (*Exercito Popular Revolucionario*) guerilla is in many ways reminiscent of the 1960s or 1970s. Almost symmetrically, the violence of the extreme right, driven by projects to take over the government has also declined and has often been replaced by forms of behavior that no longer aim at ensuring that their actors control the state but the reverse—that the state is kept at a distance from private practices. In this respect, the Italian experience is a spectacular example. In the 1970s and until the mid-1980s, the extreme right and extreme left terrorism in this country aimed to either bring down the "imperialist State of the multinationals" or create a climate propitious to a coup d'état with the aid of a "strategy of tension." Since then, the major forms of antistate violence have primarily been aimed at protecting the private economic activities of mafioso groups.

As from the 1950s, struggles for national liberation possibly associated with Marxist-Leninist orientations and assuming the form appearance of an armed struggle have often given birth to new regimes and new states; at world level, their violence is no longer as widespread today as in the 1950s–1970s era; even there are still some survivals, for example, in Europe in the experience of the Basques or in Northern Ireland, or else in the Middle East with the Palestinian Movement, and if others have emerged recently, in particular, in Chechnya. This observation does not mean that we are witnessing the end of the link between violence and nation, because this link may have other meanings than those implied by the theme of national liberation. Admittedly, nationalism, even at the heart of the most powerful countries, does constitute a major contemporary phenomena, and is often linked to extreme right themes, but is less directly associated with forms of expression characterized by violence than spontaneous discourse suggests: in Europe, at least, national populism and the rise of the radical right are phenomena that on the whole are not associated with violence to any great extent, quite simply because even if there are sporadic outbursts of violence, it rapidly enters into contradiction with the respectability demanded by a project of accession to power by electoral means. From this point of view, nationalist violence is restricted and is often more ethnic, or even racial, than nationalist as such, and associated not so much with the idea of en-suring the liberation of a nation as with protecting it from external threats and purging it of the elements that could mar its homogeneity. The idea of nation that in the past was a considerable force for emancipation tends today to be as-sociated not so much with violence as with reactive ideologies, expressed by communities or by some parts of them, whose main concern is with economic closure and cultural, even racial, purity (Wieviorka 1997:369–86).

Given the decline of the working-class movement and the loss of centrality of relationships of industrial production, any idea of a link between wide-spread social violence and the insertion of its protagonists in a structural class conflict, in the usual meaning of the term, is unlikely. Today, throughout the world, including Western Europe, it is no longer the struggle against exploita-tion, the uprising against an opponent whose relationship with the actors is one of domination, but rather the lack of any such domination, the absence of a conflictual relation, or social exclusion possibly involving cultural or racial contempt that leads to riots or more diffuse social violence, driven by anger and frustration. In this context, violence is not only a set of objective practices; it is also a representation, a characteristic that, for example, groups, including the most prosperous, may attribute, for no good reason, to other groups who are usually among the most deprived.

Finally, the most spectacular element in the renewal of violence today is constituted by the emergence of references by its protagonists to an ethnic or religious identity. These forms of identity constitute a cultural resource that may be mobilized violently for political ends; they also sometimes lie behind homicidal forms of barbarism, well beyond issues that are merely political. When references of this type, are truly inherent to the actors—and not erro-neously attributed by the media or public opinion to forms of behavior that in reality have nothing to do with them—there may be an impression of resurgence, as if the sphere of traditional or classical violence was merely be-ing enlarged as a result of favorable conditions. In fact, despite their appear-ance that is indeed traditional, even fundamentalist identities are historical constructions, often recent. Jean-François Bayart is correct in his analysis when he explains that they are, in the main, part of rational strategy on one hand, and of dreams and nightmares on the other "in which we believe because they either delight or terrify us" (Bayart 1996:10).

Generally speaking, identities constitute something new; they are produced far more than reproduced, an invention more than a tradition, and Jean Baudrillard (1995) is quite right to say that "instead of lamenting the resurgence of atavistic forms of violence, we should realize that it is our very modernity, our hypermodernity, which produces this type of violence and its special effects one of which is terrorism."

PERCEPTIONS AND REPRESENTATIONS

Violence also differs depending on whether one considers the phenomenon in its most concrete, objective forms or the perceptions of it that circulate, the representations that describe it. In Western countries, for example, France, the first fundamental characteristic of the way in which subjective violence is experienced is that today it has apparently lost all, or almost all, legitimacy in the political arena to the point of signifying absolute evil; society is unanimous in the need to absolutely proscribe and combat it, both within and without. In the 1960s and 1970s, violence could still be justified or understood by intellectuals who were themselves perhaps part of a revolutionary, anarchist, or possibly still Marxist-Leninist tradition. It could be theorized or defended with a degree of support and be tolerated in the political sphere. Some admired guerrillas and hero worshipped "Che," while others tended to extol social violence or endeavored to incite and orchestrate it. The ideas of Frantz Fanon (1961), focusing on the colonial experience, contributed to the idea of a violent rupture, a theorization that Jean-Paul Sartre radicalized in his celebrated preface to the book *The Wretched of the Earth*[2]—the same Sartre who, a few years later, encouraged the Maoists with whom he was in discussion to take the road to violent action (Gavi, Sartre, and Victor 1974). Some of the reactions at the time of the Iranian Revolution, which was acclaimed in France by Michel Foucault, constitute perhaps one of the last expressions of this current of opinion and of these political and intellectual sympathies with respect to actors having recourse to violence and benefiting from a legitimacy that was all the greater since they were responding to the atrocities and social injustices committed by dictatorial or authoritarian governments like those characteristic of Latin America until the 1980s. Since then, the intellectual and political arena in which violence could be the subject of all-encompassing, political discussion has shrunk. The phenomenon today necessarily denotes the unacceptable, and there is a very broad consensus on this. There is no serious philosophical, moral, or ethical discussion of violence, and while there may be voices emanating from "civil society" demanding that the state use its force abroad, for example, in dramatic situations concerning human rights, it is for humanitarian or ecological reasons, and any positive reference to violence is out of the question. In a world that is no longer structured on the basis of East–West bipolarity, in societies where the principle of division and conflict based on relationships of industrial production has become secondary, intellectuals faced with national or religious identities whose struggles are repugnant to them have on the whole distanced themselves from any idea of violence. This phenomenon is perhaps less true for the infrapolitical meanings of violence, when it is expressed for example by angry young people rather than for its political dimensions properly speaking. It is perhaps less obvious when violence can be associated with the lacuna or the crisis of the system and more clear-cut in matters of violence aimed at the state and the government as such.

These changes have implications that are easy to observe everywhere: as a result of lack of discussion and lack of political actors or intellectuals capable of breaking the consensus relating to violence, the latter is, of necessity, the object of perceptions and representations that are either exaggerations or underestimations.

Examples of exaggeration are to be found in the way in which alterity, cultural, religious, or any other sort of difference become objects of fantasies and fears. The actors who are assumed to embody them are likely to become scapegoats, to the extent that they are frequently attributed a virtual violence that is almost natural or innate, whereas in reality they are very far from any such thing, if such a thing were to exist. This is, in particular, the case in countries with high levels of immigration, since immigrants are often considered to be "dangerous" and whose religions, such as Islam, are often assimilated to fundamentalism. The latter is often indeed associated with extreme forms of violence, which can include the death-wish martyrdom of the Iranian *bassidji* for example (Khosrokhavar 1992);[3] but it can also be the subject of suspicions that are ultimately evidence of the extent to which a society is lacking in self-knowledge. Thus, the Oklahoma City bomb attack in the United States (April 19, 1995, 168 dead, a considerable number wounded) was in the first instance widely attributed to Islamic terrorism (which had recently struck in New York) before the country discovered that the perpetrators were two former American soldiers adhering to an extreme right ideology.

In other instances violence is underestimated; in so far as it is an extension of classical social problems or does not challenge the most fundamental modalities of domination, it is likely to be denied or banalized. Thus, to continue with the example of the United States, not only does this country have difficulty in acknowledging its domestic violence, but had to wait until the

1960s to accept the serious attention given to hundreds of the most violent pages of its history;[4] similarly in France, the social violence of small shopkeepers or farmers, characters who are firmly established in a totally respectable situation in the national imagination, is minimized in comparison with the violence that occurs in deprived peripheral urban areas and that is a subject for dramatization and considerable media coverage. Another example, once again in France, is the fact that it has taken several years for the idea to be accepted that there is a link between the feeling of insecurity, which has been widespread in this country since the end of the 1970s, and the objective rise in violence, in the form of criminality and delinquency and above all in petty forms of incivility. This idea clashed with the political sensitivities that emerged with the first presidential election of François Mitterand (1981) to have had much resonance; it appeared to be too close to the representations and security-conscious discourse of the right to be acceptable and even to be heard by the left.

Today, not only has violence lost its legitimacy in the public sphere in Western democracies, their political and intellectual debates, as well as in their capacity for armed intervention that could lead to deaths on their side but, further, it can happen that it replaces an overall approach to the understanding of both social life and international relations. In these instances, it constitutes a much more central category than heretofore in the analysis of the internal and the external, "society" and its environment. The case of France is impressive and is perhaps an exception since violence permeates the media and public opinion there: whether it be a question of the suburbs and the deprived peripheral urban areas, state education, public transport, or merely "uncivilized" acts—which are the main reason for the rise in insecurity—or Islamic terrorism, of which the most recent expressions enable the image of an internal, social, juvenile, and urban threat to be merged with that of an external threat, religious and Arabic in nature.[5]

It is possible that in the future there may be a return to the political and intellectual legitimacy of violence. This is suggested to some extent by the image of martyrdom symbolized in deprived peripheral urban areas by Khaled Kelkal, one of the protagonists of terrorism in France in the summer of 1995. Further, as we shall see below, some social violence, for example, that of angry farmers is hardly perceived as such and has the benefit of widespread sympathy in public opinion. Moreover, the rise in strength of left-wing trends of protest and the intellectual elaboration that goes along with it that can be witnessed in some countries beginning with France, might contribute, once again, to the reinvention of approaches receptive to the idea that revolutionary violence, the midwife of history, provides a way of resolving contradictions that are presumed to be at the heart of the social system. Finally, and above all, the perceptions and representations of violence referred to here primarily from the perspective of France vary considerably from one society to another, as we can see in these countries where it is tolerated or endured, being perceived as part of the normal workings of society. This is the case, for example, in Brazil or in Russia.

THE SOCIAL SCIENCES AND VIOLENCE

Various arguments are invoked in attempts to understand violence and a whole array of sociological traditions. It could also be said that there is no general theory that is capable of providing such an understanding. But, while it is possible to present the main analytical approaches to violence,[6] indicating their contributions and limits, and considering the possibilities that exist to integrate the various approaches in larger, complex theories, it is perhaps more interesting to see the change over time in the ideas that have been most influential.

At the end of World War II, for a brief period there was a dream of constructing a total approach to violence, integrating the contribution of all the social sciences—including psychology, anthropology, history—which would enable us to encompass the entire scale from the individual to international relations. Pierre Hassner (1995:83–84) has recently reminded us that this was the UNESCO project. The aim was therefore to ensure our understanding both of conflicts between fathers and sons and the tensions emerging in the Cold War. This project was a failure; while several arguments can be identified as typical of the period, the most influential in the 1950s and the 1960s, were those that hesitated between two approaches and ended by combining them. On one hand, violence was linked to the concept of conflict. On the other, it was linked to the image of crisis and then analyzed as the consequence or the manifestation of what was in some ways a pathological state of the system under consideration. Dealing with violence involved either considering that it had its place in the calculations and strategies of the actors participating in the conflict, or else in admitting that it was an indication of the inadequate integration of the actors in the system.

In the first case, violence was part of the interaction between actors capable of exercising it in an instrumental manner; it could be analyzed in the context of the approaches based on games theory or organized sets. From this perspective, violence was a virtual or real element in the working and the transformation of societal or intersocietal systems; the ideas of Thomas Schelling (1963) are a good illustration of this approach and were very influential. Considerable stress is placed on the rationality of the actors and on the fact that their decisions, including the decision to resort to violence, are interdependent.

In the second case, violence was mainly analyzed in the framework of neo-functionalism and considered to express a malfunctioning of the system and the consequences for the actors in terms of relative frustration, for example.[7] For some researchers, these lacunae and malfunctioning were related to conflict, the capacity of the actors to function in a conflictual mode, which was thought of as necessary for the integration of society or of any system of international relations. The idea here is that "conflicts can, to some extent, contribute to the integration of systems or organizations, and that inadequate integration of the latter can be a source of conflicts and of the decline into violence" (Hassner 1995:90).

This leads us to two ideas that are contradictory rather than complementary. The first is that violence may be part of a relationship in a primarily instrumental mode and part of the way in which actors communicate and relate to one another; the second is that it may, on the contrary, convey a deficit or incompatibilities in the relations, communication, and functioning between actors, and it is primarily a form of expression of this state of affairs. But we must at once add two observations. The first is that instrumental violence may be used by an actor as a way of entering a system of institutionalized relations—this is the most fundamental idea of what is known as the mobilization of resources' theory with which the names of Charles Tilly (1978) and Anthony Oberschall (1972) are particularly associated, the influence of which was considerable in the 1970s and 1980s. The second observation is that even within a structural or systemic relationship, the characteristic of violence is that it always exhibits a dimension that goes beyond the context of instrumental rationality alone, a dimension that could be referred to (somewhat superficially) as irrational, spontaneous, or expressive and that goes further than the idea of conflict—Karl von Clausewitz realized this when he defined war as "Une étrange trinité composée de la violence originelle de son élément qu'il faut considérer comme une pulsion naturelle aveugle, du jeu de la probabilité et du hasard qui en font une libre activité de l'âme, et de la nature subordonnée d'un instrument politique, par quoi elle ressortit au pur entendement."[8]

One of the best indicators of the major theoretical changes relating to the analysis of violence in the social sciences can be found since the period when it was possible to relate the phenomenon massively and directly to social conflicts, social dysfunctions, or to crises. Today the analyses increasingly stress two types of ideas to which we shall return; but expressions like individualism, subject, and subjectivization on one hand, and breakups, chaos, and decomposition on the other are indicative. These ideas are very far from the two concepts of conflict and crisis. Violence does indeed continue to be thought of in terms of the opposition between instrumentality and expressivity, but neither its possible instrumentality, nor its most extreme expressions, evoke any image of a conflict or even that of a crisis. In extreme cases for example, violence appears to become autonomous, an end in itself, a game, purely destructive or self-destructive. In some instances it thus becomes nothing more than the affirmation of the subject. The analysis must then distinguish between the system and the actors. The tendency is to focus on one or the other. In any event, their separation is observed but there is no suggestion of any mediation of the conflict between these two poles of thought. Nor are we given to believe violence is merely an indication of a deregulation of the system in question—it is much more part of a change, a radical change, an aspect that is well expressed in the frequent resort to expressions using the prefix "post" (postindustrial, postcolonial, etc.), which all designate something that has gone beyond the limits, more than just the state of a system. Violence, including its most localized or limited expressions, is either explained by changes at planetary level, the globalization of the economy, or the end of the Cold War, themes to which we shall return; or else, it is reduced to calculations or, what is not at all the same thing, to the subjectivity of the actors, in the last resort to their insanity. The analysis ranges from focusing on the system to focusing on the actor, stressing what has been destroyed and liquidated. There may be references to the social relationships of the industrial era, or the bipolar system of international relations up to the fall of the Berlin Wall, for example. But the analysis is not good at outlining conflicts or even the process of the destructuring of conflictual relationships or the malfunctioning of the system.

For there to be a conflict, there have to be actors on one hand and issues at stake on the other; there has to be a recognition that these are shared; finally, there has to be a possibility of confrontation without mutual destruction and therefore political or institutional mechanisms are required. We can only speak of a crisis if there is a system, in difficulty perhaps, but still perceptible as such. One of the reasons why violence seems to be so threatening or dramatic today is perhaps due to the rise of "antiactors," protagonists, who are outside any system of action, and in the emergence of forms of violence characterized solely by their force and strength with no possibility of relationship or dialogue between the two. It may also be because of the shortcomings in the procedures and processes that enable the functioning of the conflict, the relationship; it may also be due to the fact that the social and international systems that have worked since the end of World War II are not just changing, they are disappearing to the point that the concept of crisis is too mild to account for their destructuring. But could it not also be because some people or groups are considered to be beyond the pale? Their subjectivity is denied, broken, or destroyed by the contempt of other people and groups who are in a better situation and who refuse to recognize them as subjects.

Although there are considerable differences between the best established contemporary schools of thought, they do have something in common: the majority consider that the world is increasingly a stage without actors and attracted uniquely by the law of the jungle constituted by the market, chaos, or the clash of identities and cultures, much more than by relationships that are negotiated involving a minimum of mutual recognition. Within societies, there may be challenges to the working of the party system, with its left–right cleavages that have often become blurred, or the fairly widespread weakening of trade unionism and systems of professional relationships, the modes of management of the welfare state and, generally speaking the relationships that industrial society has invented since the nineteenth century; in international relations, the reference is to the ending of the bipolar functioning that structured the opposition between the United States and the Soviet Union or to the repeated failures of the major international organizations, starting with the United Nations and its military peacekeepers (*Casques bleus*) in Bosnia, Somalia, or Lebanon. In both instances, we need to bear in mind that institutional procedures and mechanisms often give way to the sole use of force. Not all present-day conflicts can be dealt with as they were in the past. Thus, some researchers, following Samuel Huntington (1993), speak of the "clash" of civilizations; others, in a more pertinent manner, observe that intense intercultural tensions are at work within "civilizations" and not only between them (Le Bot 1996:173–97). Some see the world as unipolar with the United States as the only power, others see it as highly fragmented, with the risk of generalized and molecular chaos, others again endeavor to outline a multipolar situation that corresponds to other ways of seeing the United States. But apart from these discussions,[9] nobody nowadays talks in terms of collective actors capable of becoming involved in conflicts or negotiations and Schelling-type political games. The majority opinion is that violence is the expression, precisely, of the incapacity of our era to implement systems with actors who are functional. It requires a lot of imagination to replace a world that is peopled by images and fears of violence and insecurity and all the excesses that these images and these fears can induce with a world of actors and conflicts. This is particularly true when a scapegoat is made of the Other, with the image of a terrorist lurking behind every Muslim. Nowadays in France it is becoming increasingly common to see the adjective "Muslim" being replaced by that of "Islamic" (in the sense of fundamentalist or militant).

Thus, both as a historical reality and a collective representation, an object of analysis and consideration for the social sciences, contemporary violence does indeed seem to be shaping a new paradigm. From a theoretical point of view, this paradigm requires that violence be analyzed in a complex theoretical arena. This includes, but also extends beyond, both the sphere of conflict and that of crisis. We have to take into consideration the subject—impossible, frustrated, or functioning outside the system and outside the norms. We also have to consider forms of behavior that, beyond the crisis, are evidence of genuine destructuring or excesses leading to chaos and barbarism.

FOUR LEVELS OF ANALYSIS

The idea of a new paradigm is therefore reinforced by close consideration of the changes that have occurred in the meaning, the perception, and the ways of analyzing violence. However this does not mean to say that a new paradigm is firmly established or demonstrated, if only because of the inflexions and reversals in trend that can always occur in historical evolution. This is why there is a need for a further set of investigations, beginning with those that may concern the changes relating to the main sources of violence since the 1970s.

In the analysis of violence, the classical approach is to distinguish between levels. In the 1960s, Pierre Hassner suggested a three-way classification. The first was that of the international system, which he said referred at that time to "the bipolar balance of dissuasion and, in Europe, to the territorial division of the two blocs" (1995:11); the second was that of states, with their internal and diplomatic concerns, and the third that of societies, within states, each with its own political system, its structures and its dynamics. This separation of levels—a technique we have already used in our work dealing with terrorism in the 1970s and 1980s[10]—enables us to think about the general conditions of change in the paradigm of violence. We shall adopt it again here, simply adding a fourth level, that of the individual, not in order to introduce a psychological dimension to our analyses, but to stress a major contemporary phenomenon, and one that has a considerable impact on the production of contemporary violence, the growth of modern individualism. At each of these four levels, there have been far-reaching changes and a consideration of these is already a useful contribution to the phenomena of violence. We can go further and be more specific if, over and above that, the analysis takes into consideration the transformations that affect the relations between the levels, their articulation, their correspondence or, if you prefer, their integration.

At the international level the end of the Cold War on the one hand and the globalization of the economy on the other have brought considerable change in violence by making local conflicts possible or more deadly, by exacerbating cultural fragmentation and the radicalization of social identities, in particular religious identities, and by accentuating the frustrations that originate in social inequalities.

At the state level, traditionally at the core of the political analysis of violence, it has been necessary to modify Max Weber's classical definition of the state as having the "monopoly of legitimate physical violence" (1958:78). Today the state is constantly outflanked both internally and externally. It has to some extent lost its classical role as the sociopolitical framework for the management of violence. Its traditional monopoly of violence has been challenged by the privatization of some of its classical functions, its inadequacies, or in some instances by the abuse of power of a number of its representatives.

But we would like to concentrate on contemporary changes in the social sphere, in the behavior of people, and individuals.

SOCIETAL CHANGES

In the 1950s and 1960s, under North American hegemony, the evolutionists developed the idea of a "one best way" according to which, throughout the world, societies were destined to embark on identical processes of modernization that were envisaged in economic terms—development—and in political terms—democratization. In this perspective, the horizon was represented by the most advanced industrial societies and, in the first instance, by the United States, and violence was expected to decline as progress gained momentum.

Today, we presume that there are alternative models of development, that economic and political progress does not necessarily entail a decline in violence; in advanced societies postindustrialization may very well coexist with intense social difficulties. In Western societies the loss of centrality of classical industry is often accompanied by phenomena of unemployment and vulnerability. The definition of the social question is no longer in terms of exploitation in production but in terms of exclusion. Employment is no longer linked to industrial growth and in this type of change, the principle of conflictual structuring of social life that was provided by the opposition between the working-class movement and capital, disintegrates. From this point on, there is a decline in trade unionism and the systems of professional relations, even in places where they were very dynamic as in Germany, or in the Scandinavian countries. The classical left-right opposition ceases to represent a social conflict at political level, political expectations become exacerbated without finding a locus for mediation, populism becomes active from Ross Perot in the United States to the *Lega Nord* in Italy or the national populism of the *Front National* in France, and the social crisis combines with the question of cultural, national, ethnic, and religious identities to nurture violence that reinforces both the tendencies to disintegration of national societies, and the various appeals that are a reaction to the disintegration of the social order.

Comparable changes are affecting the former Eastern European countries where the end of the Soviet experience is also the destructuring of a model focused on the role of labor, which provided each individual with guarantees. Many of these—jobs, housing, access to health services, leisure, basic forms of consumption, and so on—were linked with employment. But these observations should not lead us to the idea that social or political violence is directly linked to the gradual decline of social relationships specific to classical industry. While there is certainly a link between violence and these social changes, this link is not automatic and immediate, and any consideration of violence must include the elements that precipitate it. It does not emerge *directly* from downward social mobility, or crisis; thus, the riots in the declining urban areas in France or in England, and those in major American cities, are more frequently the immediate outcome of police abuse of power or inadequate legal decisions than of protests against unemployment Young people's anger and hatred is definitely expressed in a context of social difficulties, but it corresponds in the first instance to powerful feelings of injustice and nonrecognition, cultural, and racial discrimination. Unemployment and poverty, even when they are a mark of a brutal social collapse, as in the countries of the former Soviet empire, seldom end directly or immediately result in social violence—something we have known since Lazarsfeld's classical study on unemployed workers in Marienthal (1993)—but instead nurture frustrations that may possibly be expressed in an exacerbated form of nationalism, or an appeal to the return of the communists. And while they may nurture collective violence, the latter tends to be racist and anti-Semitic and associated with nationalist references, rather than specifically social or class oriented.

CONTEMPORARY INDIVIDUALISM

Individualism, as it manifests itself with increasing force in the contemporary world, is a two-sided question; its aspects may be complementary or possibly diametrically opposed. On the one hand, the modern individual wants to participate in modernity and in what it offers, the promises and the prospects offered through the media and the enticement to mass consumption, the spectacle of which is now globalized. On the other hand, the individual wants to be recognized as a subject, to construct his own existence and not be totally dependant on roles and norms and be able to put these at a distance but not be forced to do so. For example, he wishes to make choices sanctioned by reference to a collective identity without being totally subordinated thereto; he wishes to produce and not merely to reproduce.

There is nothing new about these two aspects of individualism; in a way, Emile Durkheim (1985) refers to them when he distinguishes between the individual who is characterized by the profane, and the person who is characterized by the sacred. Today they each maintain a strong relationship with violence, even at a collective level. For example, the actor of much instrumental violence is implicated for economic reasons—he wants money to consume and to buy, for himself and possibly for his family members. On a somewhat different level, violence can assume extreme forms, to which there are no limits, when related to a frustrated desire to gain access to the fruits of modernity and without there being any question of using it as a resource to achieve one's ends. This brings it closer to forms of behavior motivated by anger at nonrecognition, by the feeling of an experience of injustice, of the individual being prevented from becoming a subject, all of which can take different forms: an outbreak of rioting, a type of amusement, but also, in David Le Breton's words (1991), a very dangerous form of activity motivated by a "desire for risk," which can then become something of an initiation rite, or be self-destructive, in a reversal of the impossibility created by the system or the situation of being the actor of one's own existence. Here violence is either a quest for meaning, an endeavor to produce the self-realization formerly ensured by the culture or the institutions, a projection of the self which could be fatal, or else an appeal to an impossible or frustrated subjectivity, the expression of a person's refusal to continue being negated.

In this last instance, the rise in racism to which people are subjected in many countries is an experience that is widely considered by its victims as a profound negation of their individuality; this may then take the form of anger and escalate into violence, for example, in rioting. None of this is new, it is true, but the advances of globalization render all references to individualism much more acute than in the past—this is equally applicable to personal vulnerability, particularly when it is a question of combining the two registers, of instrumental, strategic efficiency and the construction of autonomous subjectivity (Ehrenburg 1995): nowadays we are all aware of what the modern world can offer or promise both as far as the consumption and the production of the individual are concerned, but it is very difficult to be at one and the same time the producer and the consumer of one's own existence, being efficient and rational on the one hand, and autonomous and standing aloof from social norms on the other. We find here three sets of conditions that are conducive to violence: from a purely strategic point of view, quite cynically, violence is a resource; the end result of the desire to be identified with a community may be fanaticism or warlike sectarianism. Finally, in the processes of fusion that culminate in the invention of imagined meaning as a way of resolving the impossibility of functioning at one and the same time as a consumer and a producer of one's existence, the likelihood of violence is greater when concrete means of expression cannot be found here and now.

In addition, individualism has an effect not only on the meaning, but also on the forms of contemporary violence. This seems to be one of the lessons drawn by Jean-Paul Grémy from a set of studies dealing with urban violence in France when he observes that gangs of youths or rioting crowds, in the declining peripheral urban areas, are motivated by an individualism that "makes negotiations with a view to ending the violence particularly difficult."[11]

Distinguishing between levels can therefore be helpful in the analysis. But, we should also add, that it should not lead to a division of intellectual labor, with researchers specializing in one or other level. On the contrary, any consideration of violence will gain both by giving some thought to these clearly defined subsets—the international system, the state, and so on, but also by considering their complementarity and articulation or, on the other hand, their disassociation. The above remarks lead me to make a suggestion: instead of starting at the top, in the political science tradition, with the international level where the changes, either real or imagined (globalization) are sustained by the actions of actors and societies on themselves, at least as much as they shape them, would it not be better to start at the lowest level, with individualism or the changes that affect social relationships and, in the analysis, work upward?

DOUBTS AND UNCERTAINTIES
Objective Violence, Subjective Violence

The changes briefly outlined above, which affect the four levels we have described, require sociology to study each level on its own analytically, but also in their totality. There is no such thing as an integrated sociology of violence, which posits a satisfactory unified theory enabling us to deal simultaneously with the level of individuals and their psychology, and those of society, of the state, and of the system of international relations, but that does not prevent us from endeavoring to not lose sight of the overall picture, in particular when positing the hypothesis that one of the fundamental sources of contemporary violence lies precisely in the tendency to dissociation. For example, it is tempting, on one hand, to analyze the personality of the young sicaires, or paid killers who, in Columbia seem to be motivated by a powerful desire for money and consumption with no moral considerations and, on the other, to analyze the global drug economy or the relations between the United States and Columbia. It is much more useful to demonstrate how the instrumental violence of the young paid killers in Medellin oscillates between politics and criminality and is part of a whole network of social and political relationships, at the level of the local arena, the town, the country, the continent, which are not restricted to the image of two wholly distinct worlds, the international (drugs and the drug economy), and the personal or psychological (the absence of internalized norms that makes it possible to become a paid killer) (Sarmiento 1991:60–73).

The further one pursues this type of analysis, the more useful to consider how much violence is subjective and how much is objective. When actors and social and political relationships have failed, violence fills the vacuum left between the actor, reduced in the last resort to his personality or his subjectivity, and the system, with its references to global processes symbolized by the concept of globalization. But is there really a vacuum, or is there a failure in representation? The task of sociology of violence is to highlight the lack of processes of mediation, the systems where the absence or weakening of relationships creates a space for violence. If these processes of mediation, these systems of relationship tend to be concealed, misunderstood, or ignored rather than really deficient or absent, because the society in question, its political elites, intellectuals, and public opinion refuse to learn about them and discuss them, violence has to be analyzed primarily as a form of representation, as the subjectivity of groups, even of a whole society, incapable of understanding themselves and of understanding their environment. If this is quantifiable, if it can be empirically verified that there is a lack of actors and mediation in the system of social relationships, violence is undoubtedly a strong objective reality. Here, sociology must analyze the situation and show how contemporary violence takes on new forms both in matters of subjective perceptions and in historical reality.

This is why the hypothesis of a change in the paradigm of violence also takes us back to a classical problem in the sociology of knowledge: Is the way in which we discuss violence and contemporary change, including scientific discourse, simply a function of the state of the phenomenon and its objective transformations, or is it a function of the most diverse sorts of change, which take place at the different levels that have been set out here, but in a fairly autonomous manner in relation to the facts of violence, influencing our perceptions and shaping representations that in reality have nothing to do with the concrete expressions of the phenomenon?

DISARTICULATION

If violence seems to be linked to the changes that affect not only each of the four levels chosen for analysis, but also to the overarching structures that unite them, this is primarily because when we consider them in their concrete manifestations, and not only as analytical categories, these levels no longer seem to be articulated. Here, the most obvious reference is the crisis of the nation–state with the decline in its role as the principal framework or arena for territorial, political, administrative, and intellectual or community life. Thus there is a hiatus between the scale of the problems implicated in global economic and ecological processes and the institutional tools that we have to deal with and interpret them, which are mainly those of the state.

Within each country, it is often becoming complicated to establish a strong correspondence between various policies, for example to ensure coherence between economic and commercial policies and foreign policies. Yet again, it may be difficult to reconcile diplomatic activity that may involve the state's participation in international institutions and the increasing individual awareness of the theme of human rights that may be an incentive for action well beyond the confines of the state, one that has been linked to the prerogative of international intervention. Disarticulation is most spectacular in situations where society, state, and culture were previously integrated in what, in Alain Touraine's terms, can be designated *national societies* (1992). In these societies, characteristic of the industrial era, institutions ensuring individual equality, collective solidarity, and national identity formed a highly coherent system that could be experienced as self-sufficient, and that is now being undermined by the effects of neoliberal globalization.

From this point of view, violence may be the outcome of the endeavor by certain actors to perpetuate in an increasingly artificial or deliberate manner the world they are losing; in the last resort, it is expressed by attacks on those who are accused or suspected of implementing the sociopolitical disintegration of national society and of being the vectors of the threat of cultural heterogeneity. In these instances the prime target is immigrants and, at a broader level, groups of people that are the easiest to racialize. In Europe, racism, including in its most active, most destructive, and most murderous expressions is a reaction closely associated with the refusal of the destructuring of national societies.

A WORLD THAT HAS LOST ITS WAY?

In considering the forms and extent of violence would it not be helpful to have a way of marking out areas that are relatively homogeneous in space? There are three main pathways—political (or geopolitical), economic, and cultural, or even a combination thereof—in attempting to answer this question constructively.

In the years of the Cold War, violence could be understood in terms of the bipolarity of the geopolitical division of the world. There was very little chance of its emergence, in any case of its extension and assumption of a political aspect, given that it ran the risk of challenging the fundamental equilibrium between the East and the West. Europe was at the center of this equilibrium that did not prevent serious forms of violence occurring but meant that any major political or geopolitical issue was not on the agenda. At this point, three "worlds," or subsets of countries were discernable: the West, including North America and Western Europe, the communist world, and finally the developing countries, the Third World with its very violent internal conflicts and somewhat weak and unstable states. The fall of the Berlin Wall has made it so difficult to think of the world in political or geopolitical terms that some authors have even spoken of the end of history (Fukuyama 1992).

Another distinction—this time economic—opposes the North, which was and still is rich and unlikely to be affected by serious upheavals, and the South, which is excluded from the main networks and flows of globalization and a propitious terrain for the worst forms of civil, ethnic, or other forms of violence. But the effects of exclusion are ravaging the very core of advanced societies so profoundly, and the internal differences of the countries in the South are so great that it is difficult to consider violence on the basis of this division.

Finally, a third division has recently been suggested between civilizations—that of their cultures. Violence will develop in the contemporary world between the major civilizations in the areas where they clash—this is Samuel Huntington's thesis that, as we have seen, underestimates the tensions and cultural differences produced and reproduced at the very heart of each civilization.[12]

Today, the Third World is at the center of the most developed countries, communism has collapsed and with it the idea of an East-West opposition, new powers are emerging, as in the South Pacific. Violence has appeared in a particularly brutal form in the North and especially in the former Yugoslavia; everywhere there is a mixture of cultural assertions and socioeconomic demands, everything seems confused, to the point that Ghassan Salamé (1996:21) speaks of the disappearance of the "four points of the compass." We should add that the best analysts explain that the concept of the Third World, in such constant use in the past, was a useful linguistic term that was already somewhat artificial at the time, a concept that amalgamated very different realities.

When thinking about the emergence and the development of violence in space in a differentiated manner, we realize there is no longer any strong geopolitical principle, economic distinctions are insufficient, and the hypothesis of the clash of civilizations does not appear to be appropriate. In a world that is both fragmented and globalized, the probability of serious violence at the local level is considerable everywhere and, at the same time, even highly localized problems are much more likely than in the past to be displaced, exported, and extended beyond their initial or original sphere. When violence is linked to a national cause, it can take the form of a diaspora and introduce complexity where it is least expected. For example, the question of the Kurds has become something that cannot be ignored in the internal and diplomatic life of Germany where violence may have occurred because of the presence of a large immigrant population from Turkey. Similarly, on the whole the immigrants from Algeria in France are trying hard to integrate. However this does not mean that they are insensitive to the diaspora, or even to networks, some of which function at an international level and may be linked to activities of armed violence in Algeria. Yet again, it may be possible to establish links between the crisis in a specific First World state and the crisis in a particular Third World state—a feature that emerges spectacularly if one considers the nature—not only pathetic but scandalous—of certain political or military interventions of the type that took place in Somalia. "The interventions of 'First World' countries (some in UNO form)," writes Alain Joxe, "are not pure attempts to set things right on the part of 'ordered' societies, but actions which are themselves disorganized and *disorganizing*, mirroring at the outset the 'central' crisis in the representations and the actors who are part of the legitimate level of the monopoly of violence, that of the States. There is complexity and confusion at both ends of the enterprise" (1995).

This enables us to be more specific about a new paradigm of violence: the latter must effectively be approached, henceforth, with concepts that can no longer be those of a bipolar world, or those of a world in which the economy entitled us to think of international relations straight away in terms of domination and exploitation or of varying degrees of modernization. Violence has to be understood in what is one of its radical novelties: the fact that it is both globalized—since it is subject to worldwide phenomena—and localized; general and, in Hans Magnus Enzensberger's words (1995), molecular; both worldwide and splintered or shattered. There is no inherent difference between the core and the periphery; violence contributes to the reduction of these concepts. For example, there are many similarities between the young actors of the Islamic movements in the Middle East and the angry young men in the French suburbs, whether they be Muslim or not. This unusual characteristic of contemporary violence forces us even further to focus our thinking on the individual rather than the other extreme—the sociohistorical. Violence is a challenge to us more than at any other time, not because we might be moving in the direction of worldwide chaos, or even be immersed in the heightened uncertainty of the aftermath of the Cold War, but because we have to learn to think of it in different terms, in the light of our awareness of a new historical and political dimension. We must be wary of overhasty statements in terms of "neo" or "comeback," in instances where the phenomena under consideration are either really so new that they call for a total overhaul of our categories, or else are older and more complex than these expressions, somewhat unrefined, would lead us to believe, just as we should be wary of the idea of linear forms of development or the one-dimensional consequence of specific phenomena. The globalization of the economy, for example, does not have uniform effects but tends to emphasize some trends much more than others in an ambivalent way, like those which, at one and the same time, ensure the globalization of mass consumption or televisual products and cultural fragmentation; and it is not because France has been rather slow in discovering it that it is a recent phenomenon.

VIOLENCE AND THE CRISIS OF MODERNITY

Let's assume, following the example of Alain Touraine (1992), that modernity is the product of the tension between reason and culture, between the world of the object and that of the subject, between the rational and the subjective. From this point of view, the contemporary world can be understood as being more likely to be torn between the two poles that define modernity. On the one hand, there is the world of techniques, the market, science, and the neoliberal economy, on the other that of community or sectarian identities; on the one hand, the reign of instrumentalism, calculation, and power and, on the other, cultures that are poorly treated or aggressive. On the one hand there is the system, on the other, the actors. The crisis of modernity, and in its wake, the attraction of postmodernity, resides in the total separation between the component elements of these pairs. The tension between them is the defining mark of modernity.

From this point of view, contemporary violence can be analyzed as a vast set of experiences that, in their own way, convey the postmodern tendency to disintegration and may even be its precursor. This tendency brings us to a first hypothesis that deserves to be examined: that of a dissolution of the political arena and of a distortion of the overall spectrum of violence on the basis of its political dimensions. Violence frequently continues to occupy the political level; but perhaps more than previously, we must be aware of the complementary dimensions—the forms that outflank it from above and below.

In the 1960s and 1970s, as we mentioned, political violence challenging political systems and states was indeed quite considerable. With no real social base, the terrorism of the extreme left fell within the orbit of revolutionary projects to seize power, that of the extreme right had the same aims, national liberation movements aimed at liberating a nation from foreign domination to establish their own State. Today, like yesterday, there are still numerous and large-scale examples of political violence in the world. But there is a trend at work that is by no means insignificant that is the shifting of the phenomena toward infrapolitical arenas on the one hand, and metapolitical arenas on the other. Pierre Hassner (1995) also observes this trend, noting that the key to contemporary development "seems to lie in the political deficit within present-day societies and, further, at the international level."

INFRAPOLITICAL VIOLENCE

The increasing privatization of the economy in areas where there used to be more state control, or in areas where this was traditionally the situation, constitutes wholesale encouragement to the privatization of violence, the political nature of which is attenuated or diluted. In many cases, for the protagonists of violence, the concern is not to seize power to accede thereto, or to endeavor to penetrate the political system; their concern is to keep the state at a distance so that they can engage in illicit economic activities, dealing in drugs, in stolen goods, but also in children or human organs, and so on. We thus see guerrillas who become the administrators of territories where they can be part of the drug trade, or take it over, for example in Columbia, or yet again, quite simply, exploit resources, which is not in itself illegal, but do so without being subject to state control; that is, without paying any taxes or customs duties. Actors who have been caught up in the spiral of terrorism and extreme political violence turn out in the last resort to be dealers in drugs or other illicit goods who are as interested in access to money as to political power, as the analyses of the armed struggle in Algeria suggest. Certain episodes there can only be understood in terms of conflicts between Islamic groups or between some of these groups and the armed forces for the control of a local monopoly of extortion or trafficking, the *trabendo*, which can extend to illegal goods as well as to conventional products, like food, for example (Labat 1995; Martínez 1995).[13] We also witness the development of mafias or comparable organizations, especially in the former Soviet empire, which are likely to resort to force to defend their interests; these actors are likely to strike at the State if the latter takes too great an interest in their activities—the Italian experience in the 1990s, including the assassination of high-level state officials is an impressive example of this. In Brazil, for example, where the practice of kidnapping was limited and corresponded to political aims in the 1970s, it has now increasingly become a strictly commercial enterprise. This observation applies to many other illegal and brutal extortion rackets. Privatization of violence may be part of a perversion, when those who control the legitimate use of force—the police, the army—use it for unscrupulous ends, abusing their weapons and their immunity. It is not necessarily a mark of barbarism, or the law of the jungle. But it is not very far from that, enabling unauthorized forms of behavior that can, ultimately, aim at terrorizing anyone likely to oppose the interests and the powers of the actor who exercises the force that has been privatized in this way. One of the consequences of the privatization of violence and of the increasing economic activity of armed actors is that the civil populations are subjected to it in dramatic forms, for example, in predatory raids.

Violence, linked to the control and accumulation of economic resources, is not necessarily the weapon of the poor. Thus, the outcome of a study of the economic dimensions of violence in Columbia is the observation that "the analysis, at the municipal level, of the evolution of the various organized actors involved in violence, shows that it is not so much a question of an ideological confrontation as a conflict about territory and the fruits of the most profitable economic activities. This is why conflicts and violence are more frequently encountered in the most dynamic areas and less frequently in declining areas with a low level of economic activity" (Castilla 1995:78). One question that arises here, as elsewhere, is that of the novelty of these phenomena. There again, it would appear that the principal feature tends to be their recent extension, the increase in number, a characteristic also noted by Jean-Christophe Rufin for whom "the disinvestment of the major powers and the economic disaster of numerous countries ruined by war have pushed the guerrilla movements to practice openly and on a large scale what they had become used to doing discretely and modestly. . . . The guerrillas in the 1990's tend to be based on genuine market economies, possibly involving production. . . . The change in the international context associated with the end of the Cold War has not created these new means of sustaining conflicts out of nothing. But it has undoubtedly contributed to generalizing certain practices which until then were marginal"(1996:43–44).

On a quite different level, in democracies, infrapolitical violence is also a characteristic of racist and xenophobic phenomena. The latter are illegal in the public sphere and have little credibility. When an extreme right party with a racist and xenophobic ideology develops, it is impossible for it to call loudly and clearly for violent behavior, nor is it possible for it to recognize or to support such behavior, as we see in France with the *Front National*, whose concern for respectability and being part of the political sphere forbids recourse to violence. The latter appears at the edges of the political spectrum, it endeavors to find a place there, but it is in the main infrapolitical, consisting of what the British refer to as "racial harassment" and incoherent forms of behavior.

But let us not be mistaken here. In certain instances, the infrapolitical nature of the violence may be linked to a process of degeneration; its political characteristics are overtaken by the privatization of violence for the control of economic resources, money, or a territory. In others it conveys indecisiveness on the part of the actor, as he hesitates between two levels, unsure of the one he is going to adopt. In yet other situations, it constitutes more of a prepolitical than an infrapolitical form, the beginning of a trajectory that may eventually be capable of rising to the political level. For example, at the beginning of the 1980s in Milan we witnessed young people genuinely hesitating between delinquency and extreme-left political terrorism (Camarade 1982:38). In Brazzaville the downwardly socially mobile youths form groups that, depending on the period observed, may be part of the political militia or again may be armed gangs;[14] but we also observe that in the United States, according to Laurent Zecchini (1996:2) the social anger of the "dropouts" in American society sustains the rancor that crystallizes in the form of extreme right-wing, racist, anti-Semitic militia, hostile to the federal state and international organizations, like the United Nations. The major global transformations and the crisis of states are factors that are propitious to the privatization of violence, which then becomes infrapolitical, but they are also factors that can have the opposite effect. They may for example encourage people to transform their rage or social anger into political violence. In the 1970s and 1980s, political violence primarily was a sign of the end of an era, the decline of social, political, and state institutional systems. It combined the reaction to the state order, perceived primarily as repressive, and the revolutionary appeal for change. At the end of this century, the dominant trend is social violence rather than political violence. Rioting, for example, whether on the basis of identity, ethnic origin, or religion, is all to some extent informed by a high degree of subjective unhappiness. But this does not prevent us from postulating that in the long run political violence will return and then perhaps presage a restructuring of the social, political, and state systems that are today in decline. We can thus hypothesize that the appearance of terrorism within the United States, where it seemed unlikely to occur, presages considerable political and social changes in this country and is not only the expression of a revolt against the declining federal state. But, on the whole, the major characteristic of infrapolitical violence in the contemporary world is its association with the decline of states and with practices that are part of organized crime, even with the most ordinary criminality that has increased at an alarming rate. It does not seem to be the prelude to social and political conflicts. Organized criminality is often associated with very negative opinions within the population about the state, its laws, and its police, but it is difficult to interpret this as the expression of revolts without a cause awaiting their ideological project as might be argued for the role of movements like socialism or communism in the past. It is true that at the local level some drug dealers are considered, particularly in drug-producing areas, to be benefactors who provide resources, income, and even, in some cases, minimal forms of welfare, for example, in health care. Often criminals are viewed more favorably by the population in the places where they come from than the state, the institutions, and their representatives. But it is difficult to assign the participants in organized crime the prepolitical role of forerunners of grassroots protest, or to see therein a figure comparable to that of the social bandit as analyzed by Eric Hobsbawm (1968).

But infrapolitical violence should not be restricted to its dimensions of private, instrumental violence alone; in many respects, gratuitous violence, possibly associated with a taste for risk and a desire for adventure is also part of this level, as is the endeavor to make things more meaningful, or its direct opposite, the abolition of all meaning in the pure pleasure of unbridled violence (of the type practiced by those described by Buford in his very impressive book (1990).

METAPOLITICAL VIOLENCE

Violence sometimes extends beyond the political, to become the vector of meanings that are intransigent in nature—something nonnegotiable, a religious, ideological, or ethical dimension that appears to be absolute. It then knows no bounds and the issues that it targets are so vital for the actor that, in extreme instances, he may sacrifice his own life, destroying himself for the sake of a host of meanings that, for him, have to be asserted unreservedly. Metapolitical violence is not apolitical. It is a design in which political issues are both associated with and subordinated to other issues, defined in cultural or religious terms for example, which do not admit any concessions. The crisis in modernity is highly conducive to this type of violence in which identities totally divorced from any insertion in a political type of relationship find a means of expression. The intensity depends on the degree of frustration evoked in the actor by modernity. He may have to deal with the following situations: international means of communication bring images of Western-type happiness to the most remote places, the consumption of material and cultural goods is an everyday spectacle, either on television or in the windows of shops to which entry is de facto forbidden, access to money and to the fruits of science and progress is suddenly refused or lost, or the feeling of an immense social frustration is sublimated into religious, national, or ethnic convictions. These are all circumstances in which violence may take hold of the actor and mobilize him or her in political projects in which identity becomes a resource and the political is subordinated to the demands of God or of the nation. The major Islamic mobilizations are examples of this type of action in which politics and religion are merged, with the religious element being dominant. These forms of mobilization may become quite powerful, but they may also transform into extremist movements that are no longer associated with the expectations conveyed by a religious utopia but with the consequences of failure, the catastrophic loss of meaning. In these cases they may lead the actor to sacrifice his own life—we find here the type of death-wish martyrdom discussed in the work of Farhad Khosrokhavar.[15]

We are faced, then, with two logical outcomes that are analytically distinct, but that both incorporate violence in their concrete manifestations. On the one hand, violence may signal intense social difficulties, including situations in which cultural or religious meanings in particular are asserted. In the Middle East the explanation of one of the sources of Islamism lies in the unfulfilled social aspirations of the poor. In Lebanon, in the 1970s, the adjective "disinherited" was used to account for the Shiite movement led by Imam Moussa Sadr. On the other hand, violence may be used by people who thought they could participate in modernity, or who did in fact participate therein before being ejected, left behind, victims of progress, radicalized by the feeling of an undeserved downward social mobility. The two approaches may easily merge, for example when social demands are exacerbated by the unfulfilled promises of modernity; what began as social demands is driven by frustration to increasingly express rage and fury. What was a national project is transformed into a religious one and may even be the subject of religious designs that the concept of the nation is quite incapable of fulfilling. Fury and anger then drive the actor on to the most radical forms of violence that may ultimately be capitalized upon or directed, even manipulated, by leaders or organizations with other political agendas. Martyrdom is thus a mark of collective mobilization that goes further than the political sphere; it expresses a meaning that goes beyond it. Ultimately those who are in power, possibly in a political-religious structure of government, no longer need it, for example, because it has become routinized. Violence then becomes impossible; all that remains is despair, which some transform into cynicism and others into a return to ordinary participation in social or political life.

Frustration can thus be exacerbated when it combines disappointment with modernity, rejection, and an ending of the prospects for a historical reversal of the situation that may have originated in a revolutionary or reform process on the wane. It is encountered in the most varied social situations—it is as likely to be found among landless peasants in the Middle East, attracted by the urban way of life and deeply disappointed by what it has to offer them, as among Japanese engineers who do not find the industrial firm conducive to the development of their professional lives and turn to the Aum sect. It is not simply a psychological mechanism, but the outcome of a tension between the expectations of the actor and the reality he encounters, a tension that is more difficult to bear when it is heightened by an individualism that does not find a means of expression and by the vision of a globalized world that is becoming inaccessible or that rejects him. Jean-François Bayart is right to advise us not to be fooled or naive when confronted with the "search for identity," in which identity is often merely a resource manipulated for political ends; but it can also happen that the meanings of identity extend beyond the political framework, and at the same time, escape the control of the actors who endeavor to restrict them.

VIOLENCE AND IDENTITIES

Thus, if violence does seem to correspond closely to a new paradigm, which is in its turn part of the general context of the crisis of modernity, this is because its contemporary significance seems to be more cultural than social and the work of actors defined primarily in terms of a cultural identity. Our everyday vocabulary—ethnic purification, sectarianism, fundamentalism, and so on—constantly refers to the image of movements and actors whose violence is all the more frightening as it does not admit of any negotiation, or compromise.

In the first instance we still have to distinguish between two types of meaning of identity. There are identities that are the remains of a tradition or a culture ravaged by the progress of "reason" and triumphant Western universalism. In this case, violence is primarily a form of resistance to an identity under threat. Other identities are the outcome of the work of modernity on itself, they are constructions rather than reproductions, even if their construction is the work of what Lévi-Strauss calls *bricolage*, that is to say it involves the use of disparate materials borrowed from traditions or a historical past. Violence here does not convey resistance to triumphant modernity. On the contrary, it is the expression of the crisis of modernity in which subjectivity is torn from rationality, and opposes the latter in constructing a new collective identity. In practice, identity-based forms of violence may link these two logics, but the results are more likely to be "postmodern," the outcome of the failure of modernity rather than pre- or antimodern, as is often imagined. Identity-based violence takes on a radical aspect when there is a potent combination of both the rejection of modernity and its fracture. This happens when the actor embodying them is simultaneously nostalgic for the past, for traditions that have been destroyed, broken, fragmented, but have not totally disappeared and is involved in a process of self-construction in which he is part of a postmodern communitarianism. Throughout the world, Islamism in its most murderous expressions, including terrorism, owes a great deal to this combination of references to traditions that have been lost and the construction or invention of an identity that is far from the most traditional Islam. Similarly, sects that switch to destructive, or self-destructive, violence may appear to be perpetuating a tradition, but in fact they are always an invention that may well be highly sensitive to the prevailing economic climate and the social and political environment in which they are formed.

Violence based on identity is therefore only traditional to a very limited extent. Moreover, it is always much more closely linked to social relations than the culturalist vocabulary generally used to describe it would lead us to believe. It may convey in a religious, national, or ethnic mode, problems of poverty, or frustration or else is amalgamated with these, combining social and cultural meanings. Moreover, violence very frequently tends to naturalize these meanings, often in the form of racism. From this point of view, the rise of identities is a powerful factor in the racialization of collective life; this may be a justification for violence aimed at ethnic purification.

Finally, violence connected with issues of identity, which claims to have a religious or ethnic signification, may be an expression of the failure or the inadequacies of political projects conceived of in the more classical categories of modernity, beginning with those that prioritize either the all-embracing social class and proletarian revolution or else that of the nation and the nation–state. Radical forms of Islam, in many instances, have been constructed in the wake of movements that claimed to be Marxist-Leninist, or nationalist, particularly in the wake of the failure of the Arab or Palestinian movements. This is, for example, obvious, with the rise of Islamic terrorism claiming to represent the Palestinian cause and developing in the wake of its crisis.

Contemporary violence is located at the intersection of the social, the political, and the cultural and is frequently an expression of transformation and more specifically dis-integration. It can move from one level to another, beginning for example at the social level before rising to the political level. It can, on the contrary, constitute a privatization whose strategies, once political, become purely economic, or move from issues of social frustration to the mobilization of cultural resources in a metapolitical agenda. Above all, there does not seem to be as close a link as Max Weber suggests between political/social violence and the state. For the latter, the essence of the political and even more of the state lies specifically in the state monopoly on and regulation of physical violence. At present, violence seems in fact to be much closer to constituting the reverse, the failure of the political, the mark of the decomposition of the state. The planet is in an era of mutation in which there is still considerable room for political violence in forms that are relatively classical, but where we also observe infra- and metapolitical forms of violence that constitute the most significant, but perhaps only temporary, expressions of this change. These forms of violence have a much greater impact than state-based violence, which is of necessity calculated, instrumental. They express the dual characteristic of modern individualism in which each individual, even if very young, desires to live both as a consumer and as an autonomous subject. We have referred to these forms of violence as infra and metapolitical to indicate both their difference in comparison with forms of conduct that are more classically political, and the fact that they cannot, nevertheless, be understood without referring to the political context. These forms of violence indicate the importance of a political sphere for any analysis of violence, but this sphere is itself inadequate to a complete understanding of the phenomenon. It is to be noted, however, that there are indications of new beginnings, of redefinitions that are exceedingly difficult to elaborate as they have to satisfy both individual and collective demands and harbor expectations that have themselves been considerably transformed over the past twenty-five years.

To put it more clearly, if we find it necessary to speak of a new paradigm of violence, we are not referring uniquely to the promotion of the image of a historical change—a statement that has to be qualified, since the direction of evolution is not linear and change is not the same everywhere. Nor are we simply challenging the classical categories of analysis of violence in which instrumental and expressive dimensions of violence are opposed or in which violence is either a resource in conflicts or a crisis form of behavior.

In fact, if there is a new paradigm, it is also and even mainly due to the fact that the crisis of modernity is such that the systemic conflicts of previous eras have now lost their structuring role. This fuels the decline of the political sphere. Furthermore, the breakdown in the former organizing principles means the concept of crisis is too weak to account for situations dominated by destructuring and chaos.

Seen in this light, two dimensions deserve to be stressed. The first is related to the rise in importance of instrumental violence that is observed mainly at the infrapolitical level. When there is a decline in law and order, violence functions in Hobbes's mode and is the principal resource in struggles of man against man. In these instances, instrumentality is the outcome not so much of the interplay of strategic actors involved in conflicts, but much more of the destructuring of systems of order, and therefore of crisis forms of behavior pushed to the extreme.

But there is a second dimension that is more important. This refers to the impact of the form and the meaning of violence when it is other than strictly instrumental.

On one hand, violence is a means of expressing the loss, inadequacy, or lack of conflict, the impossibility for the actor to structure his practice in a relationship in which the interaction includes a conflictual dimension. It expresses the distance or the time lag between the subjective demands of people or groups and the political, economic, institutional, or symbolic responses. In these instances it characterizes a subjectivity that is denied, broken, crushed, unhappy, and frustrated—this is what the actor, who has no existence as such, says. It is the voice of the subject when it is not recognized but tends instead to be rejected and to be, for example, caught in the net of social exclusion and racial discrimination. Seen in this light, violence is likely to erupt in the interaction or the clash of crushed or negated subjectivities. This can be observed in certain riots, in which the rioters' feeling of not being recognized evokes similar feelings among the police who feel devalorized or insulted by those whom they have to repress.

On the other hand, instead of being a negative way of expressing what a person or a group wishes to assert, violence may become a pure and simple negation of alterity, and simultaneously of the subjectivity of the individual in question; it is the inhuman expression of hatred, the destruction of the Other, tending toward the barbarism of ethnic purification or extermination.

These two sides to violence, one of which is characterized by impossible or frustrated subjectivity, the other by its absence or its loss, may very well coexist in the same actor. They may well evoke ambivalent reactions. The public may sympathize with the hurt feelings and negated subjectivity that has turned into violence and totally reject the dark and purely destructive side. These two orientations may remain passive, internalized, or they may become active, in particular in situations of interaction in which there is a mix of persons or groups who are in fact defined by similar sorts of fears, deprivation, and negation. And they are only likely to be gradually absorbed under complex conditions, the most decisive of which involve the reconstituting of exchange and communication between actors.

If violence, even in its nonpolitical, infra- or metapolitical form is constituted within the political, it materializes and takes hold in the lacunae and at the limits of political effectiveness. Where the political conditions for dynamic response are established or reestablished such violence can equally well decline or disappear as a result of an institutional processing of the demands that it harbors. Some of these conditions depend on the actors themselves and in particular on their capacity to constitute themselves as subjects who are conscious of what a political or institutional overture can bring them. An excellent example of this is the "Zapatistas" of Chiapas, who have broken with the logic of guerilla movements and are anxious to obtain a democratic form of recognition that associates a respect for human rights and for their collective identity (Le Bot 1997). Other conditions depend on the capacity of political actors to impose, by conviction or by pressure, a system of exchange of views, negotiation, and discussion. This would enable the protagonists of violence to learn how to replace violence by a relationship involving communication, even if tense and conflictual. The decline of violence often depends on a conjunction of factors. Some are specific to the actors, who must be capable of becoming subjects and of giving up behavior based on pure hatred. Others are specific to the system within which the action develops and to the power of significant actors within the system.

NOTES

1. On the "Apaches" whose fights and juvenile delinquency recall in some respects the young people in the present deprived peripheral urban areas when they angrily protest and whose experience was immortalized on the screen by the character of "Casque d'or" played by Simone Signoret (cf. Pierret 1996).

2. Fanon (1961).

3. See also his study in *Culture et Conflits*.

4. Cf. Michaud (1978), which recalls the extent of the importance of the commission set up in 1968 at the request of President Lyndon Johnson, the task of which was to go as far as knowledge permits in the search for the causes of violence and the means to prevent it, with the aim of "discovering the violence hidden behind the peaceful history of the United States."

5. Concerning this terrorism and its effects on the working of democracy and the constitutional state, readers will allow me to refer them to my book *Face au terrorisme* (1995).

6. Cf. in particular Rule (1988) and, in French, the theoretical appendix to my book, *Sociétés et terrorisme* (1988).

7. Cf. what was the most ambitious attempt and which in fact marked the end of this period, Gurr (1970).

8. In *De la Guerre*, I:28, quoted by Hassner (1995:37).

9. For a useful perspective on the basis of the American experience, cf. Mason (1995:21–55).

10. Wieviorka (1988, chapter 2 of the first part).

11. Grémy (1996:11). We should note here that there might be a difference in definition between the individualism that Jean-Paul Grémy is discussing and the definition that we have just given.

12. In Susan George's opinion, Samuel Huntington and Francis Fukuyama are part of the same ideological tendency that tends to be confirmed by the fact that both have been beneficiaries of the Olin Fund whose aim is to "reinforce the economic, political and cultural institutions on which private enterprise is based" (George 1996).

13. Cf. on the *trabendo*, Labat (1995). Martinez (1995:26) even considers that the GIA is in many respects part of the small- and medium-sized businesses and the import-export trade freed from state control and that the "guerre civile, trois ans après son déclenchement, s'apparente de plus en plus à un instrument de promotion sociale et d'enrichissement personnel"—a view that may be considered exaggerated given the de facto absence of any political consideration.

14. Bazenguissa-Ganga (1996). We find similar phenomena in numerous other urban experiences, for example, again in Africa, Marchal (1993:295–320).

15. Cf., apart from the books already referred to, Khosrokhavar (1996:83–100).

REFERENCES

Baudrillard, Jean. 1995. "Le degré Xerox de la violence." *Libération*, October 2.

Bayart, François. 1996. *L'Illusion identitaire*. Paris: Fayard, 10.

Bazenguissa-Ganga, Rémy. 1996. "Milices politiques et bandes armées: Enquête sur la violence politique et sociale des jeunes déclassés." *Les Etudes du CERI* 13 (April).

Buford, Bill. 1990. *Parmi les hooligans*. Paris: Christian Bourgois.

Castilla, Camilo Echandia. 1995. "Colombie: Dimension économique de la violence et de la criminalité." In *Problèmes d'Amérique latine* 16 (janvier/mars):78

von Clausewitz, C. 1988. *De la guerre*. Paris: Minuit.

Durkheim, Emile. 1985. Les formes élémentaires de la vie religieuse: le système totémique en Australie. Paris: Presses universitaires de la France.

Ehrenburg, Alain. 1995. *L'Individu incertain*. Paris: Calmann-Lévy.

Enzensberger, Hans Magnus. 1995. *La Grande Migration, followed by Vues sur la guerre civile*. Paris: Gallimard.

Fabrizzio, Calvi. 1982. *Camarade*. Paris: Grasset, 38.

Fanon, Frantz. 1961. *Les Damnés de la terre*. Preface by Jean-Paul Sartre. Paris: Maspéro.

Fukuyama, Francis. 1992. *La Fin de l'histoire et le dernier homme.* Paris: Flammarion.

Gavi, Philippe, Jean-Paul Sartre, and Pierre Victor. 1974. *On a raison de se révolter.* Paris: Gallimard.

George, Susan. 1996. *Le Monde diplomatique,* August.

Grémy, Jean-Paul. 1996. *Les Violences urbaines.* Paris: IHESI.

Gurr, Ted Robert. 1970. *Why Men Rebel?* Princeton, N.J.: Princeton University Press.

Hassner, Pierre. 1995. *La Violence et la paix: De la bombe atomique au nettoyage ethnique.* Paris: Esprit.

———. 1996. "Par-delà la guerre et la paix: Violence et intervention après la guerre froide." *Etudes* (septembre).

Hobsbawm, Eric. 1968. *Les Primitifs de la révolte dans l'Europe moderne.* Paris: Fayard.

Huntington, Samuel. 1993. "The Clash of Civilizations." *Foreign Affairs* (summer).

Joxe, Alain. 1995. "Nouveau paradigme stratégique: La Révolution dans les affaires militaires ou la guerre de l'information." *Cahiers d'études stratégiques* 18:85.

Khosrokhavar, Farhad. 1992. *Rupture de l'unanimisme dans la révolution iranienne.* Ph.D. diss., EHESS, Paris.

———. 1996. "Le Martyre révolutionnaire en Iran." *Social Compass* 43, no. 1:83–100.

Labat, Séverine. 1995. *Les Islamistes algériens.* Paris: Seuil.

Lazarsfeld, Paul, et al. 1981. *Les Chômeurs de Marienthal.* Paris: Minuit.

Le Breton, David. 1991. *Passions du risque.* Paris: Métaillié.

Le Bot, Yvon. 1996. "Le temps des guerres communautaires." In *Une Société fragmentée? Le Multiculturalisme en débat.* Edited by Michel Wieviorka. Paris: La Découverte.

———. 1997. *Sous-commandant Marcos : Le Rêve zapatiste.* Paris: Seuil.

Marchal, R. 1993. "Les Mooryaan de Mogadiscio. Formes de la violence dans une space urbain et guerre." *Cahiers d'études africaines* 33, no. 2:295–320.

Martinez, Luis. 1995. "Les Groupes islamistes entre guérilla et négoce: Vers une consolidation du régime algérien." *Les Etudes du CERI* 3 (août).

Mason, John. 1995. "Le Désalignement du consensus stratégique américain: Le Débat stratégique américain." 1994–1995. *Cahiers d'études stratégiques* 18:21–55.

Michaud, Yves. 1978. *Violence et politique*. Paris: Gallimard.

———. 1996. *La violence apprivoisée*. Paris: Hachette.

Oberschall, Anthony. 1972. *Social Conflicts and Social Movements*. Englewood Cliffs, N.J.: Prentice Hall.

Pierret, Régis. 1996. *Les Apaches*. Ph.D. diss., EHESS, Paris.

Rufin, Jean-Christophe. 1996. "Les Economies de guerre dans les conflits internes." In *Economie des guerres civiles*. Edited by J. François and J.-C. Rufin, 43–44. Paris: Hachette.

Rule, James B. 1988. *Theories of Civil Violence*. Berkeley: University of California Press.

Salamé, Ghassan. 1996. *Appels d'empire: Ingérences et résistances à l'âge de la mondialisation*. Paris: Fayard.

Sarmiento, Carlos Miguel Ortiz. 1991 "El sicariato en Medellin: entre la violencia politica y el crimen organizado." *Analisis Politica*, no. 14 (September/December): 60–73.

Schelling, Thomas. 1963. *The Strategy of Conflict*. New York: Galaxy.

Tilly, Charles. 1978. *From Mobilization to Revolution*. Reading, Mass.: Addison-Wesley.

———. 1986. *La France contesté de 1600 à nos jours*. Paris: Fayard,

Touraine, Alain. 1992. *Critique de la modernité*. Paris: Fayard.

Weber, M. 1958. "Politics as a Vocation." In *From Max Weber: Essay in Sociology*. Edited by H. Gerth and C. W. Mills. New York: Oxford University Press.

Wieviorka, Michel. 1988. *Sociétés et terrorisme*. Paris: Fayard.

———. 1995. *Face au terrorisme*. Paris: Liana Lévi.

———. 1997. "Quatre figures du nationalisme: La Question de la violence." In *Sociologie des nationalismes*. Edited by Pierre Birnbaum, 369–86. Paris: PUF.

Zechini. G. 1996. "Les Freemen." *Le Monde*, July 30.

6

The Case for Citizenship as Social Contract: A Tale of Two Girls

UNNI WIKAN

"How are we to get beyond the nation–state if some of our most renowned anthropological 'objects' continue to insist on locality?" Thus asks Jonathan Friedman in his critique of transnationalism and globalization as an ideology. As he points out,

> transnationalism as an ideology is something quite different than the acknowledgment of the existence of transnational social relations. It is an expression of a cosmopolitan identity with a clear political content. It is concerned to demonstrate the superiority of all forms of translocal relations to local relations.

Hence the critique of the nation–state that is voiced by the proponents of the above also includes a notion of

> a world of freedom from the shackles of the nation state . . . a freedom that is primarily, of course, a "cultural" freedom. Nation states are wrong because they misrepresent the true hybrid reality of the globalized world. (Friedman 2003)

The two girls whose stories feature below consider themselves lucky to be members of a nation–state and one that has been able to offer them protection from violence and oppression. They know what it is worth, for both of them were members of a transnational world that fractured their identities and eroded their human rights. One managed to escape after suffering a forced marriage and the curtailment of her elementary school education. The

141

other was luckier: she escaped after being drugged and beaten, kidnapped, and held captive for more than a month.

But for a nation–state at their back that upheld their right to basic human equality and freedom, both these girls would have been lost. In the following I set out to explain why that should be, and what was at stake in each of the two cases. My analysis entails a strong critique of transnationalism and multiculturalism as ideologies—not from an academic point of view but because life on the ground shows these ideologies to serve the interests of the more powerful as against the weaker members of the group. As children and females are among the latter in most societies, a focus on their situation holds the prospect of important insight.

The cases I present involve two nation–states—Norway and Morocco, but their impact carries far beyond these two. The issues I raise are transnational. They involve problems with which all liberal democracies must deal: What are the limits to cultural tolerance? How to reconcile cultural rights with human rights or the rights of parents with the rights of the child—when there is a deep-seated conflict of interest? These issues were raised with particular force in the Nadia case—a human drama that made history in Norway. But more was at stake: citizenship towered central in the events informing the case as well as in the verdict that ensued in the attendant court case. What is the meaning and significance of citizenship in a modern welfare state like Norway? What rights and obligations does citizenship confer, and what are its limitations? When dual citizenship is entailed, should it provide leniency for breaches of the law of one country when the transgressions are clearly within the bounds of law of the other? These questions and more came to the fore through Nadia's case. And they were raised with sufficient force as to make a lasting impact, significantly changing the landscape of opportunity for others struggling with some of the same dilemmas in Norway.

That immigrants have a claim to respect for their culture is an ingrained tenet of Norwegian law, as of all liberal democracies. But respect for basic human rights is also mandatory. Modern constitutions of countries as diverse as Norway, Australia (Wrede-Holm 2000), or South Africa (Chambers 2000), have in common that the problem of how to balance respect for culture with respect for human rights is adjudicated in favor of the latter—on paper. There is in principle no question of the primacy of basic human rights, namely, of the right of all citizens—regardless of gender, age, race, religion, or other criteria—to freedom and equality. The problem arises in practice, and this is where Nadia's case provides a unique lens for an insightful analysis.

Human rights, as Michael Ignatieff (1999) points out, are based on moral individualism: they are entitlements of the individual against superior powers such as the state, the church, or the family. The entrenched norms of conduct and values of such powers constitute a salient part of culture, and hence it is that the rights of the individual to choose her own future may come up against "culture." Her right to her own life may be codified as a breach of culture, or worse, a betrayal.

That parents have the right to pass on their culture to their children is something few would quarrel with. But what of the crucial and difficult issue of "the child's right to autonomy from received cultural traditions" (Shweder 1998)?[1] This—*the right of exit*—is an ingrained part of human rights, and it raises the whole difficult issue of the right of culture to protection and survival versus the right of the person to stake out her own course. Perhaps nowhere are the issues more pregnant and painful than when parents and child are concerned—as in Nadia's case.

The right of exit pertains not just to culture but to citizenship as well. It is a right that liberal democracies grant their citizens so that they can change affiliation and become citizens of other countries if they choose, and fulfill the qualifications. But not all nation–states are equally liberal. Some lay claim on their citizens for life and even in descending generations. We may term such citizenship "ethnic" in contradistinction to "civic" citizenship that can be discarded and is part of a social contract (Greenfeld 2000).[2] But what happens when the two forms of citizenship collide? What then of the incumbent's freedom of movement and expression? And what then of the more liberal country's capability to extend protection of a citizen's lawful rights?

Dual citizenship, it is often assumed, especially in academia, is an advantage in the modern world—a privilege that enhances one's life chances and facilitates globalization. The question arises: but for whom? Who stands to gain, and who to lose, by having dual citizenship, and in which combination of nation–states? The benefits, as I shall show, are not equally distributed. The disadvantages fall heavily on children, especially females. If culture is a way of distributing pain unequally in populations, as Veena Das (1990) argues, then citizenship can be equally said to do so. If communities are often characterized by a local economy of injustice, as Arthur Kleinman (1998) argues, then again citizenship is a distributor of such injustice. And not only in undemocratic nations. Norway has its share of such injustice to answer for. Aisha's story, which I shall narrate, following Nadia's, exemplifies the point; it also highlights the safeguards that must be instituted to *make* citizenship in a modern welfare state that which it should be, following Joseph Carens: "an inherited status that greatly enhances one's life chances" (1987).

By an empirical scrutiny of actual cases an insight is provided into the flesh and blood consequences of issues that are often left floating in academic thin air. I tell the stories of Nadia and Aisha to give these issues a human face, but also to throw citizenship itself into peculiar relief. I begin with Nadia's story.

NADIA'S CASE

Nadia's case was brought to the attention of the Norwegian public when on October 3, 1997, she was reported to have been kidnapped by her parents and brought to Morocco to be married against her will. It was Nadia herself who alerted a friend in Norway who called the police, and then the Ministry of Foreign Affairs. According to her own report she had been drugged, beaten, and forced into a van that had transported her, with her family, to Morocco. The journey had taken five days. She was now being held captive in her parent's house in Nadoor, and she was desperate to be set free.[3]

The Ministry of Foreign Affairs immediately took action. Nadia was a Norwegian citizen, as were both her parents. She was born in Norway; they had taken Norwegian citizenship in 1985. (Her father had come to Norway in 1970, aged twenty, her mother had joined him in 1977). Nadia was also, at eighteen, an adult according to Norwegian law. Hence her parents did not have custody of her. She was a citizen in her own right—which is why the Norwegian authorities intervened immediately. Had she been a child, the matter would have been far more complex, as we shall see with Aisha's case.

The Norwegian ambassador in Morocco was contacted and a rescue plan conceived. The ambassador would negotiate with Moroccan local authorities and Nadia's father to have her set free.

The problem was, Morocco did not recognize the Norwegian citizenship of either Nadia or her parents. In Morocco, the dictum applies: once a Moroccan, always a Moroccan, even in descending generations. Nadia, as her parents' child, was thus also redefined. In Morocco, the status of minor applies till the age of twenty for girls. And so Nadia, a Norwegian adult, became Nadia, a Moroccan child—with some drastic implications for the Norwegian authorities' ability to intervene on her behalf.

I cannot go into the full story here, which was covered in detail by the Norwegian media. For a week, each new day brought dramatic turnabouts in the negotiations between the Norwegian ambassador and Nadia's father. Nadia's father would not budge, though he promised time and again to set Nadia free and bring her to an agreed-upon spot where she would be fetched by a car from the embassy. Nadia meanwhile was reported to be suffering gravely and was mistreated in various ways. A key point of contention concerned the father's demand for a guarantee of free passage, meaning he would not be prosecuted on his return to Norway. This the ambassador could not and would not allow.

When the case was finally settled against many odds, it was probably because of an ingenious strategy by the social welfare agencies, acting in unison with the police and the foreign ministry. Nadia's parents were informed that they would lose their social welfare benefits unless they set the girl free. Though Nadia's parents were far from poor,[4] the loss was considerable: about U.S. \$1,600/month.[5] Also, the Norwegian police placed Nadia's sixteen-year-old brother in custody (*i varetekt*) and confiscated his passport pending their investigating of his complicit role in the kidnapping. (According to Nadia, he had drugged and beaten her.) These turns of events strongly alarmed the family in Morocco. So Nadia was set free and put on a plane to Norway. Shortly after she was reunited with her parents when they too came back.

On her return, Nadia's story took a new turn: She recanted everything she had said. The story of the kidnapping had been fabricated. In truth, she had gone to Morocco on her own accord to visit her sick grandmother. But when her parents wanted to remain in Morocco longer than she wanted, she despaired and pulled off the lie to marshal help. She was deeply sorry about the havoc she had created and the pain inflicted upon her family. Now she just wanted to be left in peace and be reconciled with them.

Peace was not to be. A year later the Norwegian police launched a criminal lawsuit against Nadia's parents for kidnapping their daughter and holding her captive for more than a month. The sentence ranged from a minimum of one year to a maximum of fifteen years in jail. The crown witness for the prosecution was Nadia.

Only a month or so upon her return to Norway she had contacted the police again, telling how she had been forced to pull off the story of going voluntarily to Morocco to see her sick grandmother; it had been her parents' deal for setting her free. She would take the blame upon herself and spare them from being prosecuted and perhaps jailed. But the problems with her parents had resumed on their return to Norway; her father beat and upbraided her for being "too Norwegian." She was terrified that they might abduct her once again and take her to Morocco; and *then* if she made a cry of alarm, who would believe her? She was also concerned about her little sister who might one day come to share her fate. So she saw no solution but to contact the police and cooperate with them to gather evidence against her parents.

The court case that followed was amply covered in all the media. It constituted a national event, as had the kidnapping drama a year before. Hence today, there is hardly an adult Norwegian who does not know of "the Nadia case"—*Nadiasaken*—for it made history in Norway. Because I was called as a cultural expert for the court, I followed the trial throughout five days with an extra day for the verdict. We have only limited space here to go into the court proceedings (see Wikan 2000). I shall dwell on the verdict instead, after a brief résumé of the trial.

The parents pleaded "not guilty." They had never done anything but to act in Nadia's best interests. They were trying to save her from her bad Norwegian friends. To that effect, they were willing to go to some lengths, naturally. But never to the point of beating her or kidnapping her or keeping her locked up. Nadia had always been free to do what she wanted. She had been a loved, spoiled child. Regarding the journey to Morocco, she had gone on her own accord to visit her sick grandmother. (This was in accordance with what Nadia had told on her return to Norway.) Indeed, said the parents, she had begged them to let her go against her mother's warnings that she would let her employer down by not showing up for work on Monday. The decision to travel on Sunday night had been made impromptu on Saturday night, when Nadia's father met a man who was going to drive down the next day and had five seats free in his delivery van. The telegram informing the family of the grandmother's serious sickness and urging them to come had arrived a few days before, but there had been no tickets for a flight until two weeks later. Nadia was not informed about the family's decision to travel Sunday night until earlier the same day. To her mother's delight she insisted on coming along.

"Here in court," said Nadia's father, "you think it is we who have committed a wrong. But everything Nadia tells you is just lies and falsehood. But I know that she does not mean any of this. It is her accomplices who are making her do it.[6] Nadia has forgotten the nine months in her mother's womb, the care and affection she received throughout her upbringing. . . . Now we are repaid for the kindness we as parents have shown," said Nadia's father while her mother cried openly.

But Nadia told a different story, one of having fought an uphill battle to be allowed to be what *she* felt she was, an ordinary Norwegian girl. Indeed, six months before her abduction Nadia had contacted the child welfare agencies regarding her father's ostensible abuse. As a result, Nadia was placed under child welfare custody for three months. She moved home only after her eighteenth birthday and to her father's assurances that he would not beat her. Apparently the move was voluntary. But as Nadia said in court, the project (her word) of the child welfare agencies was not her own. They were set on reuniting her with her family against her own will.

The problems resumed, they did not go away. Her brother said in court that he didn't love her anymore, not after she said that she did not want to be a Muslim. Her parents said that they had nothing against her being "Norwegian." Nadia could do as she liked, even marry a Norwegian. But they didn't like her drinking and smoking and staying out late at night. Would any parent, even a Norwegian parent? Two girls who served as witnesses for the defense confirmed this, that Nadia's parents had given her full freedom, even to marry her Pakistani boyfriend if she wanted to. But Nadia herself told a different story about being beaten and pressured to "become" a Muslim and Moroccan:

> "Did you not tell me I would have to stay in Morocco till I was married and had a baby and only then could I return to Norway?" Nadia asked her mother in a taped telephone conversation that was presented as evidence in court. "And did you not threaten me that I would have to remain in Morocco till I rotted?"
>
> "You have misunderstood me, my daughter, I was only joking," said the mother.
>
> "It is not the kind of thing one jokes about," said Nadia.

A key witness for the defense was Nadia's maternal grandfather. A cordial man who was used to receiving respect (he is a wealthy and prominent man in Morocco), he was out of place in court. Though he repeated much of the parents' story—that Nadia, who loves her grandmother so, had insisted on going to visit her, even though she would let her employer down—other parts of the parents' story left him at loss: Questioned about his wife's serious illness that had precipitated their coming urgently to Morocco, he failed to convey to the court that sense of urgency: yes, his wife is sick all the time, she has diabetes and tends to faint every so often, but he doesn't know quite how much for *he* doesn't sit at home, naturally (for a patriarch in Morocco). Anyone who had suspected that the telegram from his son, Nadia's mother's brother, had been a coverup for a mission unrelated to the grandmother's sickness, might easily have confirmed their view: as I think the prosecutor and the jury (as well as many in the audience) did.

Among other witnesses for the defense were a social worker, a friend of Nadia's brother, and a journalist who were family friends. They said they could not imagine the parents doing anything bad to Nadia, knowing them to be educated, kind, and caring people. Indeed, the defense attorneys (one for the father, one for the mother) consciously played up this quality of the parents in court. They were highly educated and cultured; would anyone of such caliber resort to the atrocities with which they were charged? The court was shown photos of Nadia's maternal grandfather's palace in Morocco, and of her parents' affluent house, as well as of Nadia's wardrobe in storage for her there. Would any family of such standing descend to such depths as was claimed? This seemed to be the message implied in the photographic display of the family's riches.

But others sided with Nadia. A crown witness for the prosecution was the Norwegian ambassador in Morocco. He painted an unflattering picture of Nadia's parents. Her father, he said, had even threatened to beat Nadia if Norway did not grant him free passage. Her mother had called all Norwegian women whores. Nadia had been close to a breakdown and had been cajoled and threatened in the worst possible ways—as all the staff at the embassy could confirm, for they had listened in on the telephone negotiations. Indeed, so irate had the father been that for much of the negotiations, Nadia had to stand in for her father.

In the end the court did not include a charge of forced marriage against Nadia's parents. For though Nadia believed that her parents had planned to have her married to a twenty-one-year-old Moroccan (whose picture she had been shown) so that he could get a visa to Norway and so that she would "become Moroccan," there was no firm evidence of this. The charge was simply that of forcibly holding someone against her will (frihetsberøvelse) for a time exceeding one month.

Both parents were found guilty. Nadia's father was sentenced to one year and three months on suspension, her mother to one year. Her father was also sentenced to pay a fine of 15,000 crowns (about $1,700) and "court proceedings costs" (saksomkostninger) of 60,000 crowns (about $6,800). Hence, the sentence was less than the legal minimum for the crime of which they were convicted: one year in jail. It was done to spare the family and further the prospects of family reconciliation.

It was the matter of citizenship that decided Nadia's fate, in more than one way. Obviously, had she not been a Norwegian citizen, the Norwegian government could not have interceded on her behalf. But also, it was of the essence that her parents were Norwegian citizens. This is clear from the writ of the verdict. It states:

> The defense attorneys have argued for acquittal on the grounds that Nadia, according to Moroccan law, becomes legally adult (myndig) only at 20 years of age. Moroccan citizens are not freed from their citizenship if they acquire another. Nadia had therefore dual citizenship. Her parents must therefore assume that she was a child/minor in Morocco, and that they were in their full right to keep her there against her will.
>
> The court does not agree. When the parents have taken the step of applying for Norwegian citizenship for themselves and their children, this implies both rights and duties. An application for citizenship means that one has decided for oneself which state one wants to be most closely connected with, if not emotionally, at least judicially. That also means that one has to submit to (innordne seg) the rules applying in this state. The parents were well aware of what the le-

gal age in Norway is. For a Norwegian citizen resident in Norway one cannot assume that Moroccan law should apply during short-term visits in that country, and especially not when she [Nadia] has been brought there against her will. The criminal offense (*det straffbare forholdet*) was initiated in Norway. . . . Forcibly holding Nadia against her will was therefore in violation of the law.

Ignorance of the law (*rettsvillfaring*), which also has been claimed as grounds for acquittal, is likewise not applicable, according to the court. Forcibly holding a person against her will is illegal in most states, if not in all. As residents of Norway, and as Norwegian citizens, [Nadia's parents] must know the rules at least in this country.

Both the subjective and objective conditions for sentencing (*domfelling*) are present, and the accused are sentenced according to the charge.

The verdict further states:

> The case arises from culture conflicts. But it is the parents who have chosen to live in Norway. After many years of residence here, they are fully aware of how Norwegian society functions, for good and bad. That they wish to maintain the customs of their country of birth is unobjectionable, so long as these customs do not come into conflict with Norwegian law. Children can develop in ways that are different from what the parents hope for. But that is the risk in having children, and—not least—in letting them grow up in a different culture. The parents have made a choice as to which country their children will be molded by. That circumstance may have such consequences as resulting in the case currently before the court. Using violence and forceful deprivation of the freedom of movement as an answer is unacceptable.
>
> The court also notes that the family continues to live in Norway and that they have two children below school age who will grow up here. Therefore, there must be aspects of Norwegian society that they, in sum, perceive as more positive than the negative ones.[7]

The verdict was a clear statement of what the Norwegian state demands of its citizens, according to the law. And it was historic. It was the first time that a Norwegian court declared, in blunt language, what *citizenship* entails. Mr. Bouras, chairman of the Islamic Council declared: "This is an insult to all Muslims. It implies that we are bushmen who do not follow Norwegian laws and rules!" Others were quoted as saying, "This is directed against us Muslims! The Norwegian state does not care about Nadia. They are just using her as a pretext against us."

Nadia's grandfather was appalled: "I thought Norway was a democracy where there was justice before the law. But this is not democracy! The judge chose to believe a young girl over her family, they sided with her. That is injustice." He presumably returned to Morocco to tell the people so and to launch a court case against the ambassador. "He even offered to send a car to pick up Nadia—from her own family!" The grandfather's honor was wounded, and he was going to correct the situation by taking the ambassador to court.

Nadia's parents appealed the verdict on the spot, but fate intervened. Nadia's father died of heart disease seven months after the trial. The Norwegian state subsequently withdrew its charge against the mother. Nadia's brother, then eighteen, tried to appeal to a rarely used section of the law to appear in his father's stead and pursue the appeal in court. But it was denied, to the mother's relief. A family reconciliation has not yet been achieved, due to Nadia's brother's rage, though Nadia may see her mother secretly. Nadia continues to live by herself at a secret address and is managing relatively well—though she is suffering greatly from her father's death. There are those who say that Nadia caused his death, But it is worth remembering that according to Islam, the time of one's death is written at birth. It is preordained.

Nadia's case presents Norway in the best possible light, if one sides with her. Those who take her parents' position would see it differently. Thanks to her membership in a nation–state that was willing and able to intervene on her behalf and put power behind its laws, she was rescued from having her freedom amputated and her basic liberties suppressed. As a transnational subject she had been travelling back and forth between Norway and Morocco since childhood; and though she treasured her times in Morocco as a child, they came to loom more gravely as she reached puberty. She is not alone in harboring such fears. As I write this (August 2000) Norwegian authorities have just issued a pamphlet to be distributed to all schools in Oslo (the capital, where the majority of non-Western immigrants live), warning girls above fifteen years of age who have problems with their immigrant parents not to travel with them on vacation to the parents' homeland. The evidence is becoming overwhelming that all too many girls have their passports taken away upon arrival in their home countries and are subsequently married by force (though the parents wait in some cases until the girl is eighteen so as not to come into conflict with Norwegian law when they apply for family reunification for the son-in-law).

We do not know if Nadia's parents actually had a forced marriage in mind for her or if this was just a threat. But the effect of Nadia's case has been to call attention to the problem of forced marriage (and not just of girls) as part of the larger problem of "the second generation" and of young people's right to be what they are: persons in their own right who are protected by Norwegian law—whatever identity they want to craft for themselves. As a twenty-three-year-old girl who escaped after being forcefully married in Pakistan said, "It is not that I want to be Norwegian, I just want to be myself." And it means more to females than to males. The latter resort to numerous expedients and recourses to make life livable that are simply closed to the female, such as easier divorce,[8] or even polygamy.[9] This is not to belittle the problems of the male. After a contact telephone was established in Oslo in the spring of 2000 for youngsters who felt threatened with forced marriage, one-third of those seeking help were young men. My point is simply that the young woman or girl stands to lose more in bodily integrity, freedom, and alternative options.

Now to highlight the gender issue, let us delve into Aisha's case. It compels attention also because it throws Nadia's case into further relief. Nadia's case is exemplary; Aisha's is more typical. Aisha's case also illuminates the situation of the girl-child—a real child, not a child-cum-adult like Nadia. Finally, Aisha's case both precedes and antedates Nadia's. Hence it helps us to see how the landscape of opportunity changed in the aftermath of Nadia's case.

AISHA'S CASE

In April 1996, Aisha, a Norwegian citizen, born and raised in Norway, was brought out of the country by her parents to their original homeland. Her parents were also Norwegian citizens, her father having lived in Norway thirty-five years, her mother a little less.

Aisha was only fourteen years old and in eighth grade in elementary school. She was a bright and diligent student despite serious problems on the home front. Her father was known to be a violent man,[10] and the children were often maltreated. (Aisha had several brothers but she was the only girl). Nevertheless, all appeals by Aisha and her teachers to the child authorities to let her remain in a foster home where she had lived for a month, failed. Not even the fact that her parents had threatened her with a forced marriage dissuaded the child welfare authorities. Aisha was reunited with her family by police escort. Two weeks later she was gone from Norway. Four years were to pass before she was heard from again.[11]

Now to throw Aisha's case into relief and highlight the gender issue, a comparison with Aisha's father is instructive. As a young man, he too was threatened with a loss of his freedom and identity, if for different reasons. That is not the issue: what concerns us here is the fact that each of them had to *do* something about their situation. Due to his drinking problem, Aisha's father had little prospect of making a career in his homeland (alcohol is prohibited in Islamic culture). He had been fired from his job with the police and seemed unable to provide for a family and reap respect in society. So he looked for an escape. And he found it in the prospects of life in a welfare society where a man's needs are taken care irrespective of whether he works. He journeyed to Norway and made a career as a social welfare client. He has done well, having saved enough to become a property owner in Morocco while his sizable family lives in good conditions in Norway. Thus he regained his honor and expanded his freedoms.

Aisha was faced with a very different opportunity situation. Like her father, she too looked for an escape when faced with a threat to her freedom and identity. She too had been socialized to think that she mattered as a human being and that her personal welfare counted. In his case, it was his North African upbringing that instilled such ideas in a man; in hers, it was her education in a Nordic welfare society committed to the premise that all humans are equal, irrespective of gender and rank. Father and daughter thus had similar compelling concerns and took similar desperate steps to safeguard their welfare and identity. He won. She was defeated. And she lost at the hands of the same nation that saved him. This was not a traditional Middle Eastern society. It was a modern European welfare state—the country in which she held citizenship from birth, he did not.

Norway prides itself on its humanitarian values. It was such values, realized in the form of practical social policies, which enabled her father to come as an alien and reap the gains of a welfare system to which he had contributed nothing. But when Aisha's welfare was most at stake, this same society let her down. To substantiate the point about Aisha's father reaping the gains without making a contribution, a word on the nature of the Norwegian welfare state is in order.

The welfare states in Scandinavia have been built over the past fifty years on the principles of solidarity and equality for all citizens. Poverty was to be wiped out and an equitable standard of living ensured for everyone. To that end, a social welfare system was instituted that would cater to the needs of those at risk for falling below a reasonable standard. Various social security benefits—in case of unemployment, illness, disability, old age—were also part of the package that the state delivered to its citizens. The difference between social welfare (*sosialhjelp*, public assistance) and social security benefits (*trygder*) was that the latter applied equally to all and were regulated by the state, whereas the distribution of social welfare is contingent on the assessment of local officials who cater to individual clients with special needs; hence there is considerably more leeway within the social welfare system. To add to these entitlements, free education and free hospital care are also provided by the Scandinavian welfare states.

In international research, the Scandinavian countries have earned the epithet of *affluent* welfare states, along with the Netherlands, New Zealand, and Canada. Norway's situation is especially benevolent. With vast reserves of North Sea oil and gas, Norway now ranks as the second richest country in the world, per capita, after Switzerland. While Sweden and Denmark have had to cut down on social welfare over the past few years, Norway has been able to expand but this is not the place to delve into that. With Aisha in mind, just let us note that the affluence trickles down to immigrants and their families too, leading some Pakistanis in Norway to bless Norway as "the most generous country in the world" (Lien 1997).

Aisha's family has been among the beneficiaries. Aisha's father could come as an immigrant and reap the gains of a welfare system to which he had contributed nothing precisely because that system is built upon the premise "to each according to his needs, not according to his contributions." Aisha's father tried a few intermittent jobs at first but soon applied for a disability pension on account of a back problem. To make ends meet, he also received social benefits including a municipal flat in an upper-class part of town. Child benefits (*barnetrygd*, which rises exponentially with the number of children one has) was of course also the family's due; so all in all the family had an "income" placing them at a good middle-class level.

Aisha's father's story serves to highlight the benefits that might accrue to an immigrant who makes it to Norway when opportunities back home are deemed nil. Not that everyone succeeds as well as he did. The immigrant record shows a range of differences. The point here is to contrast father and child, man and girl. Aisha's father could escape from his past and make it anew in Norway. His daughter is stuck between a rock and a hard place. Citizen Aisha was given far fewer rights than citizen Mustafa, her father. That one was a full-fledged Norwegian, the other a Norwegian in name only (after thirty years in Norway, Aisha's father still does not speak any Norwegian), made no difference. Gender and parental status decided the issue. Mustafa can roam the world as a transnationalist if he wishes. But can a woman? Or a girl? Aisha's case illustrates the predicament of the child. And we have still not heard her full story.

She suffered the fate that Nadia was spared: she was married by force. She was also left without an elementary school certificate, as she was held as a virtual captive in her parents' homeland, first in her father's, then in her husband's house. Her marriage took place shortly after her eighteenth birthday, eighteen being the legal minimum marital age in Norway. Aisha believes that her father feared that if he violated that, he might be prosecuted on his return, which would not have been the case. Forced marriage is illegal in Norway, but the offender is defined as the spouse, not the enforcing parent, who must be charged in a civil, not a criminal lawsuit (Wikan 2002). Also, under no circumstances could Aisha bring a husband to Norway on family reunification until she came of legal age. So for this reason too, there were no grounds to accelerate the matter.

But Aisha defeated the family. She ran away shortly after her return to Norway in February 2000, before her husband joined her. She turned up at her former school where she had been sorely missed for four years, and the school called on me for advice and help, which is how I eventually met Aisha.[12] Having been out of Norway for four years, her parents brought her back to prepare the application for a visa for her husband. "When I'm back at all," Aisha says, "it is only because I'm used as merchandise (*vare*)." It is called family reunification.[13]

Why was Aisha let down by the Norwegian authorities? Let me provide some strands of an answer. It bears mention that her school and I made strong efforts on her behalf to get Norwegian authorities to intervene after she disappeared.[14] With a large file of documents that testified to the violence Aisha had suffered at her parents' hands, and to her own desperate pleas to be saved from them, Aisha's school appealed her case to high state and communal authorities. To no avail. I too engaged myself and brought the case to the attention of the Minister of Child and Family Affairs and the Minister of Culture. I also wrote and talked about the case publicly (taking care to anonymize Aisha's identity) But in vain. Everyone who heard her case was deeply troubled. But there was nothing to do—after the fact. Only if Aisha had been spared being sent out of Norway, only then could the child have been helped.

One of the documents her school received in reply to their appeal is instructive here. A passage reads: "Because [Aisha] has gone with her family to her homeland, Norwegian jurisprudence (*rettspraksis*) does not apply to the family for the time being." Note the formulation "her homeland." Aisha's homeland was Norway, by birth, by citizenship, and by commitment. And yet she is ascribed another one by the mere fact of her parents' origin. It may have been a slip of the pen, but it is significant nevertheless. For that is precisely how Aisha felt that the child welfare authorities treated her all the way: as a person devoid of her own identity, as a mere extension of her parents. This is not how Norwegian institutions and agencies normally view youths in Norway: individuality is a capital value, embedded in the ethos of real equality. But with children of immigrants, other criteria apply.[15] And we have a form of involuted racism where children of immigrants are measured by standards that not only expect less of them but also entail that there is less to expect.[16]

With the hindsight of Nadia's case we can understand why Aisha was beyond Norwegian law at the time of her stay in her parents' homeland, and also why she was more disempowered. Nadia was an adult, Aisha was only a child—from the point of view of the Norwegian state. Hence for Norway to intervene on Aisha's part, would have meant interfering with parental rights, not just from Morocco's point of view but also that of Norway. Without clear indications that a crime had been committed, or evidence that Aisha was suffering gravely, there was no way Norway could justify intervention. And here is another crucial difference between Nadia and Aisha: Nadia managed to strike a cry of alarm. Aisha was silent. But in this Aisha is the more typical. Most of the youngsters who are abducted from Norway by their parents to be married in a foreign land, are not heard from again until they, like Aisha, apply for family reunification for a spouse. Many have been missing persons for years. And some are never heard from again, having met their death for having refused a forced marriage (Storhaug 1996 and 1998).

Aisha's case highlights the plight of the child in a multicultural, transnational world. A citizen of a European welfare state, she did not receive basic protection; indeed, such protection is becoming more and more difficult for European nation–states to extend—which is why Norwegian authorities have now gone to the drastic step of advising young people in conflict with their immigrant parents *not* to travel to the parents' homeland. The authorities know from bitter experience that "vacation" is often a code name for "forced marriage," and that once abroad, the Norwegian state's ability to help such citizens often comes to naught. The Norwegian police have no authority to investigate crimes in other countries. This pertains not only to children like Aisha, but also to the Nadias (legal adults) who have dual citizenship—despite Norway's nonrecognition of such.[17] Efforts come to naught also because some transnationals are playing by different systems and using their children as pawns in their games. The answer is not to loosen the grip of the nation–state, but to tighten it. Citizenship must become a social contract, as the verdict in Nadia's case implied. It must be a social commitment, and states like the Scandinavian ones must in larger measure be prepared to use material sanctions to reinforce obligations so that citizenship becomes more than a matter of rights. There is evidence that such sanctions work; perhaps they are the only ones that work.

Having threatened to kill her if she ran away, her father, to Aisha's surprise, voluntarily gave up her passport and marriage certificate to the police when they came to his door requesting the document. She wonders, has he learned a lesson from the Nadia case? Is he afraid that he too might be prosecuted? Aisha's parents have stayed for years in the Middle East without informing the social welfare agencies. Her father has said he doesn't mind being jailed in Norway—the conditions in prisons are good, (some immigrants speak of them as five-star hotels).

But curtailment of social welfare benefits is another matter. In this there seems to be little cross-cultural variation: people in general take care to safeguard their material assets.

To end, we may briefly ponder the question: What makes a society, which is deeply wedded to humanitarian principles, sacrifice the welfare of a young female citizen? Why was Aisha not helped before it was too late?

An abiding fear that keeps many well-meaning persons from intervening on behalf of the child is that of being called a racist.[18] *Racist* has become a "deadly word"[19] that strikes at the heart of the well-meaning Scandinavian whose cherished identity is that of world champion of all that is kind and good.[20] But there is a price to be paid for such high morality, and it is paid neither by those who pride themselves on supreme tolerance professed as "respect for their culture," nor by those who use "racist" to claim or enforce such respect. It is Aisha and others like her, persons in weak bargaining positions, who have paid the price of the cultural politics played out in Norwegian everyday life—until Nadia's case struck down like a bomb and occasioned an awakening.[21] Children of immigrants have been defined by their roots or rather those of their parents, as "belonging" to a particular ethnic group and destined to carry on its traditions.[22] As Finkelkraut observes: "It takes very little to reduce individual identity to collective identity, to imprison people in their group of origin, without ever calling on the laws of heredity" (1995).

So it was with Aisha. "Culture" did the trick. And it was "culture" that sealed her fate, making a mockery of her human rights, her citizenship, and basic human liberty.

Aisha had to step back in line and "put her uniform on," to borrow an expression by Ernst Bloch.[23] Perhaps if she had been placed with a foster family of the "right" ethnic kind, she might have been spared her final outcome. But by placing her with a Norwegian family—if by virtue of necessity because a foster family of her parents' ethnic background could not be found—the child authorities laid themselves open to accusations of racism. Concerned to set the record straight, they were relieved when Aisha's parents begged to have her back and promised to treat her well. Aisha's own desperate protests and the warnings by her teachers of an impending forced marriage were brushed aside as unwarranted suspicions. But we should be careful not to demonize child welfare workers who are doing a world of good in many cases, and are working under difficult conditions. They should both respect the culture of immigrants and safeguard the best interests of the child; they are under an obligation, by Norwegian state policies, to balance a tightrope between interests that in many cases cannot be balanced. The dilemmas and inconsistencies that are baked into official policies at the general, abstract level are left to individual social workers to resolve—often at the expense of the child. For children make less noise, they are easier to handle than adults, especially males, who often even put threats of violence behind their claims. Sweden has a famous "Sara case" in which a fifteen-year-old girl was reunited with kinsmen against her own pleas to be allowed to remain with a foster family, only to be killed by her kin.[24] Norway has had a number of cases with less tragic outcomes but similar premises at work: the child should remain with "its" ethnic group. Indeed, child care workers with whom I have talked consistently report that they are not able to offer the same protection to children of immigrant background as to other Norwegian children. Worse, they are aware of accepting acts of maltreatment of children of immigrants that they would not dream of tolerating in regard to Norwegian children. This lands them in a deep moral dilemma. Equality, irrespective of race or ethnic background, is sacrificed on the altar of culture. Children's rights and welfare are sacrificed on the altar of culture. Citizenship is sacrificed in all but a nominal sense. And the losers are primarily females.

To conclude: Nadia's and Aisha's cases present as strong an argument as I can see for the nation–state and against dual citizenship. A stronger, not a weaker nation–state is needed in today's multicultural transnational world. The freedom from the shackles of the nation–state that the proponents of transnationalism and multiculturalism as an ideology envision is a freedom at the expense of others. It is the freedom to usurp power and ride high on the liberation that such a world provides—for them. But as Ignatieff observes,

> The rights that a person has by virtue of membership in a law-abiding state are usually more valuable than the rights that a person has by virtue of his membership in the human race, and the remedies that a person has by virtue of his citizenship are more effective than those which inhere in international human rights covenants. (1999:23)

Would that responsible social scientists spend more energy on researching citizenship in practice, from the bottom up, and less on propagating a position on transnationalism from an elite viewpoint. Children and young females constitute an especially fertile field for insight that can challenge conventional positions. The question is: dare we? The danger of not daring is to blind ourselves to what is happening on our doorstep. Posterity will hold us accountable.

NOTES

1. On this point, see also Appiah (1994).

2. I borrow the distinction from Greenfeld (2000).

3. Nadia's case is presented in more detail in Wikan (2000 and 2002).

4. Nadia's parents owned a house valued at about U.S. $120,000 in Morocco that they kept as a holiday home, and the mother came from a very wealthy family.

5. Nadia's father was receiving a disability pension, due to a heart condition, and two young children had child allowances.

6. He is referring to Nadia's schoolmates and also to some unspecified journalists who he held were out to make money on her, and thus had helped her contrive the story.

7. Judgment in court case no. 98-3021 M/77, 8–10. All translations are mine.

8. See Kayed 1999. Though females have equal right to divorce by Norwegian law, Muslim women who are married by two sets of law (as are all)—*Sharia* in addition to Norwegian civil law)—encounter the problem that the husband will commonly not consent to Muslim divorce, hence the woman cannot marry another Muslim. The evidence, according to Kayed's investigation, is that the imams or mullahs (religious leaders) will uphold the right of the man to deny divorce.

9. In such cases, one wife commonly resides abroad, though cases of polygamy in Norway are also known. Getting a statistical grasp of the problem is, naturally, not possible. See further, Kayed (1999).

10. Aisha's father, a periodic alcoholic and widely known within the Moroccan community in Oslo as well as to various social welfare agencies that had catered to the family through the years, was prone to violent outbursts. He had been known to beat the children on many occasions, even the little ones. According to Aisha's own testimony to me, her mother was also very violent, resorting to beatings to discipline the children from the earliest age.

11. The story is told in more detail in Wikan (2002).

12. For the first few days, when her life was in danger, she also lived in my home, but even there she panicked from fear (her father had threatened to kill her at any cost), and so she was moved to a shelter for women in a place believed to be safe, outside the capital.

13. For a discussion of family reunification in regard to marriage in the Scandinavian countries, see Wikan (2002).

14. My own engagement with the case began when the headmaster of the school alerted me and asked me to help. He had tried to contact me just before she was taken out of the country, hoping I could get some high authority to intervene. But I was away. Next, I met with some of the school personnel who had been most actively involved in Aisha's case, and was shown all the documentation. I went public with

the case in newspaper editorials and in radio lectures and interviews. I also spoke with cabinet ministers. I was hard pressed by journalists and TV reporters to identify Aisha so that they, with my collaboration, could investigate the case and try to help bring her back to Norway. But the school was resistant, hoping at the time that Aisha's family could be made to bring her voluntarily back, and fearing that publicity might be counterproductive. Only three years after Aisha's disappearance some of the documentation was released to a journalist who pursued the school for more information.

15. I have dealt extensively with this issue in Wikan (1995 and 2002).

16. For a discussion of this argument, see Wikan (1999 and 2002).

17. According to Norwegian law, attainment of Norwegian citizenship requires the applicant to have cancelled her or his former citizenship within a year. But there has been no follow-up on that. One consequence of the Nadia case was to have this issue brought up by a member of parliament and it was agreed that the principle of cancellation must be followed up in practice. But I doubt that it is being done, the bureaucratic complexities being too great. And how to sanction breaches? These are unresolved issues.

18. I met the social workers who had dealt with Aisha's case at the invitation of the school and who arranged a half-day seminar where I would talk with them and the teachers. They wanted me to teach them about Islam and Muslim culture with special emphasis on the lives of young immigrant girls, but not to mention Aisha's case. It was simply too painful.

19. I borrow the metaphor from Favret-Saada (1980).

20. For similar observations from Denmark, see Haarder (1997); from Sweden, see Friedman (1999) and Ekholm Friedman (1998).

21. The Norwegian journalist and author Hege Storhaug also deserves major credit for having researched and written about the problem (see Storhaug 1996 and 1998). So do Nasim Karim (1996) and various others.

22. The same applies to the children of indigenous people too; for examples from the Sami in Norway, see Hovland (1996).

23. Bloch (1976:158) writes of "the right to reject [one's] uniform" (cited in Finkelkraut 1995:104).

24. For an account of Sara's case, see Wikan (2002).

REFERENCES

Appiah, K. Anthony. 1994. "Identity, Authenticity, Survival: Multicultural Societies and Social Reproduction." In *Multiculturalism*. Edited by Amy Gutman, 149–63. Princeton, N.J.: Princeton University Press.

Bloch, Ernst. 1976. *Droit naturel et dignité humaine*. Paris: Payot.

Chambers, David L. 2000. "Civilizing the Natives: Marriage in Post-Apartheid South Africa." *Daedalus* 129, no 4:101–24.

Carens, Joseph H. 1987. "Aliens and Citizens: The Case for Open Borders." *Review of Politics* 49, no 3:251–73.

Das, Veena. 1990. "What Do We Mean by Health?" In *The Health Transitions: Social, Behavioral and Cultural*. Edited by J. Caldwell et al. Canberra: Australian National University Press.

Favret-Saada, Jeanne. 1980. *Deadly Words: Witchcraft in the Bocage*. Cambridge, U.K.: Cambridge University Press.

Finkelkraut, Alain. 1995. *The Defeat of the Mind*. New York: Columbia University Press.

Friedman, Jonathan. 1998. "Globalization, Dis-integration, Re-organization: The Transformations of Violence." Paper presented to the Guggenheim research group on transnationalism and globalization.

———. 1999. "Rhinoceros II." *Current Anthropology* 40, no. 5:679–88.

———. 2003. "Globalization, Dis-integration, Re-organization: The Transformations of Violence," chapter 1, this volume.

Friedman, Kajsa Ekholm. 1998. "Globalisation and Multiculturalism." Paper presented to the Guggenheim workshop, Lund, Sweden.

Greenfeld, Liah. 2000. "Democracy, Ethnic Diversity, and Nationalism." In *Nationalism and Internationalism in the Post–Cold War Era*. Edited by K. Goldman, U. Hannerz, and C. Westin, 25–36. London: Routledge.

Haarder, Bertel. 1997. *Den bløde kynisme—og selvbedraget i Tornerose-Danmark*. Københaven: Gyldendal.

Hovland, A. 1996. *Moderne urfoldk: samisk ungdom i bebegelse*. Oslo, Norway: Cappelen Akademisk Forlag.

Ignatieff, Michael. 1999. "Whose Universal Values? The Crisis in Human Rights." The Hague: Praemium, Erasmianum Essay.

Karim, Nasim. 1996. *Izzat: For ærens skyld.* Oslo: Cappelen.

Kayed, Camilla. 1999. "Rett, religion og byråkrati—En studie av skilmisse blant muslimer i Norge." Master's thesis, Department and Museum of Anthropology, University of Oslo.

Kleinman, Arthur. 1998. "Experience and its Moral Modes: Culture, Human Conditions and Disorder." "The Tanner Lectures on Human Values." Vol 20. Ed. G. Peterson. Salt Lake City: University of Utah Press.

Lien, Inger-Lise. 1997. *Ordet som stempler djevlene.* Oslo: Aventura.

Nasar, Sylvia. 1999. "Where Joblessness Is a Way of Making a Living." *New York Times,* May 9.

Shweder, Richard. 1998. "What Is Relevant about Anthropology?" *Anthropology Newsletter* 39, no. 9:46–47.

Storhaug, H. 1996. *Mashallah: en reise blant Kwinner i Pakistan.* Oslo, Norway: Aschehoug.

———. 1998. *Hellg tvang: unge norske muslimer om kjaerlighed og ekteskap.* Oslo, Norway: Aschehoug.

Wikan, Unni. 1995. *Mot en ny norsk underklasse: kultur, innvandrere og integrasjon.* Oslo: Gyldendal.

———. 1999. "Culture: A New Concept of Race." *Social Anthropology* 7, no. 1:57–64.

———. 2000. "Citizenship on Trial: Nadia's Case." *Daedalus* 129, no. 4.

———. 2002. *Generous Betrayal: Culture and Identity Politics in the New Europe.* Chicago: University of Chicago Press.

Wrede-Holm, Vivien. 2000. "Multikulturalisme som likhet og ulikhet: En studie fra Australia." Master's thesis, Department of Social Anthropology, University of Oslo.

7

American Neoliberalism, "Globalization," and Violence

Reflections from the United States and Southeast Asia

DONALD M. NONINI

Siler City is at a crossroads. Either you get your public officials to get the I.N.S. in here and get these illegal immigrants out or you'll lose your homes, you'll lose your schools, you'll lose your way of life. . . . To get a few chickens plucked, is it worth losing your heritage?

—*David Duke, ex-Imperial Wizard of the Ku Klux Klan, speaking at a National Alliance rally, Siler City, North Carolina, February 19, 2000*

We are human beings not your scapegoat, if you are one of them (the people mass), think what you have done. . . . The robbery can't solve the problem. And one more thing, what did we do to you, so you must beat and rob us, this monetary crisis not caused by us."

—*"S.O.S. from Medan," E-mail message forwarded to Rita Ho, Flinders University, from a Chinese in Medan, Indonesia, May 18, 1998*

In entirely different ways, these messages from two very specific places reflect widely different experiences of neoliberal globalization and its connections to violence. In the first, David Duke from Louisiana, who several years ago put away his Klan robes to adopt a more respectable veneer, inveighed against the influx of Latino immigrants to Siler City and other small towns in rural North Carolina as part of his recent campaign to launch a new far-right group, the National Organization for European American Rights (NOFEAR). His fowl reference is to two poultry processing plants that employed approximately

1,400 workers, the majority migrants from Mexico, El Salvador, and Honduras, within the small town of Siler City, where Latinos now make up 40 percent of the residents. In an age of government "devolution," to use Duke's words, if not violent as such, were an incitement to the "European American" citizens of Siler City to take matters into their own hands, if either local "public officials" or the Immigration and Naturalization Service failed to do the job. In the second message, the anonymous messenger wrote two weeks after Chinese businesses and homes in Medan were burned and looted by "native" *pribumi* Indonesians, and Chinese people were beaten, raped, and killed. The riots of May 4–7, 1998, in Medan were but one of many similar conflagrations that occurred between late 1997 and mid-1998 in Chinese areas in Jakarta, Solo, Palembang, Surabaya, and other cities and towns in Indonesia. The targeting of Indonesia's Chinese minority (only 4 percent of the total population) culminated in the May 1998 riots and fires in Jakarta in which thousands of buildings were looted and destroyed or damaged by fire, more than 1,000 people killed, and hundreds of Chinese women raped. The violence came in the wake of Indonesia's political and financial crisis leading to the fall of General Suharto in May 1998. Although there was evidence of incitement of the anti-Chinese riots by the Indonesian Army as part of a broader agenda of political destabilization, news reports still made it quite clear that there was widespread and popular rage directed against ethnic Chinese as perceived national enemies benefitting from the misfortunes they saw imposed on them by the Suharto New Order regime and the International Monetary Fund (IMF)—the drastic devaluation of the Indonesian rupiah, drastic inflation in food prices, and widespread unemployment and misery, including food scarcity.

It should be evident that both episodes require attention to the active processes by which racial stigmatization as a prelude to violence takes place. What is less evident is that, in different ways, both episodes also represent contradictions between the rhetorical project of American neoliberal globalization and those economic and political processes that underlie it both within the United States and beyond and constrain its extension to the rest of the world. In this chapter, I seek to illuminate the rhetoric of neoliberalism, the transformations initiated by Western economic and political elites in its name, and its relationship to specific forms of violence. I also seek to theorize the limits of neoliberalism: to show that it does not prevail in one region of the world (Southeast Asia), to sketch out alternatives to it found there, and to suggest that it is only "global" in its pretensions to universal domination and inevitability. In fact, neoliberal globalization—viewed as a set of interconnected ideological and material processes—is unstable, incomplete, and vastly self-contradictory, all of which I hope will become clear in what follows.

AMERICAN NEOLIBERALISM AS A RHETORICAL AND MATERIAL PROJECT

What is American neoliberal ideology, and how do the contradictions between it and the material conditions underlying it historically generate the conditions for violence? Neoliberal ideology can best be seen as a rhetorical project harnessed to certain mechanisms of social control, which are at odds with the actual mechanisms by which labor, capital, and other markets work, and the outcomes they generate. Consider the following comments by a prominent member of the chamber of commerce of Durham, North Carolina. This man spoke as follows:

> When you have the kinds of businesses we have in RTP [Research Triangle Park], it automatically exposes Durham to a global economy in interesting ways. We have people in RTP that spend part of their time in England. . . . We are blessed with the Park (and the universities). The Park has really been our salvation. But there are few North Carolina roots in the Park. Most of the companies in the Park are international companies, and that is how development in this area has been since the 1960s. Now we have the benefit of a few major headquarters and other [R&D centers and production facilities]. . . . This is all testimony to how attractive this area is. They can build here at a lower cost. We have talented people, lower operating costs, and a dynamic that retains well educated people. We [the Chamber of Commerce] need to be a source of information to compete against Austin and Charlotte. It was a similar situation when were trying to get an insurance company to locate here instead of Baltimore or Louisville. . . . Image-building is an important part of it too.[1]

This is an example of the growth rhetoric of neoliberalism, and it is but one of many such instances of elite discourse in North Carolina and elsewhere in the United States. Over the past thirty years, the processes of economic and political restructuring that have occurred in North Carolina have been accompanied by distinctive processes of cultural production and the promotion of the hegemonic project of neoliberalism. The process of constructing just such a hegemony, currently under way, would establish neoliberalism as *the* dominant rhetoric of growth, prosperity, and social welfare among national, regional, and local elites in the United Staes. Alternative rhetorics do exist, but neoliberalism increasingly sets the defining framework of discussion within which the proponents for these alternatives argue.[2]

American neoliberal discourse promotes the natural appropriateness of markets in creating social "efficiency" and "progress" toward societal goals, advocates the reduction of government functions that interfere with private "free" markets—evidenced by campaigns for the privatization of government functions and by tax-reduction insurgencies—calls for the creation of hybrid "public/private partnerships," and defines a new set of societal needs around the imperative to be "globally competitive." For the United States, these include the need for citizens to receive a "world-class," "high-tech" education suited to the "information society of the twenty-first century," and the need for locales to provide a "good business climate" to attract outside investors in the global market for capital.

The rhetorical project of American neoliberalism seeks to promote a comprehensive ethos and a system of social regulation that penetrates local communities. In the United States, Britain, increasingly in some countries of Western Europe, and elsewhere that American neoliberalism prevails,[3] we can speak of "new forms of control . . . appearing in these societies, which work not through repression or welfare interventionism, but through 'assign[ing] different social destinies to individuals in line with their varying capacity to live up to the requirements of competitiveness and profitability'" (Peterson 1996:48, citing Robert Castel). Increasingly "risks" of many kinds (credit, investment, taxpayer, genetic, etc.) with market entailments come to be seen as inherent and objective characteristics of individuals falling into risk groups assessed in markets, for example, all those with a gene predisposing them to a specific disease can be identified and placed in an insurance category. The commoditization of information about individuals associated with categories of risk fosters the continuous dissemination of such information throughout the United States.

This process promotes the universalization of anxieties about risks associated with individuals, groups, and locales, and thus creates new forms of control. For instance, local elites in the United States employ a pedagogical discourse about what is wrong with their communities vis-à-vis the "global competition" (poor business climate, etc.), and in this sense we can speak of an enhanced self-consciousness of locales vis-à-vis "the globe." Castel points to the corollary of such market logics acting over time as they ramify throughout society: "taken to its extreme, this yields the model of a 'dual' or 'two speed' society . . . the coexistence of hyper-competitive sectors obedient to the harshest requirements of economic rationality, and marginal activities that provide a refuge (or a dump) for those unable to take part in the circuits of intensive exchange" (Castel 1991:294). In what follows below in the discussion of Siler City, North Carolina, we see how Latino transnational migrants are transformed into a "hypercompetitive sector" complying to the "harshest requirements" of capital accumulation. At the same time, "marginal activities" exist among those who are unemployed and underemployed—those who have been rendered redundant or at risk of being so through capitalist flexibility and "downsizing"—such as the white "European American" men to whom David Duke appeals.[4] Castel points out that such refuges/dumps have largely been formed without *directly* regulating the individuals who reside in them, who are mainly affected by the coincidence of being located within such structures (Castel 1991:294). Applied to North Carolina and other locations in the United States, this would imply that neoliberal growth rhetoric is a mode through which individuals, groups, and locales are sorted into categories in terms of their global market value and are allotted specific fates appropriate to their category of market "risk." This is beginning, in contradictory, heterogeneous and fractured ways, to occur in North Carolina: the grain is being separated from the chaff, the sheep from the goats.

NEOLIBERAL RHETORIC AND THE DISCIPLINING OF LOCALES

The rhetoric of neoliberalism itself calls for disciplining in the face of market realities and thus for internal policing, and by implication, violence when called for. For instance, the theme of the necessity for a self-disciplined laboring subject and for a disciplined "labor force" if a locale is to compete globally is ubiquitous within neoliberal rhetorics in North Carolina. The Halifax County School system recently became the first in the state to require its students to wear uniforms because, in the words of its superintendent, wearing school uniforms "levels the playing field for children," and "shows children how to handle business," and besides, school uniforms are required in both Japan and Sweden, and we know that "the performance of [their] students is exceptional."

Meanwhile, the Web site of the Fayetteville Area Economic Development Corporation in Cumberland County, North Carolina, brags: "Where else can you find an internationally trained labor force ready to jump into any situation?" The graphic shows a young white male parachuting down to the job site, wearing a business suit but with Army paratrooper boots on his feet. The Web site of the Fayetteville Area Economic Development Corporation from 1997 adds that "The area's labor supply is enhanced by the military personnel separating from active duty at neighboring Fort Bragg and Pope Air Force Base [estimated at 8,000 people per year]. This group *offers a labor source that is mission and team oriented. They are mature with a high level of discipline and technological training*" (emphasis added). What more could any employer ask for?

AN IRONY OF TRANSNATIONAL CORPORATE NEOLIBERALISM

An ironic feature of neoliberalism is that its dominant version contends that economic growth must take place through the operation of global markets, but only within a multicultural and multiracial framework of state-supported programs. This is the transnational corporate version of neoliberalism. It is worth noting that large transnational corporations, whose CEOs and sponsored think-tank intellectuals are committed to extracting their "fair share" of global markets, have come over the last two to three decades to be among the staunchest institutional supporters of affirmative action policies in the United States. This is particularly true of banking, real estate, and other branches of the finance sector. Corporate managerial and technocratic elites claim that "merit" favors the "most qualified" irrespective of race, but that historic disadvantages imposed on minority professionals must be overcome before their "merit" can be determined. Similarly, the efficiencies arising from the "natural" operation of labor and commodity markets are seen as impeded by racial discrimination that links racial minorities to poverty, thus posing an obstacle to the full incorporation of minorities as consumers into global markets, and to the recruitment of minority managers to positions that coordinate and promote such consumption. As a result, redressive policies aimed at racial minorities are deemed appropriate.

This commitment to domestic multiculturalism takes place within a larger discursive framework of "managing diversity" within a transnational setting. After all, noneconomic "irrationalities" such as racial prejudice and nationalist xenophobia in the United States impede the profitable participation by U.S.-based corporations in global markets—something not to be tolerated within the transnational neoliberal vision of export-driven economic growth. For instance, when Japanese-owned corporations kindly locate their factories in the United States and hire American workers to assemble their cars, expatriate Japanese managers should expect to be treated like "good citizens," while even if Chinese in China are deemed "Orientals," they certainly do buy U.S.-exported cigarettes, and so Americans better learn to be nice to them as customers, and understand their "customs" and "problems."

American transnational corporate neoliberalism thus adopts what Howard Winant (1994:30–31) calls the "racial project" of "pragmatic liberalism." It should be noted however that despite its commitment to affirmative action, once this commitment "levels the playing field," then the risk status of minority individuals or, say, of minority urban "empowerment zones" can be assessed by their performance within labor and commodity markets—and insofar as they are deemed "low performers" in these markets, neoliberalism promotes their marginalization. On this view, after all, the lack of entrepreneurial self-regulation by individuals, groups, and locales evinced by "low performance" casts them as undeserving of market rewards, and allots them instead to unemployment, workfare, prisons, or to the high-risk end of the municipal bond market. These represent the "slow speed" downside of Castel's "two speed" society (1991).[5]

SOCIALLY CONSERVATIVE, HOMEGROWN NEOLIBERALISM

The socially liberal version of neoliberalism favored by the transnational corporate elite with direct access to state policymakers (and indirectly to state funds) competes with a more conservative form of American neoliberalism that advocates meritocracy and individualism without redressive racial or gender policies, one promoted by regional and local elites who take neoliberal rhetoric favoring the minimalist state far more literally than do their transnationally oriented counterparts. This is because nationally redressive racial policies require proactive (and even Keynesian) state policies that contradict the ideal model of the neoliberal deflationary "pocket book" state stripped of all but the minimal functions of promoting markets and maintaining law and order. The latter homegrown version of neoliberalism corresponds to what Winant (1994) calls the "neoconservative racial project"—one that denies the contemporary effects of past and present racial discrimination and promotes meritocratic individualism "without reference to race." Claims of racial superiority are never posed as such; instead, code words alluding to supposed undesirable attributes of unspecified but very specific others ("those people," etc.) are used. Because of these internal differences over race within the larger neoliberal coalition of elites, the neoliberal commitment to racially redressive policies remains tenuous and unstable.

For instance, there are the comments of an official of the local chamber of commerce of Halifax County, North Carolina. When the ethnographer introduced herself, this man responded, "Oh, you're looking at one poor county. One rich county [Durham] and then other counties in between." He continued, "If you're looking at how this community has not grown economically, then you need to look at the leadership and the infrastructure." The ethnographer had not mentioned looking at how the community "has not grown." This was his specific word choice. He continued by telling me that the leadership is not prepared. The infrastructure is not in place. By infrastructure he means the water and sewer lines. However, in the last three years, Halifax has elected officials who are more progressively minded, yet they are still reactive. The second reason for a lack of development is the question of whether there is a qualified workforce. According to him some say "yes," others "no." Some of the industry heads that he speaks with are very satisfied with their workforce. Others are frustrated because their workers do not show up to work on time. This he sees as a problem of the educational system.

This man's arguments about why Halifax county "has not grown" is steeped within the discursive terms of reference of neoliberal rhetoric. Halifax county is compared to others, and is found wanting. Its underdeveloped infrastructure, its "reactive" yet tepidly "progressive" rather than aggressive leadership, the problem of whether its labor force is "qualified" to compete, and the lack of discipline of its school graduates are all cited as causes of the county's backwardness in the competitive race among locales to "develop" by bringing in outside capital. However, this man goes on to reveal a neoconservative racial project as he elaborates on the problem of a disciplined labor force, saying:

> All the school systems are good . . . Halifax County schools are good . . . a quality education is available for students in the county. It's the family units that these students come from that people should be concerned about. I know for myself—my parents supported me. I didn't go to school looking for affirmation from my teachers, because my parents knew the value of an education and encouraged me towards that end. Almost 50% of the parents have educations in the county and thus they can't pass on the value of education to their children.

As the ethnographer observed, this was a very "telling statement." Consistent with the neoconservative racial project, his views about the lack of discipline and "qualification" for a labor force attractive to outside investors ostensibly denies the existence of racial disparities or racial discrimination as a problem by pointing to a pathological "family unit," reflecting a widespread local elite discourse about the supposed inadequacies of certain family structures, which just happen to be those of people who are African American and very poor. This neoconservative version of neoliberalism is also evident in the forms of symbolic violence to which Latinos are subjected in Siler City, North Carolina, and it is to these I now turn, in the context of elucidating, as an example, the material processes of economic and political restructuring associated with one new industry in a supposedly "deindustrialized" United States—poultry processing.

PROCESSING CHICKENS, PROCESSING PEOPLE: AGROINDUSTRIAL RATIONALIZATION IN RURAL NORTH CAROLINA

> If Perdue Farms doesn't find a buyer for its local poultry operation and the processing plant hatchery and feed mill remain closed after mid-July, the fallout will affect more than the 800 persons losing jobs. The town of Siler City, Chatham County, a large number of farmers, and a host of other businesses all stand to be big losers in the fallout of the announcement Friday that the poultry giant is closing its facilities—a processing plant in Siler City and a hatchery and feed mill in nearby Staley (Wachs 1995).

Events like the sale of the Perdue poultry processing plant, and public anxieties over the sale, have come to dominate the rural landscapes of the southern United States over the past twenty years. They have become part of a larger process of globalization and economic restructuring that include the rationalization of rural areas through land concentration, the closings or openings of industrial and agroindustrial plants in rural areas, and the importation of cheap labor from Latin America. This has affected rural communities in ways that extend profoundly into local politics and public life with implications for new forms of violence.

In the United States, poultry, like hogs and cattle, are no longer raised by farmers, slaughtered in abattoirs, then butchered for sale by retail butchers. They are instead "processed" in production chains made up of technologically advanced, computer-controlled steps that determine the course of the animal "product" from birth to maturity to death to meat. These highly regulated and technologically intricate regimes of "just-in-time" processing extend all the way from "growing" live animals en masse in the concrete hog pens and poultry "growout houses" of rural North Carolina to the emergence of "product" in the forms of chicken "leg quarters," "nuggets," "filleted breasts," "ground turkey," or "boxed pork" in the coldrooms and shelves of supermarkets and fast-food outlets from New York to Raleigh to Tokyo (Hall 1989; Cecelski and Kerr 1992; Heffernan and Constance 1994; Boyd and Watts 1997).

Poultry processing is big business, highly profitable, and has shown a concentration of capital via mergers and acquisitions over the last several years, leading to huge oligopolies in the industry. Moreover, poultry processing, unlike beef, is an industry producing for rapidly expanding markets, increasingly with a global reach.[6] Large poultry processors like Purdue and Goldkist are conglomerates whose corporate units not only "process" the live birds into meat for specialized niche markets (e.g., Chicken McNuggets), but also breed and hatch genetically modified chicks, and produce the feed, antibiotics, and other inputs into the links of the production chain. This follows a widespread trend toward vertical integration in the American food industry over the last two decades (Heffernan and Constance 1994).

The poultry industry has been reordered into new spatial ensembles by these changes. The "branch plant" system connects contract "growers" engaged in technically coordinated poultry rearing in satellite areas, and networked to a large central processing plant that incorporates the latest electronically controlled machineries for slaughter, feather removal, evisceration, quartering, and so on, operated by abundant, cheap, and unskilled laborers.

For the current American regime of flexible accumulation, Harvey (1989) has observed the increasing employment of semifree laborers—illegal migrants, convicts, children, and others—by corporations or their subcontractors. Poultry workers' precarious legal status reinforces employers' capacities to use them—and use them up physically—to discipline them and prevent the formation of labor unions. Decisions by the industry to relocate to rural areas of North Carolina and other southern states were, after all, motivated by their reputation of hostility toward labor unions. In Siler City, there is a large, vulnerable population of several thousand transnational migrants—men, women, and children, many of whom are "undocumented" workers illegally residing in the United States, and a majority of whom are either unable to speak or read English with any fluency—available as a contingent labor force to produce and build up the differentiated products of the plants, even as they themselves are bodily broken down in the process.

TRANSNATIONAL LABOR MIGRANTS AND RACIALIZED VIOLENCE: "THEY JUST WANT PEOPLE TO WORK WITHOUT OPENING THEIR MOUTHS"

When the people, the Americans that look at me, it seems that they look at me as being different. . . . If they were to really pay attention to us, they would see that we only come to work. . . . the majority of us come to do honest work, but they don't see that, right? They don't take us into account, they place [us] in the hardest and most tiresome jobs. That's to say, they cut us down, they set us apart to one side, they don't give us equal treatment. . . . They don't treat us like the people from here. And they don't just badly treat illegals like that, the people with legal papers are also rejected by them as well.

—*Mexican* pollero *(poultry worker) in Siler City* [7]

Please do not make excessive noise at any hour. You are not permitted to use radios or TVs after 10 p.m. If you do so, your neighbor will call the police and you will be investigated. Pets such as dogs and cats are permitted in Siler City. Keeping chickens or goats within city limits is illegal. It is illegal to have garbage in your yard or to work on your car, in the street or in your driveway. . . . Drugs are illegal, and any person who sells or uses them will be arrested. Drugs are bad and very dangerous. In this country it is completely illegal for a husband to hit his wife or his children for any reason. A man who does this will be sent to jail and may lose his children.

—*Translated excerpt from pamphlet distributed to Latinos, by the Hispanic Task Force, an all-white group of Siler City, 1996*

Over the last decade, but particularly since the mid-1990s, more than 250,000 Mexicans and Central Americans have migrated from south of the border or from elsewhere in the United States (California, Texas) to work and live in the rural areas, towns, and cities of North Carolina.[8] They have come to work as tobacco and cucumber pickers, Christmas tree harvesters, construction laborers, restaurant dishwashers and cleaners, store clerks, textile factory workers, custodians, and janitors—and as workers in the poultry and hog processing plants. They have become the objects of attention due to their omnipresence in North Carolina's small towns and rural areas—noticeable to "natives" who hear them speak Spanish and perceive them through racial phenotypic generalization—they are neither white, nor black.

In Siler City two poultry processing plants as of 1996 employed 1,400 immigrants in the production work of preparing chicken broilers in the various stages of butchering, dressing, and packaging for distribution throughout the United States. For their part, Latino *polleros* in Siler City saw that the citizen-residents of the town viewed them as a "problem," or, as clear from the pamphlet quoted above as many "problems"—noisiness, dirtiness, illegality, violence, and disorderliness. For the non-Latino majority of the Siler City Hispanic Task Force, the presence of Latinos threatened the locale's inviting Southern small-town image in the global competition for outside capital. The verbiage of the Task Force pamphlet was an example of the neoconservative version of neoliberal rhetoric I alluded to earlier. The theme of Latinos being a "problem" and the imperative to "solve" it, through police coercion if necessary, was evident in other public settings as well. The racial coding characteristic of neoconservative neoliberal rhetoric was evident in the following patronizing excerpt by a white commentator from a radio newscast on the Siler City Trash Pickup: "And it's going to take an effort from everyone who lives or works in Siler City, even those who don't pay taxes here. The need to clean up their own backyards, in fact that's where a lot of the litter is coming from. Folks are moving to the area and don't appreciate our way of life, or understand our culture, you know where we use trash cans and don't throw our beer cartons out in the front yard."

Latinos, of course, got the message. The *pollero* quoted above was far from alone in his feelings of being abused. Another informant epitomized the epistemological and symbolic violence behind such euphemized imprecation with deep insight: "it seems that they [Anglos] just want people to work without opening their mouths, without problems, without enrolling their children in school. . . . I don't know. But yes, they just want the labor, but without helping them in any form or other." He infers the crucial cultural construction of a racialized U.S. nationalism: the reduction of Latino persons to labor, bodies, and body parts—an "arm," a "back"—and thus an resolute refusal to see them as human beings who felt pain and exhaustion when overworked, or as parents, or as people in need of decent housing, or members of diverse cultural communities with rich heritages. Another informant describes the silent hostility confronting him: "You can tell when you go to the store, or when you eat at a restaurant. They stare at you . . . like what's up, what are you doing here?"

Beyond such silent intimidation, *polleros* and other Latinos spoke of many instances of intimidation, harassment, and petty violence directed against them, tinging their everyday lives with fearfulness and a sense of profound vulnerability. According to our informants, the system that employed undocumented laborers in the plants worked with a kind of perverse logic: "But also because of our fear, there is a lot of repression in the plants (poultry), and fear of deportation from the INS [Immigration and Naturalization Service], even though that hasn't happened in Siler City for years. There is always the threat that the INS will come and run off all the people who don't have papers." Police—the visible representatives of the coercive state, embodied these fears on a daily basis:

> they harass you, they stop you just to see what's your business, even though you haven't committed a crime or penalty or run a stoplight or anything. They stop you just to see if you have papers, if you're legal, to see what you're doing, what you have on you, to see if you're selling something. They never stop you because you've actually broken a law, simply they stop you for being who you are, and for appearing in their rear view mirror.

Despite experiencing such violence, *polleros* sought to organize a labor union in the poultry plants of Siler City, filed workplace grievances against plant management, and engaged in other struggles to improve their condition.

To summarize, the violence in words and deeds directed against Latinos in Siler City arose from contradictions lying deep within American neoliberalism. Corporate bosses animated by transnationally oriented neoliberalism objectified Latinos as a mass "factor of production," no more (or less) than animated body parts to be used up in the "hypercompetitive sector" of poultry processing; their daily needs as human beings were "externalities" to the system of production and labor market exchanges. Nonetheless, as such, and consistent with this liberal version of "neoliberalism," corporate elites viewed them—"nonracially"—as an attractive population drawn into the new transnational labor markets created by the last two decades of economic restructuring (NAFTA, etc.), so much so that plant managers displaced an earlier generation of African American women workers in order to hire the Latinos. In contrast, those holding to a neoconservative version of neoliberalism—such as the members of the Hispanic Task force or the radio commentator quoted above—saw Latinos as deficient market actors in the *global competition between places* in which Siler City as a locale competed, rather than as a competitive advantage. And then there was the far-right rhetoric of David Duke and his many supporters in Chatham County—the majority of them middle-aged white men—poor farmers and downsized industrial workers—who have been at the receiving end of the contraction in the small-farm sector (e.g., with the loss of tobacco quotas) and the Southern textile industry over the last two decades, and were marginalized into "low-" or even "nonperforming" sectors of the economy.

"GLOBALIZATION" OR REGIONALIZATION?
PINNOCHIO'S NOSE, THE RISE OF NATIONAL CAPITALISMS
AND STATE GOVERNMENTALITIES IN SOUTHEAST ASIA

Within a broader context, American neoliberalism presents itself as a two-sided phenomenon. On one hand, it is a guiding elite ideology for harnessing instruments of control of populations in the United States to the supposed logic of "the global market." As such, it has reality effects that generate violence across differentially successful market "performers"—such as the violence by white rural Southern men against Latino migrants in Siler City. As I demonstrate below, there are similar reality effects when neoliberalism American-style manifests itself in the institutional form of economic power—the IMF—an instrument of the "U.S. Treasury–Wall Street–IMF complex" (Wade and Veneroso 1998; Weiss 1999). Wherever it is disseminated as a form of power, its discourse-made-policy seeks to drive "government" and "politics" out of the operation of the "free market economy," but instead produces social crises into which untheorized state and racial violences enter. On the other hand, neoliberalism represents the rhetorical project of U.S. and European elites that claims the inevitable and natural "spread of globalization," supposedly demonstrable wherever new national economies "open" themselves to "free trade" (or "free investment," "free currency exchange," "free movement of people," etc.). Such a claim bestows a beauty and natural lawfulness on the powers of transnational corporations as they roam the globe as exemplars of such "freedom." Thus the stentorous celebrations and declamations about a global "end to history" (Fukuyama 1992), the emergence of a "new economy" (Drucker 1992), or the decline of nation–states everywhere (Appadurai 1996) are all parts in a larger stage drama performed by American neoliberal proponents and apologists: as if presenting the play as loudly and frequently as possible could make the story it tells come true.

As a performance for an American audience, as our ethnographic evidence suggests, neoliberalism has been remarkably successful, though not completely so. Insofar as it purports to be an empirical account of the transformations of contemporary global capitalism and contemporary nation–states, it is both historically false (Hirst and Thompson 1996; Weiss 1999), and geographically limited (Hoogvelt 1997; Dicken 1998), and of course it rationalizes class and gender exploitation, threatens national sovereignties outside the United States, and is ethnocentric as well. As a performance for audiences beyond the shores of the United States, neoliberalism American style must be understood not as the removal of the state or politics from the putatively pure "economic" processes of global "market liberalization" but as a rhetorical tool of economic statecraft that combines academic and institutional cajolery with economic pressure and military threat against nation–states elsewhere in the world to accept its premises, as interpreted by American and (to a lesser extent) European elites (Gowan 1999). In short, American neoliberalism is the animating discourse for elites controlling the American state and bent on making it into the paramount "catalytic state" (Weiss 1999) in a world they seek to create anew.[9]

Nowhere else has the "Pinnochio's nose" of neoliberal proponents grown longer than in their distortions about the postwar rise of Southeast Asian capitalisms.[10] Pinnochio's nose grows longest when neoliberals make the claim that globalization spreads from the shores of the United States through the operation of the "global market" and "technology" to transform Southeast Asia into a domain of "little dragons" and "second-tier dragons," although Southeast Asia has often shown itself insufficiently grateful for the gifts bestowed upon it. Against this, let me instead point out that capitalist growth in Asia has by no means derived from the gifts of American technology. It is not globalization that has taken place but rather regionalization. The growth of Southeast Asian capitalism has been, until very recently—the onset in 1997 of the Asian financial crisis—partly autonomous from the economic and political changes associated with globalization in the United States and Europe. Although it has been connected to these changes—particularly to inflows of capital from the West[11]—it has *not* been determined by them. Instead we must ask: what are the regionally endogenous sources for Southeast Asian capital accumulation?

Much has been made of the "New International Division of Labor" (NIDL)—the internationalization of certain stages of industrial production since the 1960s (Fröbel et al. 1980). But the NIDL concept has been reworked in U.S. business-school and business-media circles into a celebration of the idealized stateless, flexible, and mobile corporations supposedly characteristic of "the new economy" American style, but that happen to be headed by Asians. One need only think, for instance, of the touting by the *Harvard Business Review* (Magretta 1998) of the Chinese family firm, Li & Fung, as "fast, global, and entrepreneurial: supply chain management, Hong Kong style," and its transpacific operation, whose CEO happened to teach for several years at the Harvard Business School, among other business fluff pieces on this firm. It is true that Southeast Asian enterprises have come to serve as subcontractors for brand-name transnational corporations from the United States and Europe committed to offshoring and outsourcing the most labor-intensive (and surplus-value-producing) phases of their production operations in electronics, computers, automobiles, steel, textiles, toys, garments, and several other lines of business. But although rapid growth in export-oriented subcontracting since the 1980s has appeared to be the other (Asian) side of the "restructuring" undertaken by corporations in the United States—hence a part of "globalization"—in fact there is only a contingent connection. Instead, Japanese transnational corporations backed by the financial powers of MITI and Japanese banks—not American or European ones—have been by far the largest such offshore investors and economic players in Southeast Asia (Machado 1995, 1997; Weiss 1999). Japan has become the postwar economic hegemony within the larger Asian macroregion. There has been regionalization and a large degree of regionally endogenous capitalist growth in "globalization" drag. This is a shift from the preponderant Cold War influence of the United States in the 1950s and 1960s, which stands as an affront to American neoliberal doctrine and the global aspirations of U.S. business and political elites. This has been seen as an insult deserving punishment—namely, the Indonesian financial crisis, below.

One must therefore ask: What are the crucial internal and external conditions that have characterized and made possible the new capitalisms of Southeast Asia? In the case of Southeast Asia, these conditions have been illustrated in an important series of country studies of the new capitalisms and state-capital relations in the recent work of Australian political economists—on Indonesia, Thailand, and Singapore, in particular (Higgott and Robison 1985). One must, however, read these analyses through the lens of an alternative Asian modernity and, in particular, through the lenses of regionally specific forms of governmental rationalities or "governmentalities" (Ong 1999; Foucault 1991). Otherwise, the very epistemic and rhetorical presuppositions of American neoliberalism—itself a form of Western liberal governmentality—might be accepted uncritically.

By "governmentality" I mean, following Foucault, a defining relationship of power between the state and its subject population. American neoliberal governmentality poses no legitimate relation between the state and its subject population other than preserving the rights of private property holders (e.g., by upholding law and order), and providing the least regulation possible of rational, entrepreneurial individuals who undertake risks by acting in national capital, commodity, and labor markets—actions that legitimately make up "society" and function optimally without a state presence. Its effects simultaneously cultivate and discipline the middle-class entrepreneurial subject. (Of course, state strategies of coercive disciplinary rationality—incarceration, institutionalization, and so on—target those who fail the test of market "performance.") In contrast, Southeast Asian liberal governmentalities, as Ong (1999) points out, have included a variety of both pastoral and disciplinary rationalities deployed toward "zones of graduated sovereignty." On the one hand, the state's leaders and bureaucracy deploy a pastoral governmentality toward favored middle-class, indigenous and global elite[12] segments of a national population (and toward their specific spaces in national territory) by guiding and caring benignly for them in regulating and promoting their privileged relation to and participation in national capital, commodity, and labor markets.[13] The state's functionaries thus act a shepherd that wisely guides its middle-class flock, the majority subject-population of its territory: hence "pastoral." On the other hand, state officials, bureaucrats, and police display disciplinary and coercive rationalities toward other, less privileged segments of the population—working-class industrial women, transnational labor migrants, and aborigines or "primitives"—who are relegated to specific spaces in the national territory, such as export-processing zones or "tribal" reserves (Ong 1999). In Southeast Asia, middle-class indigenous or global elite "individuals" therefore do not engage in risk behaviors in markets while the state gets out of the way; rather, a benevolent state protects members of vulnerable but valued groups from market hazards, uses coercion and control against less favored groups, while it also sets the broader social goals that national markets are to achieve. Arising from specific histories of colonial liberalism, Southeast Asian governmentalities have passed through two subsequent phases, that of "development" through the 1980s (Escobar 1995), and since then, "globalization," or what Ong (1999) calls a "postdevelopmental" period.

Thus the new state bureaucratic elite of independent Southeast Asian states sought to guide the national economies of the postcolonial period toward certain social goals—such as the "development" of indigenous groups, and such guidance included a direct entrepreneurial activism (on ASEAN, see Higgott and Robison 1985; Doner and Ramsey 1993; for a more general discussion, see Harris 1988). In the name of this "development," state functionaries proactively initiated export-oriented industrialization and created bases of power in cooperation with transnational, especially Japanese industrial investors, and directly and indirectly promoted domestic subcontracting in certain targeted domains of the economy—for example, semiconductors and apparel.

Guidance and care by state functionaries have been directed toward the emergent middle-class of the nation—portrayed as the "people" (e.g., *rakyat* in Malay) made up of indigenes whose autochthonous status was defined by the state's validation of specific cultural affiliations or histories of descent— for example, the association between being Muslim, a loyal subject of an in- digenous ruler, and a member of the "Malay race" in Malaysia, and so forth. Insofar as state functionaries belonged to a distinct religious or ethnic sub- group of middle-class indigenes, their guidance and care entailed promoting the interests of this subgroup over others within the overall process of capi- talist industrialization. At the same time, such "care" has also been punctuated by episodic coercive and legal disciplinings not only of working-class women, transnational labor migrants, and aborigines in their spaces, but also of middle- class renegades and women participating in progressive social movements and in heterodox religious sects whose actions challenge state metanarratives of "development" and social order (Ong 1999). For example, the paramount leaders of the Indonesian New Order state were those cliques of Javanese mil- itary officers associated with General Suharto, who presided over the bloody coup d'état of 1965–1966 in which several hundred thousand "communists" and their supporters were murdered; these officers later occupied high posi- tions in New Order government monopolies. State policies of "national de- velopment" have been couched in ways that allow these governing func- tionaries, their middle-class kin, friends, and allied members of their ethnic group to engage in economic and political aggrandizement through state sponsorship (Mehmet 1986; Robison 1985) and the use of patron-client ties (Scott 1972) at the expense of other ethnic groups.[14] For those belonging to these ruling elites and their ethnic clients, opportunities for rent seeking and speculation at public expense have been many.

Central to pastoral governmentality have been state industrial policies that seek to ensure private capital accumulation while providing fundamental eco- nomic protection to the rising middle-class indigenous segments of national populations. These policies provided an aura of "care" extending to the na- tional population as a whole. Southeast Asian governments thus sought to op- erate with financial surpluses and positive balances of payment, while their regulation of the prices of basic consumption commodities stemmed inflation and provided a bare but crucial measure of popular support for their regimes. Activist government bureaucrats played a crucial role by mediating between export-oriented industrialists and domestic banks—whose funds, accumu- lated through the savings deposits of millions of household savers, provided the capital needed to launch the formers' ambitious high-tech world-standard production and marketing facilities (Wade and Veneroso 1998). Such policies were successful in engendering export-oriented industrial capital accumulation. As a result, despite external pressures from the United States government, the World Bank, and the IMF, until the mid- to late-1980s successful and rapid industrialization allowed Southeast Asian states to set national industrial and capital-investment priorities independent of the financial strictures of "conditionality" and "structural adjustment" that the IMF imposed on Latin America and elsewhere.[15]

As noted, Southeast Asian states organized around pastoral governmentality toward their middle classes were by no means democratic, in that the logic of state formation and its connection to private capital accumulation directed coercive discipline against certain groups that were deemed to be outside the national population toward which state functionaries provided benign guidance—working-class women, communist and socialist party members, labor unionists, progressive social movement activists, and ethnic and religious separatists. In this sense pastoral governmentality generated its own forms of violence. Thus Feith (1981) refers to the "repressive-developmentalist regimes" that have characterized the ASEAN states. In the 1960s and 1970s, crucial elements of state military and police violence developed as these states militarized through the sponsorship of the U.S. and the British governments to serve as Cold War bulwarks of "Free World" power against the "fall" of Southeast Asian "dominoes" through "communist subversion." State elites collaborated with export-oriented industrial subcontractors by using their police powers to dampen labor activism and lend support to the accelerated exploitation of labor, which contributed greatly to the extraordinarily rapid economic growth in the region (Feith 1981:493, 497). Tanter (1982) continued Feith's analysis by looking at militarization within the five ASEAN states. Both Feith and Tanter emphasize the role that military and police repression played in promoting an investment climate ideal for regional subcontracting for Japanese and other transnational corporations. In an important observation, Feith points to the place of military rule and militarization in maintaining internal discipline within the heterogeneous coalitions of groups supporting ruling bureaucratic elites.

GLOBALIZATION AND ENDEMIC OR "NORMAL" VIOLENCE VERSUS EPIDEMIC VIOLENCE: DIASPORA CHINESE IN SOUTHEAST ASIA

Although as nonindigenes, diaspora Chinese have uneasily remained outside of or on the margins of the "people," or *rakyat*, which were the middle-class populations subject to pastoral protection by postwar Southeast Asian political elites, they have been crucial both to the growth of the new national capitalisms and to state formation in Southeast Asia. To the new state bureaucratic elites ruling the new postwar nation–states of capitalist Southeast Asia, dias-pora Chinese capitalists played a central but ambiguous and politically sensitive role within the "development" process knitting together the "people" with the state, that is, with these elites. While these elites acknowledged that ethnic Chi-nese played crucial roles in the commercialization and industrialization processes that simultaneously underwrote "development" and their own class aggrandize-ment, they also saw Chinese as dangerously mobile—even politically subversive—and as not indigenous, or insufficiently so, and thus not entitled to share the benefits of economic growth provided by a "caring" state to "the people."[16] In consequence, these elites placed Chinese on the edges of their national "commu-nities" through legal and administrative constraints on Chinese cultural expres-sion,[17] commercial participation, and access to educational opportunities.[18]

Wealthier Chinese capitalists have responded very differently to stigmatiza-tion from either Chinese professionals or working classes (where they have ex-isted) in Southeast Asia. The very small but extremely wealthy Chinese elites in each country have deployed their capital to form strategic alliances with factions of indigenous political elites in return for political protection in or-der to carry on business "as usual" as subcontractors for foreign industrialists or as oligopolist merchants. Behind the "caring society" and pastoral govern-mentality directed toward the middle-class indigenous segments who apoth-eosized the national population, a shadow economy has thus emerged con-sisting of widely recognized informal ties between the wealthier Chinese business class and non-Chinese state bureaucrats, taking forms such as the *cukong* "bankrolling" relationship (Indonesia), or the *Ali Baba* relationship (Malaysia)—embodied in shared directorships, silent partnerships, and lucra-tive government contracts let out to Chinese through non-Chinese figureheads. In contrast, less wealthy Chinese have been subject to state-bureaucratic preda-tion,[19] and working-class Chinese to outright police intimidation and repres-sion. Chinese petty business people or professionals have made uncertain and sometimes "losing" decisions whether to stay where they are in Southeast Asia (and risk suffering from official discrimination, or worse, political violence), or to leave for uncertain higher educational and commercial opportunities and redefined citizenships elsewhere in Asia or the Americas. Chinese workers from Malaysia—one of the few Southeast Asian countries with an (absolutely) large working-class Chinese population—long targeted by state "normal" vio-lence such as police shakedowns and verbal harassment by officials—have faced even more difficult choices: to either remain in Malaysia as the objects of such violence or to opt out of the limited choices posed to them by the Malaysian labor market by exploring transnational alternatives that are physi-cally and personally hazardous.

The contrasting strategies undertaken by Chinese belonging to different classes in response to the varying governmental rationalities of Southeast Asian states allow us to illustrate two forms of systematic violence associated with Southeast Asian regionalization and globalization processes of the last three decades. One form is the "normal" or endemic violence associated with the operation of transnational labor markets within the Asian region—stitched together by shared understandings among Asian elites about strategies of governance that apply to foreign workers defined as not belonging to the national populations of indigenes in a country. In this connection, I discuss the experiences of Malaysian Chinese labor migrants in Japan. The other form is the episodic or epidemic violence associated with, but not reducible to economic crisis brought on by the encounters between competing regions of the global economy—in this instance, the violence directed at the ethnic Chinese minority in Indonesia in 1997 and 1998 connected to the world-historical clash between the IMF, animated by American neoliberalism, and the Indonesian state, grounded, like other Southeast Asian states, in distinctively regional forms of governmentality.

MALAYSIAN CHINESE "AIRPLANE JUMPERS" IN JAPAN, SUBCONTRACTING, AND THE NATIONAL CHARACTER OF WORK

As Sassen (1988:60–64) points out, the period since the 1960s has been characterized by major transnational movement by labor migrants to "global cities" in the long industrialized countries—the United States, Western Europe, Japan. There has been the social recomposition of inner-city ethnic enclave zones in which concentrated populations of impoverished transnational sojourners reside, the creation of ties between high-tech employers (especially in financial services), subcontractors, and labor brokers who can tap into ethnic enclaves for laborers, the presence of improvised domestic and family arrangements among migrants, and mechanisms for remitting money to home communities (Sassen 1991; Sassen-Koob 1987; Cohen 1987). As with other global cities, a shared colonial history and recent investments have linked Tokyo to peripheral areas, in its case to Southeast Asia, and have led to shared regionally specific cultural practices and discourses surrounding traditions of movement, language (e.g., ideographs of both written Chinese and the Japanese *kanji* script), and patterns of sojourning being within, and in support of, these urban labor markets (Sassen 1991).[20] Certain shared conceptions of the appropriate relationship between a state, the populations who are its subjects, and resident others—similar governmentalities—were also present.

In the 1980s through the early 1990s, Malaysian Chinese laborers in Japan participated in an encompassing system of multitiered labor markets organized hierarchically along lines defined by national and cultural difference created by transnational migrations of persons seeking part-time or temporary casual work. The markets for laborers working for subcontractors—the small- and medium-scale factories and construction companies, and so forth—and for small family firms have proliferated internationally, in a highly refined hierarchical division of labor. For instance, during the same period that very large numbers of Malaysian Chinese migrated to work as casual laborers in Japan, men left Indonesia, Bangladesh, and Pakistan and migrated to urban areas of Malaysia to work as temporary laborers in construction, road building, and plantation work, while large numbers of Indonesian women entered Malaysia to provide domestic labor for Chinese and Malay family enterprises. State functionaries guiding capitalist growth have identified and sorted classes of transnational labor migrants primarily by their nationalities—indexed by their perceived cultural features—and secondarily by gender, and have assigned certain categories of foreign labor to certain types of work in specific national spaces.[21] National labor markets, as in other areas of "the economy" in Asian countries, have thus been organized not by "free market" forces, but by state bureaucrats who parse their immigrant labor forces by nationality via selective immigration controls, and apply certain practices of governance to them.

From the mid-1980s through the early 1990s, observers in Japan noted the presence of a very large number of "overstayers" from abroad—persons who "overstayed" their tourist visas for ninety days to labor illegally in Japanese cities and rural labor camps. Estimates showed a continuous and steep rise throughout this period to as many as 300,000 people until 1993, when there was a sharp contraction as the Japanese "bubble" burst and the economy fell into deep recession. By Japanese Ministry of Justice estimates, there were approximately 40,000 Malaysians working illegally in Japan in 1992. The majority of Malaysian migrants, in Chinese called "airplane jumpers," *tiaofeijiren*, were men—about two-thirds. Virtually all Malaysian airplane jumpers were Chinese, with members of the other major (official) ethnic groups in Malaysia—Indians and Malays—very uncommon.

The *tiaofeijiren* I interviewed were Chinese men in their thirties and forties.[22] Japanese employers, through their recruiters, hired them although they were living illegally in Japan, but consigned them to the least desirable work in the highly segmented hierarchical Japanese labor market. (Above them, in positions of management and skilled labor, were Japanese nationals.) They worked in jobs called "3D" labor—labor that was "dirty, difficult, and dangerous"—in construction work, factory assembly, and in small businesses such as restaurants. The work they did was often physically dangerous, as when they worked on scaffolding high above the ground to construct building walls, or was very hard manual labor, such as excavation of trenches, laying pipes, pouring and setting concrete wall forms, and similar tasks. As one informant put it, "They need semiskilled or unskilled. Like high risk, they call it unskilled or high risk." The construction firms for which most worked were subcontractors at the bottom of the contracting hierarchy of the construction industry in the Tokyo area.

In addition to serious worksite accidents, the other time of danger *tiaofeijiren* recounted with particular vividness was their entry into Japan at Narita Airport, for it was their encounter with Japanese immigration officers that would determine whether they would be allowed into Japan—initially as tourists on three-month visas. Whether they sought entry as individuals or in groups led by a labor recruiter, the stories they presented to the officials had to be credible, or else they were refused permission to enter. One, a Mr. Lau, actually cycled in and out of Japan every ninety days after entering on a tourist visa and then working. His problem, he said, was that "each time I would go in to the Japanese immigration agency and tell them my justification for wanting to return to Japan—to see the sights and to travel. I needed to come up with a convincing reason for why I wished to return to Japan, and be very polite and deferential to the official." After more than two such years of work, and after experiencing two separate workplace accidents that almost killed him, he lost his nerve, and his credibility. When he next left then returned to reenter Japan at Narita, "I was questioned by the immigration officer, who noticed on my passport that I was always in Japan as a 'tourist' for exactly ninety days. He became suspicious of my story, and wouldn't let me enter. I had to fly back to Malaysia." More commonly, men entered as tourists, then overstayed once their tourist visas expired. The story of Mr. Heng, who stayed in Japan for more than two years, suggests the more common pattern.

> I went with other Malaysian Chinese to Japan, and we later split up after we had gotten through immigration. Before that, to convince the immigration official that we were genuine tourists, we traveled via air first to Hong Kong, then on for a brief stay in China, before going on to Japan. Because we were from Malaysia, we were suspected [of seeking to enter to work], and they checked our passports and air tickets, and questioned us closely about what we were going to do in Japan.

Airplane jumpers experienced the partitioning by nationality I alluded to above "on the ground" in two ways. First, it was reinforced through the practices of labor brokers who were fellow nationals (Malaysians, in this case) but also spoke Japanese and had contacts with Japanese employers engaged in specific lines of subcontracting, for whom they provided a regular complement of day laborers, when called on. Thus, laborers were hired not only for their labor power, but also for their nationality, in a cultural division of labor in which certain kinds of work was seen as suiting certain nationalities. Second, although they worked illegally and thus had an implicitly rather than officially acknowledged presence, Malaysian workers lived separately from other nationalities together in houses or dormitories in specific neighborhoods of Tokyo, socialized together (by going out and looking around on Sundays and at other times outside work) and so distinguished themselves—both to themselves and to Japanese—as different from labor sojourners from other countries of origin.

Labor discipline was maintained both by competition for day work among laborers[23] and by migrants' fears of Japanese immigration officials. Laborers' fears of being apprehended by Japanese immigration officials were reinforced by raids of areas frequented by Malaysians and other labor migrants and by reported beatings of migrant laborers taken into custody (Komai 1993). These violent incidents grew more frequent in the early 1990s. By the early 1990s, as the Japanese economy fell into full recession, immigration policy and official practice became increasingly strict—communicating to airplane jumpers a changed perspective on who should benefit from the shrinking resources of the national economy. In 1993, the Japanese government instituted a requirement that any Malaysians intending travel to Japan first obtain a "recommended visa" from the Japanese embassy in Kuala Lumpur. The result was, as one informant said, "you need a visa to go back, but it's not compulsory. But all these are . . . I would say it is not recommended, I shouldn't use the word, because if you don't have a visa, they just don't allow you to enter. . . . But nevertheless, the incidence of just such a recommended visa as a tool, it helped curb a number of Malaysians." By 1997 the number of Malaysians staying in Japan had dropped to 12,000 from 42,000 in 1992.

In considering the perpetration of violence against transnational laborers, parallels between Chinese airplane jumpers in Tokyo and Latino poultry workers in Siler City are evident. In some ways, the material conditions in both situations were quite similar: for instance, state immigration bureaucracies selectively regulated the conditions of entry for migrants in accordance with national labor market requirements in such a way as to maintain labor discipline of transnational migrants through an enforced illegality, while pretending they were not doing so. In both, that is, the state was thoroughly implicated in the conditions creating illicit/illegal ethnic diasporas. In the American case, however, American neoliberal "civil" institutions that sort out populations and assign them to risk and "performance" categories within labor markets were fully in evidence, and this engendered the violence of one such categorical group (poor, rural white males) against another. In the Japanese case, in contrast, state officials sought to directly regulate migration in relation to the demand they perceived in national labor markets. In the course of doing so they constructed "knowledge" of the proper nationalities for the different kinds of labor needed in domestic labor markets and exercised selective strategic violence against transnational migrants whose nationalities they saw as inappropriate for the limited available work. The Japanese strategy is consistent, I would argue, with Asian varieties of governmentality that cast the pastoral state as paternalistically providing for the needs of its middle-class national/indigenous subject population, while regulating access by immigrant, nonnational workers to "its" labor markets that, after all, provide a national resource to those they have need for.

FINANCIAL CRISIS, THE IMF'S NEOLIBERAL CONDITIONS, AND "ETHNIC" VIOLENCE AGAINST CHINESE IN INDONESIA, 1997–1998

There is an emerging consensus on both sides of the Pacific that the Japanese model has failed. Countries up and down the Pacific Rim are embracing market oriented reforms in the wake of an economic crisis widely blamed upon Japanese style institutions. (Lindsay and Lucas 1998:1)

In January 1998, newspapers in Jakarta and elsewhere throughout the island of Java in Indonesia prominently displayed on their front pages the photograph of Michel Camdessus, managing director of the IMF, standing tall with his arms folded, fists clenched, towering over the sitting and stooped figure of President Suharto, who was shown putting his signature to the latest agreement with its set of "conditions" for "structural adjustment" demanded by the IMF as its price for a so-called bail out of the Indonesian economy. The photograph enraged Javanese readers, for its spatial semiotics of the "high" European versus the "low" Asian recalled the vicious didacticism of a stern colonial Dutch schoolmaster disciplining his errant Asian pupil in this latest episode of "teaching the natives a lesson." Unlike earlier episodes of colonial punitive expeditions, the lesson taught through pain took the form of economic discipline administered by U.S. and European elites, through their ventriloquist's dummy, the IMF, on Suharto and the people of Southeast Asia's most populous nation–state. As I have described above, Suharto's New Order regime, like those of other politically independent Southeast Asian nation–states, displayed the temerity of not only generating extraordinary economic growth and an attendant, if very uneven, prosperity among Indonesian citizens but actually accomplished this while it sought to independently determine Indonesia's economic growth process (Winters 1996). Indeed, this bid by wayward Asians for regional quasi-autonomous development was a generational affront to the American and European schoolmasters of international finance, which could scarcely be tolerated. The financial "caning" that punished this outrage had a *timing* that contributed as much to the pain applied as anything else. Indeed, for Camdessus and other members of Western elites, this was punishment long deferred, and so doubly sweet.[24] One does not have to be in sympathy with Suharto, a military commander who directed the murder of hundreds of thousands of his own citizens in 1965–1966 and engaged in gross abuses of both Indonesian people and natural resources during thirty years of his New Order regime, to realize that he had simply met a more formidable bully, albeit one elegantly dressed in a tailored business suit rather than in a general's uniform.

Among the "conditions" it required in return for its loans to the Indonesian government, the IMF demanded the suspension of government subsidies for fuel and electricity, the deregulation of trade in all agricultural products, a rise in Bank of Indonesia's interest rates, abolition of government import monopolies of food staples, the liquidation and reorganization of much of Indonesia's banking structure, and the removal of restrictions on foreign investments in certain sectors (IMF 1998). These conditions, which struck at the "crony capitalism" at the heart of the Indonesian shadow economy—the military/Chinese accommodation—were a double blow. First, they caused widespread misery and devastated the livelihoods of poor Indonesians by cutting off public subsidies for essential consumption goods and exacerbating the preexisting crisis by depressing business activity even further. Second, they challenged the Indonesian state's popular legitimacy and its capacities to enact a "protecting" and "caring" paternalism toward its citizen populations. It was this double *coup de monde* that led to the popular outrage against the IMF and against a humiliated Suharto in the Indonesian news media in the months of 1998 following the announcement of these policies. These representations of a domineering and viciously vengeful West, personified in the towering figure of Michel Camdessus, as it turns out, were right on target.

As these IMF conditions were being argued over and negotiated by the Indonesian government, in cities and towns in Java and elsewhere in the Indonesian archipelago, massive layoffs, inflation in the cost of foodstuffs and widespread deprivation fueled popular rage against the IMF, Suharto, and the New Order regime as a whole, but the fury was focused on a much weaker but highly visible "other"—Indonesian Chinese. In January and again June of 1998, gangs of knife-wielding youth robbed diners at several restaurants in north Jakarta's Chinatown, while food riots by Muslim youth directed against Chinese wholesalers and retailers of foodstuffs pillaged Chinese-owned stores.

In the rural town of Ujang Pandang in Suluwesi, more than 1,000 Chinese shophouses were burned to the ground and several Chinese killed or assaulted. During the period from April to July 1998, Chinese were attacked, and their shophouses looted, then set afire, in the cities of Medan in Sumatra, Yogyakarta, Solo, and Jakarta in central Java, and Surabaya in eastern Java. Catholic churches, to which many Chinese belong, were also a target of arson. The terror culminated in the events of May 12–14 in Jakarta, when thousands of Chinese shophouses were looted and burned, approximately 1,200 people were murdered, many of them trapped in buildings set on fire, numerous Chinese were publicly beaten, and hundreds of Chinese women were raped—with 168 assaults confirmed.

What was the connection between the neoliberal measures demanded by the IMF in 1998 and the "ethnic violence" directed against Chinese the same year? It would be simplistic, ethnocentric, and economistic to hold that the violence was caused directly by neoliberal IMF measures. Misery arising from economic causes does not necessarily generate violence. Violent practices such as those directed against Indonesian Chinese in mid-1998 are a cultural phenomenon depending on discourses of incitement and institutional mechanisms for execution as much as, indeed, more than on broadly shared sentiments of resentment and hurt. In this connection, certain aspects of Indonesian disciplinary governmentality must be pointed to. These include the militarization of the Javanese population for whom ABRI, the Indonesian armed forces, played a central paternalistic role through the extensive patron-client networks of favored high-level military officers. This militarization had led, for instance, to widespread acceptance among Javanese of the invasions in the 1970s of both East Timor and Irian Jaya, whose indigenous peoples were portrayed in popular media as the irredeemable "primitives," *primatif*, deserving the benefits of Javanese civilization, for example, sedentarization and Islamic missionization, coercively imposed (Sen 1994). At the same time, such peripheral groups were seen by many Indonesians as being benignly brought into the fold of the multicultural majority population guided by the pastoral state through the state ideology, *Panchasila*. Militarization among Indonesians was also central to a more broadly distributed syndrome of extrajudicial violence implicating both ABRI soldiers and civilian paramilitary gangs, such as widespread and largely unreported rapes of Indonesian women, and death-squad killings of "criminals," street kids, and other stigmatized populations—Irian Jayans, East Timorese, and Achenese (Heryanto 1999; Siegel 1998). Of course, such extensive militarization—and the deaths it caused—must be laid at the door of that paradigmatic practitioner of organized global violence: the U.S. military, with its Cold War low-intensity doctrines, its extensive training of ABRI officers in counterinsurgency methods, and its arms trade with the Indonesian military (cf. Lutz and Nonini 1999). Insofar as the U.S. military has served as a global enforcer for the neoliberal statecraft of the U.S. Treasury, Wall Street, the World Bank, and the IMF, it is responsible for far more extensive violence than that perpetrated against Chinese in 1998, although it indirectly had a hand in that.

Investigation of the worst violence directed against Chinese—that perpetrated in Jakarta in mid-1998—points, moreover, to the active intervention of ABRI operatives who incited crowds of *pribumis* to loot and burn Chinese shops, and urged on and participated in the gang rapes of Chinese women. Activists from human rights organizations who interviewed Chinese victims after the fact heard evidence of systematic incitement—repeated incidents of young men dressed in black mufti and carried in the backs of trucks, arriving in Chinese neighborhoods and leading *pribumis* in torching the buildings and assaulting their residents—soldiers, many claimed, from the infamous Kopassus special forces unit of ABRI (Volunteer Team for Humanity 1998a, 1998b).[25] Moreover, evidence collected by journalists and anthropologists (Hefner 2000) suggests that a son-in-law of Suharto, Lieutenant General Prabowo Subianto,[26] ordered Kopassus units into Jakarta's streets against Chinese, as part of a last-ditch effort by Suharto (or his supporters) to even scores against the small Chinese-business elite who had failed to support him financially in his struggle with the IMF, and to create a general political crisis that would discredit Prabowo's rival, the Armed Forces Chief General Wiranto (Hefner 2000). Not for the first time, Chinese Indonesians were being cast as outside the national population toward whom benign pastoral guidance was applied.

Where, then does this leave the IMF and its conditionality measures? To state that these measures were not sufficient in themselves to cause the violence against Chinese is not to argue that they were not necessary, logically speaking. In fact, they inspired widespread rage against the IMF, the West, and General Suharto, and his submission to them arguably was the single most important factor leading to his downfall in mid-1998. Chinese were also targeted in a discourse of incitement that cast them as an internal national enemy allied with the United States and the IMF, and widely promulgated by Prabowo and leaders of a conservative Islamic group (Indonesian Committee for Solidarity with the Muslim World, known as KISDI, its Indonesian acronym) in the weeks leading up to the violence (Hefner 2000).

In this sense, the IMF was deeply complicitous with ABRI soldiers, paramilitary gangs, Islamic conservatives, and working-class urban Jakartans in committing the violence that did take place. Its responsibility lay in a systematic policy mugging of the Indonesian government over a period of several years. Prior to the 1980s, during the years of petroleum boom, the successful national strategy of export-driven and import-substitution industrialization leading to rapid and real economic growth was "debt driven" or "debt intensive." That is, financing of industrial growth was possible precisely because of high levels of corporate debt allowing for highly leveraged investments. Foreign, that is Japanese, industrialists employed this capital to invest in advanced productive technologies, while state-owned enterprises, owned jointly by military officers in Suharto's clique and the Chinese economic elite, used it to advance short-term resource exploitation, elite speculation, graft for bureaucratic rent seekers, and payoffs to clients. What made such high levels of indebtedness possible in strategies of expansion were recycled petroleum revenues lent out by government agencies, and high levels of household savings in Indonesian domestic banks available for lending. However, in order to make these arrangements viable, the New Order state restricted corporations and banks from foreign borrowing to avoid sudden shifts of capital out of the country, which would tilt the whole system toward currency devaluation, illiquidity, asset deflation, and default (Wade and Veneroso 1998:7). These restrictions were unpalatable to foreign investors. But the loss of petroleum revenues from the oil crash of 1982 onward made it impossible for the government to maintain these restrictions, and it subsequently capitulated to the repeated demands for capital and trade "liberalization" by the IMF, the World Bank, and U.S. and European financial elites. By the late 1980s, the government had been forced to enact a whole series of laws to improve Indonesia's "investment climate" for foreign "capital controllers" by loosening controls over capital flows (Winters 1996; World Bank 1988). This then allowed Indonesian corporations and banks to build up a huge debt with European, American, and Japanese bankers—$55.5 billion by 1996—who were eager to lend out the capital recycled from the profits made from corporate restructuring in Europe, Japan, and the United States.[27] By 1997, the stage had been set for financial destabilization and social crisis. In a panic rush of disinvestment (which began in Thailand and then Korea) European, Japanese, and American banks and mutual funds called in their loans and sold their investments in Indonesian banks and corporations. Falling foreign currency holdings led to drastic devaluation of the Indonesian currency, corporations defaulted on their foreign loans, bank depositors sought to withdraw their savings, banks collapsed, corporations went bankrupt, there were massive layoffs and panic hoarding of imported staple foodstuffs and fuels.

As the "lender of last resort," the IMF was called in early 1998 to "bail out" the Indonesian, just as it was with the Thai and Korean, economies. Behind the bland mien of Michel Camdessus lay the revanchist policies of an IMF bent on punishing Indonesia, much as it was currently doing so to Thailand and Korea, for its long deviation from the truths of neoliberal doctrine. So the conditions I described above were imposed, which seriously exacerbated the crisis.

The imposition of IMF conditions goes far therefore in explaining not the hands-on "hard" physical and sexual violence committed by the Kopassus paramilitaries and their allied gangs, but instead the widespread looting and petty violence that accompanied the arsons, murders, and rapes, and made working-class Jakartans complicitous with them. In Jakarta, this is clear when listening to looters recalling the uprising of mid-May 1998: "'It was very successful,' Edy . . . said of the looting and rioting. 'It's the only way of getting the government's attention. And fuel prices have already come down'" (Kristof 1998). There are the themes of perceived inequity, unfairness, and sheer need: "Young men came to the city from the countryside during Indonesia's long economic boom, but now they find themselves unemployed and are embittered that they must struggle to survive—living in shacks while wealthy people drive by in imported cars. . . . The young men complain not so much about President Suharto as about their frustration that they are being laid off just as prices are going up" (Kristof 1998). And, "the economic crisis, some said, had made them so desperate that they were willing to do anything to obtain what they could no longer afford. 'It wasn't political,' said Iboy, a 15-year-old youth who seemed surprised when asked why he had looted clothing from a department store. 'It was because I needed things'" (Kristof 1998).

Throughout the implementation of this vastly arrogant program of revenge by the IMF in the name of "bail out," the éminence grise has been the elites of the U.S. Treasury and Wall Street. In a thoughtful assessment, Weiss (1999:xx) infers "the extraordinary behavior of the United States in the Asian region in exploiting the financial crisis to force systemic changes in the troubled economies. Acting externally to bring about structural change has been a persistent pattern in the post-war American experience." In the Asian financial crisis, the shift desired by U.S. elites was *away* from the "Japanese model," and *toward* that of American neoliberalism. Weiss states that the "U.S. administration has not merely used the crisis as a leveraging opportunity to pry open markets once closed to foreign financial institutions; it has played a critical role in deepening the crisis in the first place" (Weiss 1999:xx). The U.S. Treasury did this by purposeful inaction once its officials saw the crisis coming, by pushing the IMF to demand further capital "liberalization" precisely at a time it would do most harm, and by demanding that the IMF impose increased interest rates which would depress the economy even further (Weiss 1999).

When it comes therefore to picking a beneficiary of the suffering generated by the Asian crisis, this appears a to be a "no brainer." Within the afflicted countries, radically deflated corporate and banking assets, huge in their real value, have since early 1998 been offered up on "global" capital markets at discounted fire-sale prices by desperate leaders in Indonesia, like those in Thailand and Korea, to the scavengers of the Wall Street–Treasury–IMF complex—namely American and European finance capital, and to a far less extent, to Japanese finance capital as well. Wade and Veneroso (1998:20) comment on the sheer presumption and extent of the hijacking of assets across Asia: "There is no doubt that Western and Japanese corporations are the big winners. . . . The combination of massive devaluations, IMF-pushed financial liberalization, and IMF-facilitated recovery *may even precipitate the biggest peacetime transfer of assets from domestic to foreign owners in the past fifty years anywhere in the world"* (emphasis added). But the losses have not been merely economic, as serious as these have been, but also political, for Asian pastoral governmentalities grounded in a relationship of care between the state and its apotheosized "people" have come under a fundamental challenge due to states' failure to protect the new middle classes from the "global" threat of Western neoliberal institutions—poignantly shown in the social unrest of Indonesia, Korea, and elsewhere in Asia.

Table 7.1.   Violence and Governmentality in Three Settings

Setting	Agents	Targets	Violence Forms	Connections to Governmentality
Siler City, North Carolina, U.S., 1997	Citizen-residents (white, male, working class)	Latino labor migrants in poultry plants	racial insults, employer and police intimidation, harrassment	Amer. neoliberal governmentality: "noncompetitive" sector attacks "hypercompet." sector
Tokyo, Japan, 1992-1993	Immigration officials and police, other Japanese	Chinese labor migrants from Malaysia in construction work	raids, beatings, detentions, national insults	Asian pastoral governmentality: state officials attack migrant workers on behalf of the "people"
Jakarta, Indonesia, 1998	ABRI Kopassus units, paramilitary gangs, working-class *pribumis*	Chinese shopkeepers, merchants, professionals	looting, arson, beating, murder, public gang rape, racial insults, intimidation	IMF/American Neoliberalism encounters Asian pastoral gov'tality: army attacks on behalf of indigenes, *pribumi* citizens loot for property

Under such conditions, it may now make sense to think of global finance as warfare by other means. If so, then American neoliberal globalization specifies and represents one side's strategic rationale, template, and objective.

AFTERWORD: "GLOBALIZATION" AND VIOLENCE—A TABULAR SUMMARY

In table 7.1 on page 192, I briefly summarize the three cases of violence I have discussed, the agents or perpetrators of violence, the targets (or "victims"), the forms violence took, and their connections to governmentality.

NOTES

1. The interview materials quoted in the sections of this essay on North Carolina were collected in 1997 by Thad Guldbrandsen, Marla Frederick, and Enrique Murillo, who served as site ethnographers for the research project "Estrangement from the Public Sphere," for which I was a principal investigator. I would like to express my appreciation to them. They are in no way responsible for the interpretation of the data made here.

2. We can identify at the very least two alternative rhetorics in the U.S. context—that of social justice in which equity and growth are balanced, and a far-right rhetoric in which global and government conspiracies of domination are spearheaded by dangerous and inferior "foreigners" and minorities (Latinos, Blacks, Jews) against an unaware racial majority, as in David Duke's rhetoric.

3. For example, in multilateral organizations such as the IMF and the World Bank through which the power of U.S. economic statecraft is projected.

4. Another such marginal category is the rapidly increasingly incarcerated population of the United States, now the proportionately largest such among all industrialized societies except for Russia (Mauer 1995:114–15).

5. Even if American transnational neoliberalism recognizes the need for multiculturalism within the market place—what some have called "the united colors of Benetton"—at the same time, Asia is identified as a dangerous and powerful enemy—a theme I return to below. For instance, according to one important document: "In this new economic environment, less developed countries are formidable competitors—and not just for labor intensive products. A combination of technological innovation, investment in education, and a low-cost business environment has helped produce the 'Asian miracle' of the last decade" (North Carolina Economic Development Board 1997a:1).

6. That is to say unlike beef, which does not have the appeal of chicken and turkey as "healthy" meats for the American public.

7. Interviewed by the Mexican television film crew of "Jornado en Siler City," part of the documentary series *La Paloma*, directed and produced by Rodolfo Palma Rojo in May 1997.

8. Informal estimates gathered by epidemiologists in the Division of Maternal and Child Health of the State of North Carolina suggest that as of 1996, there were about 200,000 "Hispanics" residing in the state, out of a total population of more than 7,500,000 (Rangel-Sharpless 1996). Anecdotal evidence suggests that the number has no doubt increased substantially since then.

9. According to Weiss, "Catalytic states seek to achieve their goals less by relying on their own resources than by assuming a dominant role in coalitions of states, transnational institutions and private-sector groups" (1998:208). She sees the United States as domestically "weak" (insufficient coordination between state bureaucrats and business elites) but as externally "strong," presumably through its military power and influence over the Bretton Woods institutions, GATT/WTO, and the like. In the case of the Asian financial crisis, Weiss refers to the U.S. government as an "opportunistic hegemon" (Weiss 1999)—see below.

10. The brouhaha about the Asian "economic miracle" coming out of U.S. business schools and business journalism from the 1970s through the late 1980s (grounded in essentialist notions about "chopsticks cultures" and "bamboo networks," etc.) was as hyperbolic as the more recent Western rhetoric against the "Japanese model" in the late 1990s (on the former, see Nonini and Ong 1997).

11. Such inflows of capital from U.S. and European investors in the 1980s and 1990s may well have been a response to the enormous generation of fictive capital then being created by speculation and securitization in Western financial markets; such wealth holders sought out productive investment outlets by investing overseas—hence avoiding an "accumulation crisis" through what Harvey (1989) called "the spatial fix." Thanks to Jonathan Friedman for this insight.

12. For example, foreign expatriate managers or professionals with capital or technological expertise.

13. See also Dicken's (1998:89–90) Asian "plan-rational developmental state" whose policies he sets against the "market-ideological state" of the Reagan/Bush and Thatcher/Major regimes in the United States and Britain.

14. In the case of Indonesia, for instance, at the expense of non-Javanese, less well-off Chinese, and "Outer Island" tribal peoples, such as the aboriginal peoples of Irian Jaya.

15. The Philippines was an exception and underwent a very painful period of "austerity" measures imposed on it by the IMF and World Bank in the 1970s (Broad 1988).

16. In Indonesia, Malaysia, Cambodia, Burma, and Vietnam, Chinese since the 1960s were discriminated against because of their past reputation as commercial middlemen and petty bureaucrats forming a buffer class between European colonial rulers and indigenous elites and peasantries.

17. In Indonesia, for example, from 1965 onward, Chinese were required to adopt Indonesian surnames and were not allowed to publicly celebrate Daoist/Buddhist holidays, or to publish in written Chinese.

18. In Malaysia, government-set quotas have favored indigenous *bumiputra*, or Malays over Chinese in admission to government-operated universities.

19. For instance, small Chinese businesses in Malaysia are expected to pay exorbitantly large fees to petty state functionaries for installation of services (telephone, electricity), for business licenses and permits, and for police "protection."

20. Here, not only Japan's investment presence in Malaysia but also its occupation of Malaya during World War II and the Malaysian government's "Look East" policy emulating Japan's economic model during the 1970s were all relevant.

21. Although I cannot make the case here, I would argue that such cultural/national discriminations are functionally parallel to those identified as "racial" in the United States.

22. They came from a specific town in northern West Malaysia where I carried out ethnographic research intermittently from 1978 to 1997.

23. Such day-to-day uncertainty generated its own stress. One worker said, "There was a period of three months when work was scarce. Many days I would go out to find work, and wouldn't get any, so I would return to my room and sleep all day or watch videos. This was very difficult, and I became sad and depressed."

24. About the same time, similar punishment was being administered to Korea and Thailand for similar crimes and insults (Wade and Veneroso 1998; Weiss 1998, 1999).

25. One of the components of the violence—gang rape of large numbers of Chinese women—appears to be a strategy associated with a warfare of military terror directed explicitly at a civilian population with the aim of inflicting group humiliation and panic to flight.

26. Prabowo, when stationed a few years previously in East Timor and Acheh was widely reported to have organized civilian vigilante gangs to rape, torture, and murder villagers seen as sympathetic to their independence movements (Hefner 2000:3).

27. As noted above, large quantities of fictive capital generated by speculation in the West and in Japan, in search of new productive investment outlets, were no doubt involved.

REFERENCES

Anderson, Benedict. 1998. "From Miracle to Crash." *London Review of Books* 20, 8:3–7.

Appadurai, Arjun. 1996. *Modernity at Large: Cultural Dimensions of Globalization.* Minneapolis: University of Minnesota.

Ariffin, Omar. 1993. *Bangsa Melayu: Malay Concepts of Democracy and Community 1945–1950.* Kuala Lumpur, Malaysia: Oxford University Press.

Boyd, William, and Michael Watts 1997. "Agro-industrial Just-In-Time: The Chicken Industry and Postwar American Capitalism." In *Globalising Food: Agrarian Questions and Global Restructuring.* Edited by David Goodman and Michael Watts, 192–225. London: Routledge.

Broad, Robin. 1988. *Unequal Alliance: The World Bank, the International Monetary Fund, and the Philippines.* Berkeley: University of California Press.

Castel, Robert 1991. "From Dangerousness to Risk." In *The Foucault Effect: Studies in Governmentality.* Edited by G. Burchell, C. Gordon, and P. Miller, 281–98. Chicago: University of Chicago Press.

Cecelski, David, and Mary Lee Kerr. 1992. "Hog Wild." *Southern Exposure* 20, no. 3:8–15.

Cohen, Robin. 1987. *The New Helots: Migrants in the International Division of Labor.* Aldershot, U.K.: Gower.

Dicken, Peter. 1998. *Global Shift: Transforming the World Economy.* 3d ed. New York: Guilford Press.

Dikötter, Frank 1992. *The Discourse of Race in Modern China*. Stanford, Calif.: Stanford University Press.

Doner, Richard, and Ansil Ramsey 1993. "Postimperialism and Development in Thailand." *World Development* 21, no. 5:691–704.

Drucker, Peter. 1992. *Managing for the Future: The 1990s and Beyond*. New York: Dutton.

Escobar, Arturo. 1995. *Encountering Development: The Making and Unmaking of the Third World*. Princeton, N.J.: Princeton University Press.

Featherstone, Mike 1990. "Global Culture: An Introduction." In *Global Culture: Nationalism, Globalization and Modernity. Theory, Culture and Society*. Edited by Mike Featherstone, 1–14. London: Sage.

Feith, Herb. 1981. "Repressive-Developmentalist Regimes in Asia." *Alternatives* 7:491–506.

Fowler, Edward. 1996. *San'ya Blues: Laboring Life in Contemporary Tokyo*. Ithaca, N.Y.: Cornell University Press.

Fröbel, Folker, Jurgen Heinrichs, and Otto Kreye. 1980. *The New International Division of Labour: Structural Unemployment in Industrialized Countries and Industrialisation in Developing Countries*. Translated by Pete Burgess. Cambridge, U.K.: Cambridge University Press.

Foucault, Michel. 1991. "Governmentality." In *The Foucault Effect: Studies in Governmentality*. Edited by Graham Burchell, Colin Gordon, and Peter Miller. Chicago: University of Chicago Press.

Fukuyama, Francis. 1992. *The End of History and the Last Man*. New York: Free Press.

Goldoftas, Barbara. 1989. "Inside the Slaughterhouse." *Southern Exposure* 17, no. 2:25–29.

Gouveia, Lourdes. 1994. "Global Strategies and Local Linkages: The Case of the U.S. Meatpacking Industry." In *From Columbus to ConAgra: The Globalization of Agriculture and Food* by A. Bonanno, L. Busch, et al., 125–48. Lawrence: University Press of Kansas.

Gowan, Peter. 1999. *The Global Gamble: Washington's Faustian Bid for World Dominance*. London: Verso.

Hall, Bob. 1989. "Chicken Empires." *Southern Exposure* 17, no. 2:12–17.

Harris, Nigel. 1988. "Review Article: New Bourgeoisies?" *Journal of Development Studies* 24, no. 2 (January): 237–49.

Harvey, David. 1989. *The Condition of Postmodernity.* Oxford, U.K.: Basil Blackwell.

Heffernan, William, and Douglas H. Constance. 1994. "Transnational Corporations and the Globalization of the Food System." In *From Columbus to ConAgra: The Globalization of Agriculture and Food* by A. Bonanno, L. Busch, et al., 29–51. Lawrence: University Press of Kansas.

Hefner, Robert. 2000. "Economic Crisis and Regime Collapse in Indonesia." Paper delivered at the annual meeting of the Association for Asian Studies, San Diego (March).

Heryanto, Ariel. 1999. "Rape, Race, and Reporting." In *Reformasi.* Edited by Arief Budiman, Barbara Hatley, and Damien Kingsbury, 299–334. Clayton, Australia: Monash Asia Institute.

Higgott, Richard, and Richard Robison, eds. 1985. *Southeast Asia: Essays in the Political Economy of Structural Change.* London: Routledge & Kegan Paul.

Hirst, Paul, and Grahame Thompson. 1996. *Globalization in Question.* Cambridge, U.K.: Polity.

Hoogvelt, Ankie. 1997. *Globalization and the Postcolonial World: The New Political Economy of Development.* Baltimore: Johns Hopkins University Press.

International Monetary Fund. 1998. "News Brief: Statement by the Managing Director on the IMF Program with Indonesia." News Brief No. 98/2 (January 15). Washington, D.C.: International Monetary Fund.

Komai, Hiroshi. 1993. *Migrant Workers in Japan.* Translated by Jens Wilkenson. London: Kegan Paul.

Kristof, Nicholas. 1998. "Looters in Indonesia Say Inequality Angers Them." *New York Times,* May 18, 1998.

Lindsay, Brink, and Aaron Lukas. 1998. "Revisiting the Revisionists: The Rise and Fall of the Japanese Economic Model." *Trade Policy Analysis* 31 (July). www.freetrade.org/pubs/pas/tpa-003.html [accessed May 21, 2002].

Lutz, Catherine, and Donald Nonini. 1999. "The Economies of Violence and the Violence of Economies." In *Anthropological Theory Today.* Edited by Henrietta L. Moore, 73–113. London: Polity.

Machado, Kit G. 1995. "Japanese Foreign Direct Investment in East Asia: The Expanding Division of Labor and the Future of Regionalism." In *Foreign Direct Investment in a Changing Global Political Economy*. Edited by Steve Chan, 39–66, New York: St. Martin's.

———. 1997. "Complexity and Hierarchy in the East Asian Division of Labor: Japanese Technological Superiority and ASEAN Industrial Development." In *Industrial Technology Development in Malaysia: Industry and Firm Studies*. Edited by K. S. Jomo, Greg Felker, and Rajah Rasiah. London: Routledge.

Magretta, Joan. 1998. "Fast, Global, and Entrepreneurial: Supply Chain Management, Hong Kong Style: An Interview with Victor Fung." *Harvard Business Review* (Sept–Oct): 103–14.

Mauer, Marc. 1995. "International Use of Incarceration." *Prison Journal* 75, no. 1:113–23.

Mehmet, Ozay. 1986. *Development in Malaysia: Poverty, Wealth and Trusteeship*. London: Croom Helm.

Nonini, Donald M., and Aihwa Ong. 1997. "Introduction: Chinese Transnationalism as An Alternative Modernity." In *Ungrounded Empires: The Cultural Politics of Modern Chinese Transnationalism*. Edited by Aihwa Ong and Donald Nonini, 3–33. New York: Routledge.

North Carolina Economic Development Board. 1997. "Making North Carolina a High Performance State." http://www.commerce.state.nc.us/econbrd/default.htm [accessed November 28, 1997].

Ong, Aihwa. 1999. *Flexible Citizenship: The Cultural Logics of Transnationality*. Durham, N.C.: Duke University Press.

Peterson, Alan. 1996. "Risk and the Regulated Self: The Discourse of Health Promotion as Politics of Uncertainty." *Australia New Zealand Journal of Sociology* 32, no. 1: 44–57.

Rangel-Sharpless, Maria. 1996. "Hispanic Population Data Gathered by the Immunization Section." Memorandum, Division of Maternal and Child Health, Department of Environment, Health, and Natural Resources, State of North Carolina.

Robison, Richard. 1985. "Class, Capital, and the State in New Order Indonesia." In *Southeast Asia: Essays in the Political Economy of Structural Change*. Edited by R. Higgott and R. Robison, 295–327. London: Routledge.

Sassen, Saskia. 1988. *The Mobility of Labor and Capital: A Study in International Investment and Labor Flow.* London: Cambridge University Press.

———. 1991. *The Global City: New York, London, Tokyo.* Princeton, N.J.: Princeton University Press.

Sassen-Koob, Saskia. 1987. "Issues of Core and Periphery: Labour Migration and Global Restructuring." In *Global Restructuring and Territorial Development,* 60–87. London: Sage.

Scott, James C. 1972. "Patron-Client Politics and Political Change in Southeast Asia." *American Political Science Review* 65, no. 1:91–114.

Siegel, James T. 1998. *A New Criminal Type in Jakarta: Counter-Revolution Today.* Durham, N.C.: Duke University Press.

Sen, Krishna. 1994. "An Indonesian Film Called *Primitif.*" *Anthropology Today* 10, no. 4:20–23.

Stanley, Kathleen. 1994. "Industrial and Labor Market Transformation in the U.S. Meatpacking Industry." In *The Global Restructuring of Agro-Food Systems.* Edited by Philip McMichael, 129–44. Ithaca, N.Y.: Cornell University Press.

Tanter, Richard. 1982. "The Militarization of ASEAN: Global Context and Local Dynamics." *Alternatives* 7, no. 4: 507–32.

Volunteer Team for Humanity. 1998a. "Early Documentation No. 1." http://www.huaren.org/focus/id/072098-05.html [accessed July 30, 1999].

———. 1998b. "Early Documentation No. 2." http://www.huaren.org/focus/id/072098-06.html [accessed July 30, 1999].

Wachs, Bob. 1995. "Workers, Farmers, Local Government to Suffer." *Chapel Hill News,* May 23.

Wade, Robert, and Frank Veneroso. 1998. "The Asian Crisis: The High Debt Model Versus the Wall Street-Treasury-IMF Complex." *New Left Review* 228:3–24.

Weiss, Linda. 1998. *The Myth of the Powerless State.* Ithaca, N.Y.: Cornell University Press.

———. 1999. "State Power and the Asian Crisis." *New Political Economy* 4, no. 3 (November): 331–32.

Winant, Howard. 1994. *Racial Conditions.* Minneapolis: University of Minnesota Press.

Winters, Jeffrey A. 1996. *Power in Motion: Capital Mobility and the Indonesian State.* Ithaca, N.Y.: Cornell University Press.

World Bank. 1988. *Indonesia: Adjustment, Growth and Sustainable Development.* Jakarta, May 2.

www.fayeconomic.com "Labor Supply in Fayetteville, N.C." [accessed November 7, 1997].

8

Killing Me Softly

Violence, Globalization, and the Apparent State

NINA GLICK SCHILLER AND GEORGES FOURON

Although we have been researching and writing about Haiti for a number of years we have said little about violence. Then, suddenly, violence in Haiti directly entered our lives. In December 1999, two of our friends, Claire and her brother-in-law, Antoine, were held up in broad daylight in the middle of a traffic jam on the road from the airport in Port-au-Prince, the capital of Haiti. Claire had just arrived from New York, bringing money for medical care for her ailing mother. Armed men put guns to Antoine and Claire's head and stole all of their money as well as Claire's luggage filled with presents for family and friends in Haiti. The thieves also took Antoine's car.

No one came to help them until after the gunmen had fled. Then people on the street told them they were lucky because often the gunmen shoot their victims. When Antoine and Claire went to the police, the police were not interested in recording the details of the crime and clearly had no intention of searching for the perpetrators. Instead, they told the two crime victims, "We know where you were held up. Robberies happen in that area all the time." Claire, furious and frustrated, demanded to know why the police did not patrol the area if they knew that it was a high crime location. She was told: "But this is government business taking place here and we can't intervene. Whenever we arrest the perpetrators of these crimes, we are invariably fired from our job." This experience led Claire to join those in Haiti and in the Haitian diaspora who see security as a major issue in Haiti and link the rise of violent crime partly to the political infighting among the contenders for the Haitian presidency.

Within the past few years, the prevalence of criminal violence and the issue of public insecurity have become a major topic of debate and discussion among people of all classes. Violent crimes, which on the surface seem to be random criminal acts, may also involve the police and various political forces in a form of "government business." This situation in which random violence and targeted violence (*vyolans telegide*) cannot always be separated contributes to an atmosphere of general insecurity that makes the question of violence a central political concern not only for the local population, but also the sector of the Haitian population that resides abroad. Meanwhile, other forms of violence such as gender violence, death and violence that result from the imposition of immigration laws, and structural violence receive less public attention. Yet all these additional unmarked forms of violence contribute to a sense of a country in internal crisis, a victim of its history, culture, and politics. Haitians, political pundits around the world, and experts on globalization readily note the growth of criminal violence in Haiti and are silent about many of the other forms of violence. They do not connect the various types of violence in Haiti with the current nature of globalization.

This chapter addresses the relationship between globalization and violence. We raise issues and concerns that require further research and discussion, drawing on our observations of the current situation in Haiti. We investigate the connection between the growth of many types of violence in Haiti, the lessening of direct violence from the state, and the current position of Haiti in the global economy. We demonstrate in the Haitian case that behind the term "globalization," which is used widely to evoke an image of a neutral, powerful, impersonal, and politically disinterested economic and cultural force, stands militarily strong states such as the United States. These states dominate and compete to protect their various corporate interests in far-flung regions of the world by means of globe-spanning institutions such as the World Bank, the IMF, and the United Nations. We demonstrate that the physical and structural violence currently so widespread in Haiti is linked to the neoliberal agenda imposed on Haiti by the United States, the European Union, and "the international lending community," an agenda made palatable under the rubric of "economic reform," "the consolidation of democracy," and the "campaign against drug lords."

In our analysis and conclusions we discuss the various forms of ideology that mask the deadly relationship between globalization and violence and prevent us from understanding that the type of globalization currently popularized by the world's powerful states is a fundamentally violent and dehumanizing process. The lynchpin of this system of deadly exploitation, we argue, is the perpetuation of the notion that the world is composed of separate, autonomous, sovereign states, each responsible for their success within the global economic system. In fact most states in the world system are apparent states that maintain the apparatus of sovereignty but are stripped of the ability to develop economic structures and activities that provide for the needs of the majority of their people. Among apparent states such as Haiti, which are currently sustained to a significant degree by emigrant remittances, the ideology of sovereignty is kept alive by an ideology of long-distance nationalism (Glick Schiller and Fouron 2001). Ideologies of sovereignty and long-distance nationalism focus public concern and anger on crime and violence within each state and obscure the connections between globalization and violence. Discourses about crime and violence displace anger about the neoliberal agenda with concerns for public security and social peace.

Haiti is a particularly useful location in which to theorize about the relationship between violence and globalization. The U.S. media, politicians, and policy makers characterize the present violence in Haiti as part of the country's cultural tradition without reference to larger political and economic forces. U.S. Ambassador Timothy Carney summarized this position in a interview with Reuters in 1999, as U.S. troops left Haiti after a five-year military occupation. "Haiti," Carney stated, "has not met the unrealistic expectations of the international community since 1994. The modest advances in the economy, the real, but still fragile improvements in the police, and the spotty record in the transition toward democracy reflect Haiti's history and political style" (Bauduy 1999). However, from the moment that the Caribbean island of Hispaniola was conquered by the Spanish in 1492, Haiti has been subject to violent penetration from forces located outside its territorial boundaries (Bellegarde Smith 1990). At the same time, the current forms of violence in Haiti differ from Haitians' past experiences with violence in significant ways that allow us to focus on the current moment of globalization.

DEFINING GLOBALIZATION AND VIOLENCE

The term "globalization" is currently being used to describe the myriad of cultural, social, political, and economic processes that are integrating the world into a single system of relationships and values (Sassen 1998; Friedman 1999). In the first flurry of discussion of globalization, advocates, critics, and scholars of globalization all emphasized the novelty of the processes they were observing (Brecher and Costello 1994; Featherstone, Lash, and Robertson 1995). More recently, scholars have begun to argue that since its inception, capitalism as a mode of production, distribution, and consumption has been global in its reach and violent in its methodology. State formation during the past five hundred years has been a transborder process in which European colonization defined discrete colonial populations by differentiating the colonizer from the colonized. Modern nation–states, colonial states, and concepts of national identity were spawned through violent transborder interactions and connections (Anderson 1994; Gilroy 1991; Hall 1992; Lebovics 1992; Rafael 1995; Stoler 1989.)[1] The nineteenth century was one of intense and violent capital penetration into most regions of the world, a process that only abated with the advent of World War I.

Nonetheless, there are significant differences between the ways in which regions of the world were previously interconnected and contemporary globalization. Currently, capitalist processes are being restructured in fundamental ways in relationship to the rapid and deregulated flows of capital (Mittleman 1996:230–31). In this chapter, we maintain that the contemporary processes of capital accumulation constitute a fundamental aspect of the current historical conjuncture and that they shape the concomitant cultural, social, and political processes that accompany, facilitate, and propel this restructuring. We define contemporary globalization as this economic restructuring and its concomitant cultural, social, and political processes.

While we acknowledge that contemporary globalization is different from the processes that preceded it, we also stress that the link between violence and globalization is an old one. The colonization that spawned the development and expansion of European capitalism was achieved through violence. Conquest, slavery, rape, and pillage opened the way to the development of capitalism as a global system (Blaut 1992). The current period of globalization differs in that it is occurring at a moment in which the world is divided into formally independent nation–states; we are not witnessing worldwide strategies of territorial conquest and colonization. Instead, the leaders of a single superpower, the United States, speak incessantly of free trade, global markets, and democracy rather than worldwide domination. Therefore the links between global processes of capital accumulation and violence can and are being obscured.

Just how much violence we see around the world today depends in part on how we define violence. If we define violence as actions that are detrimental to human life, health, or well-being, then we must note that the contemporary growth of violence takes both structural and direct forms. Direct violence would seem to be more readily identifiable. It takes the form of physical attacks that leave behind the wounded and the dead. "The structural approach to violence . . . stresses the ways in which the distribution of wealth and power influence behavior" (Chasin 1998). Structural violence can be defined as deprivations of food, health care, education, and other resources necessary for human life and development that leads to physical disability, the destruction of human potential, and death. Structural violence, while it is a less visible form of the destruction of human life, can be deadly and can affect large numbers of people around the world.

At the very outset, we want to make clear that we do not write this chapter as pacifists. It is all too easy to condemn struggles for social and economic justice as disruptive and violent and define the status quo as peaceful. Under the status quo, millions face hunger, disease, and the unequal effects of police powers that are organized to protect property rather than people. We don't condemn people struggling against these conditions "by whatever means necessary." However, it is essential to analyze what we are struggling against and what we are struggling for. To this end critiques of the globalization, which link it to violence, are an essential part of any effort toward meaningful change. Mindless reactive violence, acts of vengeance or terrorism, whatever the rhetoric, is no solution.

In discussing Haiti we draw on thirty years of direct participation, participant observation, interviewing in the Haitian immigrant settlement in New York, and research in Haiti in 1989, 1991, 1995, and 1996. This research includes 224 extensive interviews conducted between 1985 and 1996 with men and women of all classes. In addition, Georges Fouron draws on his own life experience as a Haitian transmigrant, which places him in a transnational social field that connects his life in the United States with that in Haiti. To illustrate some of our points, we will draw statements made to us about various forms of violence in interviews with seventy men and thirty-nine women that we conducted in Haiti in 1996.[2] Almost all of the people we identified through a snowball sample agreed to the interview and readily discussed their relations to Haitians abroad. In answering our questions about whether they would like to migrate, people referred to both the ongoing deterioration of economic conditions and the violence and insecurity they faced on a daily basis. Their responses can serve as entry point into the various ways in which people in Haiti are currently experiencing violence.[3]

GLOBALIZATION AND THE
IMPLEMENTATION OF THE "AMERICAN PLAN."

Speaking to the National Organization for the Advancement of Haitians at Georgetown University in Washington, D.C., in July 2000, Peter Romero, U.S. acting assistant secretary of state for the Western Hemisphere Affairs set an agenda for the future of societies currently in economic and political disarray such as Haiti. He called for "consolidating democracy, promoting economic reform, and helping . . . these societies protect themselves for the onslaught of drugs."[4] Haiti, at the beginning of the new millennium, would seem ripe for such an agenda. Its political system is fractured by political discord with the various fractions warring with each other over control over the government. Haiti's economy is unable to provide even the funds to run the government much less provide basic sanitation, health, and educational services to the people. Meanwhile, a few strata of the population flaunt wealth derived from the monopolization of economic resources, employment with transnational corporations or organizations, corruption, and the drug trade. The fabric of daily life in cities and towns is rent by fear of armed attack by desperate youths, politically motivated gangs, or even the police.

On the surface, Haiti would seem to be a perfect example of a country that suffers because it has refused to fully implement the agenda for globalization promoted by the United States and the global financial institutions. U.S. politicians who wish to cut back foreign aid speak of the futility of use trying to assist countries with "no democratic tradition and with a culture of violence" and use Haiti as an example. If Haiti and similar weak states all over the world are in disarray, it would seem that they have no one but themselves to blame. And on this point, many Haitians, illiterate and well-schooled, poor and rich, seem to agree.

In the early 1980s, rumors circulated in Haiti and among the Haitian diaspora about an "the American Plan," According to rumors, the "American Plan" was a Machiavellian conspiracy devised by the U.S. government in the international lending institutions "to force Haiti to comply with U.S. economic and geopolitical needs in the region" (Wilentz 1990:269). Over the years the stories about the American plan focused on different features of the conspiracy. At one point, people emphasized that Haiti had been selected as a dumping ground for U.S. garbage and toxic wastes. And it certainly was true that in 1986, a U.S. boat, the *Khian Sea*, hauled toxic wastes from Philadelphia for deposit in a dump site outside of Gonaïves, a town located seventy miles north of Port-au-Prince. Later Haitians asserted that it was part of the American plan to contaminate the Haitians with the HIV virus to stop illegal migration to the United States and to prevent revolution in Haiti.

U.S. officials dismissed all discussion and protest against "the American plan" as unfounded anti-Americanism and a prime example of Haitian paranoia. However, there was indeed a neoliberal "development" strategy for Haiti, imposed on Haiti by the U.S. government in conjunction with globally reaching corporations, the world's strongest states, and globally acting financial institutions. We can use the term "imposed" in the sense that, although, until 1991, there was full cooperation by various Haitian regimes, much of the policy was instituted by outside governments and agencies, not by direct action of the Haitian government. And over a thirty-year period, the agenda imposed on Haiti, whether we label it "plan" or "development strategy" or "economic reform" or globalization, has devastated the Haitian rural economy and driven people to the capital city and Haiti's major towns where they look desperately for any form of low-wage work.

PROMOTING ECONOMIC REFORM:
CONTEMPORARY VIOLENCE IN HAITI

Beginning in 1967, U.S. companies began to look to Haiti to take advantage of its cheap labor and politically repressed and quiescent workers as part of the project of corporations in the capitalist core to move their production plants overseas. However, a whole new level of initiatives directed toward Haiti began in 1971, when seventeen-year-old Jean-Claude Duvalier, became the new dictator of Haiti, having inherited the regime from his father.

The U.S. strategy for Haiti was shaped not only by the general interest the U.S. government has in promoting export-processing industries in countries that provide cheap, unregulated labor but also by the particularities of its relationship to Haiti: Haiti's location, only 707 miles from the United States; the long history of U.S. economic and political involvement in Haiti; the repressive Haitian Duvalier regime that could insure low wages and no labor organizing; and Haiti's high population density (Plummer 1988). In 1982, The United States Agency for International Development (USAID) summarized the goal of U.S. economic policies in Haiti. It sought not an independent, prosperous, democratic Haiti, a goal one would imagine would be central to "international development." Rather, the United States sought through its aid a "historic change to a greater commercial interdependence [of Haiti] with the United States." This new economic development strategy was designed to increase Haiti's integration in the U.S. market in the following ways: Haiti would abandon its agricultural development programs, open its economy to U.S. interests, support the funding of private enterprises intended primarily for export businesses, and import its food from the United States (DeWind and McKinney 1988:48).

"USAID proposed the 'gradual but systematic removal' of domestic crops from 20 percent of all tilled land and their replacement with export crops such as coffee and cocoa." (Poppen and Wright 1994:25; see also DeWind and McKinney 1988). Haiti did not dramatically increase its export crops but its domestic crops were replaced. The United States flooded Haiti with millions of dollars of "Food for Peace." Food also came from European countries such as the Netherlands. This food was either given away or sold cheaply. Food produced by farmers and corporations in rich powerful countries was dumped in less powerful states, destroying local cultivation and market systems. Haitian rural producers of food crops could not compete with food from the U.S. and European "donors." Haiti, a country in which until the 1980s more than 80 percent of the population lived in the countryside, became an importer of food.[5] In 1996 a United Nations Commission reported that "Agricultural activity [had] contracted sharply (−11%), adding to the downward slide recorded since 1992. Tropical storm Gordon . . . and the undercapitalization of Haiti's rural area led to a fall in sugar-cane, banana, rice and coffee harvests. Staple food crops were also down, although to a lesser extent, as was meat output, for which the demand has been dwindling for a number of years. . . . The bulk of imports (80%) originated in the United States. One third of these purchases were food products, in particular grains, soybean oil, sugar, and beans" (Economic Commission for Latin America and the Caribbean United Nations 1996:231–32). The U.S. Department of State informed U.S. businessmen that "the US has been and remains Haiti's largest trading partner" and that "markets exist for . . . rice, wheat, flour, sugar, and processed foodstuffs" (U.S. State Department 1998:1).

This situation was worsened by pressure from lending institutions to not invest in the rural infrastructure. Investment in roads and communication in the Haitian countryside might have allowed Haitian farmers to more efficiently get their crops to market so that they could compete with the imported foods. Instead, today imported apples from Washington State are hawked on the streets of Port-au-Prince, while Haitian cultivators cannot get their fruits to urban markets.

The importation of food has been accompanied by the introduction into Haiti of secondhand clothing, shoes, and various household items. The selling of secondhand clothes and items abroad has become a big U.S. business. Clothes donated to charities are sorted, bundled, shipped, and sold to Third World countries. In keeping with the pressure of the lending institutions that provide the funds to maintain the Haitian government, tariffs that protected Haitian industries and production have been abandoned. On the surface these imports literally cover up some of the poverty and squalor of Haiti. The million people now living in Port-au-Prince, although impoverished, are not ragged and often are not barefoot. They walk down the streets, well clothed, desperately looking for some form of economic activity to allow them to feed their family. Moreover, many people are now employed in the selling of imported clothes (*pèpè*). However, the price of this refashioning of the Haitian economy has been high. A myriad of handicrafts that supported people in both rural areas and the cities have been destroyed: seamstresses, leather workers, shoemakers, hat makers, and basket weavers can no longer support their crafts. The situation is exacerbated by the flood of goods sent to sustain families from Haitians living abroad. While these goods may dramatically improve the standard of living of families assisted by remittances, they contribute to a hand-me-down, handout economy that provides few sources of steady employment. Meanwhile the imported goods give rural and urban people a sense that they have entered the global economy and fan desires for increased consumption without providing any means to obtain an income.

According to USAID, which promised that Haiti would become the "Taiwan of the Caribbean, factory employment was supposed to replace the sustenance provided by the rural economy" (Chomsky 1994a). Some export-processing factories were established. As is often the case with such industries, the few people who obtain employment were women; the men uprooted from the land were left without sources of employment. "Women in the 1980s were paid 14 cents an hour, working without health and safety protections, water, or sanitary facilities, and without the right to unionize" (Chomsky 1994a). The salary was so low that the women were unable to support themselves on the wages and certainly could not support their families. In the 1980s wages fell 56 percent while U.S. corporations and associated Haitian investors found these factories highly profitable. Among the persons who have risked their lives to flee Haiti in small boats beginning in the 1980s were people employed in the export-processing sector.[6] However, in the face of political instability that began in 1986 and continues until today, the export-processing sector has remained small (Chomsky 1994a).

To facilitate the restructuring of the Haitian economy, "development assistance" from abroad has dramatically increased over the past thirty years. In the 1970s Haiti received $384 million dollars. Between 1972 and 1981, $540 million dollars flowed into Haiti. In the five-year period of 1981–1985, right before the fall of the Duvalier regime, Haiti received $657 million in aid (Dupuy 1989). By 1995 Haiti was receiving more than this total ($730.6 million) in a single year.

At the same time, the international donors pressured the Haitian government to refinance its debt so that it could incur more debt. "In December 1994 Haiti made a commitment with the IMF, the World Bank, and the International Development Bank to use US $65 million in grants from 10 donor countries and US $18 million from the Government itself to pay off its arrears on its debts with these multilateral sources" (Economic Commission for Latin America and the Caribbean United Nations 1996:227). Since the Haitian economy did not in fact grow, in the decade between 1990 and 2000 Haiti's debt went from U.S. $800 million to an estimated $1.34 billion. Most of that debt (84 percent) was owed to the World Bank and the International Monetary Fund (Federal Research Division 1989; Haiti News Summary 2000). In June 2000, at a session of the United National General Assembly, Haiti's minister of planning requested the cancellation of this debt.[7]

Generally foreign aid and loans have ended up in the bank accounts of Haiti's political leaders, elite families, or in payment for contracts to foreign organizations or corporations. Officials of lending agencies have known about and not been deterred by the high levels of corruption and the immediate export of funds sent to Haiti, as long as the various regimes have remained compliant with efforts to restructure the Haitian economy. If loans were repaid, lenders asked minimal questions about where the money had gone and whether the interest payments represented returns on the investment of borrowed capital or further extractions of wealth from the Haitian poor through fees and taxes. Meanwhile, Haitians have become progressively poorer as repayments of the loans has drained the country of money for economic development. In 1976, 48 percent of the people were described by outside monitors to be in "desperate poverty." By 1986, this number grew to 79 percent (Hancock 1989:180). The U.S. Central Intelligence Agency (2000) estimated that in 1998, 80 percent of the population lived below the poverty line.

The result of the policies imposed on Haiti in the name of development assistance has been economic dislocation and destruction of Haitian economic life. A million people have fled the countryside and arrived in Port-au-Prince, desperate to earn a living by any means necessary. As rural people crowded into Port-au-Prince looking for work, the standard of living in the city fell dramatically. The development loans and neoliberal policies did not support the provision of public services and rural people squatted or rented single-room dwellings without sanitation or drinking water.

In 1996, approximately 55 percent of the Haitian labor force was unemployed (Economic Commission for Latin America and the Caribbean United Nations 1996:232).[8] Forty-four percent of the people we interviewed in Port-au-Prince and in Aux Cayes said that they were unemployed. This was as true of persons in their twenties as it was of persons in their sixties. Many of the older people had not had a job in years or decades. Many of the younger people had never had a job, even if they had a high school diploma or technical education. People survive by means of what they call *grapyiaj*. *Grapiyaj* means "scrambling" and if you live by *grapiyaj*, you keep yourself alive by becoming involved in many small activities. You get help from different people, making wide use of all your family ties and connections, pooling tiny pieces of resources together to give you a whole, enough on which to survive. Those who have any type of work are called on to distribute their small earnings among a broad network of people.

The poor in Haitian cities readily tell of their hunger and the losses to their family from disease. Carmelite's story was commonplace. Her life was a litany of deaths, homelessness, malnutrition, and constant courageous efforts to survive in the face of high rents and inflated food prices. She had five children by different men. Each of these relationships was an effort to find assistance in supporting her children but three of the men had died. Carmelite, age thirty, lived with her children

in a small house that I leased and it is right on the street and it is a little lean-to,
I don't even have room for the children to sleep in. You can even say I don't have
beds for them. But I leased it so that I can find a place for me to sleep with them.
It costs 350 dollars every six months (U.S. $118/6 months).

Carmelite washed clothes by hand for other families as a way of earning
money for rent, food, and school tuition for her children.

Where do I find money? I wash people's clothes. I do it in this neighborhood.
And I iron them as well. I have so many that some times I can't even do it. Sometimes I can't. Every time I wash I make six or seven dollars (U.S. $2 or
$2.30/load). I buy water. I pay for a bucket of water 1 gourde (25 cents).

Her mother or her siblings could offer little help because none has steady
work. One brother who worked as an assistant in a bakery occasionally offered
bread to the family, but he also has the responsibility of his own three children
and the rest of his family. To get the occasional handouts of bread, Carmelite
had to travel across the city—a time- and energy-consuming process. Consequently, hunger was a constant problem for her and her children. "Take today,"
she told us "I didn't leave anything for the children (to eat). If today I'm lucky
I may find a spoonful of food for them to eat and tomorrow they may stay just
like that. They are malnourished."

We must point out that not everyone in Haiti faces economic difficult and
insecurity. There are three sectors who live well. First, there is a very small
group of families described by Haitians as "the bourgeoisie" or "the elite" who
live lives of luxury and who have gotten considerably richer as the general situation of the rest of the population has worsened. Composed of a few thousand families (less than 1 percent of the population), the Haitian bourgeoisie
controls more than 47 percent of the country's wealth (Ridgeway 1994:4). Although many of these families do own land, their major wealth continues to
be based on their control of the economic transactions between Haiti and the
rest of the world. They were the major Haitian beneficiaries when Haiti was
an important exporter of coffee and other tropical products. Today, they profit
from the production or importation of building materials, the importation of
food and used clothing, and factories that produce and export goods for international corporations. Their wealth is enhanced by the fact that they continue to pay little or no taxes and their enterprises often have not paid for electricity and telephone from state-owned utilities. Living in richly furnished
houses behind secure gates, guarded by armed private security guards when
they travel between home and office or to their private beaches, the members

of the Haitian bourgeoisie live lives of privilege and conspicuous consumption in the midst of the poverty and misery. While historically many members of this class were mulattoes, since the Duvalier era increasing numbers are black. Among these nouveaux riches are families who gained their fortune from government corruption, extortion, and/or drugs. In addition, there is a small sector of middle-class people who, after struggling to obtain an education, work as professionals for the government as well as for transnational corporations and organizations.

During the 1990s the international "lending community" led by the United States increased the pressure on loan-dependent countries to open their economies. They demanded that increasing numbers of countries accept a "structural adjustment package." In order to obtain new loans, necessary both to pay off old ones and to maintain the functioning of the government, the Haitian government was pressured to cut all government supports for prices, withdraw investments from public services, and privatize all government-owned industry.[9] As a result the price of food soared, increasing numbers of people were malnourished, and the level of care at the public hospitals became even worse.

To meet the needs of the people, the lending agencies and powerful "donor" nations supported the establishment and growth in Haiti of a myriad of "nongovernment" organizations. Many of these organizations were actually funded by and answerable to governments of states other than Haiti. Others were funded by philanthropic and religious organizations. While many provided some services, training programs, tree planting, literacy education, health care, or agricultural cooperatives, they worked with no common plan or purpose or reliable system of public services. Instead they contributed to the fracturing of society with pockets of people grouped around churches or programs benefitting while their neighbors suffered (Farmer 1992, 1994). It is likely that most often persons in the countryside who already had some assets and social standing had their social and economic position reinforced (Mathurin, Mathurin, and Zaugg 1989:114). The NGOs imported into the Haitian countryside groups of professionals from abroad or from Port-au-Prince, whose lifestyle demonstrated to rural people the existence of higher standards of living and a better way of life, often without offering them access to such a life (Smith 2001). Raising the aspirations of the Haitian poor, leading them to believe that at least all Haitians would be able "to live like human beings," the NGOing of Haiti has done very little to alleviate poverty and provide any economic development which benefits the Haitian poor.

Thirty years of globalization in Haiti has intensified the levels of poverty, malnutrition, and destroyed the previously precarious systems of health care and sanitation, producing spiraling morbidity and mortality rates. The statistic that the average Haitian life span is only 51.4 years is shaped by frequent deaths of women in childbirth, as well as the high infant mortality rate of almost one infant dying for every hundred born (U.S. CIA 1999). Morbidity and mortality rates linked to poverty in Haiti are not usually described as a form of violence. Yet a thoughtful perusal of the statistics makes it clear that Haiti is a kind of killing field where death is as certain for a percentage of the population as if people were being lined up and shot systematically. Even Haitian hospitals are places of dying rather than healing since public hospitals have no clean blood, syringes, sterilization equipment, or any of the lifesaving accoutrements of modern medicine. Or as a homeless young man in Port-au-Prince told us, "There are those who are sick, if they were to go to the general hospital, even though it is a public hospital, if you don't have money, you are already dead." Drug companies market their expired medicines in Haiti and the government does not invest in any monitoring of the purity or safety of drugs sold in Haiti. In the mid-1990s Pharval, a Haitian laboratory, used a toxic substance, diethylene glycol, in the manufacturing of medicinal syrups for children. This irresponsible act resulted in the deaths of eighty children. The European drug company that had sold the contaminated medicine to Haiti was not punished.

Unwilling to sit around and die from malnutrition, lack of health care, or criminal or political violence, Haitians have been fleeing Haiti any way they can. More than a million persons of Haitian descent now live abroad, as compared to the seven million who live in Haiti, with many thousands still continuing to flee with altered documents or by small un-seaworthy boats. Large-scale emigration began in the 1960s and continues, despite increasing barriers imposed by the countries of destination, which include the United States, Canada, France, the Bahamas, and the Dominican Republic. The barriers against migration have been raised, causing people to risk their lives in their attempts to leave Haiti, despite the fact that the powerful institutions that have shaped Haitian economic policy in the past thirty years have been aware that they have left the Haitian rural population with no means to survive. The London *Guardian* reported in 1996 that the World Bank was

> privately warning that Haitian peasants could be forced to emigrate to find jobs, in sharp contrast to the Bank's public endorsement of a "people first" development strategy. Ahead of the Banks's annual meeting in Washington in a fortnight's time, aid agencies said the disclosure would undermine attempts by the Bank to recast itself as a friend of the world's poor. A draft Bank strategy paper on Haiti, which has been obtained by the Guardian, says that two-thirds of the

country's workers based on the land are unlikely to survive the free-market measures imposed by the Bank. Even if strenuous efforts are made by international organizations to secure agricultural employment, the paper concludes: "The small volume of production and the environmental resource constraints will leave the rural population with only two possibilities: to work in the industrial or service sector, or to emigrate." Geoffrey Lamb, the World Bank representative in London, said "It is simply an analytical warning of the way the trends are going. It is not our intention that people should have to emigrate" (Thomas 1996).

A significant number of those who live in the industrial centers sustain families they left behind through a flow of remittances.[10] In so doing, they help to mask the actual degree of economic devastation wrought on Haiti by the extraction of debt payments, purchase of imported food and goods, and the provision of export-processing labor. No studies of violence seem to include the death cause by immigration laws that create borders. Yet we are seeing an increasing pattern of group suicide in the form of those fleeing to the United States by small boats. When people organize to kill themselves as they did in Jonestown or recently in Uganda by taking poison en masse, at least the media and world public opinion recognize the fact. However, when hundreds of people get into small boats made out of scraps of lumber, often with no provisions, no life rafts, and no instruments beyond an old compass and head for the United States, the world is witnessing a form of violent death, with almost no word of protest either about the death or the conditions that caused it. One such voyager put the situation succinctly "Some people get to America, and some people die. Me, I'll take either one. I'm just not taking Haiti any more" (Finkel 2000).

The flight away from Haiti in small boats began in the 1970s, during the regime of Jean-Claude Duvalier. In our efforts to understand the links between globalization and violence, several aspects of the initiation of these desperate voyages must be assessed. The Haitian "boat people" are often not the poorest of the poor, since a family often has to sell land or animals to obtain a boat passage for one of its members but families take such actions because they could no longer support themselves through cultivating the land and therefore invest in this high-risk strategy, hoping to obtain support from remittances. The U.S. Coast Guard routinely captures and sinks Haitian boats on the high seas and returns the passengers to Haiti. When U.S. immigration officials discover Haitians landing on Florida beaches, they are detained and returned to Haiti. Cubans arriving in similar fashion are heralded as heroes but Haitians are labeled economic rather than political refugees and refused entry into the United States. What U.S. officials do not say, when rejecting the Haitian asylum applications, is that the United States and Western Europe played a direct role in the destruction of the Haitian economy. U.S. development officials were explicit that the policies that they encouraged in Haiti would lead to the failure of the rural economy and a flight from the countryside that would put explosive pressure on the regime unless widespread migration was possible. They admitted in their projections that at first people uprooted from the countryside would not find sufficient need for employment in Port-au-Prince and would seek to migrate (DeWind and McKinney 1988). Thus one can definitely argue that continuing Haitian migration has political roots. These roots were linked to political and economic forces beyond the control of the Haitian people. The roots of the Haitian migration and the uncounted number of men, women, and children who have drowned attempting to escape Haiti have died as a direct outcome of the restructuring of the global economy. Their deaths can be linked to the United States, European Union, and "donor agencies" "development" policies on Haiti that have devastated the rural economy, and the United States and Fortress Europe's immigration laws that make no room for the refugees from these policies. The Haitian boat people who lost their lives on the high seas, desperate to flee the oppressive conditions in Haiti, are part of the accumulating death toll of globalization.

The "economic reform" touted by Peter Romero has also increased violence against women. Since the time of slavery, poor Haitian women have earned money by selling goods in the marketplace and this tradition continues today. Among families which cultivate the land, it is the women who take the crops to market. Women in families who can no longer live on the land and have moved to towns or Port-au-Prince support their families through selling something or other in the marketplace: cooked food, secondhand clothes, or small bits of produce from the countryside or abroad.

To the extent that the economy continues to deteriorate, increasing numbers of women must exchange their bodies to feed their families. In 1996 both women and men reported to us that women are pressured to exchange sex for both blue-collar and white-collar jobs, as well as access to goods for trading in the market place or for any assistance from Haitian officials. Of the forty-two women and men we asked, 71 percent acknowledged that requests for sex were commonly experienced by women looking for work. Impoverished men and women see the complexity of this practice.

A man whose wife sold goods in the marketplace to support herself, her husband, and her three children described the situation as follows:

Q: Is it easier for a man or a woman to find work?

A: It should have been easier for men to find work, because there are many things men can do that women can't do like manual work, to lift heavy things, to work in a factory lifting heavy things. But at the end, there are no jobs. So my wife is a *komèsant* (small trader) small, small. She sells material. She buys it in the store. She gets 25–30 gourdes a day (6 dollars) profit.

Q: Do they ask for sex when a woman goes for a job?

A: Yes.

Q: Does it happen all the time that she is obligated to sleep with him?

A: Yes.

On the one hand by exchanging sex for resources poor women diminish their social standing and reinforce the elite values that see a woman's virtue as the measure of the family's social standing.[11] On the other hand, because poor women can possibly exchange sex for work, or the contacts necessary to get goods to sell in the marketplace, education for their children, or other resources, poor women have greater means of surviving than poor men. Nonetheless, the sexual violation of women must be considered a daily, destructive form of violence.

In addition, there is also a rise of crime as poor, unemployed youths grow up in a Haiti in which they have no opportunities for education or employment. In the wake of the destruction of the Haitian rural economy and large-scale migration to Haiti's cities, Haiti's urban areas have become dangerous places. Urban unemployed youths who see no future for themselves in Port-au-Prince have increasingly become involved in assaults and robberies. Gangs have grown as well as desperate youths whose violence is for hire. A whole new Kreyòl word, *zangendo*, meaning "violent desperado" has developed. The attacks on members of the Haitian diaspora returning laden with gifts and money for family in Haiti are attributed to these displaced, often armed youths. To the extent that globalization of the economy is linked to the fracturing of Haitian social life, and the loss of hope for its youth, the current crime wave can be said to also be a product of globalization.[12] Globalization has bought a violence of desperation with the poor preying on those around them, turning their anger at the injustices they face into crime, as their hopes for political solutions are crushed. The level of violence is exacerbated by the new role Haiti has assumed in the global economy, a major transshipment point for the international drug trade.

"CONTROLLING" THE DRUG TRADE AND
THE IMPORTATION OF VIOLENCE

Haiti is not a country in which narcotic or mood-altering drugs have been used for recreational, religious, or medicinal purposes. The emergence of Haiti as a major drug transshipment point and the growth of drug-related violence has nothing to do with Haitian culture and everything to do with the "economic reforms" fostered by the "consultative group" of international donors chaired by the World Bank. In the wake of the destruction of Haitian rural agriculture and handcraft industries, both the rich and the poor have increased incentives to participate in the global drug trade. This transformation began under the military generals who took over Haiti in 1986, after the grassroots movement deposed the Duvalier dictatorship and Jean-Claude Duvalier fled to France in a U.S. military jet. Since that time, Haiti has become an important platform in the Caribbean for drugs, primarily cocaine, to enter the United States (Kerry 1994). The fact that the Haitian police force is very small, underpaid, and ill equipped, has made it difficult to monitor the transshipment of drugs from South America to the United States. Paid very little, this force has readily succumbed to the temptations of the drug trade as the only opportunities available in the Haitian economy. Although, in 1997, the Haitian government drafted a master plan and created a task force, the National Drug Council, to address the "drug problem" in Haiti, drugs continue to pass freely through Haiti. In 1999, for a population of seven million people, a mountainous area of 27,250 square kilometers, and very few passable roads, the Haitian government recruited only twenty-five new officers for its counternarcotics unit. According to the National Coalition for Haitian Rights (NCHR 1999:1) not even one of these officers was placed on active duty to intercept drugs and to arrest the drug smugglers. Sixty-seven metric tons of cocaine were shipped through to Haiti in 1999, a 24-percent increase over the 1998 estimates of fifty-four metric tons. Moreover, the U.S. Coast Guard estimates that 14 percent of the total amounts of drugs that entered the United States in 1999 passed through Haiti, as compared to 10 percent in 1998 (BINLEAR 2000). Former members of the Haitian military and Haitian police seem to be implicated (Kerry 1994).

The rise in the amount of drugs that transit through Haiti, the inability or unwillingness of the Haitian National Police Force to police the country, and corruption in all areas and at all levels in the government have increased the violence experienced by people in Haiti. Armed criminals associated with the increasing drug traffic have expanded their activities in Haiti where they operate with impunity. According to the *New York Times* (Gonzalez 2000), "American officials are worried that drug related corruption has penetrated the police force and even the government. The police inspector general was transferred to a diplomatic post when he investigated several police supervisors on suspicion of helping the drug smugglers."

There is some evidence that several senators of the Famille Lavalas, which is headed by President Jean-Bertrand Aristide, are also involved in the drug trade (Gonzalez 2000:3). There has been a marked disinterest in the judicial branch in prosecuting those caught in the drug trade. Moreover, Haiti has not voted any law to combat money laundering. Occasional arrests indicate that members of the Haitian diaspora also are involved, again giving some indication that we can't talk about violence in Haiti without talking about processes that link Haiti to other places in the world.

Major drug dealers flaunt their wealth in Haiti. Throughout the country, but especially in the capital city of Port-au-Prince, evidence of the riches drugs trafficking produce is evident. For example, in a suburb of the capital named Belvil, luxury home construction has boomed conspicuously in an otherwise desperately poor country. In Port-au-Prince luxurious sports utility vehicles are ubiquitous, new gas stations dot the area, and advertisements to wire money in $1,000 installments to Colombia are boldly displayed. When Haitian officials were pressed by the international community to request bank officials to report cash transactions of $10,000 or more, their demands were not acknowledged since Haiti has no laws against money laundering and no parliament to pass these laws (Gonzalez 2000:3). The proliferation of private banks in Port-au-Prince and in the important provincial towns in a country where unemployment has been estimated at 80 percent also offers evidence that those who are engaged in the drug trade are pursuing their activities with impunity. On the other hand, those who otherwise are unable to find employment in an economy that is near collapse are looking to the rewards that the drug trade can bring to them.

However, these incentives come with significant risks. The growth of the drug trade seems to have been accompanied by the increased presence of guns in Haiti. The proliferation of guns and the certainty that those who commit violence either against other drug dealers, the police, or innocent civilians will never be prosecuted are contributing to the sharp increase in violence experienced in Haiti during the past few years. Until recently, most guns were distributed by those in political authority to forces organized to terrorize the population or extort wealth. Today, political terror is supplemented by the gun play that accompanies drug dealing and drug dealing contributes to the growing numbers of armed youths who carry out their own criminal activity. Enticed by the possibility of benefitting from the drugs they seize and cynical about the possibility that drug dealers will actually be persecuted because of judicial and political corruption and inefficiency, Haitian police officers often take the law into their own hand when they apprehend drug smugglers. The drugs are seldom turned over to the authorities and the captured drug dealers are often killed on the spot, furthering the fear of criminal violence in the country. In turn, police engaged in drug dealing become victims of drug violence. In 1999, twenty police officers thought to be connected with the drug traffic were killed in Haiti.[13]

As the economic conditions of the country continue to deteriorate, drug-related violence has intensified. For example, on April 24, 1997, a turf war among rival gangs erupted in Site Solèy, one of Port-au-Prince's poorest and most notorious neighborhood. For more than two days, drug traffickers fought openly in the slum's streets. The police, fearing for their lives and safety, failed to intervene. According the April 27 edition of *Le Nouvellist*, the clash killed at least eighteen people and injured dozens more. Around a hundred houses were burned to the ground.

When the Haitian drug trade is discussed in international organizations or by agencies of the U.S. government the problem is seen as yet another reflection of the failure of government in Haiti (BINLEAR 2000). Drug-related violence becomes linked in the press coverage of Haiti with the general chaos and poverty that are portrayed as part of the Haitian morass (Gonzalez 2000).

The history of the growth of the trade, including its early links to Haitian generals closely tied to the U.S. government should make us question the efforts to see the Haitian drug trade and its concomitant violence as primarily a problem originating in Haiti. The U.S. military and government bears direct responsibility for fostering and protecting the actors who developed Haiti as a transshipment point for drugs and the laundering of drug money. The demand for drugs that fuels the trade is a product of U.S. drug laws that criminalize use and U.S. consumers, many of them wealthy, who provide an elastic demand for cocaine. The growth of drug money as a potent force in Haitian politics, the growth of drug trade as one of the few new sources of capital accumulation in Haiti and a growing source of employment for the poor and for the poorly paid police, must be linked to Haiti's position in the global economy where those who enforce free market policies allow few economic or political alternatives. In Haiti itself, we spoke to poor people who linked the rise in drug wealth to the United States. We were told for example, "there are Haitians who got money and became big guys. [Some] . . . sell drugs. They use Haiti as a platform of transition between other countries to send to the United States." However, most Haitians did not link the Haitian drug economy and the guns to the capitalist restructuring that continues to extract wealth from Haiti. Meanwhile, the drug trade in Haiti becomes yet another reason for direct intervention in Haitian affairs by U.S. institutions or global organizations such as the Bureau of International Narcotics and Law Enforcement all justified in the name of Haitian incompetence and corruption.

CONSOLIDATING DEMOCRACY

Central to the message that Peter Romero conveyed to his Haitian audience in Washington, D.C., was the need for Haiti to consolidate democracy. In the year 2000, Haitians were lectured about democracy by the United States, the European Union, the United Nations, and the Organization of American States (Bohning 2000). Democracy in Haiti is certainly under attack and the attacks are marked by escalated levels of political violence between competing political factions, as well as a campaign of destablization by the powerful forces who have been agitating for the restoration of a dictatorship. The particular reason for the year 2000 pronouncements about the Haitian failures at democracy were twofold: first, the delay of parliamentary elections that left the Haitian President, René Préval to rule by fiat for many months, and second, after elections were held in May 2000, representatives who, according to the constitution needed to face a runoff before they could be recognized as lawfully elected, were placed in office. In protest, the opposition boycotted the elections for president in November 2000. Aristide won this election, but only a small percentage of the Haitian electorate voted, and the opposition parties declared the elections invalid and refused to recognize Aristide's second term as president of Haiti.

The actions of the Préval government and the 2000 campaign by Aristide to become president provided ample evidence of the disdain for democratic processes on the part of Aristide and his political allies in a situation in which they had sufficient control over the formal electoral processes to demonstrate that they had a mandate from the majority of the people. However, in criticizing this situation, the leaders of the United States, the Organization of American States, as well as editorial comments in U.S. newspapers totally obscured the role of the United States and the consultative group of lenders in undermining democracy. They continued to support and protect the forces within Haiti that massacred many grassroots leaders from peasants to priests and fostered political violence. Even the evidence that documented the attacks on the democratic forces between 1991 and 1994 has been held by the United States and not turned over to the Haitian government so that those responsible for the antidemocratic coup of 1991 and the ensuing violence could be prosecuted (Maguire et al. 1996). Instead those responsible for murder and torture have been allowed to settle in the United States (Kumar 1998; Malone

1998). And certainly no connections were made between the current political chaos in Haiti and the domination of the Haitian economy by more powerful states and financial organizations that have worked globally to restructure the economy of Haiti and facilitate corporate profit. These connections can be made.

Beginning in the 1980s, the Reagan-Bush administration reluctantly adopted "prodemocracy policies as a means of relieving pressure for more radical change," and "inevitably sought only limited, top-down forms of democratic change that did not risk upsetting the traditional structures of power with which the United States has long been allied" (Thomas Carothers of the Reagan administration cited in Chomsky 1994a). In so doing, they reversed U.S. policy that had used foreign aid through programs such as USAID to legitimate the brutal Duvalier dictatorship, a regime that jailed, tortured, and murdered anyone it defined as the political opposition (Trouillot 1990; Heinl and Heinl 1978). The new calls for democracy in Haiti were closely linked to the free market, rather than to increased participation of the Haitian population in the political process. In the words of the USAID, the United States has supported "processes of democratic institutional reform that will further economic liberalization objectives" (Chomsky 1994a).

However, Haitians responded to the U.S. rhetoric of democracy with a transnational poor people's movement, rooted in the Haitian countryside but supported by Haitians abroad. The goals of the movement were not only to end the Duvalier dictatorship but also to make the state responsible to the people by providing employment, public services, and citizen rights. The United States did not welcome this movement that had managed to end a brutal well-armed regime with a wave of demonstrations and strikes of unarmed people. Instead, among the first steps the United States took in 1986 after Duvalier fled to France on a U.S. military jet was to train the Haitian military in "crowd control" using antipersonnel weapons. The new ruling junta received $2.8 million in military aid during its first year in office (Trouillot 1990:222). When the military juntas that replaced Duvalier took no action against those who were responsible for the Duvalier regime's murder and torture, leaders of the grassroots movement called for an uprooting (*dechoukaj*) of the former Duvalierists and powerful families who opposed any form of equitable economic development in the country (Farmer 1994). There were also attacks on former secret police and *vodou* priests who had worked with the regime. The U.S. government denounced these attacks while continuing to fund the Haitian military, which used violent force to block the demands of the grassroots movement for social and economic justice. Even as the United States and other powers interested in investment in Haiti called for elections and democracy, they supported and equipped the armed forces opposed to any form of elected government.

When elections were held in November 1987, soldiers and paramilitary thugs with ties to the army and the former Duvalier secret police (Makout) attacked people lined up to vote in elections for a president, and scores of people were murdered (Dupuy 1997; Wilentz 1989). This occurred even though the election would not have brought to power any candidate that represented the interests of the vast majority of the population. It should be noted that the United States continued to support and train the Haitian military throughout this period, despite the clear evidence of their vicious repression of a poor people's movement and their increasing involvement in the international drug trade.

In 1990, a number of prominent leaders of the grassroots movement became convinced that gaining control of the electoral process was the key to fundamental change in Haiti, including the elimination of political terror and structural violence (Dupuy 1997). They decided that to make Haiti broadly democratic they would have to participate in the formal electoral process and they rallied public opinion in support of voting for a leader who promised to implement an agenda for social justice. Jean-Bertrand Aristide, a leader of the grassroots movement was elected president in 1990 through a massive turnout, receiving 67.48 percent of the vote against a number of other candidates (Dupuy 1997:89). For ten months, after Aristide was inaugurated in 1991, political violence subsided. We must also note that in the face of threats of a military coup and with opposition from the political classes in Haiti, Aristide insinuated that he would defend his regime and enlarge his sphere of power by supporting acts of violence including "necklacing" (placing burning tires around persons seen as enemies and burning them alive).

In October 1991 Haitian generals, who admitted that they had close ties to the CIA, succeeded in a military coup that ousted Aristide and launched an all-out effort to repress the grassroots movement. At this point the data on violence in Haiti becomes voluminous because the crimes of the military regime have been documented by Amnesty International, as well as by organizations such as America's Watch (America's Watch and the National Coalition for Haitian Refugees 1993; Amnesty International 1996). In 1994 Amnesty International reported that "in recent months, hundreds of people have been extrajudicially executed by soldiers or their civilian adjuncts. Entire villages have been massacred. Increasingly, bodies have been mutilated to sow further terror" (1994:1).

Besides direct political repression from troops trained by the United States, death and disruption came from abroad in the form of an economic embargo, imposed upon Haiti by the Organization of American States and reluctantly supported by the United States in 1991 to punish the military regime. Although the embargo was officially aimed at the junta, it was clearly destructive of the fabric of Haitian society. In the course of this embargo, "the peasants, comprising 70 percent of the population and relying largely on subsistence agriculture, experienced great difficulty in farming due to the violent nature of military rule and the lack of available and affordable inputs. . . . In cities and towns, the employment situation deteriorated as well. An estimated 143,000 jobs were lost in the private sector (this figure includes the jobs lost in the assembly sector)" (Zaidi, cited in Maguire et al. 1996:54; see also Gibbons 1999:10–11). Those who lost their jobs found no other alternatives to support their families. Access to basic consumer foods became very restricted. "In just two months, from September to November 1991, the price of a pound of rice increased 22 percent . . . the price of a pound of corn 31 percent. In three years from September 1991 to September 1994 the Port-au-Prince prices of these staples would increase 137.4 percent and 184.6 percent respectively" (USAID 1994:12). During the embargo, malnutrition increased by 61 percent, babies were thirty times more likely to die during the first month of life than before the embargo, human rights violations increased significantly, access to health care became very restricted, and state-sponsored violence increased (Gibbons 1999). The embargo against basic foodstuffs was particularly punishing because of the previous decade of destruction of food production in the Haitian countryside. Meanwhile, there was no embargo imposed on goods needed by contractors using cheap Haitian labor to produce products for the U.S. military in export-processing factories owned by industrialists who supported the coup. Responding to complaints by U.S. businessmen, Bush lifted the embargo on U.S. products such as pesticides, which were allowed into the country (Chomsky 1994b). The *New York Times* called this "fine tuning" (Crossette 1992).

Despite rapes, murder, torture, jailings, and violent attacks on poor neighborhoods that were bases of support for Aristide, the junta was unable to eliminate the grassroots movement and establish the order needed for orderly investment. Finally, the U.S. government reversed course and after several years of trying to discredit Aristide, who had fled to the United States after the coup, organized an invasion to restore Aristide to office, backed by 20,000 U.S. troops. However, this was only after Aristide had made a series of pledges to support the institutions of the neoliberal global agenda: privatization of Haiti's public corporations, reduction in spending for social programs, policies that allow the importation of various basic foods from the United States from rice to chicken, and the lowering of tariff barriers against and the maintenance of very low wages (Dupuy 1997). He also pledged to leave office at the end of his elected term, even though through most of the time he had been in exile.

Upon his return from exile on November 15, 1994, Aristide promised in a speech broadcast on *Ayti Libere:* "*sekirite maten, sekirite, amidi, sekirite a swè, sekirite a gogo to cheri*" ("security in the morning, security at noon, security at night, security a gogo, my dear"). No such security and respect for human rights materialized. Since 1994, Haiti has experienced a resurgence in armed crimes. The context for this renewal and expansion of violence is the implementation of the neoliberal policies that have flooded Haiti with U.S. food and further decreased the incomes of Haitian farmers. The resultant ever-growing misery of the Haitian population has been accompanied by the growth of the drug trade.

The rivalry between various political interests vying for control of the state also has added to the violence. This is an old story in Haiti and other areas of the world in which control of the state is one of the only routes to wealth in the uneven playing field of big power and transnational corporate capitalism (Nicholls 1996; Thomas 1984; Trouillot 1990). However, violent political rivalries in Haiti continue to be reinvigorated and fueled by outside forces. The actions and pronouncements of the United States after the initial election of Aristide in 1991, during the coup that sent him into exile, and the funding and protection of various Duvalierist forces ever since seems to contain a message to both aspiring Haitian political leaders and the Haitian grassroots movement. The Haitian state is to be returned to Haitian "political classes" that had dominated it until the 1980s' political upsurge of the poor and disempowered. That is to say, Haiti would continue as a "prebendary state" in which the state itself and its mechanisms of taxation and its sources of foreign aid and loans provided wealth to whichever political forces could control it (Dupuy 1997:21–22; Thomas 1984).[14] The only difference from the past was that in the post–Cold War era with the new rhetoric of democracy, free markets, and free trade, the political classes would now have to compete for control using the electoral process. The term "political classes" is currently being used both by the Haitian elite and U.S. government officials to refer to the bourgeoisie and urban intellectuals, usually based in Haiti but transnational in their networks and connections. Such a term excludes from consideration the rural and urban poor who made up the core of the grassroots movement that brought Aristide and Préval to power.

As the political classes have turned to trying to control the Haitian electoral process, they have used the urban poor as a lever toward power, rather than as a democratic base. The result has been escalating violence. Using a populist stance and encouraging organizations of the poor, cynical and desperate such as *Lè Chimè* (the discontents), JPP (*Jan li Pase li Pase*–Whatever happens, happens), and JTT (*Jan li Tonbe, li Tonbe*–Whatever occurs, occurs), political leaders are using intimidation and, at times force, to eliminate their opposition. These leaders include Aristide who was reelected in 2000 in a election boycotted by the opposition and most of the Haitian population. Under the guise of grassroots empowerment, crowd violence is used as a mechanism to obtain power and to keep it. In the end, Aristide's poor people's movement has been transformed into a vehicle that delivers power to his party and affiliates rather than as a means to empower the people. The opposition is no different. They also resort to arming unemployed, desperate young men to carry out assassinations, robberies, rapes, and other forms of terror to discredit the government or deliver vengeance on people who oppose the traditional political classes.

In the current moment of disorder, bands of discontents carry out acts of vindication, venting their anger on whoever opposed their will. Typical was the storming of the baccalaureate exams in July 2000.[15] When some candidates were denied entry to the exams because state officials had not issued them entry cards to which they were entitled, they beat the individuals assigned to administer the exams and threw the exams in the street to prevent other candidates from taking them.

In the midst of the violence, poor people find they have no government to turn to. They had hoped that they would be able to call on the Haitian police, trained and armed by the United States and the United Nations, to protect them from violence in their neighborhoods. Unfortunately, the police have proven to be part of the problem. In 1996, during the period of our research, many people saw the new police force as a source of protection against both criminal and political violence. Leonard, a young man who was being supported by his mother, a live-in maid, and who lived with eight other people in a house in Port-au-Prince, expressed his faith in the police and in the democratically elected government. "There is the police force to give people security. . . . The role of the state is to provide security. [The police] are fighting on the streets to avoid public chaos." The Haitian police force was established after President Aristide disbanded the military that had played the role of a domestic police force.

However, by the year 2000 many people had learned that the police provided no protection either for the majority of the people or for their person and their property. Many of the police were former Haitian military men who, during their career, had a license to kill the poor. When these troops were converted into Haiti's police force, they supposedly had been reeducated. The new police were trained by a U.S. police training force led by a former New York City police chief, with the assistance of some Haitian American police officers. New York City has consistently been a location of police violence against poor persons of color with highly armed police not punished for apparently un-provoked killings of black people, including Haitians (e.g., *Online Newshour* 2001). Converted into a poorly paid and poorly equipped police force, the for-mer military-turned-police were not prepared to be able to respect the rights of poor people and to protect them from the desperate young criminals, the "*zenglendo*," violent youths, who are increasingly armed, who steal and kill with impunity. The police are also no match for the well-armed drug smug-glers nor the inducements of the profits and payoffs of the international drug trade. And the police response to the politically fomented violence of rival po-litical leaders has been to either stand back and allow political assassinations and political destabilization to proceed or to aim their guns at the poor.

According to Amnesty International, excessive use of force and beatings too often follow arrest in Haiti. During a visit they made to Haiti in Novem-ber 1999, AI delegates received several reports of ill treatments in detention centers. According to the organization, "prison overcrowding is fostering ten-sions between detainees and guards and has created conditions that constitute cruel, inhuman, and degrading treatments in some cases" (Amnesty Interna-tional 1999). In 1999 alone the civilian mission (MICIVIH) stationed in Haiti on behalf of the United Nations and the OAS reported sixty-six killings in-volving the police force. The MICIVIH reported that disappearances, sum-mary executions, and police killings were current occurrences and that they had reached an unprecedented peak during the year. In July, the bodies of eight young people, who had been in the custody of the police for crimes they had committed, were found in Titanyen—a notorious dumping ground used by Duvalier to dispose of the bodies of his enemies. One hundred and forty-five police officers were dismissed from the force between January and Octo-ber 1999 for their involvement for trading in narcotics and human rights vio-lations; only a handful of officers was brought to justice. Although enough proof exists that the Haitian police force is involved in the killing of civilians, the American government, through its embassy in Port-au-Prince, has refused to acknowledge the role of the police in those murders. As reported by the *Dallas Morning News* of September 28, 1999, U.S. Ambassador Timothy M. Carney declared: "The key is that there is no systematic violation of human rights [in Haiti]. What is encouraging is that when there are abuses they [the police] move to address them."

IDEOLOGIES OF CONTAINMENT

In the midst of the chaos, people of all classes have begun to demand order, without an analysis of who is actually responsible for the disorder. The de-mand for order can fuel popular support for dictatorship. We had already found nostalgia for the Duvalier years among members of all classes in our 1996 interviews. Unaware of the role of the United States, the European Union, and the "international lending community" in "globalizing" the Haitian economy so that it can better serve the needs of large corporations, the Haitian poor remember that prices were lower and food was more plentiful under the Duvaliers. The vision of a Haiti based on social and economic justice becomes difficult to sustain amidst hunger and daily insecurity. Increasingly, urban poor people living without police protection in neighborhoods where desperate youths attack them, rural people who find that their efforts at forming credit associations are attacked by bandits, the Haitian diaspora who can not visit and bring money and presents without fearing for their lives, the middle class that lives fearfully behind gates, and the rich who travel with armed guards and cell phones, all focus their political energies on calls for security.

This refrain was already apparent in our interviews with poor people in Port-au-Prince and Aux Cayes in 1996. We had expected them to talk about their poverty, their lack of employment, drinking water, and decent affordable housing. They did talk about these conditions, with many people pointing out that they had not yet eaten that day. What we did not anticipate was the constant discussion of violence.

Typical of the discussion of criminal violence was that of Lourdes, a nineteen-year-old woman in Port-au-Prince who lived in a household almost entirely supported by remittances. To describe this violence that affects both the direct victims and those who find they live in an atmosphere of fear, people use the term "insecurity." Lourdes told us, "Yes, I would like to go [to the United States] because life would be better for me abroad. Life is very expensive in Haiti and it is becoming more expensive day after day. In addition to that you have the atmosphere of insecurity. People are being killed."

This theme was taken up by a second young woman, working as a clerk and living without the support of remittances or family who could help her migrate. She was equally clear that both poverty and violence were fueling migration. "To have a better life, they have to go. In Haiti there is insecurity, the cost of living is high, and in addition, there are no jobs. Nothing at all." She continued to speak about the question of personal security throughout the interview, pointing out that even those with money or migrants who returned to Haiti with money had trouble surviving in Haiti because of the daily threat of violence.

> It makes it difficult for you to live here, [unless you have money]. Once you have some money, this is the best place to live. The only thing, don't come home late

because of the insecurity. . . . What I don't like is that some Haitians who live abroad, as soon as they come to Haiti, a *zanglendo* can kill that person. They shoot them so that is why many Haitians are afraid to return. Not too long ago, someone came from abroad and he didn't even reach his house and they killed him. That is ugly. . . . He came to meet with his family and they killed him. They [the *zanglendo*] did that to three more returning migrants. . . . The same day they returned to Haiti. That is why they [Haitians living abroad] are dejected and they don't want to return. Those of us who are here, we live with fear in our hearts. Because they [the *zanglendo*] can ask you to give whatever you are carrying on you. If you have jewelry or anything else, they will take it.

Since a large proportion of the Haitian population is sustained by remittances from family abroad, and the fact that money sent to relatives then fuels economic activity such as construction and a host of services that sustain an even larger sector of the population, the possibility that the insecurity of life and property in Haiti will reduce the links between Haiti and the diaspora is understood by many Haitians to be a tremendous threat to their ability to survive at all.

The general and growing sense of insecurity and the desire for a government that will provide security spans divisions of gender, age, and location. However, the young people were the ones who were most adamant. The atmosphere of violence had marked their childhood and turned their dreams into nightmares. Although they grew up in a country that was not at war they lived within the trauma of violence.

Security was a primary concern of young people who lived in the teeming metropolis of Port-au-Prince, swollen from several hundred thousand to more than a million in the past two decades. Seventeen-year-old Augustin, a young man with only a few years of schooling, lived in Port-au-Prince with his father's sister. She was squatting in a half-built house, while trying to support herself and her own two children by butchering animals and selling the meat in the marketplace. When asked if Haitians abroad could help Haiti, Augustin said "If I would travel abroad I would help Haiti by doing something about the security problems." When asked about what the current government of Haiti could do to improve the situation in Haiti, he began with the problem of security rather than with food or employment, saying, "What I would ask the government to do is to maintain security in the country. Too many people are being killed. Thieves are killing people every day and I would like the state to guarantee security."

A much more intense verbal response to the stress of daily insecurity came from Lourdes who was able to live in a decent house and attend the university because of money sent from the United States by her aunt. She told us,

I don't see any future for this country. It needs to be reformed. Drop a bomb and kill everybody in it. Just erase it from the face of the earth and bring another nation in it. That is what I see for the future of Haiti. I don't see anything for Haiti to make it a better country. I don't see how the change will occur. I don't see it.

Even members of the cohort of young men who are growing up uneducated, unemployed, and hungry in Port-au-Prince and who are being drawn into criminal activities as a means of survival echoed the need for security. Oswald, another seventeen-year-old, linked the daily hunger that he and his friends experienced to the temptation to steal.

Things have become harder. . . . In the past we used to eat without any problems. And nowadays, very often we stay without any food at all. But I have a lot of friends, I tell them, you should refrain from taking what is not yours. I always tell them, touch what is yours, don't touch what is not yours. I do that because if later, something goes wrong, they won't point fingers at me and say that I did it. I don't want people to say I did it.

Freedom from violence also was an important theme in people's dreams of a brighter future. For example, Monique, nineteen, who with three younger siblings was supported by a mother who sold goods in the market in Port-au-Prince told us, "I would like Haiti to be beautiful. Where there is work. Where there is security. And everybody is living well." Along similar lines Yvon, twenty, who had come to Port-au-Prince from the countryside the previous year to attend school while he was supported by his mother who sold cosmetics from a fixed place in the street, told us "The state should guarantee all citizens security, nurturing, education, all those things [are] the essence of the state."

In Aux Cayes, which is sometimes described as Haiti's third largest city but is more like a sleepy peaceful town of 65,000, far removed from the disorder of Port-au-Prince, we found similar reports of violence. Lucie, twenty-three, whose parents had migrated and sent money back to Haiti to build the house in which she lived and to pay for her education, explained her desire to leave Haiti in terms of the violence in the streets.

Day after day the country is breaking down, it is in bad shape. That is why most parents want to send for their children. They don't want their kids to grow in Haiti. Haiti is no good. There is no Haiti anymore. I tell my mother, constantly day after day, the country is getting worse. There is no security. You can't go out after 8:00 at night. You have to go to bed because they are shooting all night long. You can't live in this country.

This message was reinforced by many other young people. Brigitte, twenty-one, lived on money sent by family abroad in a neighborhood where new cement-block houses, brightly painted, gave physical testimony of the transnational connections between Haitian emigrants and those they left behind. However, in her eyes, she was surrounded by the possibility of violent death.

> In the past you used to see certain things but now you are seeing them every day, in front of your eyes. If the state helped, if they gave security, these things wouldn't happen. Sometimes you may be lying in your bed and they kill you. If the state provided security, those things would not happen. . . . As time moves on, I see that Haiti has no future, because Haiti is upside down.

Some of the increases in criminal attacks may well be due to the new deportation policies of the U.S. Immigration and Naturalization Service that has been shipping individuals with any type of criminal record including traffic infractions to Haiti. Among the deportees are people with experience in the drugs trade, gangs, and theft who suddenly find themselves in a country they may no longer know and without any means of support. In this sense, one can say that at least part of the rise in violence in Haiti is directly a product of transnational forces.

By 1999, violence and security had become one of the most important political issues in Haiti. On May 28, 1999, the Chamber of Commerce of Haiti, a political force that had backed the military coup against President Aristide, organized a demonstration against the government to protest against insecurity, political violence, anarchy, and recurrent delays in organizing parliamentary elections for the next legislature. These individuals had a stake in the elections, for without a parliament, Haiti stood to lose U.S. $500 million in loans and grants.

The demonstrators were attacked by supporters of Famille Lavalas on the grounds that the demonstrators were guilty of political repression, rape, and flagrant abuses of human rights under the military regime that had expelled Aristide from power in 1991. Immediately after the demonstration ended, the police carried out an operation in the Carrefour-Feuilles neighborhood, a stronghold of Aristide's partisans. They detained and executed eleven people in cold blood, whom the police claimed belonged to armed gangs and had fired on the police officers first. Jean Coles Rameau, the Port-au-Prince police commissioner, was placed under investigation in the death of these eleven detainees (United Nation 1999:7). He tried to flee to the Dominican republic and was subsequently apprehended.

Later on, on April 3, 2000, in the same atmosphere of tension and violence, Jean Dominique, a prominent journalist was murdered as he was entering his radio station, Radio Haiti Inter, to begin his daily programs. Because Dominique was the Haitian president's counselor, the crime was automatically blamed on the opposition. As a result, supporters of Aristide attacked the headquarters of the "*Espace de Concertation*," a coalition of opposition parties that had joined forces to better the chances of winning in the impending parliamentary and presidential elections. The crowd burned the building to the ground in full view of the police, who made no effort to intervene.

If the demands for security obscure the reasons for the insecurity, they also complement other ideologies that make it difficult for people to see and respond to the links between globalization and violence. Central to the decoupling of violence and globalization is the continuation of beliefs in national sovereignty, beliefs bolstered by the rhetoric of democracy currently sustained and funded by the powerful states and the international organizations they support.

To speak about this confusing situation of independent nation–states with little actual national sovereignty, we have developed the concept of the "apparent state." Apparent states are structures of government that have a distinctive set of institutions and political procedures but have little or no actual power to meet the needs of the population. Apparent states have all the fixings of a state. Haiti has its own political system of president, prime minister, legislature, voting citizenry, government ministries, and officials. It also has its own dominant classes that for two hundred years have presented their agendas as if they speak for the Haitian nation. However, in our view, a state can only be considered sovereign when it has the power to control its internal political affairs, its economic affairs, and its relationships with other states.

At the end of the Cold War, "world leaders" proclaimed that now finally the world was composed of sovereign nations, each free to pursue their own destiny through democratic means. The U.S. and Western European governments began to fund programs to promote "democratization." Widely disseminated by the media, nongovernmental organizations, and the United Nations, the rhetoric of democracy reached into the countryside of Haiti and encouraged even those who felt alienated from the structures of their government to assume that their state was a sovereign entity.

At the same time the image of a world composed of independent nation–states was being propagated, political leaders signed agreements such as the North American Free Trade Agreement (NAFTA) and the General Agreement on Trade and Tariffs (GATT). These trade treaties, together with international organizations such as the World Trade Organization (WTO), and regional organizations such as the European Union actually function to countermand the decisions made by democratically elected legislators. The

WTO, in particular, is poised to override legislation and the regulations passed by individual governments to control working conditions and protect the health and safety of the citizens of their states. The new international agreements augment the power and interests of international conglomerates and financiers who control large amounts of capital and who wish to reduce regulation of their activities and any barriers to the global flows of currency, material, and products.[16]

Our use of the term *apparent terms* signals our position that the governments of many countries today have almost no independent authority to make meaningful changes within their territorial borders. At first we were tempted to evoke the older language of colony and colonizing power to explain the relationship of Haiti and similar countries to the United States.[17] But there are several problems in applying the older language of imperialist power and colonization to the contemporary situation. In the first place, the government of Haiti is not a puppet government. The political leaders of Haiti are not directly controlled by United States. The U.S. government and other powerful "donors" can do little to insure that any Haitian government implements the U.S. agenda. This is why Haiti is seems to be a sovereign state. Even with U.S. troops on Haitian soil from 1995 to 1999, and despite the fact that foreign loans, principally from the United States, funded the day-to-day operations of the Haitian government, the Haitian governments of Aristide and Préval refused to march in the direction set by the United States. The donors can, however, through the use of military might, the use of subversion, or the direct withdrawal of funds used by apparent states to fund their daily operations, insure that these states do not adopt any alternative economic strategies or stop the extraction of wealth via debt payment, and cannot restrict the importation of goods or significantly raise wages.

There are, therefore, clear differences between a colony and an apparent state. Haiti is not a colony of the United States because the Haitian government can resist an imposed agenda and control enough force to repress and otherwise limit the actions of its own citizens. But the formal apparatus of government and the very real struggles for power that continue to take place within it do not tell the whole story. While the governments may be able to repress their citizens and curtail dissent, their political actions as well as all their financial activities are monitored and constrained from abroad to an extent that national leaders are left with no domain in which they can actually lead. The more powerful states and global lending institutions can insure that the Haitian government doesn't implement an alternative agenda. The result is that the government does little or nothing. As the citizens of Haiti discovered when they elected Aristide, if an empowered majority through democratic elections chooses a leader who does not please the "international community of lenders," that leader will find his government destabilized and is likely to be overthrown. Sovereignty is effectively a facade if Haiti leaders do not have the power to set their own course and respond to the needs and demands of the vast majority of their people. In Haiti, as in many other emigrant-sending states, the facade of sovereignty is currently being bolstered by a reconstitution of nationalist rhetoric in the form of long-distance nationalism. "Long distance nationalism is a claim to membership in a political community that stretches beyond the territorial borders of a homeland. It generates an emotional attachment that is strong enough to compel people to political action that ranges from displaying a home country flag to deciding to 'return' to fight and die in a land they may never have seen" (Fouron and Glick Schiller, 2001).[18] This ideology, currently being fostered by the elites of states such as Mexico, the Dominican Republic, Greece, Albania, Armenia, Eritrea, and Macedonia, as well as Haiti, portray the government of a nation as based in the historic birthplace of the nation. However, the national population of the state is defined not by coresidence in a common territory but as all those who share common history and descent. Haitian emigrants who sustain families in Haiti and the multitude of people dependent on remittances and expenditures of Haitian transmigrants lend support to Haitian long-distance nationalism and efforts by Haitian political leaders to define Haiti as a transnational nation–state. In 2001, when Georges Fouron spoke to a meeting of a Haitian church organization in Queens, and introduced the term *long-distance nationalism,* the members of the congregation welcomed the term as a useful description of their ideology of belonging.

In many instances, especially among the Haitian diaspora settled in the United States, long-distance nationalism, which sustains the vision of Haiti as a sovereign state, and an identification with the foreign policy objectives of the United States go hand in hand. Typical is this statement from the National Organization for the Advancement of Haitian Americans (NOAH):

> We strongly believe that if Haitian-Americans, Haitians and friends of Haiti work closely with US policy-makers, together we can successfully develop policies that will meet US objectives as well as bring peace and stability to Haiti. Haitian-Americans have been an untapped resource in the search for peace and economic development in Haiti. NOAH/HHF (National Organization of Haitian-Americans/Haitian Holiday Festival) could be a crucial link in the development of sound practical policies that can help to resolve Haiti's conflicts and assist US policy-makers in designing coherent and effective policies toward Haiti.

Therefore, we ask that you work with us as we bring together Haitians and friends of Haiti to Washington, DC, to begin the process of understanding US development policy toward Haiti. To this end, we propose that policies be revisited and modified in order to obtain better results and hopefully make a difference in the quality of life for Haitians during this decade. Our objective is to continue to assist Haiti in becoming less dependent and more self-sufficient through public-private partnerships. The State Department's involvement in such an event will show the Haitian-American community that the US is indeed actively seeking ways to assist Haiti in achieving sustainable development.

Yet even in this statement, supportive of the U.S. State Department, there is a fault line, a desire on the part of the Haitians within the United States to see a self-sufficient Haiti. The ideology of long-distance nationalism, even as it continues to foster illusions of Haitian sovereignty, also can foster movements that oppose globalization from above and contribute to global movements for social and economic justice. This is the case because underlying much of Haitian long-distance nationalism is a long-standing conception of the state's responsibility for the people. Some political theorists have assumed that when people experience the state as repressive or intrusive and when they evade contact with government officials, they don't see themselves as part of that state. However, our research in Haiti and with Haitian immigrants in the United States showed the situation to be more complex. Of the ninety-five people we asked about the state, 75 percent told us that the state should have responsibilities to the people, providing them with employment, education, health care, sanitation, and public safety. When we spoke to people about the Haitian nation, poor people equated their nationalism with a desire for social and economic justice and linked this egalitarian agenda with their demands that the state be responsible to the people.

CONCLUSION

In 1996, on radios throughout Haiti and in the United States, you could hear the plaintive melody of a song that had made it to the top of the popular music charts. Sung by the Fugees, the song was "Killing Me Softly," a rock ballad of unrequited love, originally sung by Roberta Flack. The Fugees was a musical group whose name honored Haitian refugees including the parents of two of the group members. The fact that it was this particular song taken from U.S. rock culture that brought Haitian musicians into the mainstream of U.S. popular music and made a U.S. rock song a favorite in Haiti could be interpreted as a triumph of the globalization. Those who take this stance see globalization as a liberating process in which cultures, removed from the limitations of borders and boundaries, yield a creative hybridity. However, once we acknowledge the death and destruction that results from the relentless penetration of capital liberated from all limitations or restrictions, then the lyrics "killing me softly" take on another meaning.

Since the arrival of Columbus on the island he named Hispaniola in 1492, the people of that land have experienced violence. The history of the country of Haiti, located on the western third of the island, is a case study of the long bloody relationship between the global development of capitalism and violence. Forged from a rebellion of slave and anticolonial rebellion against France, after more than three hundred years of European colonization, Haiti certainly experienced a violent birth. After it won its political independence in 1804, Haiti began to experience interference in its economy and politics by powerful imperialist states and transnational financial interests. This interference has been accompanied by structural, military, and political violence.

In the nineteenth century, an unabashed gunboat diplomacy justified the forays of powerful capitalist interests with the support of their governments into defensive and weak economies. In the era of neoliberalism, imperialist domination is no longer the order of the day. Instead of colonial domination and a world divided into empires, we seem to live in a brave new world of independent states connected to each other by a free market. In the twenty-first century, all states are challenged to open up to this flow of capital so that the lives of all their citizens will be improved. If instead of prosperity, misery accompanied by violence results, we are led to believe that the fault must lie in the corruption of a country's leaders or in the country's antidemocratic culture. People of impoverished states, according to this received wisdom, have no one to blame but themselves for the violence that is destroying them.

However, when we take an unflinching look at the results of the current capitalist restructuring, using Haiti as a case study, we see that the growing violence and the extraction of wealth from apparently independent states are an integral component of contemporary globalization. To benefit from their penetration into the various "independent" world economies, the transnational corporations need stability. While they prefer a stable political regime, their bottom line requirement is a stability of understanding. They need to insure that there is no challenge to the dominant explanation for poverty and misery that points the finger of responsibility at the people of each individual country and their leaders, rather than at the processes of global capitalist restructuring and the people reaping billions of dollars a year profit from this restructuring.[19] It is often the case, and this has certainly been true for Haiti, that the world's powerful states and financial institutions achieve a stability of understanding by destabilizing the apparent states that they penetrate.

In this chapter we dissected the globalization agenda promoted by the world's major power under the guise of promoting economic reform, consolidating democracy, and protecting societies from the onslaught of drugs. We demonstrated that this agenda can be directly linked to the direct and structural violence currently being experienced by the Haitian people. However, the links between violence and globalization are obscured by ideologies that portray states such as Haiti as sovereign states. This logic makes it possible to place the responsibility for the current political chaos, corruption, and disorder in Haiti primarily if not solely on the backs of the Haitian people and their leadership. Most of the people we spoke to did not see their problems as personal failure. They blamed either Haitian leaders or the Haitian people as a whole for the problems of Haiti. Not seeing that their state is only apparently sovereign, and noting the obvious corruption of their leaders, increasing numbers of people in Haiti are calling for a strong dictatorial state that will stop the violence.

A new global discourse about violence displaces anger about globalization with concerns for social peace at any price. In states that serve as the base for global corporate power such as the United States, antiviolence discourse can lead to demands or more policing, even in neighborhoods where police deliver yet another form of violence against poor and disempowered people. In a country such as Haiti, a public demand for the government to provide security can fuel public support for dictatorship. When people experience disorder and violence without an understanding of its root causes and when they become impatient with the delayed advance of economic progress and political stability, they can easily be persuaded that military rule or that a strong undemocratic government is preferable to democracy. As insecurity mounts in Haiti, people have begun to say we need a brutal leader who can impose the death penalty and control violence by violence.

While power to attend to the needs of the majority of the people has been stripped from the state apparatus in Haiti, strong militarized states linked to globally extended capitalist interests rest at the core of the globalization processes. Underneath the promised prosperity and freedom contemporary globalization is delivering death and destruction to poor people around the world. Friedman (1999:373) reminds us, for example, that underneath the debates about globalization lies

> the presence of American power and American willingness to use that power against those who would threaten the system of globalization from Iraq to North Korea. The hidden hand of the market will never work without a hidden

fist. McDonalds can not flourish without McDonnel Douglas, the designer of the US Air Force F-15. And the hidden fist that kept the world safe for Silicon Valley's technologies is called the U.S. Army, Navy, and Marine Corps.

There are, however, contradictions that underlie the contemporary period of violent globalization. The grassroots movement in Haiti that previously stood up to dictatorship was part of a global movement for social and economic justice that has not vanished but has been reborn. This movement has begun to put a face on contemporary globalization, identifying the role of the World Bank, the International Monetary Fund, the G7 nations, and the centrality of the U.S. military in sustaining a worldwide system of wealth expropriation and violence. To date, it has succeeded in forcing changes in rhetoric rather than in fundamental policy, so that in places like Haiti the World Bank now has reversed itself and speaks of the need for rural development and health care, although still supporting the privatization of public services (Malone 1998; Gibbons 1999). The struggle continues.

NOTES

1. A related literature outlines the global dialogues of race that effected the everyday forms of state formation throughout the world (Dikötter 1997; Gilroy 1993; Stepan 1991). We could draw examples from China, Latin America, and Europe that document subaltern discourses of blood and link those discourses to the conflation of race and nation made global in the nineteenth and early twentieth centuries.

2. At the time we were interested in the degree to which those who stood outside the ruling and elite circles accepted the view being popularized by Haitian leaders that Haiti was now a transnational nation–state so that persons who had migrated, settled abroad, and become U.S. citizens, remained Haitians. In our writings, we argued that one of the outcomes of globalization was a continuation of nationalist ideology in many emigrant-sending states but in the form of a reconstituted ideology of the nation that included emigrants as part of the national population (Basch, Glick Schiller, and Szanton Blanc 1994; Glick Schiller and Fouron 1991; Glick Schiller, Bash, and Blanc Szanton 1992; Fouron and Glick Schiller 1997).

3. An analysis of the frequency with which those Haitians we interviewed used the word *violence* to describe their daily life experiences revealed that while the word was not totally absent from their vocabulary, they used it rather sparingly. Either because they were careful not to antagonize those who were using violence against them or because this word had different connotations for them, we found that when they spoke about acts of violence used against them. They utilized euphemisms such as

ensekirite (insecurity), *gwo ponyèt* (belligerent), *ak banditis* (banditism), *atanta* (attempts at people's lives), and *krim* (crime).

4. Speech delivered on July, 13, 2000, at Georgetown University to the National Organization for the Advancement of Haitians. www.haitionline.com/2000/713.htm.

5. Meanwhile USAID described the decline of Haitian agriculture as if this outcome was inevitable and natural, stating "agriculture slowly and inexorably deteriorated" (1986:5).

6. On September 22, 1980, while Duvalier and his U.S. allies were celebrating the twenty-third anniversary of the regime, 116 Haitian men, women, and children who could endure no more poverty and state-sponsored violence and oppression crowded a rickety boat and set sail for Miami. Near Cuba, the boat began to take on water and the boat captain decided to land on a deserted island called Cayo Lobos. Abandoned by the captain, who managed to flee with the derelict boat, the passengers were left without food, water, or the means to reach a more hospitable land. When the Bahamian government, under its jurisdiction, twice notified the Haitian government of the plight of its citizens, Haiti remained unmoved and unconcerned. Frustrated and enraged by the callousness of the Haitian government, the Bahamian government finally captured the Haitians, returned them to Haiti, and forced the Haitian government to take them back. Upon their return, some of the refugees were interviewed and they revealed that although they had jobs, they were not earning enough to support their families. As workers in the U.S.–owned factories, they were making a mere $1.50 a day, from which their employers often deducted the cost of miserable meals. The Cayo Lobos incident brought together the elements of an immoral and iniquitous exploitative equation, to wit, the Haitian repressive system, the rapaciousness of the U.S. corporations operating in Haiti, the U.S. immigration laws, and the threat of death that they face on that island (Abbott 1988).

7. While some degree of fiscal reform after the return of Aristide meant that in 1995 tax revenues were almost three times higher than in 1994 and represented more that 5 percent of the gross domestic product, more than this was needed to service the debt. "Interest payments on the domestic and external public debts represented 6% of current expenditure" (Economic Commission for Latin America and the Caribbean United Nations 1996:227).

8. The USCIA (2000) estimated that in 1999 the unemployment rate was 70 percent and that "more than two-thirds of the labor force do not have formal jobs."

9. As of 2001, the struggle over the state-owned phone company and electric company continued. With no program of investment or modernization, the state-owned phone company has almost stopped working and is being replaced by private phone companies that use satellite technology and cell phones. USAID and the World Bank "employed a private PR firm to run a U.S. $900,000 campaign to convince Haitians of the benefits of privitization" (*Ecologist* 1996:2)

10. Estimates of the size of remittances vary greatly. In 1999 a *Washington Post* story stated that "Haiti's economy has been helped by the estimated U.S. $600 million a year that Haitians outside the country send to relatives" (Kovalkeski 1999:A16).

11. See Karen Brown's (1991) account of "Mama Lola's" life history for a description of the circumstances that compel this kind of exchange. See Glick Schiller and Fouron (2001) for a description of the status system in which poor women who are economically independent are seen as sexually accessible and therefore have low status.

12. This is not to deny that Haiti has a long history of political violence, which we will discuss below. However, today political violence extends beyond those targeted as enemies of the regime. It is a violence of destabilization whose targets are random; vying politicians struggling for power encourage robberies and murders or have no interest in preventing them.

13. See www.amnesty.org/ailib/aipub/2000/AMR/23600100.htm.

14. Dupuy argues that between 1986 and 1988 the World Bank and USAID "wanted to create a modern state in Haiti that would respond to the interests of capital and, simultaneously, devise and implement policies that would facilitate the accumulation of capital and open Haiti to foreign trade and competition" (1997:22). However, we feel that the political messages and actions of these forces countermanded any policies designed to reform the Haitian state.

15. Official exams that take place during the last two years of high school.

16. For an example of the limitations on national sovereignty that arise from international banking projects within various states see Johnston and Turner (1999). Girón and Correa (1999) have provided a useful discussion of the implications of financial deregulation that "has made it gradually impossible for nation–states to control their money supply or credit."

17. For an alternative approach to the one advocated here that uses the concept of "coloniality" proposed by Peruvian sociologist Anibal Quijano to describe the

current position of formerly colonized states and their migrant populations, see Grosfoguel and Georgas (2000) and Quijano and Wallerstein (1992)

18. In this definition we have built on but expanded Anderson's use of the term (1993; 1994). We develop our concept of long-distance nationalism in our book *George Woke Up Laughing: Long Distance Nationalism and the Apparent State.*

19. See, for example, a description of the current political understanding of Africa's problems detailed in the story "As Hopes Wither, More Africans Turn on Leaders" (Swarns 2001).

REFERENCES

Abbott, Elizabeth. 1983. *Haiti: An Insider's History of the Rise and Fall of the Duvaliers.* New York: Touchstone.

America's Watch and the National Coalition for Haitian Refugees. 1993. *Silencing A People: The Destruction of Civil Society in Haiti.* New York: Human Rights Watch.

Amnesty International. 1994. *Haiti: On the Horns of a Dilemma: Military Repression or Foreign Invasion?* AMR 36/33/94. www.amnesty.org/ailib/aipub/1994/AMR/363394.AMR.txt.

———. 1996. *Haiti: A Question of Justice.* Amnesty International Report AMR 36/1/96, January. www.amnesty.org/ailib/aipub/1006/AMR/236000196.htm.

———. 1999. www.amnesty-usa.org/news/1999/23600799.htm, November 2.

Anderson, Benedict. 1993. "The New World Disorder." *New Left Review* 193 (May/June): 2–13.

———. 1994. "Exodus." *Critical Inquiry* 20 (winter): 314–327.

Aristide, Jean-Bertrand. 1994. Speech broadcast on *Ayti Libere*, November 15 (tape recording in files of Georges Fouron).

Basch, Linda, Nina Glick Schiller, and Cristina Szanton Blanc. 1994. *Nations Unbound: Transnational Projects, Postcolonial Predicaments, and Deterritorialized Nation–States.* Amsterdam: Gordon and Breach.

Bauduy, Jennifer. 1999. "U.S. Troops Pack Up, Haiti Questions Invasion Worth." Reuters, printed in nozier@tradewind.net.

Bellegarde Smith, Patrick. 1990. *Haiti: The Breached Citadel.* Boulder, Colo.: Westview.

BINLEAR (Bureau of International Narcotics and Law Enforcement Affairs). 2000. *Haiti on the Edge.* Washington, D.C.: International Narcotics Control Strategy Report (March).

Blaut, James. 1992. *The Debate on Colonialism, Eurocentrism, and History.* Trenton, N.J.: Africa World Press.

Bohning, Don. 2000. "OAS Official to Visit Haiti for a Dialogue on Elections, Recognition of Vote at Stake." *Miami Herald,* Thursday, September 21.

Brecher, Jeremy, and Tim Costello. 1994. *Global Village or Global Pillage: Economic Reconstruction from the Bottom Up.* Boston: South End Press.

Brown, Karen. 1991. *Mama Lola: A Vodou Priestess.* Berkeley: University of California Press.

Charles, Carolle. 1995. "Gender and Politics in Contemporary Haiti: The Duvalierist State, Transnationalism, and the Emergence of a New Feminism (1980–1990)." *Feminist Studies* 21, no. 1:8.

Chasin, Barbara. 1998. *Inequality and Violence in the United States: Casualties of Capitalism.* New York: Humanity Books.

Chomsky, Noam. 1994a. "Democracy Enhancement, Part II: The Case of Haiti." *Z Magazine,* July/August, zena.secureform.com/znet/zmny/zmay.cfm.

———. 1994b. "Introduction." In *The Use of Haiti,* by Paul Farmer. Monroe, Maine: Common Courage.

Crossette, Barbara. 1992. *New York Times,* May 28.

DeWind, Josh, and David McKinney. 1988. *Aiding Migration: The Impact of International Development Assistance on Haiti.* Boulder, Colo.: Westview.

Dikötter, Frank, ed. 1997. *The Construction of Racial Identities in China and Japan: Historical and Contemporary Perspectives.* Honolulu: University of Hawaii Press.

Dikötter, Frank, and Alex Dupuy. 1989. *Haiti in the World Economy: Class, Race, and Underdevelopment since 1700.* Boulder, Colo.: Westview.

———. 1997. *Haiti in the New World Order: The Limits of the Democratic Revolution.* Boulder, Colo.: Westview.

Dupuy, A. 1997. *Haiti in the New World Order: The Limits of the Democratic Revolution.* Boulder, Colo.: Westview.

Ecologist. 1996. "The Ecologist Campaigns and Updates." *Ecologist* 26, no. 2:1–2.

Economic Commission for Latin America and the Caribbean United Nations. 1996. "Economic Survey of Latin America and the Caribbean, 1995–1996." Santiago, Chile: United Nations.

Farmer, Paul. 1992. *AIDS and Accusation: Haiti and the Geography of Blame.* Berkeley: University of California Press.

———. 1994. *The Uses of Haiti.* Monroe, Maine: Common Courage Press.

Featherstone, Mike, Scott Lash, and Roland Robertson. 1995. *Global Modernities.* London: Sage.

Federal Research Division of the Library of Congress. 1989. *Haiti.* Area Handbooks Division. Department of the Army. lcweb2.loc.gov/cgibin/query/r?frd/cstdy@field(DOCID+ht0001), December.

Finkel, Michael. 2000. "America, or Death: At Sea With 44 Haitians Willing to Get Here at Any Cost." *New York Times Magazine,* June 18, 48–53, 66–67, 82–83, 94, and 99.

Fouron, Georges, and Nina Glick Schiller. 1997. "Haitian Identities at the Juncture Between Diaspora and Homeland." In *Caribbean Circuits: New Directions in the Study of Caribbean Migration.* Edited by Patricia Pessar. Staten Island, N.Y.: Center for Migration Studies.

———. 2001. "All in the Family: Gender, Transnational Migration, and the Nation–State." *Identities: Global Studies in Culture and Power* 7, no. 4:539–582.

Foweraker, Joe. 1995. *Theorizing Social Movements.* London: Pluto.

Friedman, Thomas. 1999. *The Lexus and the Olive Tree: Understanding Globalization.* New York: Farrar, Strauss, and Giroux.

Gibbons, Elizabeth. 1999. *Sanctions in Haiti: Human Rights and Democracy under Attack.* Westport, Conn.: Praeger.

Gilroy, Paul. 1991. *"There Ain't No Black in the Union Jack": The Cultural Politics of Race and Nation.* Chicago: University of Chicago Press.

———. 1993. *The Black Atlantic: Modernity and Double Consciousness.* Cambridge, Mass.: Harvard University Press.

Girón, Alicia, and Eugenia Correa. 1999. "Global Financial Markets: Financial Deregulation and Crisis." *International Social Science Journal* 160 (June): 183–94.

Glick Schiller, Nina, and Georges Fouron. 1991. "'Everywhere We Go We Are in Danger': Ti Manno and the Emergence of a Haitian Transnational Identity." *American Ethnologist* 17, no. 2:329–47.

———. 1998. "Transnational Lives and National Identities: The Identity Politics of Haitian Immigrants." In *Transnationalism from Below*. Edited by Michael Peter Smith and Luis Guarnizo, 130–61. New Brunswick, N.J.: Transaction Press.

———. 1999. "Terrains of Blood and Nation: Haitian Transnational Social Fields." *Ethnic and Racial Studies* 22, no. 2:340–66.

———. 2001. *Georges Woke Up Laughing: Long Distance Nationalism and the Search for Home*. Durham, N.C.: Duke University Press.

Glick Schiller, Nina, Linda Basch, and Cristina Szanton Blanc, eds. 1992. *Towards a Transnational Perspective on Migration: Race, Class, Ethnicity and Nationalism Reconsidered*. New York: New York Academy of Sciences.

Gonzalez, David. 2000. "Drug Runners are Finding the Going Easy in Haiti." *New York Times*, July 30, p. 3.

Grahm, Pamela. 1996. "Nationality and Political Participation in the Transnational Context of Dominican Migration." In *Caribbean Circuits: Transnational Approaches to Migration*. Edited by Patricia Pessar, 91–126. Staten Island, N.Y.: Center for Migration Studies.

Grosfoguel, Ramon, and Cloe Georgas. 2000. "'Coloniality of Power' and Racial Dynamics: Notes Towards a Reinterpretation of Latino Caribbeans in New York City." *Identities: Global Studies in Culture and Power* 7, no. 1:85–125

Guarnizo, Luis Eduardo. 1997. "The Emergence of a Transnational Social Formation and the Mirage of Return Migration among Dominican Transmigrants" *Identities: Global Studies in Culture and Power* 4, no. 2: 281–322.

Haiti News Summary. 2000. "Haiti News Summary." July 14. HaitiNewsSummary@aol.com.

Hall, Catherine. 1992. *White, Male, and Middle Class: Explorations in Feminism and History*. New York: Routledge.

Hancock, Grahm. 1989. *Lords of Poverty: The Power, Prestige, and Corruption of the International Aid Business*. New York: Atlantic Monthly Press.

Heinl, Robert Debs, and Nancy Gordon Heinl. 1978. *Written in Blood: The Story of the Haitian People, 1492–1971*. Boston: Houghton Mifflin.

Johnston, Barbara, and Terrence Turner. 1999. "The American Anthropological Association, The World Bank Group, and ENDESA S.A.: Violations of Human Rights in the Pangue and Ralco Dam Projects on the Bío Bío River, Chile." *Identities, Global Studies in Culture and Power* 6, no. 2–3:387–434. Special issue, "Ethnographic Presence: Environmentalism, Indigenous Rights, and Transnational Cultural Critique." Edited by Peter Brosius.

Kerry, U.S. Senator John. 1994. "Drugs and the Haitian Military." In *Decoding the Crisis*. Edited by James Ridgeway. Washington, D.C.: Essential Books/Azul Edition.

Kovalkeski, Serge. 1999. "Haiti's Dual Economy Lets Most Scrape By: Offically Jobless, 70% of Workers Must Improvise." *Washington Post* Foreign Service, Monday, October 4, A16. From nozier@tradewind.net.

Kumar, Chetan. 1998. Building Peace in Haiti. International Peace Academy. Occasional Paper Series. Boulder, Colo.: Rienner.

Lebovics, Herman. 1992. *"True France": The Wars over Cultural Identity, 1900–1945*. Ithaca, N.Y.: Cornell University Press.

Le Nouvellist. 1997. "Rival Gangs in Site Soley" April 24:1.

Maguire, Robert, Edwige Balutansky, Jacques Fomerand, Larry Minear, William G. O'Neill, Thomas Weiss, and Sarah Zaidi. 1996. "Haiti Held Hostage: International Response to the Quest for Nationhood, 1986–1996." Thomas J. Watson Jr. Institute for International Studies and the United Nations University. Occasional Paper no. 23. Providence, R.I.: Brown University.

Malone, David M. 1998. *Decision Making in the UN Security Council: The Case of Haiti*. Oxford, U.K.: Clarendon.

Mathurin, Allette, Ernst Mathurin, and Bernard Zaugg. 1989. *Implantation et impact des Organisations non gouvernementales: Context général et étude de cas (Haiti)*. Genève: Société Haïtiano-Suisse d'Edition.

Mittleman, James. 1996a. "The Dynamics of Globalization." In *Globalization: Critical Reflections*. Edited by James Mittleman. Boulder, Colo.: Lynn Reinner.

National Organization of Haitian Americans. 2000. "Schedule for Haitian American Summit." Washington D.C., September.

NCHR (National Coalition for Haitian Rights). 1999. *Haiti on the Edge.* www.Nchr.org/hrp/INLEHaiti99.htm.

Nicholls, David. 1996. *From Dessalines to Duvalier: Race, Colour, and National Independence in Haiti.* Rev. ed. New Brunswick. N.J.: Rutgers University Press.

Online Newshour. 2001. "Police Shootings." ww.pbs.org/newshour/bb/law/ jan-fune01/police_shootings/timeline2.htm.

Plummer, Brenda. 1988. *Haiti and the Great Powers 1902–1915.* Baton Rouge: Louisiana State University Press.

Poppen, Cinny, and Scott Wright, eds. 1994. *Beyond the Mountains, More Mountains: Haiti Faces the Future.* Washington, D.C.: EPICA.

Quijano, Anibal, and Immanuel Wallerstein. 1992. "Americanity as a Concept, or the Americas in the Modern World System." *International Journal of Social Sciences* 134:583–91.

Rafael, Vincente. 1995. *Discrepant Histories: Translocal Essays on Filipino Cultures.* Philadelphia: Temple University Press.

Ridgeway, James. 1994. "Introduction." In *The Haiti Files: Decoding the Crisis.* Edited by James Ridgeway, 3–4 . Washington, D.C.: Essential Books.

Sassen, Sakia. 1998. *Globalization and its Discontents: Selected Essays.* New York: New Press.

Schaeffer, Robert. 1997. *Understanding Globalization: The Social Consequences of Political, Economic, and Environmental Change.* Lanham, Md.: Rowman & Littlefield.

Scott, James. 1985. *Weapons of the Weak: Everyday Forms of Peasant Resistance.* New Haven, Conn.: Yale University Press.

Smith, Jennie Marcelle. 2001. *When the Hands are Many: Community Organization and Social Change in Rural Haiti.* Ithaca, N.Y.: Cornell University Press.

Smith, Robert. 1998. "Transnational Localities: Community, Technology, and the Politics of Membership within the Context of Mexico-U.S. Migration." In *Transnationalism from Below.* Edited by Michael Peter Smith and Luis Guarnizo, 196–240. New Brunswick, N.J.: Rutgers University Press.

Stepan, Nancy Leys. 1991. *"The Hour of Eugenics": Race, Gender, and Nation in Latin America.* Ithaca, N.Y.: Cornell University Press.

Stoler, Anne. 1989. "Making Empire Respectable: The Politics of Race and Sexual Morality in the 20th Century Colonial Vultures." *American Ethnologist* 16, no. 4:634–60.

Swarns, Rachel. 2001. "As Hopes Wither, Africans Turn on Leaders." *New York Times*, Sunday, February 25, A1, 6.

Thomas, Clive. 1984. *The Rise of the Authoritarian State in Peripheral Societies*. New York: Monthly Review.

Thomas, Richard. 1996. "Bankers Forcing Migration." *Guardian* (London), Monday September 16, from haitisupport@gn.apc.org.

Trouillot, Michel-Rolph. 1990. *Haiti: State against Nation: The Origins and Legacy of Duvalierism*. New York: Monthly Review Press.

United Nations. 1999. "Situation of Human Rights in Haiti." *General Assembly Report*. New York: United Nations.

USAID (United States Agency for International Development). 1986. "Project Paper, Haiti: Export and Investment Promotion." Project Number 521-0186.

———. 1994. *Monitoring Report* 3, no. 12 (October).

USCIA (United States Central Intelligence Agency). 2000. *The World Factbook 2000*–Haiti. www.cia.gov/cia/publications/facbook/geos/ha.html.

United States State Department. 1998. "Background Notes: Haiti, March 1998." Bureau of Inter-American Affairs. http://www.state.gov/www/background_notes/haiti_0398_bgn.html.

Wilentz, Amy. 1990. *The Rainy Season: Haiti Since Duvalier*. New York: Simon & Schuster.

9

Sorcery and the Shapes of Globalization Disjunctions and Continuities

The Case of Sri Lanka

BRUCE KAPFERER

Sorcery and witchcraft have reemerged as important phenomena of anthropological interest. The main reason is that in many parts of the world very contemporary crises having to do with the forces of globalization and the collapse of modernist projects are refracted through discourses of sorcery and witchcraft. Anthropologists and historians have conventionally demonstrated such functional reasons underlying sorcery and witchcraft practice. It is never merely fantastic or mystical but images the conflicts and tensions that are ever present in political and social worlds. They symbolize the personal terrors born of such realities and in various ways symbolically express the changing structures of practice and violence of daily life. The "logic of witchcraft" as Gluckman (1956) explained following Evans-Pritchard is in the capacities of sorcery and witchcraft to realize in personal experience the shape of larger structural processes.[1] They can maintain a continuing relevance to ever-changing historical contexts because they have "a genius for making the language of intimate, interpersonal affect speak of more abstract social forces" (Comaroff and Comaroff 1999:286). In this view sorcery and witchcraft are enduringly modern and are not to be conceived as atavistic survivals. They are the fabulations of contemporaneity. If the figurations of the sorcerer and the witch are absurd distortions they are so as mirrors of the absurdities, irrationalities, and wildness of lived realities, of the "logic" of the real in its apparent rationality and irrationality. Such aspects are likely to be at a height at key transitional moments, at periods of chiasmus or crisis or rupture, which is how many characterize the local effects of globalization on populations worldwide.

If sorcery and witchcraft have been reinvented as foci of everyday concern in many cultural realities affected by current globalization, so have well-tried anthropological perspectives. Once again sorcery and witchcraft are barometers of social change and conflict as, too, is their imagination integral to the restructuring of social realities, often in innovative directions. The very imaginaries of sorcery and witchcraft and their functional equivalents in numerous other kinds of occultic practice worldwide, as Comaroff and Comaroff (1999) show, are often driven in that human concern to comprehend that which refuses common sense or escapes personal reason yet in such practices is domesticated or tamed to such reason. That old wine is being poured into new bottles is not to be disparaged, it is matured and mellow after all. But the claim is strong that the current revitalization of anthropological interest in sorcery and witchcraft is radically different from earlier approaches even if it does repeat them in salient ways. This is so because the phenomena are grounded in distinct empirical circumstances (a view that is assimilable to earlier approaches) and, more importantly, because the analytical terms are different. Previous perspectives were driven in a modernist anthropological project, one that overprivileged order and coherence, was too emphatic on a rationality/ irrationality opposition and was too committed to constrain such avowedly mysterious and volatile forces to the powers of reason. Moreover, such perspectives in their bid to de-exoticize witchcraft phenomena, as, for example, did Gluckman (1956), somehow shored up an anthropological primitivism as well as, paradoxically, refusing to address the nature of the phenomena in their existential fullness. In other words, sorcery and witchcraft were sustained as prerational survivals in their rationalist unmasking and not seen through and through as the creations of modernity and, in fact, discontinuous from previous cultural formations even if they apparently took their shape.

Such argument is promoted in post-structuralist, postmodernist, and post-colonial discourse in anthropological circles that is itself often, and inescapably so, a product of the globalizing processes upon which it comments.

The general point that I am making is that important approaches to the phenomena of sorcery and witchcraft have not necessarily removed themselves from what are conceived of as the limitations of prior perspectives. Their dissolution into the general rubric of the occult, for example, both sustains as it expands a view of the irrationality of sorcery and witchcraft in the terms of a logical-positivist social science and destroys local specificity and, yes, potentially significant difference.[2] The terms *sorcery* and *witchcraft* are difficult because of their use in discourses of dominance and, too, because of the attachment of a Victorian mysticism to them—one that owes much to the scientific and secular rationalism of the time. Geschiere's (1997) sensitive and locally contexted discussion of modern sorcery in the Cameroons has an air of a rationalistically born mysticism about it. This, indeed, could be the product of the modernity of which Geschiere writes, especially as he concentrates on elites, but this is not sufficiently historically grasped. He stresses the importance of addressing the nature of the extraordinary forces and powers in sorcery that excite participants but goes no further than reporting a personal sense of the uncanny.[3]

Sorcery and witchcraft are still trapped in mainly an externalist and still largely Western-dominant, rationalist conception of them. It may well be that the practices of what are described as sorcery and witchcraft are infused with a rationality and its obverse mystical side born of modernizing processes occasioned in colonial and postcolonial processes. What was once held as external is now internal (the different is now the same), a powerful implication in some contemporary analyses, but this requires demonstration rather than assertion.

The insistence that modern practices of sorcery and witchcraft are thoroughly modern "discontents" does not necessitate their discontinuity or radical disjunction with "past" or "traditional" practices. This seems to be the argument of some contemporary perspectives (almost an ideological insistence). Of course, the terms *sorcery* and *witchcraft* gloss a great diversity of practices and it might be expected that some relatively old practices might coexist with totally innovative ones. Because they have been reproduced through time does not mean that they are any less modern than the completely new or innovative ones. Not only does this type of implication (modernity as disjunctive) ingrain most of the difficulties of earlier anthropological antimonies (tradition versus modern) but it can miss the possibility of specific features of the dynamics of sorcery and witchcraft practices that motivate their reinvention. It is a dimension of their structure of practice as well as the general projects of such practice that are integral to their reproduction and also change through historical time. What I am saying is that there may be continuities, as well as discontinuities, in the formations of sorcery and witchcraft practices and that the continuities are central to their very modern force. This does not mean that the practices are static or unchanging or that the populations that engage in them are bound to an essential irrationalism, a view, incidentally, that is far from avoided by more recent approaches to these phenomena.

An investigation of the continuity and discontinuity of sorcery and witchcraft practices involves a greater attention to historical forces than I think is the case where they are understood as epiphenomena or as merely reflective of sociohistorical processes at base. Sorcery and witchcraft are integral within historical dynamics and not merely as their expression or reflection. Latter kinds of interpretation usually involve culture and society distinctions, with society being active and culture almost a secondary and often passive remainder, a mere product. Thus in a variety of approaches, sorcery and witchcraft are simply the ageless terms of the irrational or, in slightly less generalist terms, the personal reflexive expression of the abstract: a logic of causation that fetishistically grasps general processes in personal terms and in languages of individual victimhood and scapegoating. These are treated as almost "constant" features of sorcery and witchcraft and recur as their defining features regardless, for example, of whether the analysis is of European "witch crazes" or contemporary instances of witch hunting in modern societies experiencing the turmoil of globalization. Very different historical moments reduce to the same broad cultural functional form. I do not deny the importance of these perspectives but note that they are as applicable to a great many other forms of practice that also tend to be classed as irrational whether this be "cargo cults," millenarian sects, movements of religious revitalization, or the engagement in poor scientific method (see Gluckman 1956; Polanyi 1958; Feyerabend 1978).

What I suggest is that there may be other "logics of practice" involved in what is frequently too easily glossed as sorcery and witchcraft, often specific to the diverse forms that they take. These may account for their apparent continuity or reinvention. Furthermore, more than merely expressions of irrationality or confusion or uncertainty (another catchall of understanding to which theoreticians of globalization appear attracted, see Appadurai 1996) they may already frame in the dynamics of their symbolic structure the shape of critical dimensions of the force of larger contemporary processes.[4] These dynamics are not necessarily produced out of the present so much as they discover original force and practical relevance within present historical circumstances. This original force is central to the continuity of certain practices (as well as discontinuities) that nonetheless have vastly different import than they may have had in their realization at some previous time.[5]

These preliminary remarks can be expanded with reference to material on sorcery and witchcraft in Sri Lanka. Here, as in many other parts of the globe (see Geschiere 1998), what are described as sorcery and witchcraft practices according to some are on the increase, although this is far from an unproblematic observation.[6] What is incontestable is that they are certainly more observable. This is especially so in the context of the emergence over the last century of a sorcery god known as Suniyam. Destructive sorcery, that explicitly directed to cause another injury, hurt, and sometimes death, was normally a covert practice in Sri Lanka. These days it is often performed in the open at publicly frequented shrines consecrated to Suniyam. Some scholars have found this extraordinary because such violent sorcery is done at temples where Suniyam is brought into association with the Buddha, the arch symbol of nonviolence. They have taken this fact as a sign of modernity par excellence, a modernity, moreover, that manifests as moral decline (the inversion of Buddhist principles) and increasing social disorder (see Obeyesekere 1976, 1981; Gombrich and Obeyesekere 1989). This kind of argument, of course, risks a repetition of earlier functionalisms in anthropology that conceived of modernization and social change as disruptive of coherent, once integrated, sociomoral systems. A classic and much debated study using sorcery as an index of anomie along similar lines is Redfield's (1941) study of the city of Mérida on the Yucatan peninsula. It is a style of analysis of which many anthropologists both past and present would be acutely critical. There is too much negativity in the representations both of the social realities explored and in their modes of expression, such as sorcery.

Suniyam's shrines are modern inventions, the history of their establishment dating from the latter part of the nineteenth century. They are located mainly in Sri Lanka's bustling capital city, Colombo, but also in other commercial centers along the seaboard to the south and southeast of Colombo. The development and proliferation of these shrines and, too, the appearance of an innovative custom whereby domestic shrines are raised to this god, seems to coincide with several political and economic factors including extensive urban migration and the development of powerful Sinhala merchant classes that often endowed the shrines and became patrons and occasionally devotees of the god. It is significant that major shrines to Suniyam are situated at critical points of entry and egress of both people and products into the urban and national economies. He is a god that has a close affinity to the recent courses and transmutations in the island's history effected through the advent of capital and its current globalizing energy.

Moreover, there are features of Suniyam's particular potencies that refract dimensions of the structuring of power (and its crises) both under the conditions of British colonial rule and in the circumstances of a postcoloniality that has seen a weakening of the postcolonial state and a shift toward the new centers of imperial power in North America. Thus the construction of Suniyam as an enshrined god begins at the peak of British colonial power during which most Sinhalese were alienated from direct administrative and political control over their affairs. There are critical dimensions of Suniyam's potency that are oriented to penetrate into those domains of power that can not otherwise be immediately reached and influenced. This alienation continues for many into the postcolonial context. Suniyam's popularity has increased in the last twenty or so years (gauged by the considerable number of new shrines that have erupted in this period). This coincides with major reorganizations of the political economy of the island (attendant on IMF and World Bank demands for structural adjustment). This has involved some weakening of state power (even though it has undergone greater centralization) and a reduction of its protective capacity (the state even turning destructively against its own populations), all of which has been exacerbated by the ongoing Tamil-Sinhala ethnic war (see Cleary 1997). These processes and changes call forth a god of Suniyam's extraordinary powers; a god whose magical force can intervene directly in the ever-changing fortunes of daily life and, perhaps, more than match the overbearing forces that threaten to crush the very terms of everyday existence.

CONTINUITIES AND DIFFERENCE IN
SORCERY PRACTICE: RITE AND SHRINE

The Suniyam of the modern urban shrines is clearly continuous with major practices that have a long history in Sri Lanka stretching back to precolonial times. This does not deny the modernity of the shrines in any sense and especially the fact that the forces engaged in their formation are thoroughly connected with political and economic forces vital in transitions into postcoloniality. However, contextualizing the modern incarnation of Suniyam within other practices of often considerable historical depth and resilience expands an understanding of the current significance of Suniyam and the apparent resurgence of sorcery as a phenomenon of postcoloniality and globalization. What may be described as the current transmogrification of Suniyam, his particular potency as a fabrication of modernity is thrown into relief by exploring his continuities *and* discontinuities with other practices. The setting of Suniyam worship in a larger context will also indicate a reassessment of the import of what are referred to as sorcery practices, which in my view fails to realize their differentiated character.

The modern urban Suniyam of the shrines has a distinctly double aspect. Iconographically he is represented as a being who is simultaneously destructive and protective and/or beneficial. In his right hand he holds a sword (*kaduva*) of judgment and in his left he carries a broken pot (*kabala*) in which burns the fire of destruction. In his mouth, Suniyam bites the viper of sorcery's annihilation. The doubleness of Suniyam's form, the heightened sense of ambivalence and ambiguity that the enshrined figure of Suniyam projects, is consistent with how sorcery is often described in the ethnographic literature and not for Sri Lanka alone. Sorcery is a volatile force in which beneficence as much as destruction are inseparably intertwined. In Sri Lanka the destructive capacities of sorcerers are thoroughly part of their healing work and the modern Suniyam is largely a phenomenon born of the ritual healing traditions for which Sri Lanka is widely known (see Wirz 1954; Kapferer 1983). These traditions engage cosmological and mythical themes that are vital throughout the extremely varied and always changing religious and ritual practices of Sinhalese, most of whom describe themselves as Buddhists.

It must be stressed that sorcery and Suniyam are embedded within Sinhala Buddhist cosmology and its practices. Although Suniyam (and sorcery) enshrined may manifest an original form, Suniyam (and sorcery) is in no way antithetical to well-established Sinhalese practices and occasionally those that might be regarded unproblematically as being Buddhist.[7] The cosmological embeddedness of sorcery practice not only helps to understand why certain kinds of sorcery (actually antisorcery practice appears to be proliferating) but also why the term *sorcery* in anthropology is often a woefully unsatisfactory gloss for what sorcery practice is about—either in the present or the past. All this demands fuller explication.

The name of the god/demon Suniyam name is derived from one of the most common words for sorcery, *huniyam*, from the Sanskrit *sunya* (void, negation, emptiness). The word is conventionally used for charmed or magical acts and objects designed to have a destructive or blocking (and occasionally, protective) effect. Although few apart from Buddhist monks or ritualists professionally concerned with sorcery are aware of the deep religious resonances of such a notion of *sunya*, the concept has considerable import in long-standing religious thought involving various Buddhist and non-Buddhist traditions that have swept through the region over millennia. The implications contained in the concept of *sunya* are realized both in everyday experiences of what are described as sorcery and in those experiences constituted in ritual contexts. People will grasp as sorcery experiences that appear to them to sweep aside the apparent basis of their lives and to open up a chasm underneath: a life-threatening illness, marital desertion, the death or disappearance of a loved one, the risk of imprisonment, the theft of one's belongings, a shaming slight or event of personal humiliation, and so on. Perhaps a term for sorcery in more common usage than *huniyam* is *kodivina* or just *vina*—action. The notion relates to widespread understandings present within abstract Buddhist thought but, more important, also part of ordinary everyday commonsense assumptions that recognize that any action, however innocently directed, involves the potential of ill even disastrous effects. *Karma*, the law of cause and effect, in which all actions and events are interconnected is also highly relevant to *vina* or sorcery, perhaps contributing to what may appear as an intense concern among many Sinhalese with sorcery and with what they see to be at its root—envy and jealousy (*irishyava*).

Such concepts indicate the enormous ontological reach of sorcery. Sorcery is at the center of the human existential condition arising out of the very participation of human beings in realities shared with others. It is the force of destructive contingency wherein the very circumstances and life projects of human beings become subject and vulnerable to the actions of others. Sorcery, as a force ultimately inseparable from the situations that human beings create and live, constitutes vital themes in the major anti-sorcery rite of the Suniyama (see Kapferer 1997). This is a rite performed in domestic space that seeks to address the full range of malignant sorcery practice, turning this practice back to its source. The immense cosmological themes of this nightlong ritual elaborate well-known Buddhist creation myths, concentrating on the story of King Mahasammata's institution of the original political and social hierarchy of the world and the event of the first attack of sorcery, whose victim is Mahasammata's queen. The figure of sorcery (Vasavarti Maraya who in myth appears as Mahasammata's double) manifests in his extreme annihilating form at the moment the world order is created. In other words, the human formation of social existence brings forth the specter of the sorcerer, who is revealed by his exclusion from body and world through the moral and social recreation of human beings that Mahasammata's constitutional act symbolizes. Toward the end of the ritual performance, when the political and social order has been restored—after the victim has been cleansed of sorcery's pollution and made regenerate (and regenerative, for the victim is effectively made into a "world maker" and is recentered in Mahasammata's axial position)—a ritualist in the guise of the archdestroyer, Vasavarti, makes a threatening appearance. This is meant to indicate Vasavarti's impotence (sorcery's impotence) in relation to the victim, restored and reempowered; but it also signifies the inevitability of sorcery's more potent return, manifesting the fact of its embeddedness within the very orders and practices of social existence. The Suniyama as a whole is structured as a sacrifice, one in which the victim is effectively reborn and ontologically regrounded in a life world and liberated from the coils of sorcery's destruction.

The magnificence of the Suniyama in its practice of mythological themes reveals sorcery, at least for many Sinhalese, as a force that strikes at the vitals of the human-created orders of human existence. Moreover, sorcery destroys the very ground of reason, returning human beings to an existence before Mahasammata's act when human beings acted outside reason and were motivated, if unconsciously, out of self-interest alone. In the Buddhism of the Suniyama the sorcerer is the unbridled self outside control and beyond all morality. This is an orientation that, in the context of the Suniyama, is also applicable to the victim in the grip of sorcery and awaiting ritually mediated release. Within the process of the rite, sorcery victims are presented as quite literally bound in the immobilizing coils of sorcery, which are cut away. Thus, victims at the start of the Suniyama are symbolically situated in the position of Mahasammata's queen but in the course of the rite systematically moved into a ritual building (Mahasammata's palace that both symbolizes Mahasammata's created world order and is the womb space, *gaba*, of both victim and world regeneration). Effectively the victim travels from the amoral space of sorcery's destruction into a moral realm of a political and social order commanded by the Buddha virtues. I add that this shift is in itself generative. That is, the victim symbolically repeats Mahasammata's constitutive act. It is the victim's action that is reconstitutive of a morally right and socially ordered reality.

There are apparent continuities between the urban Suniyam and the Suniyama rite. They share much in the symbolism and the dynamics of their practice. Many of the shrines were built by artisans from one of the main caste communities, the *bereva*, which is largely responsible for the Suniyama and other closely connected healing rites (or exorcisms) still commonly performed in villages along the western and southern littoral of the island. Some (but by no means all) of the priests (*kapurala*) at the urban shrines are from the same community. The image of the urban Suniyam itself is a hybridization, on the one hand, of dynamic aspects of the energy of *huniyam/suniyam* in the Suniyama and other related long-term ritual traditions (in certain ways a concretization of them) with, on the other hand, representations of Prince Oddisa, the archsorcerer and the archsacrificer.

In mythology, Oddisa is the creator of the healing traditions commanded by the *berava* ritual specialists who routinely perform the Suniyama rite and, indeed, conceived as the person who invented the Suniyama to overcome the sorcery of Mahasammata's queen. Oddisa is described in myth as both a destroyer of kingdoms and the force of their protection; a figure who is the enormous face of the contradictions upon which existence (and sorcery) are founded. Oddisa is such a furious and completely ambiguous power that as some myths relate he causes even the most powerful of the gods to tremble. His huge consuming and destructive potency (Oddisa is described as having an enormous all-ravenous mouth) is what calls forth the ordering force of the cosmic entirety and ultimately the supreme potency of the Buddha, which calms his fury and turns Oddisa protectively in the Buddha's way.

In the Suniyama, the ritualists, in the guise of Oddisa, enter within the maw of sorcery's energy-summoning cosmic powers of Buddha and the universe whereby they turn back destructive sorcery to its source. The unity of Oddisa with Suniyam in the rite is effectively realized in the dynamic form of Suniyam at the shrines where in some respects plaintiff's before Suniyam become their own ritualists and, Oddisa-like themselves, enter within Suniyam's potency.

They join with Suniyam's conversional, rebounding, and turning energy variously punishing the sources of their anguish and/or gaining Suniyam's assistance and protection in their projects.

There are obvious similarities between the urban Suniyam shrines and the Suniyama ritual. Rite and shrine grasp sorcery as nothing less than a defiling and fracturing violence at the root of existence, of person, and of world into which void (*sunya*) the orderings of ordinary existence collapse. In both cases Suniyam (or Oddisa/Suniyam as he is referred to in the rite and also occasionally at the shrines) is the active agency effecting the emergence of such totalizing force.

The totalizing dynamics of shrine and rite is integral to their being regarded as antisorcery practices of ultimately the most potent kind.[8] As such, both practices bring the victims of anguish within a morally unifying space that in its process (for the dynamic of shrine and rite is a building of moral space) brings benefits to the plaintiffs and visits destruction on those who are or who might be instruments of anguish. I stress the fact that the shrines and the Suniyama rite are not seen as sites for the perpetration of destructive sorcery. Rather, they are regarded as places where redress is made when persons are under the duress of sorcery. This is so even though destruction is the great potency of their sorcery-overcoming force. It is because both shrine and rite are centers for antisorcery practice, are moral foci for all their destructive possibility, that they are public places and not places of secrecy, otherwise a characteristic of sorcery practice.

The Suniyam shrines should not be understood as transpositions or transformations of the Suniyama rite. They are contiguous practices in a continually elaborating and diversifying cultural field and mutually influential because of their contiguity. The Suniyama rite is a practice that has strong documented evidence for its performance in precolonial times but it is, of course, changing and with respect to the historical forces that have influenced the emergence of the shrines. Moreover, the symbolic innovations of the shrines have influenced aspects of the continual reformation in practice of the Suniyama rite. What I draw attention to is that each, perhaps as a function of their differences and the way they refashion elements contained in the other, develops or highlights critical aspects that may be condensed or suppressed in the other yet are vital to understanding its current appeal or import. This is a theme to which I will return subsequently.

Before I do so I want to consider another set of sorcery-related and shrine-centered practices that are relevant to those at the Suniyam shrines. I discuss the *bandara* shrines for a class of demonic gods in whose category Sinhalese often place Suniyam and Prince Oddisa. The *bandara* shrines in their distinction, yet relatedness, to the Suniyam shrines point up the current significance of the latter as a new development yet expanding or realizing new possibilities in dynamics already present in previous forms. Both the Suniyam shrines and especially the *bandara* derive their force through the imaginary of the state and the relation of the historical circumstances of such an imaginary to the exigencies of personal living. They manifest different orientations to their imaginary of the state and particularly the force of distinct kinds of globalization in the invention of their difference but also in the formation of a similar dynamics. Again my concern is to insist on the differentiated character of what are generally taken to be sorcery-related practices.

THE *BANDARA*: THE MAGIC OF THE STATE IN CRISIS

The *bandara* are a category of powerful supramundane beings relatively lowly placed in the Sinhala Buddhist cosmic hierarchy. They are often extremely violent and dual in aspect, punishing and protective. One of the more intriguing features of these beings is that they manifest human potencies and while regarded as gods are conceived of as having once been human beings, usually officers of state power (the meaning of *bandara*), who, moreover, often met a violent death.

There are innumerable *bandara* gods and these appear to have emerged under a great diversity of different historical contexts of state formation, stretching far back into Sri Lanka's precolonial past. Most descriptions of the *bandara* concentrate on those connected with subdivisions of the Kandyan kingdom, the last stronghold of Sinhalese that fell to the British in 1815. Most of these *bandara* are now inactive, though some figure as personalities in the dramas of ritual performance.[9] Here they are manifested as ambivalent, liminal gods, often alternating absurd, comic aspects, with a dangerous and violent manner. They are beings who in ritually structured processes of the formation of a cosmic hierarchy mediate disordering and ordering forces. The ritual role of the *bandara* indicates a trace of perhaps their greater importance in precolonial times, until the establishment of British colonial hegemony and the formation of a relatively stable bureaucratic order constituted around a centralized and alien administrative/military power.

One feature of precolonial states in Sri Lanka up until the fall of the Kandyan kingdom was their fragility. They were continually subject to internal disruption and to conquest from neighboring kingdoms. Their political dynamic was one akin to what both Tambiah (1976) and Geertz (1980) have described for "galactic" or "theater" states whose endemic instability and constant threat from the periphery was masked by grand ritual ceremonial that accentuated the divine ordering powers of the king and the gods. Histories of ruling dynasties (e.g., Mahavamsa, Culavamsa, Thupavamsa Rajavaliya) describe the continual internal strife, rebellions by erstwhile subject kingdoms, and repeated invasions from southern India (see also Obeyesekere 1984). Kings at the center were routinely overthrown by rival lords, often by their own kin. Indeed, the British conquest of the last king of Kandy was effected by the British manipulation of this dynamic (see Davy 1821). The overall point is that the *bandara* gods expressed a political world in constant dynamic flow, one of highly porous borders, repeated changes in political fortunes, ahierarchical disruptions, and forces of rehierarchialization.

Among the more powerful *bandara* gods are those collectively known as the seven or *hatara bandara* whose shrines are located along the western seaboard of the island. This is part of the island most vulnerable to foreign invasion and settlement from south India throughout recorded history. The myths of origin of these coastal *bandara* describe their violent beginnings, their powers of making alien disruptive forces conform to internal orders, and their aggressive ability to guard and police their territory. The coastal *bandara* appear to express these features even more strongly than those connected, for example, with the Kandyan kingdom. This fits with the western coastal region being the most intensely affected by continually disruptive ordering/reordering forces, indeed, of a long period of globalizing dynamics in which the colonial penetrations were the most recent instance.

The more powerful *bandara* are conceived of as being historical personages, human beings who met a sudden violent end, and who effectively could be seen as "lords of the marches" whose work it was to resist violence in the interests of state order and to maintain territorial borders against violation. New *bandara* have been created since the colonial conquest and in postcolonial circumstances and maintain some of the distinctive characteristics. Keppetipola, a leader in the 1918 rebellion against the British and executed by them became a *bandara* (see Peiris 1950:421; Obeyesekere 1984:287). More recently, if only for a relatively brief period, the prime minister of Sri Lanka, assassinated by a Buddhist monk in 1959, became a *bandara*—worshipped as Horagolle Devata Bandara. *Horagolle* refers to his territory, the plantation estates owned by him and his family. (Bandaranaike's daughter is currently the president of Sri Lanka.) Apart from the violence of his death, Bandaranaike is most significant for ushering in an era of Buddhist nationalism. He was an intensely territorializing postcolonial nationalist figure marking Sri Lanka as a political order to be protected for Sinhalese and for Buddhism.

It is in the context of the reterritorializing "localism" of postcolonial nationalism, at once a reaction to the globalizing force of colonial powers and one that encourages a population to conceive of personal disruptions as a function of external and alien threats, that the coastal *bandaras* especially, have once again arisen in popularity. This is so with Taniwalla Bandara, whose shrine is located on the coast north of Colombo. He was once a prince famous for his defeat of foreign Hindu and Muslim pirate traders in the fifteenth century and who was killed in the course of his violent work (Bell 1920). Taniwalla's shrine, a place for cursing and sorcery, is located in an area of much contemporary ethnic tension, in a borderland where Sinhala merge into Tamil populations. Another *bandara* shrine of growing importance is that of Rajjaruvo Bandara (alias Devata Bandara, which tends to be a generic title for a number of different *bandara*), inland from the southern town of Galle. Rajjaruvo is a form of Phussadeva, the champion of King Dutthagamani, the hero of the sixth-century Chronicle of Sinhala kings, the Mahavamsa. In local traditions, the area of the shrine is located close to a site where the Sinhala king, Valagamba, hid and regrouped his forces to resist the invading Colans from south India. The since assassinated president of Sri Lanka, Premadasa, created Rajjaruvo's shrine into a National Heritage site. Sinhalese come from all over the island to this shrine to win Rajjaruvo's judgment against their enemies, especially those suspected of crimes for which there is insufficient evidence. Even the local police sometimes bring suspected criminals before Rajjaruvo in order to force an admission of guilt.

I remark that the above *bandara* largely experienced their resurgence in popularity after 1977, when the IMF/World Bank instigated a series of political and economic infrastructure reforms that altered the circumstances for ordinary lives. State welfare support (including food rationing) was curtailed and privatized (the postcolonial NGO phenomenon taking over welfare functions from the state). After 1977, with the defeat of the left coalition under Mrs. Banadaranaike and the election of the United National Party under Junius Jayawardene, internal markets were opened up for international competition and there was a high influx of new capital and hitherto highly regulated consumables. The political economy of daily life was radically and speedily altered, old social orders were threatened and new ones came suddenly into being (Gunasinghe 1984; Kapferer 1988). This was also the context for a radical intensification of nationalism among the majority Sinhalese who pressed for more safeguards in an extremely labile situation. Nationalist localism and ethnic communalism were exacerbated by the very globalizing forces that simultaneously contradicted such localism even though globalization conditioned it. Thus peasant populations and urban poor who had been protected under an earlier nationalism (that initiated by the assassinated SWRD Bandaranaike and very influenced by the processes that had won independence), with the

new forces of global economic and political incorporation, now found themselves disadvantaged in skill, education, and in language and opened to the
unmoderated oppressive potencies of "the market."

While a previous postindependence nationalism had powerful economic
and institutional effects (even though it most often acted through colonially
established infrastructures that drew their efficacy from within a regulated
and relatively coordinated colonial political economy of Empire), the period
after 1977—which is the start of the postmodern, postcolonial globalization
situation for Sri Lanka—is marked by ideological rupture. By this I mean that
the cultural assertions and appeals to "tradition" were relatively disconnected
from the political and economic forces that were vital in shaping everyday
realities. There was an increasing fetishization of national culture and
tradition—particularly by the agents of a weakened state—which was in inverse proportion to their capacity to change real-life circumstances, especially
through such assertions. Despite the fact that the British "invented traditions"
or created them through a restructuring of what they regarded to be indigenous institutions of order, this action was integral to the formation of their
bureaucratic secular state (see Cohn 1983 for the similar example of India)
and was relatively tightly integrated. Postcolonial Sri Lanka was/is marked by
a return to "authenticity," a nationalism of the revivalism of the past, which is
driven more and more into a crisis of the state whereby nationalist ideology
and a resort to violence is driven into a failure of state institutions of control,
to a large extent fomented by globalizing forces.

The reappearance of the *bandaras* is consistent with globalizing forces in
which there is a crisis of power and particularly of state power, a demand for
its ordering force in conditions in which it is most vulnerable to failure, and
where the energies of disruption appear to be external. The *bandaras* reflect
the weakness of the state and at the same time augment and compensate for
the inadequacies and vulnerabilities of the state. The agents of the state even
turn to their support—as is suggested in the state recognition of the potency
of Rajjaruvo Bandara—in an effort to regain a failing power.

If the *bandara* are the creatures of globalizing forces, they manifest a similarity in dynamics and do not reflect, of course, identical forces. They are neither mere constructions of the historical present disconnected from the past,
to be reduced to the terms of a contemporary presentism, nor instances of the
power of the past to maintain its relevance in the present. In my view, they are
simply culturally at hand whose current import has expanded because they
happen to inscribe a dynamic in their form, and in associated practices, that
discover an original relevance in the historically distinct circumstance of a
postcolonial globalization.

Bandara are Janus-faced, simultaneously destructive and protective. They are punishing gods who redress the wrongs done to victims who address them. They set things to right. Their world is a world of victims who achieve the satisfaction of seeing those who have caused them anguish in turn made to suffer and brought to book. One instance I witnessed involved a woman who brought another, suspected of being involved in adultery with her husband, before the fierce Rajjaruvo calling upon the bandara to exact punishment if indeed guilt was there. The victim followed her accused home watching closely for any sign that the punishment was taking effect. Another occasion was when members of a Buddhist community association arraigned a suspected thief before the judgment of Rajjaruvo. Restitutive, restorative, and protective demon gods, the *bandara* are fixers who force an order. They are officers of the state (the very meaning of the *bandara* term)—the potent extensions of weakened orders, perhaps the magical arm of the state.

I have argued that the *bandara* have reemerged as the paladins of state power in the circumstances of the decline, retraction, and vulnerability of the state and its agents. They are the instruments and manifestations of statelike order, of state mediated law and rule in conditions where there is a failure of the power of state institutions or where they are in some way or another unable to operate in the interest of citizens. The *bandara* augment the power of the state; they are integral to its interests and to those who desire the protection of the state even in the crisis of its failure. They manifest the magicality of the state as a paradox of its weakness.

THE DIFFERENCE AND ORIGINALITY OF SUNIYAM'S POWER

While the *bandara* augment or extend the state, Suniyam may be better seen as its contingency, even its conditionality. Suniyam is both that force that, on the one hand, is external to the state, the potency of its disruption and destruction, that which refuses its orders and limitations, and, on the other hand, that which calls forth, demands, the state, but not merely as a powerful order, rather as a moral and truly protective order. Suniyam manifests, virtually causes, the Buddha. This is the sine qua non of his appeal, the vital core of his potency. Furthermore, Suniyam is the energy of social creation and formation, as he is also the force of its destruction. This he can achieve despite the state and even independently of its existence. Suniyam is beyond the state.

These dimensions of the modern Suniyam of the shrines are conveyed both in the popular myths of Suniyam and in the dynamics of practice at his various urban locations. The stories of the modern Suniyam are variants on the corpus of Oddisa myths that relate to the Suniyama and other rites commonly performed in peasant areas. Conceived in India beyond the perimeter of the state, in a situation of carnal lust and primordial desire, Suniyam destroys his father's state, going on to consume neighboring political orders and devouring their inhabitants. Eating his way through India he arrives in Sri Lanka where he confronts Ananda, Buddha's chief disciple, who recoils before his fury. This manifests the Buddha who is able to cool Suniyam, bringing him round in ultimate defense of the Buddha's moral order. I might note that other supporters of the Buddha, the Guardian Gods of Sinhala Buddhist cosmology and protectors of the state, cower before Suniyam's onslaught. It is only the perfection and potency of the Buddha himself that restores an order that the fury of Suniyam enforces (see Gombrich and Obeyesekere 1989; Kapferer 1997).

This story is possibly of recent invention, constructed in a climate of disruptive and great transformational processes attendant on the globalizing forces of colonialism and its aftermath. It expresses the threat to the state and its vulnerability. Such sentiments are exacerbated in the current intensity of a Sinhala Buddhist nationalism fueled in the ongoing outrages of the Tamil-Sinhala ethnic war, a nationalism that receives renewed energy in the very weakening of the order of the state, as a function of the vagaries of global politics and economics. The connection between the emergence of Suniyam, the kinds of stories that surround him, and a religious-ethnic nationalism should not be understated. Thus some of the potency of Mulu (root) Suniyam, the original Suniyam from whom Suniyam priests at the urban shrines receive their permission (varam) and power, derives from the location of his shrine in an ethnic borderland to the north of Colombo where Tamil-speaking communities merge into Sinhala settlements. This is a zone of violence (integral to Suniyam's transgressive force) and a place of conversion from foreign externality to local internality. The stories surrounding the shrine, which was established in the 1920s, a period of growth in Sinhala ethnic consciousness, state that this is the place where Suniyam halted his passage from India and protectively settled down.

But the feature of the recent stories of Suniyam that I stress is Suniyam as the extraordinary power of the outside, who is able to penetrate within and, furthermore, converts and reforms from within. My interpretation has some resonance with my brief account of the Suniyama rite that I described earlier and that has relevance for understanding the Suniyam of the shrines. In the Suniyama the victim of sorcery for whom the rite is performed is in a violent and polluted state because he or she is the victim of sorcery. Sorcery is what has metaphorically at least cast the victim out of state and community. The victim starts the ritual progress to Mahasammata's palace, the temple and womb of the state from a position of destruction at the margins of state and community (see Kapferer 1997). This practice has some similarity with routine practices at the urban shrines, which themselves tend to be located in what are described as violent neighborhoods or in marginal areas (often of conversion and transition) at the edge of the city. Here the victims of anguish go to places that are away from their routine sites of religious practice and distant from or at the margins of their own habitual lives. At the shrines they curse and rage at the sources of their anguish, effectively cast off the passivity and pollution of their victimness, and thrust themselves back toward a world in which they have often felt isolated and excluded in their suffering. It is the violence of the shrines and the fact that victims seek redress through violence that distinguishes this practice from the work of the Suniyama. This rite in a more orthodox Buddhist vein attempts to seek the reconstitution of the victim through a cleansing of violence rather than by means of violence (see Kapferer 1997).

The practices at the shrines catch up, expand, and transmute dynamics that are already a feature of other sorcery rites—especially those of antisorcery. Thus the Suniyama rite engages victims in a practical elaboration of sorcery myths describing the connection of the anxieties and suffering that sorcery acutely expresses as intimately associated with the formation of state and society. Moreover, it is the imperfection in the state, the breaking of its internal harmonies, that return anguish to its people, making them external to its order through its disorder. There is an intimation of the violence of the state (Vasavarti Maraya, violence supreme, assumes the identical form of Mahasammata) and that the barriers and restrictions of its internal ordering produce the force of sorcery. The activities at the Suniyama shrines reveal further implications of such practical ritual discourse.

About half the cases I collected at the shrines involved problems with government agents and agencies. Many were engaged in both civil and criminal court cases or had difficulties with the police or other powerful persons in the scheme of things. They expressed not merely uncertainty as to outcome but a sense that the instrumentalities of power and the state were in an exclusionary and violent relation to them. Suniyam's violence, a transgressive barrier-destroying force, was engaged to break into the offices and minds of government bureaucrats—into regions where the plaintiffs at the shrines believed they had no access through influence or situation. Suniyam's potency in these instances is to turn the minds of the powerful in the state and in the society to win favorable action and decision: to sway the mind of a magistrate, to stop police persecution, to secure a bank or housing loan, to get a job. The violent face of the sorcerer, mirroring the threat of the agents of power, turns back toward that which apparently excludes, and forces an entry.

A common (if debated) observation on sorcery in contemporary contexts is its "egalitarian" and antihierarchical force. That it is nothing other than a politics of envy born in the conditions of expanding social inequalities and growing poverty, which are intensifying in the globalizing context of such economically impoverished worlds as Sri Lanka. The proliferation of the urban Suniyam shrines support such observations and sorcery as an expression of the dangers and violence of class forces among others that infuse all regions of social and political reality. But it is the antihierarchical, system-leveling, barrier-breaking energy of Suniyam that is invoked at the shrines, not for any equalitarian or redistributive desire, but rather as the means of intruding into regions of ordering power that have been increasingly closed off and have become more hidden, secluded, secretive, and exclusive. Contemporary processes of economic restructuring and of privatization have sharpened lines of social and political differentiation. Institutions and organizations of power in the public and private spheres have become more distant from the general population and have placed greater restrictions on access. Persons of authority and influence are harder to reach. All of this is exacerbated in a climate of fear fueled by social unrest and a violent war that encourages tighter state control and the frequent abuse of power by its agents. The state appears to many to have violently turned against its own populations necessitating that they too must assume violent transgressive form.

One instance among many of the state in violent relation to its citizens was the 1989–1990 popular youth uprising organized by the Peoples' Liberation Front (Janatha Vimukthi Peramuna). Official estimates of the number killed by military and paramilitary action are in the region of 60,000, but the toll is probably higher (see Kapferer 1996, 1997). In a few short months more Sinhala were killed by their own government than have been killed in years of ethnic war with separatist Tamil groups. The Suniyam temples were crowded with anxious relatives angrily exhorting Suniyam to punish the instruments of state who had killed or else to help discover some news of those who had apparently disappeared. As with most curses and pleas before Suniyam, his help is demanded as meritorious action, worthy of the Buddha's morality that turns the violent Suniyam on the Buddha's path. Suniyam becomes an instrument of the state's reform and moralization.

Suniyam's apotheosis as a form that enables him to encompass numerous dimensions of a critical and practical discourse engaging the state and its citizens is the invention of historical forces acting on particular cultural materials. But his realized form is not a mere reduction to historical context. Suniyam's creation as a form thoroughly relevant to contemporary processes and anxieties is historically produced but this is also nonabritrary. The diverse

original import that Suniyam manifests is a consequence of historical forces
acting within the dynamics of cultural materials that, a) already were centrally
positioned within political consciousness; and b) had implicit within their
processes a dynamic import that was powerfully available to the transmuta-
tional work of later historical forces. Historical developments discovered the
nature of their impetus and significance through a reworking of dynamic implications already present in available practice. This process is not a repetition
of the same but rather the invention of a difference, often radically disjunctive
from earlier forms, that through its difference is, nonetheless, continuous with
such forms of practice.

The emergence of Suniyam as a thoroughgoing being of modernity and
globalization, able to grow and find renewed relevance within the many directions and twists these processes take, arises out of the globalizing and modernizing formation of colonialism. The building of Suniyam shrines began
apace with the firm establishment of British colonial rule, which enabled the
relatively unchecked pursuit of a modernization project. The resulting urbanization, industrialization, social disruption, and population flow are all clearly
central to Suniyam's formation. But the political effect of the colonial conquest following the British overthrow of the Kandyan kingdom in the creation
of Suniyam demands attention.

Prior to the conquest the control of sorcery was integral to the power of the
state. In Kandy, to engage in sorcery practice was treated as a crime against king
and state and was punishable by death. Annual ceremonies for the renewal of
the power of the kingship and the king included rites of antisorcery. Current
performances of the Suniyama rite incorporate key events that were also crucial in the state rites of kingship (see Seneviratne 1979). The British ending of
the kingship recreated such rites as symbolic presentations of British hegemony and removed sorcery from state control. With the British, sorcery was, in
effect, deregulated, placed outside the state and simultaneously opened up, as
it were, to public use. Major rites of antisorcery were disestablished and dis-
lodged from one critical practical value of maintaining the integrity of the
kingship and the hierarchical social order that it defined. Performances of the
Suniyama, in the political conditions of the kingship, were largely confined to
families of high rank and status in a social order hedged about by caste rules
defining power in relation to the kingship. This changed rapidly and rites such
as the Suniyama became popularized and freed up to express the new political
and economic anxieties and interests of shifting caste alignments and new class
formation occasioned by British domination. The Suniyama, and other rites
like it, became more generally associated with empowerment and also involved
in other innovative developments, such as the proliferation of the Suniyam

shrines. They became an instrument not just in the expression of changes in the distribution of political and economic power but also agencies of its production. What I note, in particular, was the potentiality created in history for certain symbolic practices, such as antisorcery rites, to expand and shift the import of a dynamic, already present within them.

Implicit in the Suniyama rite and in its body of traditions is a critique of the state, that a diversity of problems in the realm of the state is part of the entropy of the state and the penetration into its center of alien all-consuming force, that also alienates those once protected in the order of the state. Those so alienated are victims of the state and are placed in a relation of reciprocal violence. This is the nature of the identity that is established between malevolent sorcerers and their victims. The context of the colonial conquest, I suggest, intensifies this sense, opening the way for the establishment of a more powerful identity between the violence of the sorcerer as a being of the outside, on the one hand, and the violent situation of the colonized who are now more excluded from control over state power, on the other hand. The division between the state and the population it controls is more clearly marked. New and stronger barriers are erected calling forth the transgressive potency of a Suniyam.

This was, and is, linguistically marked in the Sinhala concept of *kaduva*, the sword that divides and separates. It is a concept that was applied specifically to the situation of colonial rule and continues into the postcolonial era to indicate the cleavage between state and the larger population. The English language was conceived of as the *kaduva* of the state. In postcolonial contexts this recognition of the separating, including and excluding, potency of English has reappeared as a consequence of global forces where English is the primary medium mediating relations to the outside facilitating new class fractionalization. Such contemporary cosmopolitanization, which divides the local from the global, constitutes an intensification of class tension and feelings motivating the violence of exclusion.

Different moments in globalization (colonialism and postcolonialism) have created not just a closer identification between large sections of the Sinhala population and the violent Suniyam, but have influenced the revaluation of his violence. His violence is turned from being a largely negative force, if ambivalent, into a strong positive force. The polluting, poisonous, power of sorcery is not something that must be cleansed (as in the Suniyama rite) but directly and immediately engaged as the instrument of beneficence. The negative and positive polarities of sorcery are more tightly fused into one overridingly positive energy. This is the central feature of the image of Suniyam at the shrines, as I have described. Moreover, I note, he bears the *kaduva*, his sword of judgment and reconstitutive sacrifice. In the contexts of the shrines, this is no more the sword of judgment of the agents or agencies of the state in power, rather the constitutive power of those who are denied (even momentarily) a potency or a sovereignty by state or other social and political processes. Through Suniyam the supplicants at the shrines become arbiters of power, a moral and violent power, that for them has otherwise been adbicated and potentially turned against them.

There is a relation between the emergence of nationalism and the emergence of the sorcery shrines. Both perceive suffering as rooted in the decline of state power and moral and protective potency as a function of alien intrusion and dispossession. Perhaps the violence of each is a mirror in a different register of the potential and moral impetus for violence of the other. Some of the convergence is conscious, nationalist practice expressly catching up themes present in the sorcery rites. Episodes from the *Suniyama* rite are performed at times of Buddhist and nationalist celebration, as at Vesak. But I stress the convergence of sorcery and nationalism as driven in globalizing forces and in the fact that they are thoroughgoing energies of the forces of modernity that have realized particular potency in cultural materials at hand.

In the case of the sorcery shrines, while they constitute original practices, their originality is conditioned in certain aspects of sorcery—already present in its practice—that is realized through the very inventions and transmutations that are effected in the contexts of the shrines. In many instances they revalue as positivities what otherwise are regarded as the negativities of sorcery, what is at the root of its danger. This is so in the positivity attached to Suniyam's violent and transgressive force and in his rhizomic capacities, the potency of sorcery to break through difference and to course along the lines of relatedness and the ability of sorcery to shape itself to any circumstance or eventuality it encounters. The Suniyam of the shrines is certainly the equal to the diversity, shifting, and uncertain dimensions of modern, urbanized realities. He is thus a representation of modernity but, nonetheless, a representation created by acting on the nature of sorcery to create what sorcery may represent as also its very potency. Suniyam and sorcery are not merely expressions of processes that exist independently of them but the realization of the forces of such processes by means of a reconfiguration and revaluation of the dynamics of sorcery. The dynamic of sorcery captures those potencies present in context and engages them to the purposes to which it is aimed. Thus sorcery manifests the potencies of what it represents. One common use to which Suniyam is put, among the myriad, seemingly inexhaustible uses, is to open relations where there are none, especially in business contexts. He is employed to create desire in others—sometimes explicitly to make them consume—and to force and to make business deals solid. Traders often regard him as their facilitator and protector.

Obeyesekere (1976) demonstrates Suniyam to be a highly pragmatic being, thoroughly bound up with human practical concerns. He draws attention to this being as drawing its potencies from his ordinary, secular, involvements. This, I think, requires even stronger emphasis than Obeyesekere gives. Suniyam is not to be categorized with other powerful gods in the Sinhala pantheon, a tension in Obeyesekere's analysis. Indeed, Suniyam's distinction in the pantheon, his recognition as a new form, disjunct from other beings in Sinhala cosmology, is implicit in the organization of representations in at least one of the major Suniyam shrines in Colombo. Here he is set apart from other representations of beings in the Sinhala pantheon. These are shown worshipping the Buddha. They are contained in a glass case as if to be protected from Suniyam's furious (and contaminating?) secular presence.

Suniyam expands what is an aspect of the *bandara* and is a transmogrification of what is the most obvious aspect of sorcery. This is sorcery as no more and no less than the powerful constitutive and destructive force of human beings per se. He is the apotheosis of human power, in a way the manifestation of what Durkheim (1976) imagined to be the true nature of religion. As with Durkheim's view, Suniyam is a creature of a world given to the processes of a rational secularism, the magical means for the achievement of its reason even against the energies of unreason that such a world unleashes. My earlier description of Suniyam as a reformation of the archsorcerer and sacrificer, Oddisa, makes sense in the context of modernity and globalization that fetishizes individuality and human potency. Oddisa is regarded as nothing other than a human being and, in the myths, as the capacity of human beings to reconstitute themselves and their circumstances through sacrificial action.

The apotheosis of human beings in the urban reinvention of Suniyam parallels similar historical processes surrounding the worship of the Buddha. Secularization has resulted in a divinization of the rationalism of modernity. Over the past two centuries, Sinhala Buddhism has gone through a series of revitalizations that have reinvented Buddhist thought and practice, especially among the urban middle class, as the epitome of a secular and scientific rationalism. It built within implications already within Buddhist thought and practice to create a thoroughly humancentric and rationalized understanding of the Buddha and his practice. The Buddha became the ideal of rational man in absolute command of circumstance and intensely appropriate to a bureaucratic, technical, and capitalized world conditioned in colonialism and after. Suniyam is a product and refraction of a similar if more popular process, the potency of the real in contrast to Buddha as the truth of the ideal. He is the extraordinary (re)constitutive and destructive force of human being realized as the creator of his own circumstance, outside and above the circle of the gods. Perhaps he is still the destructive secret hidden behind the ordering face of human power (as the Mahasammata story of the Suniyama rite presents in the malevolent sorcerer's appearance as the world ordering king). But through the historical forces of secularism, rationalism, and a gathering individualism, Suniyam has been refigured as the image of practical rationality and power on the same path as the Buddha has achieved. Thus, in the pleas for his assistance at the shrines, supplicants express the wish that he will become a future Buddha. Suniyam is indeed the image of demythologized realities, of the differentiating and fragmenting world of modernity. Here, too, his dimensions as a being of sorcery are significant, available to such historical formation. For sorcery's very ambiguity is the expression of a construction of the reality of human existence as grounded in the dynamics of division and differentiation, a critical aspect of his enshrined image also vital in his constitutive/sacrificial energy. Suniyam is the modern myth, the myth indeed of demythologizing processes as well as of their power.

It is in Suniyam's difference—in his modern concretized, concentration of human potency—that he manifests a continuity with what sorcery always already was, sorcery as the quintessence of the human formation of human social and psychological existence. This is the force of the great antisorcery rite, the Suniyama. It literally works in that void between personal extinction and recreation (a sense of the Sanskrit word *sunya*) regenerating the person as an active potency in the formation of his or her social world. This rite destroys the destructive forces as it renews the person and this is certainly a dynamic that continues into the shrines. The activity of the shrines builds within that which is not only a major discourse of rites of sorcery long integral to a diverse cultural field of practices but also intuitively recognized by those who participate in what is often too easily glossed as sorcery. Supplicants before Suniyam become immersed in the very heat of the dynamics of creation and destruction that is nothing other than the energy of human sociality, of social formation that both overcomes suffering as it also must create it. When entering the shrines people enter a space where they can engage in a dynamic of extending or recapturing their own human potency from within the very wellspring of its formation. Suniyam is a potency of the tragedy of social existence and the aporia of its impossibility. It is this impossibility that the magic of sorcery recognizes and from which it draws its appeal and extraordinary force.

SORCERY AND THE POSTCOLONIAL CONDITION

There is a sense of surprise among anthropologists and others at the apparent "return" of sorcery practice in numerous globalizing and postcolonial realities.

Some older arguments are being replayed even though there is a concern to distance understanding from earlier perspectives and to insist that sorcery should be grasped through an attention to current crises of state power and social existence in the globalizing circumstances of the postcolonies. My discussion of the emergence of the Suniyam shrines and related sorcery practice supports much recent analysis. However, much of this analysis remains overcommitted, in my opinion, to the rationalist frames of interpretation that the scholars concerned may otherwise wish to separate themselves from. Thus in order to make postcolonial sorcery sensible Jean and John Comaroff invoke the rationalist comparativism of Gluckman (1956). If South Africans are irrational in their sorcery they are no more nor less irrational than New Age occultists or those economic theorists struggling to maintain their theories in the face of unpredictable developments in global markets. Sorcery is the shape of irrationality everywhere you look. What appears as different is really the same. Geschiere's assertion of sorcery as harboring the uncanny (1997)—to which he claims the rationalism of earlier scholars paid little attention—risks reproducing a mysticism that is the child of a Victorian scientific rationalism. There is a concern to escape the exoticism of previous anthropology that either celebrated radical difference to the point of ignoring similarities or that was so narcissistically enamored with its own explanatory powers that it refused the possibility that there are some areas of human construction and experience that are beyond explanation, at least in the terms of an earlier anthropology. Such orientations still risk and can legitimate a refusal to examine the phenomena in question both as they appear and on their own terms. An anthropological blindness is sustained that refuses what is otherwise apparent on the very surface of the phenomena in question and crucial to establishing similarities and differences from other apparently like phenomena.

The sorcery practices I have discussed in Sri Lanka are far more than mere sorcery and certainly not reducible simply to the uncertainties, ambiguities, failure in knowledge, or irrationality that are still being repeated in anthropological discussion. They certainly refract crises in organization of power in the state in the circumstances of globalization and, too, forces engaged in the reformations of social life and its anxieties. What I have shown is that the practices that are glossed as sorcery in Sri Lanka are highly differentiated. The term sorcery often subsumes and fuses too much difference. Although Suniyam and the *bandaras* achieve a new relevance and an originality in current globalizing processes they are relatively distinct processes that manifest in the same general conditions. The *bandara* and Suniyam refract the crisis of the state in different ways although there are continuities between them. When they are explored for what in fact they manifest on the surface of their representation and practice, calling them sorcery seems to deny much of their import. Indeed, it is by attending to the details of what these practices overtly present (for what may appear as their depth is already at their surface) that their resurgence and general appeal may become more clear and less surprising. They may indeed share a similarity with other practices elsewhere, for example, in their fetishism of human self-creation in the circumstances of its denial by state and globalizing forces. Such a fetishism is provoked in the rationalism of widespread processes of modernity. But this rationalism also brings to the fore in the Sri Lanka context a particularity of sorcery as engaging with the dynamics of sociality and social (re)formation that is also accentuated in the very fluidity of globalizing urban realities. The fetishism of personal power is directed against organizations of power that condition it and overcome it. Here I stress that later historical processes bring out dimensions of practices that may have been already vital to them, but manifested differently. In other words, what is treated as sorcery is "always modern" and although its practice may be originally constituted in the present it is not necessarily unconnected with the dynamics of older practices or of other contemporary practices. Moreover, this observation indicates that it is important to consider other related contemporary practices as well as what appear as older practices in order to comprehend the modern (an approach that the presentism of some analyses may well admonish). And vice versa, for the modern may make thoroughly obvious what other approaches may have overlooked in their exoticism and in their celebration of the traditional.

The analysis I have presented seeks to avoid an essentialism that finds in sorcery a fundamental property that is independent of its construction in the diversity of historical processes. This I think is more the problem of perspectives on sorcery that regard it as irrational without much thought beyond its expressivity. Different histories and contexts come to beat out the same insistent rhythm. The sorcery practices I have described are formed and reformed in their differences and similarities through historical forces. These forces have set down particular dynamics that can come to have an energy or implication or potential value that can be separated from its context of initial creation. As such, and perhaps through processes of original transmutation, it can have discovered within it a new relevance and, in fact, an original possibility.

I am suggesting that particular resurgences or reconfigurations of sorcery practice have occurred because of the dynamics that have been historically constituted within them. In other words, there is a process in such practice that impels its reinvention relevant to particular contexts. In globalizing contexts human beings acting intuitively approach particular available practices. They become creatively active in remolding them and in so doing make particularly manifest what they had, in my view, correctly intuited as their possibility.

One final point. What is described as sorcery for Sri Lanka reveals much of the experiential complexities of current globalizing processes. In this too, it appears highly appropriate to those scholarly orientations increasingly demonstrating their relevance for the understanding of postcolonial and postmodern circumstances. The sorcerer is a powerful Nietzschean metaphor as it is for Deleuze whose discussions of repetition and difference (1994) have influenced my discussion. This suggests that major perspectives on postcolonial realities and globalization have, if they are not ideologically internal to the phenomenon, intuitively recognized an identity between sorcery and their orientation to reality. Suniyam and sorcery in the Sri Lanka context is already postmodern and certainly in the situation of contemporary history demands the kind of perspective I have attempted. I underline the character of his representational potency as a being founded in difference, a creature of the void beneath whom there is nothing, but who can generate all manner of appearance, rhizomically travel in any direction, refuse all boundaries, yet invent new ones in a continuously diversifying reality.

NOTES

I wish to thank Jonathan Friedman and the participants at a seminar held on aspects of globalization under the auspices of the H. F. Guggenheim Foundation in 1998 in Lund, Switzerland. Ideas in this chapter have been further developed in seminar discussions with anthropologists at the universities of St. Andrews, Bergen, and Helsinki.

1. Jean Comaroff and John Comaroff (1999) quite explicitly reiterate Gluckman's (1956) functionalist expansion of Evans-Pritchard and more than adequately match his brilliant capacity to move rapidly from ethnographic specifics to global generalization. They share Gluckman's drive to demystify and to reveal the universal commonalities behind the superficially different and, too, Gluckman's concern to reveal the irrational in the rational. Engaging a logic of functional equivalence sorcery and witchcraft in Africa, for example, operates in ways similar to the imaginaries in the West of Satanic sacrifice, flying saucers, or the mysticism of New Age.

2. Englund and Leach (2000) have developed a powerful critique of positions that argue for too radical a discontinuity and for the importance of considering developments through their transformation or redefinition of local cosmologies and routine, culturally centered and taken for granted, orientations to existence. Gulbrandsen (2003) in an excellent discussion of ritual murder in Botswana takes a

similar stance. The overemphasis on disjunctive processes misses vital aspects of local reconstructions that assist the understanding of the phenomenon as a whole.

3. Geschiere's sense of the uncanny and empowering force of witchcraft is portrayed by his recounting a moment in the darkness of a Cameroon forest with his assistant when his car broke down (1997:1). He then develops the notion of empowerment and pursues the subversive and leveling dimensions of sorcery as a feature of its very modernity. This is an excellent argument and there are strong parallels with what I pursue in this chapter although, as the reader will see, I will insist that the very disjunctions manifest a structure of continuity and the importance of investigating more deeply the cultural dimensions of "empowerment" in the context of the failure of power in contemporary circumstances. It is likely that the Sri Lanka situation that I discuss is very different from the Cameroonian one. However, Geschiere (1998) insists that his perspective is generalizable in the terms that he develops it.

4. Jean and John Comaroff are particularly critical of approaches to globalization that gloss too much and do not consider ethnographic variation in some detail. They refer to much discussion of globalization among anthropologists and others that treat ethnographic information superficially as "Anthropology Lite" (1999:294). Their point is well taken although they might run a little close themselves, as Englund and Leach (2000) suggest. Their use of the word occult increases exponentially the already too-inclusive word sorcery, as used in much anthropology. My own discussion here does not necessarily avoid the risk.

5. My entire discussion around this theme draws very strongly on my interpretation of Gilles Deleuze's argument in *Difference and Repetition* (1994; see also Kapferer 1997).

6. This is a quantitative judgement that is difficult to demonstrate. It may well be that sorcery-related practices were always common but have changed so that they are now in the open and thus give the appearance of an increase. But even in this case it is not so much of an increase but the appearance of a new form.

7. An example is the nightlong *pirith* chanting of sacred Buddhist texts by monks at the houses of persons who understand themselves to be afflicted by malign sorcery. The *pirith* chanting banishes the malevolent agents.

8. What is antisorcery might be regarded as the most potent kind of sorcery precisely because it is the very encompassment of all manner of violent destructive sorcery. This is where even rites like the Suniyama—conceived as a nonviolent rite in terms of a Buddhist ethos—discover their paradox, for they are ultimately the most

destructive of rites. This is indicated in the concluding stages of the Suniyama when the archsorcerer, Vasavarti Maraya, makes his appearance. He manifests a virtual riot of destruction. Indeed, the destruction of the rite that occasions the apotheosis of the victim who effectively transcends the violence results in the harbinger of sorcery's violence engaging in self-destruction.

9. Rites to the goddess Pattini engage dramatic performances that involve *bandara* (Obeyesekere 1984) as do other healing rites or exorcism (Kapferer 1991).

REFERENCES

Appadurai, Arjun. 1996. *Modernity at Large: Cultural Dimensions of Globalization.* Minneapolis: University of Minnesota Press.

Bell, H.C.P. 1920. "Prince Taniyavalle Bahu of Madampe." *Journal of the Royal Asiatic Society,* Ceylon branch. 28:36–53.

Cleary, Seamus. 1997. *The Role of NGO's Under Authoritarian Political Systems.* London: MacMillan.

Cohn, Barney S. 1983. "Representing Authority in Victorian India." In *The Invention of Tradition.* Edited by Eric Hobsbawm and Terrence Ranger. Cambridge, U.K.: Cambridge University Press.

Comaroff, Jean, and John L. Comaroff. 1993. Introduction to *Modernity and Its Malcontents: Ritual and Power in Postcolonial Africa.* Edited by Jean Comaroff and John L. Comaroff. Chicago: University of Chicago Press.

———. 1999. "Occult Economies and the Violence of Abstraction: Notes from the South African Postcolony." *American Ethnologist* 26, no. 2:279–303.

Davy, John. 1821. *An Account of the Interior of Ceylon and of Its Inhabitants.* London: Longman.

Deleuze, Gilles. 1994. *Difference and Repetition.* Translated by Paul Patton. London: Athlone Press.

Englund, Harri, and James Leach. 2000. "Ethnography and the Meta-Narratives of Modernity." *Current Anthropology* 41, no. 2:225–39.

Feyerabend, Paul. 1978. *Against Method.* London: Verso.

Geertz, Clifford. 1980. *Negara.* Princeton, N.J.: Princeton University Press.

Geschiere, Peter. 1997. *The Modernity of Witchcraft.* Charlottesville: University of Virginia Press.

———. 1998. "Globalization and the Power of Indeterminate Meaning: Witchcraft and Spirit Cults in Africa and East Asia." *Development and Change* 29:811–37.

Gluckman, M. 1956. *Custom and Conflict in Africa.* Oxford, U.K.: Basil Blackwell.

Gombrich, Richard, and Gananath Obeyesekere. 1989. *Buddhism Transformed.* Princeton, N.J.: Princeton University Press.

Gulbrandsen, 2003. "The Discourse of 'Ritual Murder': A Critique of State Leadership in Botswana." In *Beyond Rationalism.* Edited by B. Kapferer. New York: Berghan.

Gunasinghe, Newton. 1984. "Open Economy and Its Impact on Ethnic Relations in Sri Lanka." In *Sri Lanka: The Ethnic Conflict.* Committee of Rational Development. Delhi: Navrang.

Kapferer, Bruce. 1983. *A Celebration of Demons.* Bloomington: Indiana University Press.

———. 1988. *Legends of People, Myths of State.* Washington, D.C.: Smithsonian Institution.

———. 1991. *A Celebration of Demons: Exorcism and the Aesthetics of Healing in Sri Lanka.* Washington, D.C.: Smithsonian Institution.

———. 1996. "Remythologizing Discourses: State and Insurrectionary Violence in Sri Lanka." In *The Legitimization of Violence.* Edited by David Apter, 159–88. London: Macmillan.

———. 1997. *The Feast of the Sorcerer.* Chicago: University of Chicago Press.

———. 2001. "Ethnic Nationalism and the Discourses of Violence in Sri Lanka." *Communal/Plural* 9, no. 1:33–67.

Obeyesekere, Gananath. 1976. "Sorcery, Premeditated Murder and the Canalization of Aggression in Sri Lanka." *Ethnology* 14, no. 1:1–23.

———. 1981. *Medusa's Hair.* Chicago: University of Chicago Press.

———. 1984. *The Cult of the Goddess Pattini.* Chicago: University of Chicago Press.

Polanyi, Michael. 1958. *Personal Knowledge: Towards a Post-Critical Philosophy.* Chicago: University of Chicago Press.

Peiris, Ralph. 1950. *Sinhalese Social Organization.* Colombo: Ceylon University Press Board.

———. 1956. *Sinhalese Social Organization.* Colombo, Sri Lanka: Ceylon University Press Board.

Redfield, Robert. 1941. *Folk Cultures of the Yucatan.* Chicago: University of Chicago Press.

Seneviratne, H.L. 1979. Rituals of the Kandyan State. London: Althone.

Tambiah, Stanley. 1976. *World Conqueror, World Renouncer.* Chicago: University of Chicago Press.

Taussig, Michael. 1987. *Shamanism, Colonialism, and the Wild Man.* Chicago: University of Chicago Press.

———. 1999. *Defacement: Public Secrecy and the Labor of the Negative.* Stanford, Calif.: Stanford University Press.

Wirz, Paul. 1954. *Exorcism and the Art of Healing in Ceylon.* Leiden, the Netherlands: E. J. Brill.

10

Imagining Monsters

A Structural History of Warfare in Chad (1968–1990)

STEVE REYNA

In 1990 Idriss Déby, once head of the army in Hissen Habré's government, then head of his own national liberation movement, engineered a number of military victories against Habré that drove his former boss into exile in the Novotel in northern Cameroon. Déby then assumed the presidency in December 1990. Since that time perhaps seven national liberation "armies" have formed and operate in southern, northern, eastern, and western Chad. All seek to do unto Déby what he did to Habré. In the east-central portion of the country, armed gangs—called *N'Katha Zulu* by wags in the capital—murdered, pillaged, and sold their loot in neighboring Sudan. The French felt obliged in 1992 to send military assistance. There were massacres of suspected rebels by government troops just north of the capital in 1993. Abbas Koty, a former chief of staff in Déby's regime, led a coup attempt in October 1993. There was speculation as to whether the state in Chad would disintegrate, again![1]

The military has a "central role" in Third World states (Cammack, Pool, and Tordoff 1993:133). This chapter, using the case of Chad, and placing it in the context of globalization, suggests that Third World militarism has not been fully imagined and that it is time to start thinking in terms of monsters.[2] Specifically, it argues that a process that constitutes a particular organization of violent institutions has escaped the notice of students of globalization. This organization is named a AIV-GIV Hydra (Autonomous Institution of Violence-Government Institution of Violence). Readers will discover that it, and its logic, are truly monstrous. The chapter further contends that this monster has occurred in other Third World states, occasionally provoking their descent into anarchy. The existence of processes producing such monsters raises the question of whether Third World states are currently undergoing a structural history that is different from that of the modern Great Powers. This investigation is made using a structural history approach. A word is in order concerning the approach.

GLOBALIZATION AND MONSTERS
The fundamental problem in Chad is above all a structural problem.

—*Moïse Ketté (FBIS 1994)*

Who is Moïse Ketté, and why is he important? We shall get back to this gentleman in due time, but first we need to contemplate globalization and monsters; because the former appears driven by the latter. Globalization is for many commentators, the most important social phenomenon currently occurring in the world. Further, it is understood to be the consequence of structural behemoths whose logic lead them to operate at higher frequencies and in greater numbers of ways throughout the globe. The term *logic* is used in this text to refer to what a structure does. Processes of operation fulfill structural logics. Thus, drilling is a process that fulfills a dental practice's logic of dental hygiene.

The behemoth behind—that is, the social structure that globalizes—is not a Hobbesian state, but rather a titanic Grendel of multinational enterprise distributed across such states. The globalization Grendel voraciously consumes resources to satisfy a logic of capital accumulation. So, in the present intellectual conjuncture, commentators struggling to influence opinion are globalization-monster experts. These experts have divided into two: "Friends" and "Enemies" of the monster camps.

However, two sorts of opinions tend to be *shared* by members of both camps. The first of these is that globalization is a recent phenomenon; starting in the 1960s and picking up speed thereafter as a result of technological changes that have come to be known as an "information revolution." The second opinion is a sort of *über*-determinism. *Über*-determinisms stress one set of causes at the expense of all others, even though those who make such determinisms really know that there are other, important causal elements in what they are trying to explain. Sociobiology, for example, is an *über*-determinism, accentuating genes as the cause of all things in the human condition to the exclusion of all other factors. Globalization experts tend to exhibit two sorts of *über*-determinism. Either they interpret the globalization Grendel as a monster pretty much entirely animated by culture, as tends to be the case with certain anthropologists (Hannerz 1992), or they insist that it is pretty much entirely driven by the technological and economic capabilities of a postindustrial capitalism, as tends to be the case with some economists (Hilferding 1981). Both of these views can be challenged.

Let us begin with the age of globalization. A number of different theoretical perspectives compellingly argue that capitalism has had a global dynamic since the very beginning of the capitalist era. After all, if capitalism is endless accumulation, then its accumulative appetite will eventually include all regions of the world. Certainly capitalist enterprises, and the coerced labor enterprises to which they were linked, spread through much of the world, especially the New World, during a merchant capital phase (ca. 1500–1780). This expansion came to include vastly more of the world, especially in south, southeast, and east Asia, during an industrial phase (ca. 1780–1960), and has enormously spread still farther during a postindustrial phase. So globalization is old, because one aspect of the making of the modern world from 1500 until the present has been geographic expansion of different morphs of the capitalist Grendel.

I am interested in challenging the cultural and technoeconomic *über*-determinisms on the general ground that they overly simplify complex structural situations. Specifically, they oversimplify by ignoring that there has been an enormous amount of warfare during the making of the modern world. I believe that the structural transformations that have occurred during the making of modernity have been just as much about violence as they have been about culture, technology, or economy. Elsewhere, I have argued (Reyna 1998) that globalization gurus have their monsters wrong. The modern world was made by a complex of economic and political structures that resulted from a cloning of Hobbes's behemoth (the state) with Adam Smith's Grendel (capitalism). The resulting Behemo-Grendelian monster is a *military-capitalist complex*. Cloning occurred through trial and error among the competing polities of Atlantic Europe. Spain and Portugal, in the 1500s and 1600s, tried and erred in making such a monster. In the 1700s and 1800s, France tried and lagged, especially as compared to Holland and England. By the end of the Napoleonic Wars, Great Britain had emerged as the most powerful Behemo-Grendelian. In the nineteenth century this monster spread across the Atlantic to the United States and east to Germany.

The military-capitalist complex used military force to facilitate concentration and accumulation of wealth in capitalist institutions and the resulting economic wealth to facilitate the concentration and accumulation of violent force in the central government. These mutually reinforcing dynamics are termed *logics of predatory and capital accumulation*. These logics resulted in globalization in the sense that a society that had perfected them relentlessly sought to utilize more and more of the world to accumulate more and more of the means of production and destruction. Countries that rigorously followed these logics tended to become especially wealthy and powerful. They tended to be called *Great Powers*.

Predatory and capital accumulation during the mercantile and industrial phases, among other things, involved the expenditure of violent force to conquer areas. These areas, especially in what has become known as the Third World, became colonies. Cultural, legal, and governmental institutions in colonies functioned to concentrate capital formation among the Great Power's capitalist firms. This process of conquest, colonization, and wealth extraction was *imperialism*. Imperialism was an especially rapid form of globalization. By 1900 imperialist Great Powers had conquered and turned most of the world into some form of colony.

Then, for reasons that are beyond the scope of this chapter, the Great Powers decided to abandon imperialism as a way of running the dual logics of predatory and capital accumulation. These decisions came after World War II. Between then and roughly 1960 most colonies received their independence. This, then, inaugurated a new era for the behemo-Grendelian monster, that is, the military-capitalist complex. This poses the question: "What is happening out there in the former colonies in the contemporary era of globalization?" This leads us back to Monsieur Ketté.

Ketté, the leader of a rebel movement in southern Chad, is correct. The "fundamental problem" in Chad is "structural." But I believe Chad's problem is shared by others in the Third World, especially Africa. The problem is occurring because these areas are having a different structural history in the current phase of globalization than that earlier experienced by the Great Powers. Specifically, what appears to have changed is the emergence of a type of relations of domination that inhibits the concentration and accumulation of violent force within the government, while encouraging its dispersion and accumulation. The notion of *relations of domination* requires introduction in order to understand the argument that makes this point plausible.

Societies may be represented as networks of organizations of power. Understanding how such networks are constituted and how their constitutions change depends upon two related notions, those of force and power. Actions do not simply occur. Rather they happen because something has the power to make them happen. *Power*, the ability to make things occur, ultimately results from the exercise of force, which is the utilization of combinations of different resources that can generate different outcomes. Force is not power. *Force* is that which makes power. The amount of powder in a cartridge has to do with its force. The fact that the bullet when fired penetrates six inches has to do with its power. Force is not always violent. Missionaries exercise nonviolent force that has the power to convert some. Crucifixion is an exercise of violent force that has the power to slow conversion.[3]

Individuals who are utterly alone posses only the force of their single bodies. Social structures, on the other hand, stockpile resources that give them, relative to individuals, enormous endowments of force. Thus it is organizations that effectively possess the force that can be exercised to generate different powers. This implies, if history is the temporal ordering of actions, that it is exercises of force in networks of social structures which generates the powers that produce the actions that are history. Such a history is a structural history. History involves an analysis of *relations of domination*, which are the structures in which certain actors control, that is, dominate, other actors in a population. Domination requires force and this, as just suggested, is exercised by institutions with resource endowments. Such endowments, including capital, people, tools, raw materials, and the knowledge of how to combine these to attain ends might be conceived of as a means of domination. The military-capitalist complex is a type of relations of domination whose fields of force have global reach.

Organizations with interacting actors, as in the state, exercising different forces, constitute a *forcefield*. Actors exercising force against each other to control each other are in conflict. Weaker actors expending force to frustrate stronger ones are exhibiting *resistance*. More powerful actors, whose exercise of force results in their control over weaker actors, have dominated the latter and have established relations of domination in fields of force.

Anarchy, as here defined, is a situation in which the operation and distribution of forces in a field of force are such that it is not possible to produce stable relations of domination. Processes in fields of force in which force is accumulated within a particular institution are those of *concentration*. Processes in which the reverse occurs, and force is diffused among a number of institutions, are those of *dispersion*. Sometimes the dispersion of violent force, in conjunction with continued accumulation of that force, can raise resistance to levels where it is impossible to establish enduring relations of domination, provoking a *violent anarchy*. This is a situation where actors in conflict resist each other using violent force. The monster creating such anarchy produces truly unimagined states.

I argue that the structural history of certain Third World countries in the current phase of globalization has produced such a monster. The argument is developed as follows. A history of the postcolonial Chadian state is provided in the following section. Next, the possibility that this history might be explained in terms of ethnicity and nationalism is discussed and rejected. Then there is a demonstration of how great and regional powers instituted a dispersion and accumulation of violent force that made the state an anarchic field of violent force in Chad. A final section puts the instance of Chad in a comparative context, suggesting that what happened in Chad is the development of an AIV-GIV Hydra. This is the new monster on the block which, though currently unimagined, may be ravening elsewhere in the Third World.

A brief word is in order about Chad. It is a large country of 1,284,000 square kilometers, roughly twice the size of France, that occupies most of what is known as the central Sudan. There has been a tendency of both officials and scholars to imagine this region as composed of two very different parts—a north and a south. The latter region is to the south and west of the Shari river. It is an area of relatively well-watered savanna, occupying perhaps a fifth of the country with about one-half its population of approximately six million. The major ethnic groups in the south prior to colonization were stateless, non-Muslim Sara and Masa speakers.

The north is a far more arid region. The extreme north—in a rough parallelogram running from the Tibesti mountains to the Ennedi Highlands to the Wadai plateau to Lake Chad—is desert. Immediately south of the desert is a Sahelian zone. Most of the ethnic groups in the north were Muslim. Camel pastoralists, called Tubu, controlled the desert. Cattle pastoralists, who tended to be Arab speakers, practiced transhumance south of the Tubu. Stretching from west to east in this zone were a string of precolonial states such as Bagirmi and Wadai. Chad was colonized by the French starting around 1900. It was they who first imposed a state organization over the north and south and who dominated the two regions from their capital in what is today N' Djamena. Independence was granted in 1960.

UNIMAGINED ENDINGS

Chad, thus, has been independent for thirty-four years. During this period there have been five presidents: François Tombalbaye (1962–1975), Félix Malloum (1975–1979), Goukouni Oueddei (1980–1982), Hissèn Habré (1982–1990), and Idriss Déby (1990–present). Particulars of each ruler's reign are described in order to establish the existence of a distinctive praxis in Chadian politics.[4]

An election was held a year prior to independence (1960) that was won by the *Parti Progressiste Tchadien* (PPT), whose head—Tombalbaye—had the right to become the first president of the fledgling republic. Throughout 1961–1962 Tombalbaye disposed of all his southern party rivals. In 1963 he turned against the northerners. At the same time, he made the PPT the sole legal party and himself president for life. At this point many of those who would rebel against Tombalbaye fled the country.

A national liberation movement called the *Front de Libération Nationale du Tchad* (FROLINAT) was formed in 1966. Two rebel fighting forces were created: *la Première Armée*—that operated in east-central regions, and *la Deuxième Armée*—that fought in the extreme north. France supplied up to 3,000 troops to support Tombalbaye's *Armée Nationale Tchadienne* (ANT) between 1969 and 1971. These troops employed tactics that emphasized the use of air power for ground support, tactics that resembled those that the United States was using at the same time in Vietnam. The French won every engagement and were gratified by the success of their 20-mm helicopter-mounted cannon.

Qaddafi gained control of Libya in 1969 and, though initially wary of FROLINAT, he had come to see it by 1970 as useful to his ends. With the support of Soviet-bloc nations, especially East Germany, the First and Second Armies were trained and armed by the Libyans (Buijtenhuijs 1978). When the French ceased direct military intervention in June 1971, the strengthened FROLINAT forces crushed the ANT. As a result, Tombalbaye was assassinated (1975) by elements of his own security forces.

Tombalbaye was replaced by his former chief of staff, Malloum, who governed as the head of the *Conseil Supérieur Militaire* (CSM). The forces opposing Tombalbaye had not been defeated and they continued to oppose Malloum. However, a split occurred in the Second Army, with its former leaders dividing it into two new forces. One part became the *Forces Armées du Nord* (FAN). This was led by Habré, a former official in the Tombalbaye regime. The other part became the *Forces Armée Populaire* (FAP). This was commanded by Goukouni, the son of the head (*derdé*) of the Teda, and only major leader who was not an ex-official. Malloum would be supported by the French. FAN and especially FAP would have Libyan assistance.

During the first three years of the Malloum regime French military support for the CSM gradually eroded. Libyan support, especially for the FAN, greatly increased. FAN troops continued to receive training from the Libyans as well as sophisticated arms such as SAM missiles and incendiary phosphorous mortars. As a result of this situation, Malloum was routed by 1978. However, by this time Habré and Goukouni were in conflict with each other over Libya, with the latter pro- and the former anti-Qaddafi. A defeated Malloum sought to profit from this split by inviting Habré to join his government. Habré did so, infiltrated FAN into the capital, and overcame Malloum (when the French deserted him) in 1979. However, a year later Goukouni, massively supported by the Libyans and their Soviet bloc allies, fought Habré in the streets of N'Djamena.

This combat was witnessed by a U.S. military person who was a veteran of Vietnam. He described the fighting as more intense than he had experienced at Hué during the Tet offensive. Habré, unable to stand against an estimated

200 Soviet T54 and T55 tanks, was driven for the first time into exile at the Novotel in the northern Camerouns.[5]

Goukouni, then, proceeded to rule in 1980, presiding over a government known as the *Gouvernement d'Union Nationale de Transition* (GUNT). However, the FAN had not been destroyed. On the Sudan/Chad border Habré would enlarge, rearm, and retrain his forces. U.S. support during this period seems to have been decisive. One source estimates that U.S. $100 million in military aid was delivered to the Sudan destined for the FAN (Joffe 1986:95). Habré was of interest to the Americans because his anti-Libyan stance was seen as a useful instrument for Reagan's anti-Qaddafi policy. A CIA–backed FAN marched largely unopposed during the dry season of 1982. The French remained neutral. GUNT was evicted from the capital in June of 1982. Habré was declared president.

Just as Goukouni could not destroy the FAN, Habré did not destroy the GUNT; and it immediately plotted armed opposition, finding a willing ally in Qaddafi. By early 1984 an army was created, the *Armée de la Libération* (ANL). This was organized in two main fronts. In the north were units that ultimately descended from Frolinat. These included the FAP, firmly under the control of Goukouni, and pro-Libyan. There was also a revived First Army, the CDR (which through late 1984 provided 60 percent of the GUNT's manpower), the *Volcan* Army, and the FAO. There was also a non-Frolinat contingent in this northern front. These were soldiers from Tombalbaye's ANT led by a southern leader, Colonel Abdul Kadir Kamougue, who had been a officer in Tombalbaye's military and who was then Goukouni's vice president in the exiled GUNT. Kamougue's men supplied about 25 percent of the GUNT's manpower through the end of 1984.

After assuming the presidency, Habré had sent his forces into southern Chad to establish authority. The troops led by Déby were involved in atrocities that precipitated the creation of purely southern guerilla movements. These were called *codos*, an abbreviation of commandos. There were at least six of these by the middle of 1984: the *Codos Rouge, Vert, Espoir, Noir, Vert Aigle*, and *Cocotier*. Most *codo* fighters came from the defunct ANT. Though originally autonomous, the *codos* agreed in October of 1984 to unite with the GUNT. Thus, by 1984 Habré faced a considerable coalition of ANL forces. This, however, was their high point.

The ANL was supported by Libya. In 1986, with very considerable assistance from the Soviets and East Germans, Libya invaded northern Chad, ostensibly in support of its allies. This had a double effect. On the one hand, a number of GUNT leaders went over to Habré because he, compared to Qaddafi, was viewed as the lesser of two evils. On the other hand,

Libyan invasion brought both the French and the Americans strongly into Habré's camp. French, American, and Chadian personnel campaigned together throughout 1987. When it was over, a tenth of Libya's army was lost and "Fred," an American of unknown connections, was busy "turning" Libyan prisoners into a contra force.

The extent of great power involvement at this time was considerable. Since 1983, when the French became firmly committed to Habré, they were estimated to have spent on the order of $500,000 per day defending him against the ANL (James 1987:81). During the period 1986–1987, when Goukouni was defeated, the French were reported to have spent $100 million in Chad (James 1987:22). These were the largest French military operations since the Algerian War (Lemarchand 1984:65). U.S. support during the 1986–1987 period was also substantial. It rushed in "$25 million worth of military aid in addition to the regular $5 million in military assistance. . . . At times giant American Hercules C-130 cargo planes landed on an almost daily basis in N'Djamena, ferrying in military supplies in the form of trucks, guns, ammunition, and Redeye anti-aircraft missiles" (James 1987:21). It is most implausible that Habré could have defeated the GUNT coalition without the help of his great power friends.

However, even in victory, opposition to Habré reemerged swiftly from elements of his own administration. He had originally come to power with considerable assistance from Idriss Miskine, who had led a rebel group from the Guera. Miskine died in 1984, officially as a result of "malaria," though it was widely believed that he had been killed by a unit of Habré's secret service known as "the Vultures." As a result, persons from the Guera in Habré's government became disaffected and formed in 1987 a rebel force called the *Mouvement du Salut National* (MOSANAT).

The architects of Habré's success against the Libyans had been two persons often said to be Zagawa. The first of these was Hassan Djamous, who had been the chief of staff in the war against Libya. The second was Idriss Déby, the army commander. Fearing that they might perish as Miskine had, Djamous, Déby, and the then interior minister, Itno, staged a coup on April 1989. It failed and Itno and Djamous paid with their lives. Déby fought his way to the Sudan. There, after receiving "money and military equipment" from Libya, he created a rebel force, the *Mouvement Patriotique du Salut* (MPS) (*Africa Confidential* 1989:8). The MPS united with MOSANAT. This force is reported to have received assistance from Togo and Burkina Faso (*Africa Confidential* 1990e:4).

Habré, for his part, concentrated his forces aggressively in the heart of Zagawa territory in early 1990. He did this with military assistance from Zaire, Israel, Iraq, and the United States (see *Africa Confidential* 1990e:4–5; *Africa*

Confidential 1989:4). If there was not a formal U.S./Israeli/Iraqi alliance to aid Habré, there was certainly an "informal" working relationship. The level of U.S. support for Habré at this time is unclear. He is described as having "close connections with the US" and as employing "former U.S. Marines as personal bodyguards" (*Africa Confidential* 1990b:3). Nevertheless, on November 25 there was a spectacular defeat of Habré at Iriba. A month latter Habré was on the road again, to the now familiar Novotel.

The pattern appeared to repeat itself in the early 1990s. There are currently probably seven rebel movements that seek to destroy Déby's government. The most important of these is the *Conseil de Salut National pour la Paix et la Démocratie au Tchad* (CSNPDT) located in southern Chad. This is headed by Moïse Ketté, who was a member of Habré's notorious secret security service. The CSNPDT is described as "growing" in 1993 (*Africa Confidential* 1993:6). A spokesman for the group, said to number 7,000, announced in September of last year, "We are prepared to die, they will have to exterminate us" (FBIS 1993:1).

In the region near Lake Chad the *Mouvement pour la Démocratie et le Développement* (MDD) is operating. This group seems to have been created by Habré. It is described as having an "impressive range of military hardware" (*West Africa* 1992:69). The MDD, nicknamed the Khmer Rouge, is said to be made of largely of members of Habré's old secret police and his army. It is described as wealthy and as supported by the CIA (*Africa Confidential* 1993:6). As a result of the raids of groups like the CSNPDT and the MDD there is again talk of the "fragmentation" of Chad (5).

Every president's rule, save for that of the current officeholder, has ended in his violent overthrow. These unintended endings, at least from the vantage point of the dispossessed president, are the signature of Chadian political praxis. They involve an alternation between disintegration, toward the end of a reign, and reintegration at the beginning of a new reign. The structural history of the Chadian state is one in which governments have lacked the ability to dominate rebel movements. Five times the government has had its domination unravel as taxes went unpaid, as officials also went unpaid, as roads crumbled, as schools closed, and legal cases went unheard. If, as defined in the first section, violent anarchy is a situation in which there are unstable relations of domination in fields of violent force, then Chad regularly descends into such anarchy. Readers should understand that nobody in Chad intended this situation. This poses the question, why the unimagined anarchy?

ETHNICITY

More often than not journalists and scholars have attributed the civil wars that make and unmake presidential regimes in Chad to essentialist tribal or ethnic conflicts.[6] Such explanations are only convincing if, indeed, the belligerencies just described have been ethnic. War may be said to be "ethnic" if two conditions are satisfied. The first of these is that the immediate cause of hostilities involves disputes between existing ethnicities. The second condition is that hostilities are performed by institutions of the ethnicities in conflict.

Belligerence is sometimes initiated in Chad as a result of confrontations between ethnicities. However, the casus belli described earlier appears to have been the political defeat of an official. FROLINAT'S founders had been ousted by Tombalbaye. Habré rearmed FAN after 1980 because he had been ousted by Goukouni. Déby organized the MPS because he had been ousted by Habré.

Hostilities also occurred as a result of anticipated political gains. Habré, for example, had been a relatively low official in the Tombalbaye regime. However, he switched sides and went over to Frolinat in the early 1970s because he seems to have calculated that he could rise farther as an organizer of FROLINAT forces.

It should equally be noted that the civil wars did not involve the institutions of ethnicities. Neither the armies of precolonial states like Bagirmi or Wadai, nor the kin-based militia of acephalous ethnicities such as the Sara were mobilized to fight the wars of high officials. Rebel fighting units were trained in the case of FROLINAT by Soviet-bloc specialists in unconventional, low-intensity conflict. Some of Habré's soldiers were probably trained by gentlemen like "Fred," that is, by U.S. specialists in unconventional war. These units once trained were led by ex-officials who organized them along bureaucratic lines, influenced by contemporary notions of guerilla war.[7] Certainly the soldiers of different rebel forces tended to be drawn from the ethnicities of their leaders. However, rebel forces were never uniquely constituted by a single ethnicity (Magnant 1984:48).[8]

Further, recruitment appears to have been as much from a specific educational category as from ethnicities. Throughout Chad there are young men who have had some formal education, but who have been obliged to stop schooling prior to finishing high school. Education gives these men aspirations beyond the local community. Many, in fact, dream of becoming *fonctionnaires* (officials). Economic conditions dictate that such men become largely underemployed urban laborers or that they return to their rural kin's land, where they become ordinary *meskin* (poor folk). To such men, joining a liberation army is a way of becoming "somebody." Rebel forces, thus, tend to be led by ex-officials who command soldiers that are would-be officials.

It is true, as the conflicts have continued, especially during and after the time of Habré, that some Chadians report that different ethnic groups are in conflict. Southerners may say that they are warring against Goran or Zagawa.

Northerners may relate they are warring against Sara. However, the evidence provided in this section, at least concerning the period roughly from 1960 through the late 1980s, suggests that neither condition needed to qualify Chad's wars as ethnic conflicts is satisfied. Put bluntly, Chadian presidential wars have not involved tribes fighting tribes over primordial tribal affairs. They have involved officials, ex-officials, and would-be officials fighting each other for control over the state. The anarchy, then, has not been the result of ethnic fratricide.

Nevertheless, new, postcolonial conceptions of ethnicity appear to be emerging in Chad. What is distinctive about these new conceptions is that vast areas of north and south, which were previously conceived of as having many different tribal ethnicities, are now reinvented in terms of overarching, regional ethnic affiliations. Northerners tend to get lumped as Zagawa, southerners as Sara. This means, because people from the north have generally been in conflict with people from the south, that there is an increasing ethnic element to the belligerence. There may be something of an irony here.

Wars that began as nonethnic clashes in a country with numerous ethnic groups have gradually evolved into such conflicts as whole regions have been reimagined ethnically. However, these are not essentialist ethnic squabbles because they are not about something in the primordial essence of Chadian tribes that was there before colonialism and exists after it. They are wars for domination of the contemporary state and, because northerners have squabbled with southerners for this control, it has been useful to give terminological recognition to this material reality.

NATIONALISM

It might be argued that at the heart of the anarchy are nationalist ideologies.[9] Specifically, it could be hypothesized that the different actors in Chad's internal wars possess competing national aspirations and that these, in large measure, provoke the violence. So attention turns to the ideological discourse of important actors.

An essential similarity between all the presidents and most of their opponents, even as they tried to kill each other, is that they have been nationalists. Institutions of the state and rebels have functioned to create and diffuse emblems, rituals, and discourse championing their image of a Chadian nation. A sense of how inventive this nationalist imagery has been can be acquired if one explores the ideological discourses of Tombalbaye. He, in a nicely tailored French suit, appealed to all Chadians in a 1961 speech, saying "Before being Arab, Muslim, Christian or Sara, we are Chadians." He went on to promise the nation the gift of "*la vie moderne*," which would be achieved through "*développement*" (Le Cornec 1963:315). Thus at the very beginning of Tombalbaye's rule nationalism is expressed in a discourse of modernization—one being espoused vigorously at the time by French technical advisers to his government, who probably wrote the text of his speech.

By the end of the 1960s, with the rebellion making the greatest headway in northern, Islamic areas, it was clear to all that the government needed to attract Muslims. So in 1972 the president, a Baptist, made the pilgrimage to Mecca; perhaps at the instigation of Ba Abdoul Aziz, a Mauritanian who served as Tombalbaye's advisor on Islamic matters. Afterward he exchanged his suit for the robes worn by Muslims and styled himself *el-hadj*. Thereafter his appeals for national unity had an Islamic ring to them.

However, by late summer 1973 Tombalbaye was concerned to create a truly Chadian nationalism. At the end of August the PPT was dissolved and replaced by the *Mouvement National pour la Révolution Culturelle et Sociale* (MNRCS). This new party's job was to invent tradition—lots of it, and fast. The MNRCS was inspired by a similar movement occurring at the same time in Mobutu's Zaire. Operating incessantly over the radio, this cultural revolution demanded a "*retour aux sources*." Gone was the Tombalbaye of modernization. Out was *el-hadj*. In was the new Tombalbaye who spoke in terms of *tchaditude*.

There were echos in *tchaditude* of the *négritude* that had been important among African and Caribbean intellectuals in the 1920s through the 1950s. *Négritude*, however, sought to celebrate universal qualities shared by all blacks. *Tchaditude* was far more particularistic—it was about Chad and Tombalbaye. It was a "Chadian socialism." According to one document of the time, this "was not a socialism based on that of Karl Marx. Chadian socialism has far more respect for the religious element that is one of the mental structures of the Chadian people" (Bouquet 1982:147).

In this *tchaditude*, the president was no longer merely a president. He was *Ngarta, le Guide*. He traveled now in the presence of his *Grand Griot* (Great praise singer) who always sang the qualities *du Guide*, such as "*Ngarta, champion des champions! Il connait tout, sans papier!*" and even in English "*Ngarta, number one!*" The griot's chants were echoed endlessly on the radio. Tombalbaye, then, had concocted three variations upon a nationalist discourse, and it did him no good. His opponents shot him in the belly and left him to die. They did so in the name of nationalism. Frolinat, for example, which had been the key rebel organization in the struggle against Tombalbaye, stated that one of its major goals was the "unity of the Chadian nation."

Mallourn and the CSM would stress an ideology of "*réconciliation nationale*" that welcomed all into the "*grande famille tchadienne*." Malloum's chief opponent at the time was said to be "above all a nationalist . . . uncompromising in his determination to build a nation state"(Lemarchand 1984:65). When Habré seized the government he made the day he came to power "National Liberation, Unity and Martyrs' Day." Further, to disseminate his nationalism he created the *Union Nationale pour l'indépendance et la Révolution* (UNIR), a party that in certain ways harked back to the MNRCS.

Déby today governs with a strongly nationalist ideology. Further, in response to the urging of both the French and the Americans, he has organized a *Conférence Nationale Souveraine*; one that seeks to institute more "democratic" means of attaining his nationalist goals. Nevertheless, the two major rebel movements—Habré's MDD and Ketté's CSNPDT—attack Déby on the grounds that his is a defective nationalism and theirs is not.

Thus, the major political actors on all sides have consistently justified their actions on the basis of some form of nationalist ideology. Such evidence, of course, is consistent with a view that nationalism provokes Chadian conflict. However, I am skeptical of this view for reasons outlined below. The proposition that "Chadian nationalisms provoke conflict" is causal. Causal statements express the existence of spatiotemporal orderings of events and of the fact that in these orderings, antecedent events produce subsequent events (Miller 1987). This means that for a causal statement to be supported by evidence there must be observation of 1) spatiotemporal ordering, and 2) the production of subsequents by antecedents. This would mean for the proposition under evaluation that 1) Chadian nationalism occurs first in time and that the conflicts occur subsequently, and 2) that it is the nationalism that actually produces (i.e., causes) the conflicts.

Evidence bearing upon the preceding is as follows. A number of persons, such as Ibrahim Abatcha, were members of a party called the *Union Nationale Tchadienne* (UNT) in the early 1960s. This party, which has been called neo-Marxist, was in opposition to Tombalbaye's PPT. All parties save for the PPT were dissolved in 1962. This sharpened UNT strife against Tombalbaye. So the leadership of the UNT decided to draft a policy statement, written by Abatcha, that presented its position. Events soon moved quickly. There were anti-Tombalbaye riots in 1963 that were violently suppressed.

This made anti-Tombalbaye leaders, including most of the leaders of the UNT, flee Chad. These exiled leaders met in Nyala in the Sudan and created Frolinat on June 22, 1966. A "*programme politique*" was adopted at this time that, according to one commentator, was identical with that of the 1962 UNT policy statement (Buijtenhuijs 1978:123). This statement was the inception of FROLINAT'S version of Chadian nationalism. The point to grasp is that those who would be Frolinat leaders were in conflict with Tombalbaye as far back as

1962. As a result of this, as a part of creating an organization to combat Tombalbaye violently, they also formulated a statement that would become their nationalistic justification of this combat. Thus spaciotemporal ordering appears to be the reverse of what the proposition predicts. Instead of nationalism provoking conflict, conflict produced FROLINAT'S nationalism.

This spaciotemporal sequencing of conflict and ideology seems to repeat itself through the succeeding presidencies. When Tombalbaye was replaced by Malloum in 1975, Goukouni and Habré were already involved in a bloody war with Malloum's government. Consequently they devised and broadcast over their radios endless discourses that discredited Malloum and praised themselves on nationalist grounds. Similarly, when Goukouni drove Habré from Chad in 1980, the two were in the midst of a most violent war. As a result Habré invented his own brand of anti-Goukouni ideology. The early anti-Tombalbaye discourse of FROLINAT complained that Tombalbaye sold out national sovereignty to the French. Habré, taking a page from this tactic, constructed Goukouni as a dupe of the Libyans and promised true national liberation if he were allowed to rule.

When Déby fled for his life to the Sudan in 1989 he was in the midst of a violent confrontation with Habré. His response was to create the MPS, and then, using MPS sources, issued an angry discourse suggesting that Habré was a tyrant who had sold out his country to the Israelis and the Americans. Déby, of course, promised that with him good times and national autonomy were just around the corner. In Chad, then, it seems that conflict causes those who are party to the conflict to invent nationalistic tradition, rather than the reverse. Nationalism does not appear to be a cause of Chad's anarchy.[10]

ACCUMULATION AND DISPERSION OF VIOLENT FORCE

How then does one account for the cycling between dis- and reintegration? I begin to answer this question by documenting changes in the means of violence. FROLINAT, in the earliest days of rebellion against Tombalbaye, had perhaps a hundred partisans who fought for the most part with lances. There were then less than a thousand soldiers in Tombalbaye's army. By the time of Habré's rule in 1986 and 1987 there were perhaps 20,000 soldiers in different liberation armies armed with everything from tanks, to missiles, to phosphorous mortars. Habré may have had up to 25,000 people in his army. By the mid-1990s the two major rebel movements in opposition to Déby were reporting that they have 10,000 soldiers while Déby was supposed to have an armed force estimated to number 50,000. In 1966 there were probably less than 1,000 government and rebel soldiers. In 1994 there were well over 60,000 such soldiers. In 1966 these troops were poorly armed. In 1994 they possessed a ferocious array of the most modern weapons. A first finding is that there has been a spectacular accumulation of the means of violence in postcolonial Chad.

The accumulation of violent force has not been associated with its concentration in the hands of the central government because of the continual creation of rebel military institutions that started forming during Tombalbaye's rule. These may be characterized as *autarkic*.[11] The term *autarkic* means self-sufficient. Rebel groups were self-sufficient in the sense that they were not part of the Chadian government. They had their own organizations, ideologies, administrative procedures, and resources in soldiers and weaponry for performing their violence. The term *autarkic* does not mean that the rebel movements were uninfluenced by Chadian government institutions. Indeed, the Chadian military did whatever it could to render the rebel bands as dysfunctional as possible. Most important, government military units sought to influence the rebel movements by killing their soldiers. This and the previous paragraph document that the means of violence in Chad, roughly between 1960 and 1990, were dispersed across a number of autarkic and government military institutions. This means that the structural history of postcolonial Chad has exhibited a logic of both the accumulation and dispersion of violent force.

Autarkic institutions of violence (hereafter AIV) exercise their violence to compete for control over the state. The existence of such institutions means that the government institutions of violence must resist their autarkic competitors. Three necessities result. First, contests for control of the state must be violent. Second, as AIVs win, the state tends to disintegrate. Third, when AIVs have won, they become government institutions of violence, allowing the state to reintegrate. The preceding means that the fields of force in Chad are not only dispersed, they are unstable. Such a structural history has implications for relations of domination. Specifically, it means that AIVs are able to exhibit enormous resistance to the government. Five times this resistance has been so great that the government has lacked the means to overcome it. Thus in independent Chad, dispersed fields of violent force have produced periodically bloody anarchy.

Why has this occurred? There appear to be two important determinants of postcolonial Chadian structural history. The first pertains to the accumulation of violent force. The enormous growth in local institutions of violence resulted from international competition for regional influence.[12] France, Libya, the United States, the Soviet Union, East Germany, Israel, Togo, Burkina Faso, the Palestinians, Nigerians, Zairois, Egyptians, and the Sudanese have continually provided military resources to both liberation and government armies. However, the major suppliers of arms, training, and at times soldiers have been France in aid of the ruling regime;[13] Libya, in promotion of the rebels; and the United States, in support of whoever opposed Libya.[14]

One military observer posed the question, "how can impoverished Chad afford to fight?" He responded to his question by noting, "the simple answer, of course, is that it can't. The war is being paid for by the French and the Americans" (Coxe 1988:166). The United States, it will be recalled, is reported to have spent on the order of $100 million to rearm Habré in the early 1980s. The French then spent about $500,000 per day between 1983 and 1986 defending Habré. The Israelis, Iraqis, and Zairois have operated in many ways as surrogates of the Americans. In sum, Great Power actions to influence Chad allowed both the government and the rebels to accumulate violent force. It has been the arming of both rebels and government troops that dispersed the accumulating violent force, and made for the instability in the fields of force. To the extent that the Great Powers created this instability, they were responsible for the anarchy it produced.

Chad is among the poorest, least developed peripheries of the periphery, which poses the question, "Why the French and American interest?" There are, I believe, two answers to this question. The first is geopolitical and the second is more directly economic. Both answers ultimately bear upon the well-being of French and American capitalists. An American diplomat once confided to me that Chad is a "back door" to the Middle East and southern Africa. If, for example, he went on, Libya were to "destabilize" Chad, then it would be far easier to undermine Egypt and the Sudan as well as Zaire and southern Africa. If Egypt were destabilized, Western, and especially U.S., control over Near Eastern oil might be in jeopardy. Similarly, if Zaire and southern Africa were removed from the Western "camp," a number of raw materials classified as of "strategic" importance to industry might be at risk. So French and American strategists insured better control over raw materials by holding the line in Chad. Access to such materials, of course, is not a matter to which capitalists are indifferent. Then there is the matter of Chad's direct value to Western industry. As one commentator notes, "The key to French interest is the south's petroleum" (*Africa Confidential* 1993:6). It has been suspected since colonial times that Chad is rich in mineral and oil resources. Oil was discovered in commercially exploitable quantities by the early 1970s. This was in two areas: around Lake Chad, where the MDD operates, and in the south near the town of Doba, where the CSNPD is active. The southern oil reserves are considerable. Exploitation of these by a U.S.–European consortium made up of Elf and Chevron under the leadership of Shell is supposed to begin in five years. French and U.S. military investments in Chad allow them to protect the interests of Elf, Chevron, and Shell, thereby helping these companies to maintain healthy profits.

If great powers like the United States and France made possible the accumulation and dispersal of violent force, local class structure provided the motivation to use them. Most Chadians, probably some 80 percent, are subsistence or semisubsistence cultivators. There are a few merchants and very, very few manufacturers and employees of multinational corporations. The only occupation that permits the accumulation of wealth is that of the *haut fonctionnaire*. The high salaries combined with sweet political deals enjoyed by such officials allow them to acquire capital. This is typically funneled into local land and businesses as well as into international investments in capitalist enterprise. There are really only two choices in such a class structure. One can remain a desperately poor food producer, or one can become a bureaucrat. Given such choices, Chadians strongly desired to become and remain officials, even if this means taking a turn at participating in an AIV.

A NEW MONSTER IN GLOBAL FIELDS

Apter and Rosberg—experienced students of African politics—following a review of some of the difficulties analysts have had understanding the postcolonial African state, suggest that it is now "time for a new round of reconceptualizing" (1994:4). I argue below that the findings concerning Chad recur throughout the Third World, that these comparative findings indicate commentators have overlooked a significant aspect of the structural history of the Third World, postcolonial state, and, finally, that efforts to think about what has been overlooked constitute Apter and Rosberg's desired reconceptualization.

Table 10.1 summarizes data concerning the existence of AIVs in African wars since 1960. A number of points of clarification are in order concerning the table. First, it includes data from forty-one Saharan or sub-Saharan African countries. Excluded are island states, such as Madagascar, and extremely small, and hence atypical, ones, such as Djibuti. States included in the table fall into one of two categories: those where there have been AIV wars against the central government, and those where such wars have been absent. (Just as there are autarkic institutions of violence, abbreviated as AIV, so there are government institutions of violence, abbreviated as GIV.) War is said to have occurred if AIV/GIV combat has led to at least one hundred deaths.

Table 10.1.   Incidence of AIV-GIV Warfare in Africa (1969–1993)

AIV-GIV War Present	No AIV-GIV War
1. Somalia (Adam 1992)	1. Lesotho (*AC* 1986a)
2. Guinea (*AC* 1986b; Lemarchand 1992)	2. Gabon (*AC* 1990a)
3. Burundi (*AC* 1990c)	3. Central African Republic (*AC* 1991a)
4. Senegal (*AC* 1990d)	4. Ivory Coast (Amondji 1986)
5. Chad (this chapter)	5. Tanzania (Lugalla *PC*)
6. Gambia (*AC* 1991b)	6. Botswana (Holm and Molutsi 1992)
7. Sierre Leone (*AC* 1992a)	7. Zambia (Decalo 1998)
8. Liberia (*AC* 1992b)	8. Malawi (Decalo 1998)
9. Rwanda (*AC* 1994a)	9. Ghana (McFarland 1990)
10. Uganda (Avrigan and Hovey 1982)	10. Kenya (Decalo 1998)
11. Congo-Brazzaville (Ballif 1993)	
12. Congo-Kinshasha (Young and Turner 1985)	
13. Guinea-Bissao (Cabral 1974)	
14. Sudan (Daly and Sikainga 1993)	
15. Equatorial Guinea (Fegley 1989)	
16. Mozambique (Finnegan 1992)	
17. Namibia (Innes 1977)	
18. Burkina Faso (Jaffré 1989)	
19. Mauretania (Marchesin 1995)	
20. Zimbabwe (Martin and Johnson 1981)	
21. South Africa (Mokoena 1993)	
22. Mali (Pietrowski 1991)	
23. Niger (Charlick 1991)	
24. Nigeria (Stremlau 1978)	
25. Angola (Rusk 1987; Spikes 1993)	
26. Ethiopia (Tiryneh 1993)	
27. Western Sahara (Hodges 1983)	
28. Eretria (Selassie 1980)	
29. Cameroon (LeVine 1974)	
30. Togo (Decalo 1987a)	
31. Benin (Decalo 1987b)	
Percentage	
76%	24%

The table justifies the following three points. First, AIV-GIV wars have been extremely widespread throughout Africa, occurring in 76 percent of the states. Second, AIV/GIV war has been extraordinarily bloody. In the fourteen countries where such wars have been the most severe, approximately 3.6 million people have perished through the mid-1990s (Reyna n.d.). Third, great and regional powers have contributed to these wars, having been involved in 74 percent of them. Such findings support the conclusion that AIV/GIV wars, nurtured by great and regional powers, and the anarchy they provoke are a monstrous fact of postcolonial, African life.

AIV/GIV wars have been frequent in other areas of the Third World. They have arisen throughout South America since the success of the Cuban Revolution, most notably currently in Colombia. They dominated Central America in Guatemala, El Salvador, and Nicaragua during the 1980s. The different liberation movements of the Middle East and North Africa, including contemporary fundamentalist ones, have pitted AIVs against their governments. Since the success of the Chinese Revolution such wars occurred throughout Asia in the Philippines, Sri Lanka, Malaysia, Indonesia, and the various fragments of what was Indochina. AIV/government war has been rare among great powers, with the major occurrence being the long-standing conflict in Northern Ireland.

Great and regional powers have been involved frequently in these wars with involvement often exhibiting a Cold War logic, for example, if a communist state supported a Third World AIV, a noncommunist state would support that country's central government and vice versa. In sum, AIV/GIV war, enabled in part by great and regional powers, intending either to facilitate or resist the interests of capitalists, has been common throughout the Third World.

What are the implications of the preceding? It was noted that it is commonly understood that "military control has increased in the world's states over the last thirty years" (Tilly 1990:205), and that this is especially true in the Third World (Jackman 1976). Such a realization poses the question of the structural properties of this militarism. Here the literature has emphasized the existence of coups d'état and the subsequent occupation of nonmilitary posts by military persons.[15] It is true that generals have moved from being merely generals to being generals who are also presidents. This is certainly an important structural process; one of consolidation, where nonmilitary offices come to be occupied by military personnel, conflating their nonmilitary with their military functions.

However, the findings of this chapter indicate that another structural process has been occurring at the same time. This has been a "leaking" of institutions of violence out of the realm of government into that of civil society. Thus, not one, but two, processes seem to characterize the recent structural history of states, and this second process has gone unimagined in the discourse concerning their militarism. This previously unremarked structural history exhibits a dynamic *different* from that which occurred during the making of the modern European state. The structural history of these powers between A.D. 1500 and A.D. 1900 involved the evolution of fields of force in which violence was increasingly accumulated and concentrated within specialized, military institutions of the central government (Tilly 1990). Aristocrats became Don Quixotes, while revolting peasants, such as those reputed to have infested Sherwood Forest in the Middle Ages, were disarmed and sent packing to the factories.

Why might the preceding be important? Think monsters, and recognize that recent globalization has involved the provision of violent force by Great Powers to both AIVs and GIVs in Third World countries. This has been a structural history that produces a curious structural monster. Remember the Hydra, the many-headed horror that Hercules had to kill during his labors? What has emerged in the Chads of this world is a new sort of Hydra. Imagine one of its heads to be a GIV. Next imagine the other heads to be AIVs. Then imagine all the heads, connected to the body of the country, weaving and bobbing, endlessly striking at each other. Let us call this monster the AIV-GIV Hydra.

Currently globalization is characterized by resource depletion as a result of the increasing consumption of raw materials by capitalist enterprises as they follow the logic of capital accumulation (Reyna 1991). This occurs at a time when the world is being populated by AIV-GIV Hydras whose fields of force feature a greater propensity to decide issues violently. Thus, global fields of force may consist of a few Great Powers, whose Behemo-Grendelian monsters, experiencing difficulties in capital accumulation, may be twitchy, among a swarm of AIV-GIV Hydras—armed and ready to rumble. Such a conjuncture in global fields of force may mark the outset of a postmodern era of violent anarchy.

THE DISASTERS OF WAR

We have been speculating on the future. In conclusion let us contemplate the present by attending that most civilized of events, an art exhibition. Toward the end of his life, the Spanish artist Goya produced a series of etchings that have come to be known as *The Disasters of War*. Each of the eighty etchings records a different abomination of the Napoleonic Wars in Spain. The last of these etchings contain images of monsters attacking humans. For example, plate number seventy-two, "The Consequences," shows a vampirelike creature sucking at a human body. One dresses up, goes to the exhibition containing this print, and thinks, "Oh, what imagination, how creative," secure in the knowledge the monsters are unreal, prior to ambling off to the reception with its succulent brie and chilled chablis.

But we now know better. AIV-GIV Hydras marching to logics of bloody anarchy ravage Chadians, regardless of what anyone might intend. Chad is not alone. The Behemo-Grendelian monsters of Great Powers have given up formal imperialism for the promoting of AIV-GIV Hydras among lesser powers, as they go about the business of structuring the Third World to the satisfaction of capital. Such fosterings—be they in Ethiopia, Somalia, Colombia, Nicaragua, El Salvador, or Guatemala—create the disasters of war. We patronize the arts, so civilized, swilling brie and chablis. We point our fingers at the Nazis, satisfied that they were evil, so we are not; unimagining of the monsters we create.

NOTES

1. For reasons that will become clear later, in the text I prefer not to use the Weberian definition of the state (1958). Rather, a *state* is understood to be a territory in which there are two sets of institutions, those of a central government and those of the civil society, where the government in varying degrees attempts to dominate persons within the civil society. States "disintegrate" when the organs of the central government either cease to function or barely function. They "reintegrate" when these begin to operate again.

2. Use of the term *imagined* in the text, though suggested by Anderson (1983), should not be construed as acceptance of his views. Indeed, an implicit position of this chapter is that much of what goes on in social life comes as an unimagined surprise.

3. A relations of domination approach to structural history is presented in Reyna (1994a). Discussion of precolonial relations of domination in Chad are addressed in Reyna (1994b). Changes to the relations of domination during the colonial and postcolonial periods are analyzed in Reyna (n.d.).

4. Discussion of the Chadian civil wars roughly between 1966 and 1980 can be found in Buijtenhuijs (1978), Bouquet (1982), Chapelle (1980), Reyna (n.d.). Accounts of post-1980 events can be found in Boyd (1984), Joffe (1986), Kelley (1986), Lanne (1987), and May (1990). For events in the 1990s I have relied upon my own interviews.

5. The exact extent of Libyan/Soviet-bloc support for Goukouni is unknown. However, it has been suggested by one source that some 14,000 Libyan troops were withdrawn from Chad on November 4, 1981 (Lemarchand 1984). These troops were conventionally armed with considerable Soviet bloc logistical support.

6. Buijtenhuijs (1978) argues from the perspective of northern Chad in favor of treating Chad's civil wars as ethnic conflicts.

7. The First Army in the mid 1970s had acquired modern weapons and uniforms. It divided its zone of operations into seven *wilayas* (military commands). There was a military council that supervised the operations of the different commands. Each

wilay was represented on the council by its commander and a delegate elected from its soldiers. Soldiers were given extensive training in guerilla operations, often from their own leaders, who had received such training from Middle Eastern or Soviet-bloc specialists. A twenty-page manual explained to the soldiers their responsibilities and the punishments that would be incurred if they were derelict in the execution of these operations. Weber (1958) would classify such a fighting force as bureaucratic.

8. Sometimes it is said that this or that liberation army is composed of Goran, Sara, or Hadjerai tribesmen, as if each of these terms designated a single, discrete, and fixed ethnicity. They do not. The terms *Goran, Sara,* or *Hadjerai* are generic expressions applied by outsiders that classify in common different peoples with different and changing ethnic identities. The word *Goran,* for example, was used by Chadian Arabs, with whom I lived in the early 1970s, pretty much as a pejorative to describe anybody living in the desert. Kreda, Zagawa, Teda, Daza were all lumped together as Goran. Then, as today, a Zagawa knows that she or he is not a Teda.

9. Discussion of ideology and nationalism in the context of Chad can be found in Magnant (1984) and Ciammaichella (1990).

10. Michalon has argued that authoritarian or dictatorial actions were encouraged in Chad in order "to break up traditional societies . . . and thus allow the emergence of national feeling" (1979). My view of the matter is different. During the late 1960s and 1970s, the period about which Michalon writes, there was little effort at least on the part of the state to "break up" ethnicities. Local governments had difficulties getting into the countryside to do the breaking up, either because they lacked the resources to do so or they were denied access by the rebels. Further, throughout this time the state was preoccupied with defeating rebels and did not want to create additional problems by provoking local communities. However, the espousal of nationalist sentiments gave a person legitimacy that allowed him or her to be a major political actor. Such actors soon became involved in violent contests for control over the state, whose very violence provoked authoritarian actions. In this view dictatorial practices are an unintended consequence of "hardball" politics, rather than an intended result of a strategy to create nationalism.

11. *Autarkic,* as used in the text, means that rebels are independent of the central government in the sense that they are not part of it. This obliges government to exercise force to control such institutions.

12. Great power strategies vis-à-vis Africa are discussed in Foltz and Bienen (1985).

13. Some discussion of the role France in Chadian military affairs can be found in Cox (1988).

14. The full story of Libya's involvement in Chad is untold. However, an account of it until 1981 can be found in Neuberger (1982). Description of French/Libyan competition in Chad can be found in Somerville (1990). There are only anecdotal accounts of the U.S. role in Chad.

15. An introduction to this literature can be found in Cammack, Pool, and Tordoff (1993:133–69).

REFERENCES

Abi-Saab, G. 1978. *The UN Operation in the Congo, 1960–1964.* London: Oxford University Press.

Adam, H. 1992. "Somalia, Militarism, Warlordism, or Democracy?" *Review of African Political Economy* 54:11–27.

Africa Confidential. 1986a. "Lesotho: Uneasy Nuptials." *Africa Confidential* 27, no. 7:7–8.

———. 1986b. "Guinea: The General's Hand." *Africa Confidential* 27, no. 16:3–6.

———. 1989. "USA/Chad: Target Gadaffi." *Africa Confidential* 30, no. 1:1–2.

———. 1990a. "Gabon: Ethnic Intrigue." *Africa Confidential* 31, no. 7:2–3.

———. 1990b. "Chad: Operation Rezzou." *Africa Confidential* 31, no. 9:2–3.

———. 1990c. "Burundi: Buyoya's Rubicon." *Africa Confidential* 31, no. 20:2–3.

———. 1990d. "Senegal: Crisis in Casamance." *Africa Confidential* 31, no. 23:1–2.

———. 1990e. "Chad: Habré Out, Déby In." *Africa Confidential* 3, no. 24:2–3.

———. 1991a. "CAR: Conciliation or Clampdown." *Africa Confidential* 32, no. 15:6–7.

———. 1991b. "Gambia: Heroes No More." *Africa Confidential* 32, no. 15:7.

———. 1992a. "Sierra Leone: Junior Officers Jump the Gun." *Africa Confidential* 33, no. 9:3–4.

———. 1992b. "Liberia: The Forces in Contention." *Africa Confidential* 33, no. 22:3–4.

———. 1993. "Chad: Finding Oil in Troubled Waters." *Africa Confidential* 34, no. 4:5–6.

———. 1994a. "Rwanda: Civilian Slaughter." *Africa Confidential* 35, no. 9:5–6.

———. 1994b. "Rwanda: A Double Agent." *Africa Confidential* 35, no. 10:7.

Amondji, M. 1986. *Côte d'Ivoire, le P.D.C.I. et la vie politique de 1945 à 1985*. Paris: Harmattan.

Anderson, B. 1983. *Imagined Communities: Reflections on the Origin and Spread of Nationalism*. New York: Verso.

Apter, D., and C. Rosberg, eds. 1994. *Political Development and the New Realism in Sub-Saharan Africa*. Charlottesville: University of Virginia Press.

Avrigan, T., and M. Hovey. 1982. *War in Uganda: The Legacy of Idi Amin*. London: Zed.

Ballif, N. 1993. *Le Congo*. Paris: Karthala.

Bouquet, C. 1982. *Tchad: Genèse d'un conflit*. Paris: Harmattan.

Boyd, H. 1984. "Chad: A Civil War without End." *Journal of African Studies* 10, no. 4:119–26.

Buijtenhuijs, R. 1978. *Frolinat et les révoltes populaires du Tchad, 1965–1976*. The Hague: Mouton.

Cabral, A. 1974. *Guiné-Bissau: Naço African Forjada na Luta*. Lisbon: Nova Aurora.

Cammack, P., D. Pool, and W. Tordoff. 1993. *Third World Politics: A Comparative Approach*. 2d ed. Baltimore: Johns Hopkins University Press.

Ciammaichella, G. 1990. "Ciad: conflittualità permanente e ricerca di un identità nazionale (xix–xx sec)." *Oriente Moderno* 9, no. 1/6:110–35.

Chapelle, J. 1980. *Le Peuple Tchadien: Ses Racines, sa vie quotidienne et ses combats*. Paris: Harmattan.

Charlick, R. B. 1991. *Niger: Personal Rule and Survival in the Sahel*. Boulder, Colo.: Westview.

Cox, J. T. G. 1988. "Chad: France in Africa." *Army Quarterly and Defence Journal* 118, no. 2:161–67.

Daly, M., and A. A. Sikainga. 1993. *Sudan's Civil War*. New York: St. Martin's.

Decalo, S. 1987a. *Historical Dictionary of Togo*. Metuchen, N.J.: Scarecrow Press.

———. 1987b. *Historical Dictionary of Benin*. Metuchen, N.J.: Scarecrow Press.

———. 1998. *The Stable Minority: Civilian Rule in Africa.* Gainesville, Fla.: FAP Books

FBIS (Foreign Broadcast Information Service). 1993. "Rebels Threaten to Sabotage Oil Exploration Project." FBIS-AFR-93-178. Springfield, Va.: National Technical Information Service.

———. 1994. "Government Said Satisfied with Talks." FBIS-AFR-94-039. Springfield, Va.: National Technical Information Service.

Fegley, R. 1989. *Equatorial Guinea: An African Tragedy.* New York: Peter Lang.

Finnegan, W. 1992. *A Complicated War: The Harrowing of Mozambique.* Los Angeles: University of California Press.

Foltz, W. J., and H. S. Bienen. 1985. *Arms and the African.* New Haven, Conn.: Yale University Press.

Hannerz, U. 1992. *Cultural Complexity: Studies in the Social Organization of Meaning.* New York: Columbia University Press.

Hilferding, R. 1981. *Finance Capital: A Study of the Latest Phase of Capitalist Development.* London: Routledge & Kegan Paul.

Hodges, T. 1983. *Western Sahara: Roots of a Desert War.* Westport, Conn.: Praeger

Holm, J. D., and P. Molutsi. 1992. "State Society Relations in Botswana." In *Governance and Politics in Africa.* Edited by G. Hyden and M. Bratton. Boulder, Colo.: Lynn Rienner.

Innes, D. 1977. "Imperialism and the National Struggle in Namibia." *Review of African Political Economy* 9:44–60.

Jackman, R. W. 1976. "Politicians in Uniform: Military Governments and Social Change in the Third World." *American Political Science Review* 70:1078–97.

James, F. 1987. "Habre's Hour of Glory." *Africa Report* 32:20–23.

Jaffré, B. 1989. *Burkina Faso: Les Années Sankara de la révolution à la rectification.* Paris: Harmattan.

Joffe, E. G. H. 1986. "The International Consequences of the Civil War in Chad." *Review of African Political Economy* 7, no. 6: 91–104.

Kelley, M. P. 1986. *A State in Disarray: Conditions of Chad's Survival.* Boulder, Colo.: Westview.

Lanne, B. 1987. "Quinze ans d'ouvrages politiques sur le Tchad." *Afrique Contemporaine* 144:37–47.

Le Cornec, J. 1963. *Histoire politique du Tchad.* Paris: Librairie générale de droit et jurisprudence.

Lemarchand, R. 1984. "Putting the Pieces Back Together Again." *Africa Report* 27:60–67.

———. 1922. *Burundi: Ethnocide as Discourse and Practice.* New York: Cambridge University Press.

LeVine, V. 1974. *Historical Dictionary of Cameroun.* Metuchen, N.J.: Scarecrow Press.

Luckham, R. 1993. "French Militarism in Africa." *Review of African Political Economy* 24:55–85.

Lugala, J. 1995. Personal communication. Anthropology Department, University of New Hampshire, Durham.

Magnant, J.P. 1994. "Peuple, ethnies et nation: Le Cas du Tchad." *Droit et Culture* 8:29–50.

Magnant, J. P. 1984. *La Terre sara, terre tchadienne.* Paris: L'Harmattan.

Marchesin, P. 1995. *Tribu, ethnies, et pouvoir en Mauritanie.* Paris: Karthala.

Martin, D., and P. Johnson. 1981. *The Struggle for Zimbabwe.* New York: Monthly Review Press.

May, R. 1990. "Internal Dimensions of Warfare in Chad." *Cambridge Anthropology* 13, no. 2:17–27.

McFarland, D. M. 1990. *Historical Dictionary of Ghana.* Metuchen, N.J.: Scarecrow Press.

Michalon, T. 1979. "Le Drame du Tchad et l'héritage colonial de l'Afrique: L'Echec de la greffe Jacobine." *Le Monde diplomatique* (avril).

Miller, R. W. 1987. *Fact and Method.* Princeton, N.J.: Princeton University Press.

Mokoena, K. 1993. *South Africa and the United States: A National Security Archive Documents Reader.* New York: New Press.

Neuberger, B. 1982. *Involvement, Invasion, and Withdrawal: Qaddafi's Libya and Chad 1969–1981.* Tel Aviv: Shiloah Center for Middle Eastern and African Studies, Tel Aviv University.

Pietrowski, M. 1991. "Cessation of Tuareg Repression, Respite or Resolution." *Africa Today* 38:41–47.

Ranger, T. 1985. *Peasant Consciousness and Guerrilla War in Zimbabwe.* Los Angeles: University of California Press.

Reyna, S. P. 1991. "What Is to Be Done?" In *The Political Economy of African Famine.* Edited by R. E. Downs, D. O. Kerner, and S. P. Reyna. Philadelphia: Gordon and Breach.

———. 1994a. "A Mode of Domination Approach to Organized Violence." In *Studying War: Anthropological Perspectives.* Edited by S. Reyna and R. Downs. New York: Gordon and Breach.

———. 1994b. "Predatory Accumulation and Religious Conflict in the Early 19th Century." In *Studying War: Anthropological Perspectives.* Edited by S. Reyna and R. Downs. New York: Gordon and Breach.

———. 1998. "The Force of Two Logics: Predatory Accumulation in the Making of the Great Leviathan, 1415–1764." In *Deadly Developments.* By S. Reyna and R. Downs. New York: Gordon and Breach.

———. n.d. "Domination in the Absence of the Means." In *Paths of Violence: Destruction and Deconstruction in African States.* Edited by G. Bond and J. Vincent. New York: Gordon and Breach.

Rusk, J. D. 1987. "Warfare and Human Rights in Angola and Mozambique." *Africa Today* 34, no. 4:33–43.

Selassie, B. H. 1980. *Conflict and Intervention in the Horn of Africa.* New York: Monthly Review Press.

Somerville, K. 1990. *Foreign Military Intervention in Africa.* New York: St. Martin's.

Spikes, D. 1993. *Angola and the Politics of Intervention.* Jefferson, N.C.: McFarland.

Stremlau, J. J. 1978. *The International Politics of the Nigeria Civil War, 1967–1970.* Princeton, N.J.: Princeton University Press.

Tilly, Charles. 1990. *Coercion, Capital, and European States.* Oxford, U.K.: Basil Blackwell.

Tiryneh, A. 1993. *Ethiopian Revolution 1974–1987.* New York: Cambridge University Press.

Watts, M. 1991. "Heart of Darkness: Reflections of Famine and Starvation in Africa." In *The Political Economy of African Famine*. Edited by R. E. Downs, D. O. Kerner, and S. P. Reyna. Philadelphia: Gordon and Breach.

Weber, M. 1958. *From Max Weber: Essays in Sociology*. New York: Oxford University Press.

West Africa. 1992. "Chadian Affairs." *West Africa* 3878 (January 13–19): 69–70.

Young, C., and T. Turner. 1985. *The Rise and Decline of the Zairian State*. Madison: University of Wisconsin Press.

11

"Trouble Spots"

Projects, Bandits, and State Fragmentation

STEVEN SAMPSON

WHAT GLOBALIZATION *DOES*

Understanding what globalization is can be best achieved by observing what globalization does. As a minimal definition, globalization is the increasing transnational movement of capital, goods, people or ideas, and cultural practices; this process is now so accelerated that these resources, groups, ideas, and practices now seem to circulate without any specifically localized base, taking on, as it were, a life of their own. Hence, we have global companies, international organizations, diasporic populations, and transnational mafias. The actors in the global arena area international managers, NGO activists, diaspora middlemen, diplomats, humanitarian aid workers, migrant laborers, political refugees, "Executive Outcomes" mercenaries, and transnational smugglers. Global practices exist in an ideological environment marked by discourses of democracy, privatization, modernization, human rights development, "one world," consumer hunger, multicultural diversity, environmental protection, conflict resolution, peace building, institutional building, diaspora, ensuring "security," "global organized crime," self-determination, national identity, empowerment, and the term "globalization" itself.

Understood as long-distance or transnational contacts, globalization is certainly nothing new; after all, missionaries, traders, crusaders, pioneers, migrant laborers, and conquering armies, with their affiliated social and ideological paraphernalia, have been crossing borders for centuries, with devastating consequences for local societies. Nor is awareness of the "outside" very new to the non-Western societies, which have borne the brunt of colonial or imperial expansion, slavery, plantations, mines, white settlers, or the imposition of European religions and languages. What is new is the speed, intensity, variation, and increasing pervasiveness of these contacts, all of which affect local societies and allow certain groups new cultural expressions and political possibilities.

At a human level, globalization widens the horizons of time and space for some people, turning some into the global elite of symbol producers, knowledge mediators, discourse creators, security demanders, and fun seekers; on the other side, global processes operate to turn others into truly global proletariats who follow the flow of capital as international managers, consulting engineers, bridge and tunnel builders, and a host of migrants, refugees, or bandits. The difference in possibilities entails uncertainty, such that globalization creates its own social and existential crises (Bauman 1998).

How do global processes affect the territorial units known as states and those citizens who identify with their states? A conventional wisdom is to regard globalization as undermining states, such that "outside forces" act to "destroy the fabric"—to use the common metaphor—of local societies and economies; the motif could best be described as "colonialist" or "imperialist." The familiar examples are McDonaldization (Smart 2000, Ritzer 1996), American pop culture, uncontrolled migration, organized crime, all of which operate as invaders or homogenizers. Traditional structures based on kinship and neighborhood or long established societal arrangements based on citizens' allegiance to the state are seen to be undermined. The indigenous population is confronted by immigrants, some of whom are simply parked there (Turner 2002, chapter 2 of this book).

Along with the motif of globalization as colonizing and destroying states, we may speak of a second motif, of "development" or "empowerment." Transnational communication and common interests spawn global movements toward democracy, human rights, environmental awareness, and civil society; these movements penetrate across borders leading to an empowerment of civil society and the undermining of oppressive or bureaucratic state control. Under the watchful eye of the international human rights community and of "global civil society," states that deny rights to citizens can now be sanctioned, denied aid, isolated, or even bombed. Democracy does not simply "flow." It is also imposed by the real power differential of some states over others.

Seen in this light, globalization relates to states and to local society in terms of either new threats or new possibilities. Confronted with the entry of new resource inputs, some local elites (within either the state or society) see their possibilities threatened, others see them expanded. Viewed in local terms, the "outside" is something to be latched onto as a kind of resource. When local elites come into conflict and new elites form, we may view this as the differential utilization of various global "waves." The empirical question is which group jumps on which wave: say, humanitarian aid, beauty contests, or refugee smuggling, to name three. For those unable to seize these opportunities, the global becomes a threat to our "way of life" and bulwarks against it must be constructed. These take the form of various kinds of localist movements: environmentalism, anti-Brussels referenda, anti–World Bank demonstrations, religious fundamentalism, regional separatism, anti-immigrant movements, xenophobia, and at times, banditry.

Common to both the colonialist/McDonaldization and empowerment discourses of globalization, however, is a view of a state seemingly powerless to deal with these outside forces. I will argue that this view of globalization is simplistic. It is simplistic because it views the existing states as undifferentiated, static, and passive. Rather, we should see global forces in terms of their ambivalent relationship toward the state, a relationship that can both undermine and consolidate at the same time. States, I will argue, are not going away, but in the new globalized environment need to be redefined. To see states simply as being "fragmented" is not enough. We need a more complex understanding of the "forces" by which states are ostensibly being undermined and by which other formations are being formed.

GLOBAL FORCES AND THE STATE

The idea of globalization as simply undermining local power is simplistic because it is predicated on an idea of states as passive objects of outside forces. Some of the problem is rhetorical, insofar as globalization is constantly articulated in terms of "forces," "streams," "flows," that is, as dynamic impositions on some kind of seemingly stable order (Hannerz 1992; Barth 1989; Appadurai 1991, 1993). In this view, "clashes" between the forces and the state must inevitably occur (Barber 1995). What is forgotten is that states are composed of people, actors. And that these actors within states can co-opt or utilize global resources, global actors, and global ideologies for their own diverse ends. In the discussion of the undermining of states by international organizations and global forces, this dimension has been missing. In celebrating the wave of democracy or multiculturalism, or in our anxiety about global illegal migration or organized crime, we have overlooked the tenacity of states to *reorganize themselves* in the face of new market forces, political sanctions, cultural impositions, Internet, human rights accusations, support for guerrilla forces, and so on.

Here I propose to view states as resource-using groups, in which one of the key resources is public legitimation. Other units besides states (NGOs, private security forces, mafias, private firms), can also carry out state functions (e.g., citizen protection, provision of welfare services). What states do is carry them out in terms of a "public" project. When states use their resources in ways of which we approve and that resemble our own concepts of states, we use terms like "administration," "public sphere," "good governance," "dialogue with civil society," "political system," and "bureaucracy." Such states have flags, diplomatic representations, airlines, ministries of education, post offices, currencies, infrastructures, and programs for development. When those groups acting on behalf of the state use their resources in ways that are not readily transparent to us, we speak of "weak state," "clans," "corruption," political underdevelopment, "politics of the belly" (Bayart, Ellis, and Hibou 1998) or "criminalization of the state" (Chabal and Daloz 1998). Such states may certainly possess the same institutions as above, but the ministers are busy plundering their own ministries, the mail never gets delivered, the airlines are run by foreigners, and the infrastructure, if it functions at all, is a vehicle for personal enrichment. In extreme cases, when even the trappings of states are absent, we speak of "collapse" or "mafia" or "ethnic/tribal" warfare.

This chapter retains this view of states as simple networks of interests that happen to legitimate themselves as public institutions. It examines two global processes that seemingly undermine the state. The first is "global civil society" as embodied in local civil society/NGO development programs, what I call "the world of projects." The globalization of democracy and local NGO "capacity building" are about a specific kind of formation called "project society." States respond to project society by trying to co-opt project resources or undermine the NGOs who use them insofar as these NGOs may threaten state power.

The second global threat to the state is global organized crime, banditry, outlaws, which for want of a better term I will call "mafia." Mafia seeks to undermine state authority by competing with its control over territory, appropriation of funds (extortion replaces taxation), and monopoly on violence. Bandits, mafiosi, pirates, smugglers, money launderers, and the rest of "global organized crime" seemingly operate on the margins of states, but insofar as they participate in an international traffic of contraband goods, services, and people, these bandits are certainly transnational. Project society and bandit society (mafia) are two sets of global structures that tend to both undermine and consolidate state power.

In choosing to concentrate on these two global manifestations, it does not mean that people have no other strategic options. A variety of other responses to global processes are possible: movements of national identity, social movements, or "weapons of the weak" (Castells 1997, Scott 1985). The point here is to see project society and bandit society as two prominent manifestations of the ambivalence of globalization. It is this ambivalence that creates globalization's new classes of winners and losers, and that reproduces the kind of fragmentation and existential insecurity that can also lead to violence. Democracy and ethnic enfranchisement, for example, can be seen as empowerment, but they also fragment kinship and status hierarchies leading to new kinds of warfare. The emergence of nongovernmental organizations may be salutary for articulating citizen needs, but more NGOs does not necessarily mean a more democratic political culture.

Finally, project society and mafia society are not necessarily separate from each other. Project society has become a resource base for organized crime and corruption, as numerous scandals about EU aid in Southeast Europe, Scandinavian aid in East Africa, and French relations with its former colonies now attest (Verschave 2000). Sometimes these scandals and resources become so chaotic that states disappear. When this happens, project society and bandit society seem to compete to fill the gap of providing security and redistributing resources. This competition for resources brings with it its own form of violence, in the form of intimidation, kidnapping, and murder of officials working for "the international community." Those places we now call "trouble spots" are places in which various mafias are battling each other and where state resources are nonexistent. But they are also objects of international humanitarian assistance, peacekeeping operations, and global human rights concern. One might even define a "trouble spot" as a field in which project society and bandit society compete for sovereignty. As an example of this complex interaction between project society and bandit society, take the following e-mail sent to me by a colleague working in Geneva, who in late 1998 (before the second Russian invasion) offered me some advice about going to Chechnya:

> Steve, I am sure that I am not the first one to tell you this but, DO NOT GO TO CHECHENYA. I was working in Daghestan, I had 4 of my colleagues taken hostages in Chechnya. It was 106 bad days. Then I had this good friend [Marc] who said he had "special arrangements" [to remain safe] and did not care. He got caught. He managed his way out, but had 2 fingers cut. Then I met with [John,] who thought he was outside the sphere of the Chechen bandits' operations. He is still in a basement, after 9 months. One other thing. When my colleagues got caught, they were taken from the Daghestan border, through all Chechnya, crossing all checkpoints without any problems. We are not talking here about isolated groups of bandits but rather organized crime networks with strong relations with political circles. It became obvious to me when I had to deal with the case. And you must have heard that they have entered Georgia and

are threatening UN staff there. And do not think I have anything against the Chechen people. On the contrary, I enjoyed working with them very much and I had good friends there. But it is just not worth the risk. OK, you might have come up with a special plan that you think will make you invincible. I am sorry, I've heard this before and I do not quite believe it anymore. Even with OSCE. But if you take this risk, I would be very interested to stay in touch with you.

Of interest here is not the violence per se, but that the violence now affects members of the international community. Between 1996 and 1998, thirty-nine U.N. workers have been killed over the last two years. In the Caucasus, international humanitarian actors in 1996 suffered fifty-eight "total incidents" of murders, kidnapping, attempting kidnapping, shooting incidents ("targeted and untargeted"), assaults, armed robberies, local staff deaths, and expatriate staff deaths (Hansen 1998). Communications like this, from someone on the front lines of the international community's project society, reflect the kind of structures we are dealing with: on the one hand, well-endowed international organizations with "missions," mandates, and resources acting on behalf of a consortium of advanced states now known as "the international community"; on the other hand, paramilitary groups, and groups of bandits, especially in ex-communist areas, that seem to operate with impunity: not only kidnapping for political reasons but increasingly kidnapping for money. The problem is not kidnapping as such, it is that "they are even going after U.N. people now." Things are getting out of hand.

Northern Albania, eastern Bosnia, sections of Kosovo, the northern Caucasus, large portions of Africa, and now East Timor and the border areas (where U.N. staff were recently murdered) are all places of fragmented political units. Except for Chechnya, they are objects of massive international assistance. These areas are now the loci of "bandit society" on the one hand, and "project society" on the other. This means that we will increasingly see a kind of triangle between existing fragile states, the bandits challenging them, and the project society trying to hold the states accountable. All three social structures—states, project society, and bandit society—are competing for resources. All organize opportunities for elites to latch on to these resources. But all three are also creating insecurity for the people caught in the middle.

We may therefore envision modern states as specific groups of people availing themselves of specific types of resources, material, social, and knowledge. In the case of projects, the resources clearly come from outside, while in the case of mafia they may also come from transnational criminals operating abroad. What is new about new elites is how they avail themselves of the resources offered by the world of projects and the world of bandits. People may enter project society or mafia society. In between the international world of projects and the expanding, border-crossing local mafias are hapless citizens trying to find solutions. Let us therefore explore how states are affected by the two worlds, beginning with democracy assistance and NGO projects.

DEMOCRACY ASSISTANCE, CIVIL SOCIETY, AND NGOs

"Democracy" is one of the most essential of global "ideoscapes" (Appadurai 1993). Yet it is not simply a flowing of norms and principles. It is also a set of practices. Along with privatization, rule of law, human rights, and European integration, "democracy assistance" forms the cornerstone of the processes of "transition" now taking place in Central and Eastern Europe (Carothers 1996, 1999). Promoting and consolidating human rights and democracy is now a prerequisite for receiving aid. Democracy assistance began in Latin America decades ago and is not a major part of the transition in Central and Eastern Europe, the Balkans, and elsewhere. As a carrot and stick set of practices, it involves transfers of massive amounts of money, the training of promising leaders, the establishment of institutions, and the building of political parties and organizations. Democracy assistance may focus on direct aid to parliaments and election support, by aiming at reform of public administration and training of public servants at central and local levels, and most commonly, through civil society, NGOs, and institution building. This assistance is invariably administered through activities called "projects." While humanitarian aid projects are meant to meet a particular material or medical need in a group, democracy, human rights, and civil society projects are both more abstract and long term: they are meant to build a developed citizenry that can promote and consolidate democracy. Civil society assistance, which will be the focus here, is supposed to build a strong NGO sector.

"Civil society" has a long philosophical pedigree in political theory. In the late 1980s, the term "civil society" was used largely to connote society's opposition to repressive regimes in Eastern Europe or elsewhere. Over the last decade, however, civil society has become a category of democracy assistance focusing on activities of social self-initiative organized by networks, groups, and formal organizations. Since donors tend not to give funds to informal groups or engaged individuals, "civil society" as a donor category is restricted to organized voluntary associations such as political parties, trade unions, church organizations, press and media, informal networks, and particularly voluntary associations, also called NGOs.

Since political parties and trade unions have their own separate aid programs and specific donors, since most aid is secular, and since aid to informal networks is risky for legal/accounting reasons, the funding category known as "civil society" is usually limited to support for media and voluntary organizations. Media aid centers on training journalists and funding what are considered to be "independent" TV and press; the idea is that an informed public provides for a better democracy.

The vast majority of civil society assistance, however, goes to nongovernmental organizations. Such organizations may be known as well: nonprofit organizations, not-for-profit organizations, voluntary associations, "ideal organizations" (Swedish), associations, foundations, charities, trusts (Britain), interest organizations, grassroots organizations, civic organizations, civil society organizations, and so on. NGOs lie between the state and the market and are thus known as the "third sector" (Salamon and Anheier 1996).

An NGO, no matter whether it is a small group or a large interest organization, is usually considered to have certain basic characteristics: it does not seek state power (i.e., nongovernmental), it has a voluntary element, it is autonomous in decision making, nonprofit (though it may have income), and it is juridically constituted. The "NGO sector," as it is called, has its own dynamics: organizations rise and fall, some evolve into parties, some become fronts, others become profit-making firms, some unite into umbrella organizations, others split into competing organizations. While NGOs exert great efforts for government to recognize their importance in helping to formulate or implement policy, governments seek to construct NGO registration systems or regulatory frameworks. Funding questions are crucial, since NGOs want government grants or the possibility to earn income by providing services; governments, for their part, want to ensure against "abuse" of NGOs' charity status.

From a democracy assistance viewpoint, building a strong NGO sector means initially supporting the increase in the number of NGOs, in the number of sectors covered, and in their professional quality. It involves moving from "first-generation" NGOs based on humanitarian aid or direct grassroots needs to "second-generation" NGOs, which are "professional," "self-supporting," and policy related. First-generation NGOs may provide aid, second-generation NGOs conduct advocacy campaigns and lobbying. "NGO assistance" involves strategic support, funding, training, and goal-directed activity consistent with the NGOs "mission"; this activity takes the form of "projects." Although there may be questions as to whether the increasing number of NGOs represents a valid index of democratic development, there is no question that NGOs are now the vehicle for the expansion of projects as a way of life (Sampson 1996, 1998).

PROJECT LIFE

Projects are specific activities implemented by a group of actors having a specified goal over a limited period of time. In this sense, they are the opposite of "policy." Projects are inherently temporary. They either end or evolve into new projects; rarely do they evolve into state-administered programs or policies. Most "pilot projects," presumably forerunners for permanent programs, inevitably "crash."

From a globalization perspective, project life may be viewed as a form of "traffic" in which resources, people, and ideologies move between west and east/south, or between center and periphery. In this sense, projects are global, but the traffic is not equal in all directions. Projects are not just about the movement of resources; they are also about control.

Projects invariably require money, and money is allocated according to priorities set by Western donors. In democracy assistance projects, money and strategies flow from wealthier, more democratic countries to poorer, less democratic countries; the expression often used is "democracy promotion" or "consolidation of democracy." Those who "invest" in democracy are Western governments and their aid agencies, international organizations like UNDP, Western NGOs (many of which are government funded), and privately-funded NGOs such as Soros, Ford, Mott, Carnegie, and other foundations. In practice, funds flow from a few major centers in Western Europe and the United States, from various international organizations, and then proceed east or south. The flow of funds is mediated by a host of implementing organizations, such as large government-funded NGOs in the home country, government offices, some private consulting companies, or by aid-oriented NGOs that already have field offices abroad and have obtained the implementing contact in open or closed bidding (e.g., Oxfam, Danish Refugee Aid, or Save the Children). Take, for example, the World Bank's effort to pursue gender equality in Bosnia. This led to the Bosnian Women's Initiative (BWI), which received earmarked funding by USAID. The BWI was a set of projects to be implemented by various in-country NGOs. In eastern Bosnia, the organization Scottish European Aid (SEA) is charged with soliciting and controlling applications by local Bosnian organization to conduct BWI-funded projects concerning gender-related issues. SEA handles project administration. One of these projects, submitted by the Human Rights Office Tuzla (HROT), targeted women refugees returning to their home cities in Muslim and Serb parts of Bosnia (Sampson 2001). The project, called "Towards Democracy," was a series of ten seminars in which the women acquired training in various subjects ranging from property rights, family law, and conflict resolution. HROT received funds for bus transport, meeting hall rental, meals, and photocopying and the making of a video. On completion of the ten seminars, HROT submitted a report to SEA, which is responsible to the USAID office funding the BWI secretariat. Following this, HROT has submitted another application to conduct a similar project in Serb regions of Bosnia. The Bosnian Women's Initiative is a typical project system, and in fact a similar Kosovo Women's Initiative is now operating in Kosovo with $10 million of USAID funds.

The search for money and the mechanics of project administration are complicated. Under such conditions, with the rapid deadlines, convoluted bidding requirements, and difficult accounting procedures, donors are hesitant to allow local organizations in the target country to run large projects. At most they can play a minor role as "local assistance" on the implementation side.

Project society is more than money, of course. Together with the money come consultants and specialists who provide inspiration, project management, monitoring, and evaluation. Some consultants are part of organizations or of a consortium of organizations consisting of chains of main partners and subcontracting partners. Other consultants are recruited on a short-term freelance basis for a given number of man-days to carry out tasks such as "project identification," "staff training," or "interim evaluation."

Donors begin their activities with a project identification or project appraisal mission. This mission is invariably entrusted to a Western consultant. Here the possible "target groups" are identified and a "needs analysis" conducted. This involves visiting the country, contacting those with knowledge of potential partners, and interviewing them about their needs and assessing their competencies. In early stages, a crucial activity is identifying the other donors to "coordinate." Concretely, it involves finding out who is doing what project, or whether there are other projects open for bid. Sometimes the target group is the vulnerable group itself (e.g., homeless children, refugees without housing), but just as often the target group may be the NGO or group of NGOs that is supposed to be helping a vulnerable group. The goal of such NGO projects may be direct humanitarian aid, which is the case in acute, conflict situations. In post-conflict situations, however, the aid takes on a more abstract form known as "capacity building" or "institutional development" (Sampson 2001). Capacity building involves donations of office equipment and the "transfer of skills" from the implementing partner to the target NGO or group. Transfer of skills takes place by conducting project activities or by training. Training may include courses lasting days or weeks. Typical training activities focus on fund-raising, project management, staff or board training, public relations, dialogue with government, and so on.

Every project involves a foreign or local donor and a "partner" in the target country who carries out implementation. Most donors manage to find a suitable "partner," but often the best potential partners are oversubscribed, that is, they tend to be the most skilled NGOs in the capital city with experience in managing projects. Project inputs, whether it be donations of office equipment, training or support for "capacity building," and project grants must be empirically variable: there must be concrete outputs to make the project convincing to the donor office back home. Much of the training involves explaining to the "partner" how to handle budgets and file reports according to the donor's needs, training the NGO's board of directors or its staff. The donor supplies expertise in the form of "expatriate staff," local experts, trainers, and volunteers whose sole job is to build capacity among the local staff and counterparts in the receiving country. After some time, the donor may change priorities (blaming it on "the system"). Donors can "leave," and in order to ensure the "sustainability" of its partner, leaving evolves into a suitable "exit strategy."

One may envision the structure of project life in two ways: as a flow of resources, people, and knowledge, and as a set of concentric circles.

As a flow of traffic, the relationship between donors and recipients in the world of projects is one in which some resources go from West to East/South and others go in the opposite direction. From the West comes money, suitably transmitted in complicated tranches and often transferred by circuitous routes in countries where banking systems remain primitive. Along with money comes traffic in people: expatriate consultants, foreign project managers, and the short-term evaluators and trainers. These individuals often go from country to country, and much of their job is spent talking with other donors, an activity called "donor coordination," or with government officials to smooth entry. Government officials, not being donors, are useful to smooth the administration of the program, and increasingly as copartners in applying for EU, World Bank, or UNDP funds.

The West-East traffic in money and experts is partially balanced by a circulation of promising local project managers to conferences, meetings, internships and training in the West. From Eastern Europe, thousands of NGO activists, journalists, and officials have been on shorter or longer trips abroad for training and to see with their own eyes how democracy works. In Denmark, to take a single example, the government-funded Democracy Foundation has spent about U.S. $100 million over ten years to bring thousands of foreign NGO activists, local officials or teachers, social and health workers to examine how counterparts work in Denmark. Other programs run by foreign governments have concentrated on NGO leaders, journalists, and government officials. The socialization of local NGO activists into the world of projects proceeds with their acquisition of the discourse of global civil society, which takes place as they go about attending training courses, meeting donor representatives, applying for money and managing projects.

Let us instead look at the world of projects not simply as a flow of money, people, and concepts, but as a system of hierarchical concentric circles. At the center of the circle are the elite organizations in the West (donors) and their funding policies (suggested by knowledge producers who help define strategy). This inner circle can be seen as the most abstract type of knowledge. At the periphery is concrete, local knowledge of real people with real problems; in the periphery are the "needs" and the sought-after "target groups," including that most peripheral of target groups, "the vulnerable groups," such as refugee women, the handicapped, or traumatized children.

Knowledge is not only located at the center, however. The periphery is also a site of key information simply because donors may be visiting their projects. Kosovo, an international protectorate where more than three hundred international organizations are operating, is rife with donors coordinating projects and sounding each other out. In practice, this means an enormous amount of meetings and follow-up memoranda.

While project life is certainly an example of global flows, viewing projects as a hierarchy of power circles reveals globalization with *power*. Resources, people, and ideas do not simply "flow"; they are sent, directed, channeled, manipulated, managed, rejected, monitored, and transformed on their journey eastward by the myriad of middlemen at the source, on the way, and in the local context. The world of projects is about control over money, knowledge, and ideas.

Control over money, for example, involves who is allowed to apply, who is allowed to spend, and who must do the accounting. Most Western programs require that the Western organization be accountable. While Western aid organizations may be spenders "in the field," at home they are supplicants. This is why most of the funds spent on offices, hotels, restaurants and publications are centered on communications and information with the home office or donor.

Control over project personnel is carried out by the Western consultants and project directors, some of whom fly in, others who are resident. Such control entails the recruitment and management of additional foreign consultants, local staff managers, and support staff. The Western donor representative networks with various other donors, diplomatic missions and local government officials in order to ensure "transparency."

Control over knowledge involves deciding whom to tell about what; in the world of projects, knowledge involves deadlines, budget lines, key words on applications, the major conferences being held, and coordinating time schedules with others. At the local level, knowledge control involves knowing which donor is about to give out funds.

Finally, since most Western donor consultants are pressed for time, there is a continual monitoring of the next bid, project, or upcoming trip. The hierarchical relations of the project system are best expressed in the various use of time of foreign consultants and the invariable waiting time for others. Meetings must be scheduled rapidly and rescheduled when the others are also involved in meetings. Meetings with donors and foreign organizations take precedence over meetings with locals or supplicant NGOs, which means that some people are kept waiting. With more information, the number of meetings increases, which means more rescheduling and more waiting. Logistical problems—local traffic, bad weather, phones that don't work, lost messages, power blackouts, delayed flights, unexpected project application deadlines necessitating couriers—create a pressure-cooker atmosphere in which the foreign consultants are constantly moving and the hapless target group is endlessly waiting.

The final type of control in the project system is control over concepts. Ideas do not simply travel; they are sent, received, and manipulated. And ideas rarely travel alone. They are attached to resources. The activity of projects is to attach ideas to activity, and activity requires money. It involves an understanding of donors and the identification of a target group and an implementing partner. Establishing such partnerships between a donor and implementing partner organization is not difficult if there already exists a network, an NGO, or a government office with an idea about, say, establishing crisis centers for battered women, a legal aid office, or an anticorruption bureau. The problem for the donor comes when these potential implementing partners do not exist. If they do not exist, then they must be created.

Creating such NGOs may be called "institutional development," "capacity building," or at times "cloning." In many cases the international donor or NGO simply uses its local secretariat to create a local NGO. Cloning of NGOs is a typical exit strategy in many former Eastern European countries. It ensures a role for the parent organization, facilitates continuity of funding for the newly created local NGO, and deals with the postpartum sustainability problems after donors go elsewhere.

Project society is not simply fly-in, fly-out missions and the hunt for funds. Local NGOs also actually do things. In cases of successful projects, NGOs begin to carry out key services that ameliorate the damaging effects of uncontrolled markets or that supplement the government social programs. NGOs help to publicize new laws so that people know their rights; human rights NGOs may be paid to conduct training of judges or prison officials in international human rights provisions. Environmental and health NGOs may carry out surveys on specific problems, while educational NGOs may procure textbooks and youth NGOs sponsor counseling. In this sense, NGOs take on state functions, and donors may recognize NGOs as key actors in the development process. As long as the functions between NGOs and the state are clearly delineated, there is no conflict; when they are overlapping, state officials may frequently become jealous of the attention paid to NGOs. In Western polities, strong states and strong interest groups go together; in societies in transition, project society may pose a threat to the state.

The above description of project society would on first site appear as a typical case of globalization undermining the state. The tensions between state officials and the NGO sector are illustrative. Ministers and state functionaries may complain that there are too many NGOs, that "they" are getting "our" aid money. Isolated cases of NGO overspending or inefficiency are used to smear the entire sector. Government officials may complain that many local NGOs tend to have better office equipment than most government offices. Salaries for NGO staff often exceed what one can make in a local or central government ministry. The intimate relations between NGOs and Western donors are also an object of some jealousy in some of the poorly paid, poorly equipped, government offices.

Looking at project society from outside, some state officials devise various strategies to tap into project resources. The most widespread method is for state organs to clone their own NGOs, called GOs and quasi-NGOs (or QUANGOs, a term made popular in Thatcher's Britain as an instrument of privatization). Throughout Eastern Europe, for example, it is common to find government-sponsored youth, sport, environment, and women's groups, some of which may be politically affiliated, others funded by or otherwise linked to the government. In former times, such organizations would have been called "fronts" but many such organs do not have a specific political profile; rather they are a means of procuring aid resources. Deloz (1998) notes that in the post–Cold-War era, Western aid can no more be procured on the basis of strategic anticommunism, rather, aid funds flow in as a result of donors' faith that the government is promoting democracy, building civil society, pursuing development, and ensuring human rights. The GOs can put on a good presentation for a potential donor and then garner the necessary funds for their activities. Invariably much of the money goes informally to government officials who may sit on the boards of these foundations, while other funds are used for the invariable foreign trip or political campaign.

A second strategy by which state actors attempt to tap into the resources of project society is for government officials to sit on the boards of various NGOs as an indication of state-civil society "partnership." This practice is not in itself objectionable, since public officials may be genuinely interested in the project and can become a lobby for the organization's mission within the government. An NGO helping handicapped youth could benefit from a board member who worked in the Ministry of Health. More often, however, state officials' participation in the NGO sector provides government with access to knowledge about donor priorities and the means by which to channel eventual donor funds away from civil society organizations and directly into government itself. Throughout Eastern Europe, for example, one sees the emergence of government offices for "civil society partnership" or "NGO coordination." These offices or secretariats are now the object of intense donor interest. (Curiously, no such offices exist in Western Europe where the association sector is too large and too diverse to be the object of any kind of coordination beyond very specific sectors like "women," "youth," "development," or "environment").

Finally, governments may actively seek to undermine the activities of NGOs by imposing barriers to their cooperation with foreign donors, limiting income generation, or other kinds of harassment. Some social assistance and humanitarian aid organizations can operate unhindered, since they are viewed as a supplement to state activities. Other NGOs, particularly in human rights, law, media, environment and anticorruption, may be regarded as adversaries of state agencies who see them as "political." This conflict is exacerbated as NGOs become more influential in their lobbying and "advocacy" activities.

Project society, in its civil society variant, may thus pose a threat to the state organizations in which it penetrates. Those in the state may either seek to exploit the resources of the project society or to oppose it. What I term "project society," however, is not a single actor but a set of practices with its associated sets of resources, social groups, and ideological constructs. The global character of project society and the strength of NGO networks means that efforts to attack or subvert a local NGO may bring on unwanted international attention to the offending government. Calling international attention to abuses is particularly the case for organizations defending human rights, since offending governments can be quickly embarrassed in international fora.

Project society is thus a threat and a resource for states. In this context, one may differentiate between "weak" and "strong" states in terms of their ability to adapt to or co-opt project society. Strong states have strong, but well demarcated NGO sectors; there are many interest organizations and policy makers listen to them. Weak states tend to be either actively opposed to project society, or they tend to overtly try to subvert it by the creation of quasi- or shadow NGOs. With unclear boundaries, states and project society have a tendency to undermine each other. Instead of partnership there is conflict.

It is precisely this unclear boundary between sectors that characterizes the relationship between states and mafia.

MAFIA AND BANDITS

States are supposed to provide law enforcement, basic services, and protection over a given territory. State sovereignty is legitimated internally by accountability to citizens, and externally by other states in the form of "recognition." A sovereign state can legitimately appropriate income through taxation and can monopolize the use of violence in the form of police and armies. A "weak state" is a political unit that does not generate sufficient legitimacy, where taxation or law enforcement is conducted privately or where it is contested. A vacuum of order and legitimacy turns such states into "trouble spots."

Trouble spots are sites of "disorder" because groups compete to exert the kinds of powers that states normally exercise. Violence is privatized and protection and taxation are carried out by coalitions based on territory, ethnicity, kinship, or political-ideological affiliation. The competing coalitions may include neighboring states and various nonlegitmated actors known as "rebels" or "bandits."

Thomas Gallant, in a synthesis of bandit studies, has redefined bandits and mafia as "military entrepreneurs," a clear parallel to Blok's "violent entrepreneurs" in Sicily and to Volkov's "violent entrepreneurship" in Russia (Gallant 1999; Blok 1974; Varesse 1994; Volkov 1999). Common to such groups is the provision of various illegal goods and services, especially the supply of "protection," which includes protection from other mafias (Gambietta 1993). In functional terms, there is little functional difference between the security provided by states and the protection provided by bandits; the difference is that states rely on public legitimacy. Similarly, there is little functional difference between illegal mafias that provide protection and the legalized private security agencies (both tend to recruit from the same social pool). Volkov (1999) notes the similarity between the two in Russia.

In one sense, then, mafia is a form of state; in another it is simply illegal business. Where the state becomes privatized so that it is the instrument of privatized enrichment, we might speak of the criminalization of the state. Mafia-type organizations, whether they operate in Europe or in the former Soviet Union, the Balkans, or Latin America, specialize in the sale, export, and reexport of valuable commodities, be they drugs, stolen cars, arms, cash, or illegal sex workers, or other migrants.

Most of the research on mafia and banditry, and recent reports from Eastern Europe, link the presence of organized crime with state corruption (Bayart, Ellis, and Hibou 1998; Wedel 1998; Volkov 1999; see also Council of Europe and Southeast Europe Anticorruption program at www.nobribes.org, www.coe.org, and www.sepa.org). The debate on transnational organized crime has overlapped with the conceputalization, especially in Africa, around the concept of the "criminalization of the state." In the latter paradigm, illegitimate activities are carried out not only by criminal gangs or bandits outside the state, but by the state apparatus itself in the form of functionaries and their retinues, by groups of privatized police, or by rogue army units that live by intimidation, plundering, or smuggling. States are simply the loci of business transactions; what is sold is either state supplies or protection from prosecution.

Criminal activities within the state apparatus are not simply found in Africa, however. Many postcommunist countries reveal examples of criminal activity: the corruption of state bureaucrats in awarding licenses and contracts, particularly to foreign firms; the emergence of small feudal dictators in the Caucasus region; the privatization of state companies into the hands of former state managers who then plunder the firms for their wealth; and various smuggling activities carried out at border crossings, ports, and airports. There are continual reports of the smuggling of illegal goods, arms, money, and refugees with the complicity of local police, border guards, and armed forces (a typical case being the planeloads of contraband cigarettes caught at Bucharest's military airport, fuel sent by Albanians into Serbia during the Bosnian war embargo, or the transport of Kurdish refugees and drugs between Albania and Italy). Smuggling occurs in the context of local warlord regimes that exist only because local leaders have the cooperation of (or in fact are) the police authorities. This is clearly the case in parts of Albania, in eastern Bosnia, and the Caucasus. Where smuggling is uncertain, bandit activity may also include the plundering of civilians by paramilitary units, as has taken place in Bosnia, and is now going on in Kosovo in the form of burglary and robbery.

The "criminalization of the state" paradigm thus includes a range of activities: corruption, privatization of state function, and other criminal behavior carried out by state functionaries. However, there are two major problems with the "criminalization of the state" paradigm. First, the criminalization concept is overinclusive. It equates criminalization *of state functionaries* with *lack of state control* over criminal activity generally. In this case, Chicago during the gangland era of the 1920s could be an example of a "criminal state." Here I would argue that there is a difference between criminal activities carried out within a central state apparatus and using its facilities (corrupt officials, etc.) and criminal activities carried out by competing warlords or local bandit chieftains. If we define a weak state in terms of its lack of "reach"; the state simply lacks enough authority "out there," such that banditry occurs in the periphery while the center remains uncorrupted. However, we could also define a weak state as one in which state functionaries lack a "public service ethic," that is, the various groupings in the state resonate to their own morality (e.g., clan, region, party, etc.; the issue is not lack of ethics/morality but lack of an ethic *of public service*). In the case of this kind of weak state, there is a lack of ethics and of authority: there is corrupt/criminal behavior at the center and bandits at the periphery. The "criminalization of the state" paradigm relies on a weak state but does not tell us what constitutes such "weakness."

A second problem of the "criminalization of the state concept" is that it operates with a reified definition of "state" as a functioning, legitimate institution, somehow above society, rather than as simply an alternative set of resources used by specific actors. Here the problem lies in a concept of state that may be good for political theory or establishing state/society contrasts, but is so abstract as to be useless. We need to know more about how state actors are recruited, how these sets of actors achieve recognition as legitimate states that represent society, and how alliances and conflicts are forged within the state apparatus. Since states are by definition hierarchical organizations of authority, we need to know how people define their belonging in this hierarchy: When do local representatives of the state become local militants against the center? How is a public service ethic constructed and how does it degenerate? When is a state a self-aware group of administrators and when is it just a platform for gangs plundering public resources? Perhaps the "criminalization of the state" concept can provide a window to understanding the complex processes related to state definition, concepts such as "sovereignty," "territoriality" and "legitimacy," and "monopoly on the use of force." But this requires that "criminalization of the state" be seen as more than just "crime committed by state functionaries." Seen as a process, state criminalization can be seen as a form of privatized authority; corruption can be viewed as a form of political influence (Scott 1972). Let us therefore look more closely at the way in which mafia and banditry make a state.

WHEN IS A STATE CRIMINAL?

Criminalization of the state exists if actors in higher positions in central administration—politicians, ministers, generals, officials—act to pursue private interests. This betrayal of public trust is known as corruption. Corrupt behavior exists on a continuum that may start with helping family members get a job to channeling millions into a Swiss bank account. Following definitions of Scott (1972) or Heidenheimer (1989), corruption entails that primordial loyalties (nepotism) or private gain (money) take precedence over a public ethic (honest administration). This public ethic *may never have been present*, in which case criminalization is simply the continuation of tradition under a new guise. Alternatively, the appearance of more serious corrupt behavior could denote a decline of public spirit, a form of *political decay* in which primordial loyalties become resurgent; in the latter case, corruption is not a cause of state decline but a symptom. Indicators of the relative level of corruption are based on reporting by implicated actors. The anticorruption NGO known as Transparency International, for example, collects reports of foreign businessmen giving bribes in various countries and publishes a corruption index.

Empirically, corruption occurs in the Caucasus, parts of the Balkans, and in central Africa, where state and political leaders have both private armies and carry out their own entrepreneurial activities; under the rhetoric of human rights and democracy, they siphon off funds to pursue private projects. In such sites, certain market mechanisms are restricted; foreign businessmen must go through state channels to obtain contracts, which leads to the bribing of state officials or various forms of speed payments or intimidation. From eastern Bosnia to west Africa, political leaders establish state firms siphoning off funds for the import of cigarettes, fuel, oil drilling, or construction permits. In Sierra Leone and other African states, private armies are involved in the diamond trade (Traub 2000), while in Russia, military units have for long been dealing in the export of arms and precious metals from Russian ports. In Mexico, the "narco-state" joins drug smugglers, police, and border guards (Massing 2000). In the north Caucasus area, one can envision the kind of pipeline blackmail that will occur as oil is shipped from the Caspian port of Baku westward through various small enclaves each controlled by nationalist or bandit groups demanding protection money. The link between national liberation movements, banditry, and state security is illustrated with the fate of the Kosovo Liberation Army (KLA). Part of the KLA has become an official police force under the tutelage of the international community, another part a political party seeking state power, and still other sections operate as independent bandit groups intimidating or corrupting local officials and robbing aid missions with military precision. Liberation armies, political projects, local protection, and banditry come together.

The criminalization of the state paradigm centers on state functionaries carrying out a particular kind of illegitimate activity: bribe taking, favoritism, pilferage, nonenforcement, establishing personal fiefdoms or hidden companies. A more productive approach would be to view these central functionaries as entrepreneurs controlling a given public domain and to contrast them with 1) other elites or warlords controlling a territory (town or region), and

2) network coalitions that cross borders and conduct illegal trade, that is, mafia. Criminalized states would thus include a variety of actors: state officials invoking a public service ethic or "democratic" rhetoric; warlords utilizing military structures to extract taxes, perhaps invoking the rhetoric of "self-determination" or regional separatism, and the bandits acting as businessmen using illegal methods. The criminalized state would consist of state officials conducting business and private coalitions enforcing (their own) laws using violent means. Let me describe these various actors in more detail:

1. Corrupt bureaucrats working within the central state apparatus. These people link foreign networks and local warlords by taking a percentage in the form of bribes, providing protection or assistance by national armies, or by looking the other way. Such individuals and cliques exist in most Eastern European and postcommunist countries, particularly in ministries most resistant to reform, as in industry, raw materials (forestry, energy), defense, and even foreign trade. Their activities are frequently exposed by "scandal," invariably by a disgruntled subordinate who had not been included in the network, or by a political rival. In Romania, for example, millions of cigarettes were smuggled into the country by way of the military airport, with the complicity of officers from the army and border police and airport authorities. Clearly, somebody had not been paid.

2. Local warlords, that is, local politicians or military commanders who with their loyal troops/police may control (legal/illegal) production, trade routes, and smuggling. Where warlords are strongest, they manage the police or have own paramilitary functions, often in the same ethnic or regional autonomy; and they have good connections to the corrupt bureaucrats above. This is the case in the southeast Asian Golden Triangle, in northern and coastal Albania, in parts of Bosnia and Kosovo, and even in some of the regions of the already truncated states of the Caucasus. To take one example, Albania's clans and territorial networks became stronger after the central state apparatus collapsed in 1997 and the weapons depots looted. In Bosnia there have been local territorial warlords divided on ethnic and political lines, including the Muslim separatist enclave around Bihac. In Kosovo, the divisions are by town, with various KLA units running various towns and plundering parts of the citizens affiliated with the opposition or who do not pay protection.

   Some of these warlords end up taking over the state apparatus or regional government, as in eastern Moldova, which has been effectively under the occupation of the former Soviet 14th Army. In much of the former Soviet Union, former communist leaders have now emerged as regional chieftains; hence, the devolution of the Soviet Union into smaller units was basically a "transition from socialism to feudalism" (Humphrey 1992; see also Verdery 1996).

3. Local mafias, that is, networks of illegal entrepreneurs who move resources via unofficial channels, plunder state resources, or provide state functions (protection, including protection from other mafias) within local areas. In order to intimidate citizens, what amounts to demonstrations of authority, local mafias need the protection of local politicians and warlords. Often such local mafias are known as bandits.

4. "Organized crime," wider networks of illegal entrepreneurs who move resources across regions and countries or between sectors (e.g., smuggling drugs, transporting stolen cars, moving illegal refugees). These networks need not only the collusion of local warlords in their own areas, but also those along the route (harbors, border zones) as well as the aid or passivity of central corrupt officials. The emergent measures to "combat organized crime" are centered upon this category.

The four types of actors described above, called either "clans" or "local mafia," or "organized crime," are often conceived as a "state within a state." Indeed, like states, they 1) control allocation and redistribution of public resources; 2) collect taxes (extortion, protection money); 3) provide security to legitimate business or to the public; and 4) use force or the threat of force against those who contest their authority. Yet seeing them as ersatz states is not a complete picture, since they are also businesses, albeit illegal. Mafias are thus not the same as the state, insofar as the pyramid organization is not codified into law and they do not seek to sanctify a public sphere. Mafias, as it were, have no "mission." They involve private interests and network coalitions. Hence, for all the rhetoric of ancient tradition, loyalty, code of silence and honor, these coalitions can be extremely unstable, as so much intramafia violence attests.

Insofar as mafias obtain a monopoly on force, they come to resemble the state, at least within the region where they have the monopoly. Mafias may impose order, but they are also entrepreneurs. Like global businesses everywhere, mafias compete with other mafias for access to resources, for example, cheap transport routes, sectors, customers, and middlemen.

An analysis of the criminalization of the state must begin with some description of which actors are pursuing what goals using what means. Criminalization of the state is not just about corrupt bureaucrats or decadent presidents. It is about state functionaries, warlords, and mafia networks who make choices on the basis of strategies and allegiances. This means that grouping a whole set of processes as varied as smuggling, bribery, private security services, counterfeiting, embezzlement, pilferage, and so on, solely because they are illegal may not be the most effective way of understanding them (Harris 1996). In the same fashion, viewing the state as somehow prey to a criminalized "outside force" depicts the state as somehow divorced from the processes taking place in society. In the case of states versus mafia, the representation is one of "order" versus "chaos." Let us not forget the fact that states may be extraordinarily chaotic and that mafias may impose order.

What we are in fact speaking of are alternative coalitions competing for legitimacy and support. States may be able to invoke legitimacy in terms of public accountability; mafias, however, may have more resources at their disposal due to bonds of trust and reciprocity and primordial ties. Following Tilly (1985), the mafia with the greatest support receives the "prize" of legitimacy as the state. Strong states are those coalitions where the legitimacy to extort is uncontested; such coalitions invoke ideologies of "public service" and represent themselves as "the bureaucracy" or "the system." If weak states are simply gangs or coalitions pursuing interests, strong states are coalitions that represent a clientele. This representation is called "legitimacy," and with legitimacy comes the authority to invoke a public service ethic. It is the authority to invoke order "in the name of" the people, the nation, the State of California, and so on. When the claim to representativeness is publicly contested, we speak of politics. When it is contested at the level of practice, by people switching loyalties, we end up with "corruption," with "conflict between public and private spheres." It is here we descend to level of "weak" or "soft" states (Myrdal 1968). If criminalization of the state is the result of mafia "penetration," this only begs the question of why mafia or private moralities can penetrate some states and not others. It is one thing to assert, as does Tilly, that the state is just the mafia that wins out in imposing order. The question remains that order is imposed not simply by force but also by some kind of representational link with a public. How does mafia become "the public sector"?

THE CONCEPTUAL PROBLEM OF STATE:
"MAFIA KINGDOMS" OR "WHITE-JEEP STATES"

In circumstances of globalization and of globalism, of project society and mafia coalitions, what do we mean by states? Generally, we define states in terms of some kind of public apparatus that extends itself over a territory, and is recognized as legitimate and sovereign by some other state. A state is about territory, sovereignty, power, representation, public sphere, and recognition.

States also have ritual trappings. The "Kingdom of Denmark," where I happen to live, has the trappings of a kingdom—the Queen's castle, processions, feudal-style estates, and even soldiers in brightly colored uniforms who march past my window every day at 12:30 P.M. Tourists who come to Denmark think it is a little kingdom. They visit the castles and watch the changing of the guard. But the "Kingdom of Denmark" is in fact a democratic welfare state where real power lies not with the monarch but with state administration, banks, trade unions, political parties, and a host of interest organizations.

In the Kingdom of Denmark, the queen is only a queen in a symbolic sense. Symbols and trappings are important, but cannot be confused with more substantive sources of power and decision making. Now if kingdoms like Denmark can really be modern states, what appear to be modern states might in fact really be kingdoms: mafia kingdoms, warlord statelets, and so forth. This is the case, I think, in several African states, and is certainly the case in northern Albania, and parts of Bosnia and Kosovo, and with much of the Northern Caucasus. In all these areas, warlords and modern chiefdoms, many of them clan-based, live off of cannibalizing foreign aid, privatization of former communist activities, and the facilitation or smuggling of goods, people, drugs, money, or arms. All these states have post offices that sell stamps, ministries of finance, and police, but they do not deliver mail, the treasuries are empty, and the police are for sale to the highest bidder. Some are mafias with territory. Kosovo is an occupied country under foreign administration, its judiciary and police under severe suspicions for corruption and incompetence.

If we concentrate on the trappings of the state rather than the mechanisms of power, we overlook fundamental differences between these kinds of formations and European welfare states with their large public sectors, uncontested legitimacy, and civil-servant castes. What kind of state do we have when the treasury is empty, when the national post office does not deliver mail, when the army belongs to the leader as his personal police, and when local police extort money instead of protect people from thieves? What if the bureaucracy only sells its services instead of performing on the basis of salary, or if basic public services are lacking once we leave the main towns? What if there is no public service ethic? What is the much sought-after recognition by other states is limited to paying customs duties by Western aid agencies and by representatives of project society? Where exactly is the state but in its trappings, symbols, and rituals?

These kinds of states (call them "mafia kingdoms" if you will) are different in terms of the way in which resources are procured and distributed. Resources are mobilized and distributed according to territorial loyalties or clan ties rather than a "public service ethic." Compliance is assured not by the force of law, but by the threat of force. Efficient administration is facilitated by paying corrupt bureaucrats. And representativeness gives way to being a "member," being "silent," or being in an opposing mafia, clan, or faction.

Mafia kingdoms have their trappings of power. And they have the rhetoric of a neutral public sphere, of "local government," efforts to "reduce bureaucracy," respect for "human rights," administrative or economic "reform," and pursuit of "development" as defined by the donors' agenda. But the rhetoric is but an instrument for procuring the resources offered by project society. In a situation in which states exist only as "trappings," social life consists only of mafia kingdoms manipulating "the world of projects." When even these trappings disappear, the state collapses, services fall apart, and the central government is besieged by local warlords coming in from the periphery. There comes the call for aid from abroad, and we obtain the meeting of mafia kingdoms and international project aid. We get "trouble spots."

WHITE-JEEP STATES

How do we distinguish mafia kingdoms from "normal" states? One way is to try to use the traditional definitions to define a state: sovereignty over territory, the ability to provide basic services, to impose order (security) and to collect taxes. It appears that for many so-called states, these functions are carried out in areas much more limited than the ostensible state boundaries. If I were to draw a map of the Albanian state in terms of the aforementioned basic state functions, it would have a strip going from the airport to the center of Tirana, and then a one-square-kilometer block linking the two major hotels, the embassy quarter, the World Bank/UNDP headquarters, the government buildings, a strip west to the coastal city of Durres, and some additional vectors to major foreign aid sites and military installations. This would be the "daytime Albanian state," that is, the territory where "Albania" can supply minimal services and protection to its citizens and foreign residents. The "nighttime state" would be even smaller, as travel along main roads outside Tirana is hazardous and in the hills and provincial towns power lies in the hands of various informal authorities—clans, bandits, warlords, customary law. In the spring of 1997, when the Albanian state collapsed completely and arms stores were looted, the nighttime Albanian state was so small that no one was allowed on the street after 9 P.M. In effect, the state had no "reach." People stayed in their homes, foreigners in their hotels, and one heard the sound of gunfire as each resident let potential thieves know that he, too, had a Kalashnikov. Similar daytime/nighttime contrasts can be seen in towns of Kosovo, some of which even had 6 P.M. curfews. In numerous other areas of the world, notably west Africa, there are similar complaints about "security" or "crime."

From a territorial-sovereignty definition, one might say that in Albania, in the Caucasus, in parts of eastern Bosnia, in Kosovo, and in much of Africa, the state extends to where you can no longer drive your white jeep (white jeeps being the icon of "the international community" and of project society). We might call such places "white-jeep states." The white-jeep state, therefore, has little to do with the official boundaries of the state as shown on maps or codified in treaties. Rather, the white-jeep state is delimited by how far one can drive one's jeep until one is:

a) forced to pay tribute to keep going,

b) where one gets robbed

c) where one must turn back because the area is otherwise unsafe due to rebels, or because the road is impassable.

In the case of a) tribute, and b) robbery, it is simply another "regime" that has taken over taxation duties; while in the case of the impassable road c), the state is unable/unwilling to maintain order or infrastructure.

Normally, we encounter such barriers to state sovereignty on the borders between one state and another. Such boundaries mark off the limits of state sovereignty and the beginning of a no-man's-land or war zone between recognized states. Today, however, we increasingly find such zones within the territorial borders of states, in zones where officially recognized states, mafia kingdoms, and project societies simultaneously operate; or to use the vehicular metaphor, we have an increasing number of areas with official state cars and police escorts, the mafia's stolen Mercedes, the brown jeeps of international peace-keeping forces (NATO), and the white jeeps of the international humanitarian/project community. (In Albania it was revealed that local officials were in fact driving around in stolen vehicles, and in Bosnia the international organizations now take the logos off their white jeeps, the idea being that this gives them some kind of protection; yet another instance of the kind of magical thinking going on in the world of humanitarian aid.)

We tacitly acknowledge the real boundaries of state authority when we talk about traveling to a "secure" or "unsafe" areas. Some ostensible states consist largely of unsafe areas, here understood as areas where someone with resources does not require a police escort. But if the state has no resources to provide services or maintain public order, why even call it a state? Here I think we are all too enamored of the trappings of statehood without analyzing its substance. Our tendency to reify "the state" as a single actor and complain about "the evils of the bureaucracy," only exaggerates this abstract gap between state and society. The state, instead of being seen as coalitions legitimating themselves via the public sphere, is demonized as "the system," what Herzfeld (1997) calls "secular theodicy." The "criminalization of the state" paradigm maintains this fiction of the reified state as unified, floating above, and as an agent.

States have long had problems ensuring territorial sovereignty. Feudalism solves this problem by pyramids or "trees" of loyalties. The limits of the feudal state formation are the limits of these loyalties. In modern times, state sovereignty often covers lowland towns and peoples. As states develop, state coalitions obtain the strength to integrate or neutralize more independent groups in the hinterlands, borderlands, or in the more inaccessible highlands. Such periods are exceptional. In the Balkans, highland peoples were both border-crossing bandits and nationalist heroes who led revolts against central state oppression. On the coasts, the distinction between pirate and privateer was whether the state had granted a concession to plunder competing states (Bax 1997; Gallant 1999; Bracewell 1992). In central Asia, new leaders have emerged as the USSR declined. Limited sovereignty at the edges of central power is not new. Central states are always under pressure from other informal alliances.

What *is* new are the new resources that accrue to being recognized as a state by the international community. The international community not only exerts moral and political pressures. It is a pool of resources giving aid. Recognition by other states brings with it the possibility to exploit project society. This is truly the "success story" of African criminalization of the state as described by Bayart, Ellis, and Hibou (1998), Chabal and Daloz (1998), Verschave (2000), and others. Foreign recognition once founded on Cold War considerations is now replaced by recognition of the state as pursuing development and democracy. Local mafias gaining access to power in the center, with the corrupt bureaucrats, is now less important than *becoming a center*, no matter how weak. This means that mafias have an interest in becoming states; the many breakaway republics in the former Soviet Union, especially in the north Caucasus, are examples of this tendency, as are the regional wars in the Horn of Africa.

The *struggle for recognition* seems to replace sovereignty in the contest for making out what is a state. States are simply those units recognized as states. States do not have to provide territorial security, collect taxes, provide services, or monopolize violence. They just have to have the trappings. In a discursive sense, declarations about human rights and democracy become more important than actually *ensuring* human rights or democracy. It is such declarations that help facilitate the entry of project society and NGO development. It is declarations of this kind, and the Western aid agency's or the NGO's decision to "go in" to Bolivia or Somaliland or Abkhazia, which sets in motion the traffic in project resources and power struggle about how to utilize them.

In this struggle for recognition as a state, powerful clans, warlords, and networks do not count; warlords and mafias may fulfill state functions and control wide stretches of territory in white-jeep states, but they cannot obtain aid. International assistance is given to local organizations recognized by "states," no matter how small or powerless these states are, and much aid can be administered only by "national governments." This means that mafia coalitions have an imperative to seek recognition as states, which can be done by struggling for recognition as separate cultural or regional movements. The impetus is there for mafias to take on territorial-nationalist-popular ambitions.

The link between organized criminal activity and nationalist struggles is not uncommon. Most nationalist or regional struggles against corrupt central governments, especially those not supported by Western governments, often rely on illegal activities to procure arms and raise funds. Recent accusations of IRA, Kosovo-Albanian, Kurdish, and other such smuggling operations are therefore not without some foundation.

Mafias, therefore, can also be nourished by the forces of global identity politics, such that they achieve recognition as speaking for a "people." Mafia coalitions can also be nourished by appropriating the resources of project society (as has apparently occurred in the mafiaization of civil society groups in Russia, penetration of war veterans groups, and exploitation of NGO laws for illegal enterprise, that is, racketeering; see Williams 1996). The ability of mafia to appropriate global resources means that we must view globalization not simply as decapitating the state from the top, nor should we see mafia as truncating the state from below. Rather globalization, here understood as the decentralization of capital, movement of resources, and mediation of discourses, creates new conditions and new resources available for state formation. It enables mafias to struggle for recognition—and succeed. It facilitates the entry of project society. And it allows for criminalization to be not just something that "happens" to good states but to be a force in state formation and reproduction.

It is in the world's "trouble spots" that the relationship between state formation, criminalization, and project life is most transparent. It is here that the brown jeeps driven by local armed forces or peacekeeping troops pass the white jeeps of the international aid community, the official cars of the Minister of Public Order, and the shiny new Mercedes driven by the local warlord or mafia chieftain. When the international community provides assistance to such trouble spots, it is under the pretext of giving resources to the formal, central state. In reality, it is to a coalition that only occupies state offices. Hence, aid to "Albania," "Kirghizstan," or "Senegal" becomes controlled by a few corrupt bureaucrats and administered by local elites and their networks, with the complicity of local criminals. Aid to privatization in Russia, administered by Harvard University, was controlled by the Chubais "clan" that channeled the money into private accounts and eventually emerged as consultants to the world of projects (Wedel 1998). In Kosovo, aid to police training in Kosovo goes to placate political factions and violent groups that would otherwise be preying on the new society from outside.

This aid eventually takes the form of projects, and it is via projects that the bandit society and the state come together. Globalization brings project society into a mediating role between bandit society and the state. Trouble spots are places where project society has completely replaced the state, and where project society's jeeps cannot travel, bandit society operates. The relationship between central states, project society, and mafia kingdoms can stabilize, but often this requires some demonstrations of power on either side to mark off domains of authority; hence, the violence that characterizes trouble spots: terrorist attacks on the center, kidnapping of once immune U.N. functionaries whose fingers are chopped off to demonstrate the kidnappers' seriousness, peacekeeping troops' attempts to arrest criminals, and the incipient local state campaigns to wipe out organize crime, cut off smuggling routes, and so on.

The future of Eastern Europe, the Balkans and the former USSR reflects a combination of First and Third World conditions. In the capitals, in the more developed regions, and along secure arteries through which flow essential goods and transport we will have a "European regime." Here "Europe" is understood as relative public order, welfare services, market economies, strong administration, and an active, publicly oriented citizenry. Daytime and nighttime states will overlap and jeeps travel unhindered. In other regions, typically in the highlands, the peripheries, and along border zones, we have banditry and warlords plundering their own regions and exacting tribute from those who pass through, whether they be smugglers or EU aid projects.

Globalization processes produce various kinds of white-jeep states in which project society and mafia kingdoms interact. This interaction may have various degrees of boundary creation marked by violence. Mafia kingdoms may exact tribute from project society in the form of creating false NGOs or embezzlements in local project offices where expense accounts are falsified or seminars invented. Other resources may be extracted by theft or more violent means, including kidnappings of international community representatives; there will be more "missing fingers" until the groups doing the kidnapping achieve recognition.

In such trouble spots, the transnational networks of mafia entrepreneurs expedites people, money, arms, drugs, goods, and services across borders, aided by corrupt bureaucrats and warlords who help facilitate the movement of these transnational flows. Aid money flows in as "anticorruption programs" and "civil society development"; there are programs to "combat organized crime," and this enters into the very criminalization process that aid is supposed to hinder. Global processes of both the project and the mafia type help create "states," but these states are not necessarily coterminous with sovereignty or control; they are states only in terms of their trappings or their recognition by other states or donors. They are states that attract projects. But it should be emphasized that these states are no more than coalitions of actors who utilize public resources under varying degrees of popular legitimacy.

CONCLUSIONS: IT'S ALL GLOBALIZATION'S FAULT

As an imposing force on the state, the globalization concept assumes a stable state order that is somehow destabilized. States, we are told, are being fragmented by forces beyond their control, a fragmentation that generates efforts to reassert control and redraw boundaries leading to violence. Project society, as a manifestation of global resources, certainly replaces some state functions from above just as local mafias may threaten state order in the provinces or in certain sectors. The question, however, is whether these functions or order existed in the first place.

The purpose of this chapter has been to show that the relationship between states, projects, and bandits is both simpler and more complicated than it appears. Simple in the sense that what we call states are no more than groups of individuals utilizing specific sets of resources, including means of obtaining legitimacy and recognition. More complicated in the sense that states, projects, and bandits are not necessarily antagonistic or mutually exclusive. Project society can also be used by the central state to consolidate power. Mafia and banditry can help consolidate the state. And the triangle between states, projects, and the uncivil society we call mafia can be mediated by state-centered coalitions.

Seeing states as only groups of people with access to specific kinds of resources compels us to rethink the various conceptions of "informal" relations that are usually seen as lying in between state institutions. The informal is viewed as somehow less legitimate, less stable, as something that corrupts or perverts states. Instead of conceiving of the criminal, the violent, the informal and the corrupt as something occupying the vacuum of the institutional, what Eric Wolf (1966) called the "interstices," it is more fruitful to reverse the priorities. Let us conceive of the state *as filling gaps where the informal sector does not operate.* Those coalitions that achieve recognition as states have done so by virtue of their ability to mediate between other informal coalitions. They use their legitimacy and international recognition to play mafia chieftains and warlords against each other. Some states are mafias with international recognition, others are mafias with both local legitimacy and international recognition, thereby gaining access to the resources of project society. Mafias, however, act like illegal companies while simultaneously appropriating state functions. In this way, mafias actually compensate for the inadequacies of the state and the market. Insofar as they fill the vacuum between state and market, mafias act like an ersatz civil society. In their uncivil way, mafias are the ultimate non-governmental organization.

Weak states exist in an environment of project society and bandit society. Those involved in the coalitions that we call "the state" can mobilize other kinds of resources, including the legitimacy and recognition that comes from invoking a public sphere based on administration, representation, citizenship, and national mission. They can do this more effectively by utilizing the resources of project society and bandit society. Strong states are those that utilize both, under the guise of public service. They appropriate or co-opt project funds, utilize the mafia networks of trust and loyalty, but maintain the state's monopoly on violence. Strong states do not eliminate primordial ties; they organize them.

States are therefore not simply the mafia that wins, since states are supposed to have some kind of public project while mafias and warlords pursue private interests. When states fail to impose themselves on the local, privatized mafias, we get "trouble spots." Trouble spots are characterized by decentralized violence. Yet it is not enough to say, as does Bax (1997) in discussing Bosnia, that this violence is a result of "decivilization processes" linked to decline of the state or that there are "cycles of violence" between dependent groups. What is it that makes states weak in the first place? Why does informal organization sustain itself even when formal organizations collapse? Why are states and project society undermined by primordial ties of kin, ethnic, region, or religion?

We observe here two contradictory processes: primordial ties seem to undermine the state and corrupt project society, while global projects and states try to replace primordial ties with those based on civil society or citizenship ties. In some cases, global project society succeeds, but this success is better understood as people latching onto new kinds of resources, the kind that project society offers. This entails changing loyalties, and the various social groups in the global world are indeed people who have forsaken local loyalties to join another world. Like Freemasons, traveling merchants, international civil servants, gypsy academics, and human rights activists, they have evolved "other priorities." To the extent that peoples' private projects overlap with global discourses, we speak of "development" or of the "power of globalization." Global forces, abstract as they are, appear in people's everyday practice: the young Albanian NGO activist who must decide whether to visit her grandmother back in the village or attend the conference in Geneva. Where there is conflict between the private and global projects, we speak of corruption or criminalization. "Transnational organized crime" is but the linkage of such private projects. It is the mirror image of "global civil society."

Just as we must be more concrete in understanding "the state," we must also stop assuming the automatic strength of primordial ties. Under conditions of transnational movement of resources, people, and ideological constructs, when does kinship, friendship, trust, ethnicity, regional affiliation, and so on, become unimportant? Why do promising intellectuals in the Balkans organize and run NGOs? Why do young men and boys in Africa leave their families to join rebel armies led by warlords or ethnic leaders? Perhaps it is not the "pervasiveness of the informal" that should be problematized, but the demise of informal loyalties, those unique settings we call "institutions" or "bureaucracy." The threat of globalization is precisely this threat to informal ties. It can turn locally grounded leaders into global project office managers in a new world; and it provides the impetus for local mafias to aspire to state power, preferably with the necessary public ethic and rhetoric of democracy. The conventional wisdom is that globalization undermines states in the form of projects and bandits. But fragmentation is only part of the story. Projects and bandits do not just threaten states; they are now helping to constitute them.

NOTE

I would like to thank the participants at the Harry Frank Guggenheim Foundation conferences on Globalization and Violence for stimulating discussion, and especially Jonathan Friedman for valuable comments on earlier drafts of this paper.

REFERENCES

Appadurai, Arjun. 1991. "Global Ethnoscapes: Notes and Queries for a Transnational Anthropology." In *Recapturing Anthropology: Working in the Present.* Edited by Richard G. Fox, 191–210. Sante Fe, N.M.: School of American Research Press.

———. 1993. "Disjuncture and Difference in the Global Cultural Economy." In *Global Culture: Nationalism, Globalization and Modernity.* Edited by M. Featherstone. London: Sage

Barber, Benjamin. 1995. *Jihad versus McWorld: How Globalism and Tribalism Are Reshaping the World.* New York: Random House.

Barth, Frederik. 1989. "The Analysis of Culture in Complex Societies." *Ethnos* 54:120–39.

Bauman, Zygmunt. 1998. *Globalization: The Human Consequences.* New York: Columbia University Press.

Bax, Mart. 1997. "Decivilizing Processes and the War in Bosnia." *Ethnologia Europaea* 28:116–132.

Bayart, Jean-Francois. 1993. *The State in Africa: The Politics of the Belly.* London: Longman.

Bayart, J.-F., S. Ellis, and B. Hibou. 1998. *The Criminalization of the State in Africa.* Oxford, U.K.: James Currey for the International Africa Institute.

Blok, Anton. 1974. *The Mafia of a Sicilian Village: A Study of Violent Peasant Entrepreneurs.* New York: Harper.

Bracewell, Catherine W. 1992. *The Uskoks of Senj: Piracy, Banditry and Holy War in the Sixteenth Century Adriatic.* Ithaca, N.Y.: Cornell University Press.

Carothers, Thomas. 1996. *Assessing Democracy Assistance: The Case of Romania.* Washington, D.C.: Brookings Institution.

———. 1999. *Aiding Democracy Abroad: The Learning Curve.* Washington, D.C.: Carnegie .

Castells, Manuel. 1997. *The Rise of the Network Society.* 3 vols. London: Blackwell.

Chabal, Patrick and Jean Pascal Daloz. 1998. *Africa Works: Disorder as a Political Instrument.* Oxford, U.K.: James Currey for the International Africa Institute.

Gallant, Thomas W. 1999. "Brigandage, Piracy, Capitalism and State-Formation: Transnational Crime from a Historical World-Systems Perspective." In *States and Illegal Practices.* Edited by Josiah McC. Heyman, 25–62. New York: Berg.

Gambietta, Diego. 1993. *The Sicilian Mafia: The Business of Private Protection.* Cambridge, Mass.: Harvard University Press.

Hannerz, Ulf. 1992. *Cultural Complexity: Studies in the Social Organization of Meaning.* New York: Columbia University Press.

Hansen, Greg. 1998. *Humanitarian Action in the Caucasus: A Guide for Practitioners.* Providence, R.I.: Watson Institute for International Studies.

Harris, Olivia, ed. 1996. *Inside and Outside the Law.* London: Routledge.

Heidenheimer, Arnold, ed. 1989. *Political Corruption: Readings in Comparative Analysis.* New Brunswick, N.J.: Transaction.

Herzfeld, Michael. 1997. *Cultural Intimacy: Social Poetics in the Nation State.* New York: Routledge.

Humphrey, Caroline. 1992. *The Transition from Socialism to Feudalism*, ms. Forthcoming.

Massing, Michael. 2000. "Mexico: The Narco-State." *New York Review of Books*, June 15, 24–29.

Myrdal, Gunnar. 1968. *Asian Drama: An Inquiry into the Poverty of Nations*. New York: Pantheon.

Ritzer, George. 1996. *The McDonaldization of Society*. Thousand Oaks, Calif.: Pine Forge Press.

———. 1997. *The McDonaldization Thesis: Explorations and Extensions*. London: Sage.

Salamon, Lester, and Anheier, Helmut. 1996. *The Emerging Non-Profit Sector*. Manchester, U.K.: Manchester University Press.

Sampson, Steven. 1983. "Bureaucracy and Corruption and Anthropological Problems: A Case Study from Romania." *Folk* (Copenhagen). 25:30–55.

———. 1996. "The Social Life of Projects: Importing Civil Society to Albania." In *Civil Society: Challenging Western Models*. Edited by C. Hann and E. Dunn, 121–43. London: Routledge.

———. 1998. "Exporting Democracy: Preventing Mafia, the Rebirth of Eastern Europe in the Era of Post-Post-Communism." In *Collective Identities in an Era of Transformations*. Edited by K-G Karlsson, Bo Petersson, and Barbara Tonrquist-Plewa, 151–86. Lund, Sweden: Lund University Press.

———. 1999. "The Power of Abstract Concepts: Authority in the World of Democracy Consulting." Paper presented at American Anthropological Association Meetings, Panel on Anthropology of Authority, San Francisco.

———. 2001. *Evaluation of Human Rights Office Tuzla* (HROT). Copenhagen: Danish Center for Human Rights.

Scott, James. 1972. *Comparative Political Corruption*. Englewood Cliffs, N.J.: Prentice Hall.

———. 1985. *Weapons of the Weak: Everyday Forms of Peasant Resistance*. New Haven, Conn.: Yale University Press.

Smart, Barry, ed. 2000. *Resisting McDonaldization*. London: Sage.

Tilly, Charles. 1985. "War-Making and State Making as Organized Crime." In *Bringing the State Back In*. Edited by Peter Evans, Dietrich Rueschmeyer, and Theda Skocpol. Cambridge, U.K.: Cambridge University Press.

Traub, James. 2000. "The Worst Place on Earth." *New York Review of Books*, June 29, 61–66.

Turner, Terence. 2002. "Class Projects, Social Conciousness, and the Contradictions of Globalization." Chapter 2 of this volume.

Varesse, Frederico. 1994. Is Sicily the Future of Russia? *Archives of European Sociology* 35:224–58.

Verdery, Katherine. 1996. *What Was Socialism and What Comes Next?* Princeton, N.J.: Princeton University Press.

Verschave, François-Xavier. 2000. *Noir silence: Qui arrêtera la Françafrique?* Paris: Editions Les Arènes.

Volkov, Vadim. 1999. "Violent Entrepreneurship in Post-Communist Russia." *Europe-Asia Studies* 51:741–54.

Wedel, Janine. 1998. *Collision and Collusion: The Strange Case of Western Aid to Eastern Europe 1989–1998.* New York: St. Martin's.

Williams, Phil, ed. 1996. *Russian Organized Crime: The New Threat.* London: Frank Cass.

Wolf, Eric. 1966. "Kinship, Friendship and Patron Client Relations in Complex Societies." In *The Social Anthropology of Complex Societies.* Edited by M. Banton, 1–22. London: Tavistock.

12

State Classes, the Logic of Rentier Power and Social Disintegration

Global Parameters and Local Structures of the Decline of the Congo

KAJSA EKHOLM FRIEDMAN

It is becoming commonplace today to locate the social sciences of development within a larger perspective in which development is more clearly understood in terms of the ideological discourses of the global system. There has been cause to ponder the many disasters of development agencies, but there is also cause to ponder the theoretical failure of critical approaches such as the Dependency Theory that predicted that development in the form of capital export to the underdeveloped world was merely a means to the intensification of the process of peripherialization. Some complained that the problem with Africa was, in fact, the lack of capital rather than its abundance. The Asian NIC countries and China today are more powerful counterarguments to the Dependency Theory since their economic success is very much a product of such capital transfers. It is crucial to examine more closely the mechanisms involved in the articulation between specific polities in the global arena. Congo-Brazzaville is the target of this analysis of active underdevelopment. It traces the forms of state-class power in this process and argues that the current violent crisis are the end results of the dynamics of a particular political economy.

ECONOMIC CRISIS IN SPITE OF OIL

During the 1980s it became clear that most countries in sub-Saharan Africa were in deep economic crisis. The optimistic visions of the 1960s were never realized, nor was foreign aid able to alter the downward trend. Many African countries were much worse off than they were at independence.

The Congo is no exception. The country, situated in west-central Africa, north of the Congo River, the Congo had about two million inhabitants, at least before the civil wars of the 1990s, in an area of 342,000 square kilometers. The industrial sector is more or less limited to oil. A great deal of money has been spent on state enterprises, both industries and state farms, but their performance was poor in the 1970s and even worse in the 1980s. Production of food for the domestic market as well as crops for export was decreasing. Agriculture was limited to two very different domains—modern farms, most of them state owned and peasant agriculture. Congo had one of the highest rates of urbanization in Africa, roughly 60 percent, which was absurd given the lack of available jobs. Large parts of the country were depopulated. Whole villages had disappeared and many of those that still survived harbored only social categories that could not survive in town—old people and abandoned women with small children who had been forced back to the village in search of food. Congo's external debt per capita was one of the highest in Africa. But it also had among the highest number of Mercedes per capita in the world.

The Congo referred to itself as a Marxist-Leninist state under the PCT, the Congolese Labor Party (*Parti Congolais du Travail*). But in a country where there was no real working class and where the domestic basis of political power was the military, the name of the party was misleading to say the least.[1] Political meetings, covered by TV, often ended with the singing of the *International* by representatives of the state class and the army. The president raised his right fist and shouted "*Tout pour le peuple*" and the others responded "*Rien que pour le peuple.*" In 1989, people in Brazzaville joked about the new version being "*Rien pour le peuple.*" Brazzaville was heavily militarized. When the president left his palace, large parts of the town were closed and guarded by armed soldiers; the cortege was protected by soldiers sitting back-to-back in jeeps with their machine guns directed toward both sides of the street, ready to fire.

Oil was found offshore in 1968 and extraction started in 1972. The country has had huge oil revenues since then. And yet it is no exaggeration to say that people were much worse off in the 1980s than twenty years previously. Congo's growth in GDP at the beginning of the 1980s did not affect the majority of the population to any significant extent. It gave rise to impressive buildings and a class of rich politicians with money in Swiss banks and conspicuous consumption in Brazzaville and Pointe-Noire. But it did not lead to economic development, and it did not improve the living conditions for the people. Production was carried out by foreign companies in joint ventures with the Congolese state—ELF Congo (French-Congolese), Agip Congo (Italian-Congolese), and AMCO (American-Congolese). In 1973 production amounted to two million tons and in the middle of the 1980s to more than five million. What happened after that was controversial. If it is true that production was seven to eight million tons, the country's oil revenues could not possibly be as low as was officially claimed. For some years the state advertised the idea that it no longer had any money to spend, which was accounted for by the shrinking dollar and lower oil prices. Schools, the university, the health care system and low- and middle-income salaries were deteriorating due to the lack of money. In 1990 there were open accusations about part of the oil revenues going directly to the president.

In this first section, I will take up three interrelated elements. The first is a brief overview of the economic history of the area in order to demonstrate that the situation had truly deteriorated since 1970. There was a period of economic development after World War II up to independence, which was maintained and even accelerated during most of the 1960s. The second is an analysis of the political system as the structural ground for Congo's underdevelopment. It is evident that African countries with a socialist and Marxist-Leninist orientation have failed miserably in economic terms. I will argue that this is due to a structural problem, most clearly developed in one-party systems but that may exist in other countries in sub-Saharan Africa as well. This structural problem has to do with the survival of the traditional African political organization. Africa was certainly influenced and transformed by European colonization but not as thoroughly as one might imagine. After independence it successively rid itself of foreign influences and there was a gradual Africanization of European institutions. The third element captures the effects of the political system on various aspects of the economy, primarily rural production. I will here take up material from my study of cooperatives and individual peasants in the southern part of the country and illustrate the problems from the peasants' point of view. Finally, I will touch upon the ongoing democratization process as a response to the economic crisis.

ECONOMIC BACKGROUND

Historical material indicates that the Congo was relatively wealthy and already quite developed at independence. Its wealth emanated partly from its position as a transit country for trade toward Chad, Central African Republic, and Gabon, and from its position as center for the colonial administration of AEF. But part of it came from the relatively high level of industrialization. Congo exported industrial products, such as sugar, soap, cigarettes, shoes, and so forth, to neighboring countries. The development of light industry continued until the end of the 1960s when it was suddenly interrupted. It seems plausible to connect this deindustrialization with the military takeover in 1968 and the proclamation of Marxism-Leninism as the official ideology. But it is, of course, possible that the tendencies were there before and that it took a while for them to fully manifest themselves.

For centuries, this part of Africa experienced a devastating trade in slaves that drew attention away from productive activities. However, from about 1860 to colonization, a rapid expansion of agricultural production for export took place (Ekholm Friedman 1991). This development came to an end with the colonization in 1885. Large tracts of land were given as concessions to European companies with rights of tenure and exploitation in exchange for a fixed annual payment and 15 percent of the profits (Cornevin 1986:23). This first phase of the colonial period, up to 1920, was characterized by the collection of rubber and ivory. The concessionary company only took what nature offered spontaneously, and no transformation of the indigenous economy took place. The weak performance of the concessionaries has been attributed to low population density, the lack of adequate infrastructure, the generally low level of development, and their own deficiency of capital (Bertrand 1975:80; Cornevin 1986:23)

The second phase of the colonial period, from 1920 to 1945, is characterized by the elimination of the big consessionary companies and the development of forest exploitation and commercial agriculture. Forestry developed in the Kouilou region and early became the most important export category. The more substantial investments in agriculture did not appear until after the World War II. *Les colons* settled primarily in the Niari Valley where they found an area with relatively high fertility, large tracts of flatland, and transportation facilities (Vennetier 1963, 1965). Here they started monoculture in peanuts and later developed a more diversified agriculture in combination with cattle. Cattle was introduced after 1947 and a number of ranches appeared, both private and government owned. The biggest industrial enterprise, SIAN (Société Industrielle et Agricole du Niari), started with mechanized monoculture in peanuts, supplying the whole country with peanut oil. Later, it turned to sugar and supplied not only the entire Congolese market but also exported its product to Congo's neighbors within the subregion.

Amin (1969:128, 56) emphasizes Congo's relatively high degree of industrialization at independence and he even characterizes the third phase of the colonial period, from 1946 to 1960, with the development of light industry. Even Bertrand (1975:218) makes the remark that Congo, at independence, had a relatively large number of agricultural industries, but he adds the word "paradoxically," as if it were an anomaly. Both Amin and Bertrand, faithful to their Marxist orientation, distrust, in general, an "export-dependent" economy. Their view of the economy of a developed country is like a biological organism, the different parts of which are interrelated and integrated and has its own internal dynamics. To Bertrand, Congo's economy, in spite of all the industries, "lacks internal dynamics," it lacks "a national motor" (198, 199). An economy must be "self-centered" and "auto-dynamic" according to them both, meaning that it should produce for its own needs, be governed by local demands, and that the driving force should be found within the country. It is, however, very clear from their material that the Congolese economy, at independence, displayed a very promising pattern. The industrialization process was then accentuated during most of the 1960s. The value of total exports increased from six billion CFAF[2] in 1960 to twelve billion in 1968, of which 50 percent came from forestry. Agricultural products, mineral products (lead, zinc, copper), and oil accounted for only a minor part, while industrial products toward the UDEAC (for which figures are known), such as sugar, tobacco, beer, oil, soap, and so on, constituted 28 percent of the exports. Sugar did very well in the 1960s. The export value was 700 million CFAF in 1960 and 1.5 billion in 1965. After 1966 Congo even exported refined sugar to Zaire, France, and Iraq, and molasses to France and the Netherlands (Amin 1969:110).

This is an important aspect of the Congo's postcolonial history, as it seems to indicate that an early process of industrialization was interrupted around 1970. The investment rate was also very high during the 1960s. The state accounted for almost 50 percent of industrial investments after 1965 (Amin 1969:75). Private investments were made in oil prospecting, sugar, forestry, and industries (Guichaoua 1989:28). It is even possible to discern a positive change in the investment pattern from the period 1960–1963 to the period 1963–1968. During Youlou's regime the investment distribution followed the general pattern for African countries, that is two-thirds to infrastructure, transportation, social services, and administration, and one-third to directly productive activities. During the following period, 1963–1968, the former kind of investments was reduced to 50 percent to the benefit of directly productive investments. Investments in industry increased from 15 percent to 29 percent. On this point the Congo was doing very well, not only compared to the average of the continent but also compared to countries such as Ivory Coast and Senegal (Amin 1969:75). A great number of state enterprises were established during Massamba-Débat's regime at the same time as he explicitly opposed the idea of nationalization as a way of improving economic conditions of the country. The wave of nationalizations in the Congo did not happen until Ngouabi's regime.

Around 1970 Congo lost many of its regional functions at the same time competing industries were established in the neighboring countries. Bertrand (1975:198–99) writes about "a serious recession" in 1970–1971 due to the appearance of competing industries for beer, cigarettes, soap, and sugar in surrounding areas. Figures for the production of sugar show an abrupt fall after 1969. The sugar industry is an example of capital flight from the Congo at the end of the 1960s. SIAN was owned by Grands Moulins de Paris. After 1967–1968 it started to close down its activities in the Congo while moving its production to other countries within the UDEAC. Competing activities, for instance sugar plantations, were established in neighboring countries that formerly depended upon the Congo. The various companies in the Congo did not renew material or even maintain the plantations, and in 1970 the Congolese state felt prompted to nationalize (Bertrand 1975:218). After that production fell abruptly.

Foreign capital thus abandoned the Congo around 1970, apparently as a reaction to the political situation. The military coup happened in 1968 but the situation had been aggravated somewhat earlier by the conflict between the government and the army and the killing of opponents to the regime. Massamba-Débat had no control over the army and when he tried to get rid of Captain Marien Ngouabi, the army took over. Marxism-Leninism was adopted as state ideology by the military regime at the beginning of 1970, and the USSR and Eastern Europe became models for the political system. Bertrand says in his work of 1975, which was apparently written in 1972 judging from the statistical material, that the most important part of the Congolese industry was then dying at a fast rate (218). Private capital did not want to stay or invest, and state enterprises functioned miserably. It is worth noting that the unwillingness of foreign capital to invest in the Congo (outside the oil sector) is shared by today's politicians with big money, honestly or dishonestly earned. "Where is the oil money?" is a question that has never been answered in a satisfactory way. When preventing oil money from entering the sphere of production in the Congo, the Congolese state class is, one could say, as rational as was foreign capital that fled the country at the end of the 1960s.

THE POLITICAL SYSTEM
The State's Disengagement from the People

The African state has been discussed by a number of political scientists (Hyden 1983; Jackson and Rosberg 1982; Markowitz 1977, 1987; Sandbrook 1985). The best portrayal is the one of privatization. Politicians and civil servants do not occupy functions of a state apparatus as in the West where they have to separate their private interests and economy from those of the state. The Congolese state was and is, instead, a social group, a network of personal alliances, much more like the mafia than a Western state. In the Marxist-Leninist period it was not expedient of the IMF to suggest privatization. Hydro Congo, one of the largest state enterprises, was transferred to one of the president's clan brothers as private property, apparently in order to please the IMF.

A strong state was, according to official ideology, an absolute prerequisite, not only for economic development but also for the development of socialism

and the liberation of the masses. Around 1985, when the state was pro-
nouncedly more Marxist-Leninist than today, it was claimed that the Congo
was in transition from neocolonialism to socialism (see Goma-Foutou 1985;
Mouamba 1985). Workers and peasants cannot play their historical role without a strong state, it was claimed, as they are opposed by a number of "reactionary classes"—French imperialism of course, but also indigenous "classes,"
such as the national bourgeoisie and the "feudal lords." "Feudal lords" are, in
this context, clan chiefs administering land that belongs to their kin groups.
There has never been any real feudalism in Central Africa since land always
belonged to the larger clan unit. The official view of the crisis of the 1980s was
very much in accord with the Dependency School. It was blamed on external
factors that were beyond the control of the political elite. Congo's development problems and the suffering of the poor was, according to this political
ideology, caused by imperialism and the malfunctioning of the capitalist system. The political leaders were powerless against such vicious forces, but they
were doing their best and in due time they would undoubtedly solve all the
problems.

The reality was very unlike the political ideology. The state had not been
able to promote any economic development, and worse, it constituted the
principle obstacle to development. Nor had the Congolese state contributed to
the liberation of the "masses." According to the official model the political
leaders were true servants of the people, constantly listening to the people's
voice in order to learn about their needs and wishes. I cannot judge if this extreme falsification of the relationship between rulers and people appeared
more convincing in the early 1980s; it was, in any case, laughed at in 1987 and
not even commented upon in 1989. The political elite was (and is) a ruling
class that represented no one but itself.

The Congo can be seen as composed of two more or less separate spheres
(not including the oil company Elf): *the state*, dominated by a ruling class controlling all the resources of the country; and *the popular sector*, where people
are left to survive on their own. The ruling group had simply disengaged itself
from the people, in spite of rhetorical assurances to the contrary, and it
formed an enclave in the country with its own economy, culture, political
party (the only party), and the military (Ekholm Friedman 1990a, 1990b).
The inflow of money derived from three main sources: export revenues
(mainly oil), aid, and foreign loans, all controlled by the state. It was not dependent upon ordinary citizens in any significant way, and it could therefore
turn its back on them. The Marxist model of the relationship between classes,
in which they mutually condition each other's existence, was based on realities of nineteenth-century Western Europe. Here the relationship was quite

different. The upper class was not so extraordinarily wealthy because it exploited the working class but because it controlled all the valuable resources of the country and all the money that was channeled through the state from the outside world. In Hyden's (1983) view the African state is weak because the people, protected by its "economy of affection," is strong and self-sufficient. My view is rather the opposite. The Congolese state is strong, much too strong and self-sufficient, and that forces people to survive on their own, in other words to develop and maintain an "economy of affection" (Hyden 1983).

The Congolese state was based on two main pillars, the military and alliances with foreign interests. The coup d'état in 1968 brought the military into the political arena. Both presidents Yombhi (1977–1979) and Sassou (1992, 1997) were from the ranks of the military. It was often emphasized by his critics in Brazzaville that Sassou started as a schoolteacher and was enrolled in the reserve during a period when there was a high demand for military personnel. He had, in other words, no military merit. The unofficial figure for the number of soldiers in the country was 20,000 to 25,000. Most of them were stationed in Brazzaville and Pointe-Noire, an indication of their principal purpose (to maintain order). Congo also had a dreaded secret police, whose agents were, according to rumor, trained by Securitate, Stasi, the Libyans, the Abu Nidal group, and so on. The ruling class was intimately connected to various metropoles of the world system and a great deal of the money that was generated in the Congo, or obtained from the outside, was exported to these areas, in the form of consumption and above all in investments, the purchase of real estate, and savings in foreign banks.

The popular sector was more or less cut off from the self-sufficient state. There were, of course, a certain number of salaried jobs and some money trickled down from the ruling group. But most people did not have an income. The fact that in 1987–1988 there was still no widespread starvation was an effect of the clan system and of the subsidy on bread (made of imported wheat). Every income created a group of dependents tied to its earner. The decline of the Congolese countryside is an illustration of the impossibility of development in a situation of isolation.

Money was concentrated in very few hands. It entered the central sector of the country, and there it remained. The political elite had virtually all the money and so few people could only eat so much. Moreover, the Congolese upper class was not satisfied with Congolese food but preferred to buy canned peas from France and apples from Spain in air-conditioned supermarkets where they could also find a variety of French cheeses, different kinds of ham and pâté, vintage red wines, and champagne. Food was imported, not because of agricultural problems, but rather because imported food was what people with money most desired. Thus the buying power of the country was only to a limited extent directed toward its own producers.

The domestic market, in turn, was very limited due to the fact that ordinary people had very little money. The buying power in the popular sector was not adequate to enable the peasants to sell their agricultural products. Congo's decreasing production of food was not primarily a consequence of lacking a capacity to produce but rather of the structure of the market. While people were undernourished, searched for food in garbage heaps, and stole their neighbors' hens and manioc from others' fields, there was an overproduction of food. A great deal of food rotted because revenues were so limited. Congolese products were, furthermore, undercut by cheaper food smuggled from Zaire (in Brazzaville) and Cabinda (in Pointe-Noire), where national currencies were valued lower.

Traditional African Kingdom under Marxist-Leninist Flag

Why did African states declare themselves Marxist-Leninist around 1970? Why this interest in Marxism-Leninism? One way of answering this question is that it suited the state class perfectly, as it did in Eastern Europe. It legitimized state class power. The state was to control the whole economy, there could not be more than one party, no competitors were allowed, all attempts at organizing from the bottom were illegal and counterrevolutionary. Marxist ideology was perfectly adapted to the political elite when it came to the identification of the main enemy of the people and the revolution. It has been used against entrepreneurs of various types, what Amin (1969:147) called "the embryonic local bourgeoisie." This initial class of "capitalists" was jealously fought in the name of Marxism-Leninism and downgraded to petty traders.

But Marxism-Leninism was extraordinarily compatible with the Congo at a deeper level by masking the fact that the Congo still, to a large extent, was politically structured as a traditional central African kingdom. The precolonial kingdoms were composed of a number of structurally isomorphic local units, hierarchically related to one other through exchange. "Tribute" was transferred from lower ranked groups to higher ones, and in the other direction there was a distribution of foreign goods obtained through external trade. All the different units were more or less complete societies, so to speak, with their own economic and political structures. The central, or highest ranked, unit was larger than the others. It had more people, more slaves, more of everything, but it was not structurally different. Its position was based upon the monopoly over external trade, that is, over the inflow of resources from the outside world. Under traditional conditions it still depended upon the other groups for its social reproduction; it needed their resources and production for its participation in the international system. Those kingdoms were composed of long chains of such hierarchically related groups. The principal strategy of a central African king was to use his resources in expanding the size of his own group and in establishing and maintaining alliances with other groups.

President Sassou's ruling group resembled the central unit of the kingdom in various respects. It still constituted a world of its own, with no national consciousness or concern for the country as a whole. The president had a monopoly over external exchange. There was no distinction between the private and public economy. The ancient kings controlled domestic resources and external trade in a way that we would define as clearly private. European trade goods went first to the king who then distributed them among his vassals. This is how the Congo's resources were dealt with in the postcolonial era. Part of the oil revenues were first transferred to president Sassou and from him to his vassals. There were still hierarchies in which wealth was distributed from higher to lower ranks in exchange for loyalty. Another characteristic trait of a traditional African kingdom is that political power ideally should be conquered by *the king-and-his-men*. In myths about the origin of the Kongo Kingdom, the founder was first made king by his men and then, together, they crossed the river to conquer the new land. The political system was ideally established by military means and the king was, above all, a conqueror. The Congo's military regime can, thus, be said to be rooted in the traditional system. Kings were always, by definition, both wealthy and militarily powerful. This same pattern can be found following colonization when the "king" was, in reality, deprived of political power but where battles for the throne and the king's exceptional power were articulated in ritualized form.

The main difference between the ancient kingdom and the contemporary Congo is the self-sufficiency of the central group. The ruler might now be said to directly control the principal resources of the country, in the name of Marxist-Leninism, and he does not need the rest of the country for either tribute or alliances.

Marxism-Leninism thus suited the African structure very well. It fit into traditional Congolese political thought and practice. This is strikingly apparent if we look at the notion of "collective ownership." In both cases it implies that the ruling group or the management of a state enterprise could control and absorb all generated wealth. This constituted a critical problem, as we shall see below, not only at the level of the state and state enterprises but also in peasant cooperatives.

The Hierarchical Clan Structure of the Congolese State/Society

The Congo's political system was, in spite of the segregation between the state and popular sectors, a pyramidal structure. The country was, according to its constitution, a Marxist-Leninist one-party system. The political organization and the party were two parallel structures that extended from top to bottom, embracing the country as a whole. Before the summer of 1990 when the national union adamantly contested the regime and finally declared itself independent of the party, the political structure was untrammeled by conflicting interests and was, on the contrary, hierarchically encompassing; the party (with its Bureau Politique and Comité Central), government at the top, all the various "mass organizations," and the army were subsumed under their dominance.

The National Union and the National Youth Organization had more autonomy during the 1960s but were subsumed under the hegemony of the party at the beginning of the 1970s and were controlled by the ruling group through loyal clan brothers in leading positions. The population at large was controlled through the various mass organizations. All women, for example, were included in the URFC, the women's organization. There were four different categories, workers, peasants, tradeswomen, and housewives/members of associations. The party, or rather, male members of the ruling group, appointed female leaders of the URFC and its four sections. Ordinary women were ordered to meetings, receptions for visitors, and political spectacles under the threat of punishment. The URFC is thus part of the power structure and not a "social movement" in the Western sense where people organize themselves around specific common goals.

At the end of the 1980s, ordinary people looked upon the state as another world. It was inconceivable to think of the state as their instrument, that politicians could be their representatives. The call for *multipartisme* (a multiparty system) and democracy did not come from the people. When the hierarchy finally came apart, the fracture occurred very high in the pyramid, within the ruling organizations themselves; the party, the Bureau Politique, the Comité Central, the army, the Union, and the Youth Organization.

In all the ruling organizations there were members of the Sassou clan in top positions, but there were also others, from other ethnic groups, in what seemed to be a fairly stable structure of alliance. But suddenly the others revolted. In some cases it is evident that the Sassou clan abused its dominant position, for example in the army where high military officers climbed the career ladder not by possessing real military merit, but by being clan brothers or conspicuously loyal. Such was also the case at the university where a number of "researchers" and "teachers" had no formal qualifications.

The breach in the pyramid between the state and the popular sector was clearly experienced (and clearly observed by anthropologists) in the agricultural sector. The "cooperative movement" was officially represented as a hierarchical organization, starting at the top with the Ministère du Développement Rural and then following the political-administrative structure, the Direction Régionale du Développement Rural at the regional level, and the *secteur agricole* at the district level. Cooperatives were located, of course, at the bottom of the hierarchy. Correspondingly there was a Union des Paysans (UNPC) represented at the various territorial levels. In reality the hierarchy was divided in two, an upper segment composed of wealthy politicians and civil servants without any experience of peasant life, living in Brazzaville or Pointe-Noire, and a lower segment composed of poor peasants. The top was very distanced from, but also quite unconcerned with, the life of the ordinary peasant. In the middle there was a level of poorly paid agricultural advisors in charge of immediate contact with the cooperatives. The breach in the hierarchy was suffered by these men and women as they were supposed to help the cooperatives by identifying problems and seeking to implement solutions. When car and gas could be obtained they might visit the cooperatives; they wrote reports in which the situation of the area was described and analyzed, reports that were sent up through the hierarchy. And after that nothing happened because no one was interested. When the peasants became angry after sitting with their bags of paddy waiting for the agents of the marketing board, they had no one else to attack but the agricultural advisors. When a representative of this category arrived in a village in the Kindamba district, she feared that she would be beaten by angry peasants. "You come here to talk to us; you better talk first to the rice that has been standing here since last year." They forced her to enter the hut where the unsold rice was kept.

She understood their anger, and also the insuperable difficulties of her own work.

> The peasant usually does what you tell him to do, but afterwards, when his products are not bought, he gets angry and when he gets angry, it is not the president who is on the spot but I. I am the one who has made him to work. The president, he just gives his *mots d'ordre*. We carry them out. But then, the producer will ask us why their products are not bought.

The peasant union revealed the same pattern of hierarchy, with high-ranked party members at the top with no experience of rural life whatsoever and a lower level of true representatives of the peasants, frustrated in the same way as the agricultural advisors because their work seemed quite meaningless. Cars belonging to projects, donated by international organizations, were frequently used privately by the *chefs*. In Kinkala, the Union Régional des Paysans had, on paper, three cars at its disposal, two Mercedes-Benz trucks and one Toyota pickup, all of them donated by the UNOP (*Rapport annuel* 1987:10). None of these cars were, however, available at the time of my stay in 1988. The president of the union, a man in his late fifties, was expected to visit cooperatives within a large area but no car was made available. He deemed that he was too old to walk and he later left his position in anger.

The Effects of the Political System on Economic Performance

The political order had a major impact on state enterprises, entrepreneurial activities, and foreign companies. State enterprises were established, modern equipment bought, but very little production took place. "While our ancient kings built palaces and pyramids, our modern presidents erect steel mills and hydroelectric dams," said Mazrui in an article about Africa in general and Uganda in particular (1988:339). He calls the new structures "temples"; "because like temples they are built in faith rather than through rational calculation." In the Congo's case it is clear, however, that these "temples" were not only for the gods; they were first and foremost a constant source of private wealth for the political elite. And why should they bother to produce when they could get what they wanted more easily? All state enterprises were failures. Private farms, owned by whites, were nationalized at the end of the 1960s and gradually deteriorated. A number of state farms and ranches were also established in the later period, with the same negative results. Modern agricultural equipment, imported from various countries in the West and in the East could be observed abandoned throughout the country. Some of it had never been in use. Instead of generating income for the state, these enterprises constantly needed funding from the state (see Atipo 1985). The very high wages and other exorbitant payments to the management would be enough to explain the failure. But to make it worse, the directors of these state enterprises apparently embezzled funds continuously. Private capital fled the Congo in the 1970s and has not come back, except in the oil sector. It was unclear what kind of deal was struck between the oil companies and president Sassou although it has now become increasingly apparent since the major scandals involving Elf have come to light (Verschave 2000). There was at the end of the 1980s very little private foreign investment in other sectors of the economy.

The entrepreneurial class that emerged in the 1960s, was overcome by the political elite. Free "capitalists" were few and usually involved in a number of different activities simultaneously, as an attempt to escape the long arm of the cleptocracy.[3] At the same time the members of the state class themselves entered all sorts of entrepreneurial activities. Everything that generated money was absorbed: gas stations, bakeries, pharmacies, transports, import businesses, hotels, and restaurants. It is important to notice, however, that the political class did not become entrepreneurial merely by conquering entrepreneurial activities. Its members were quite incompetent in these activities in the same way as they were incompetent at running state enterprises. They identified sources of wealth, appropriated them, pillaged them, and when problems arose they looked elsewhere for another game.

One of the few joint enterprises that existed, established in the late 1980s and not yet gone bankrupt, was the cement factory SOCICO in Loutete. It was owned by Scandcem, a Norwegian-Swedish company in a joint venture with the Congolese state. This enterprise provides an excellent example of how difficult it was for companies to operate in the Congo. When they became a target for the state class, there was no national legal system to protect their interests. The management did not know from one day to the next which rules were operative. New laws and taxes were often introduced and the companies were often forced to pay fines for "crimes" whose significance could not be understood. All this made the situation unbearably insecure, while the political elite continuously attempted to plunder their revenues.

Scandcem entered the Congo in 1987 after the old factory in Loutete had been rebuilt (following a fire). At that time cement was imported from Spain by SIASIC, a company of uncertain composition. According to the management the company would probably not have gone in at all if initial information about the market had been correct. The Congolese state provided an absurdly optimistic view of how much cement the factory would be able to sell. This created serious problems from the very beginning. It also turned out that SIASIC was maintained in spite of the fact that cement was now produced in the country. There was even an agreement that entitled SIASIC to buy cement from SOCICO at the cost of production. In 1988 the factory could not sell its cement. SIASIC "bought" (on credit) about 30 percent of the cement while it continued to import cement from Spain. The Loutete factory found itself in the position of supplier to SIASIC. SIASIC even had a monopoly on the Brazzaville and Pointe-Noire markets. SOCICO was only allowed to sell cement freely in the rest of the country, which was quite meaningless since there were no buyers. Collapse was near at hand. Scandcem issued an ultimatum and it was decided that all imports of cement should stop and that SIASIC should pay for the cement that was bought from SOCICO. In 1990 the problems still prevailed however. Several boats arrived in Pointe-Noire with cement, and the Loutete factory still had to sell between 20 percent and 30 percent of its output to SIASIC.

SOCICO was, of course, an important production unit in the Congo that ought to have been supported and encouraged. Of its five to six billion CFAF in turnover, three billion went back to the state. In addition to the jobs that were created in Loutete, SOCICO was the country's largest consumer of oil, electricity, and transportation. All three were remarkably expensive in the Congo, which made it impossible for SOCICO to sell its product to neighboring countries. Instead of being supported it was constantly balancing at the edge of catastrophe. And why did it continue to exist? Why had it not yet been forced to close down? The management's guess was that it would look bad for the IMF and the World Bank and that the Congolese state was in such a situation that it had to take their opinions into account.

In the pure model of a capitalist country the state has no economy of its own, no (or relatively few) resources of its own but is, instead, dependent on the taxation of capital and labor. Politics and economy are two separate spheres, even if the state may play an active role in supporting and regulating both production and markets. In countries such as the Congo there is no economic bourgeoisie separated from the political elite. Instead the political rulers control the resources and use them for their own purposes as if they were part of their private economy. A person who obtains control over a state enterprise by political means, through kinship or friendship, has a very different interest in the enterprise than a private entrepreneur. The latter has no other security but his enterprise and he must therefore ensure its survival. His own position is intimately linked to the well-being of his company. The Congolese executive in charge of a state enterprise is not dependent in this way. He acts from a predatory position and for him the enterprise is only a means of personal enrichment. He does not need to concern himself about its well-being. When he has emptied it of its capital, it has served its function. He is ready for his next prey. To him it is only a question of using the opportunity while in power to despoil, in his own name or in the name of cousins and other decoys. His life at the top may be uncertain. He does not know how long he will remain in power and therefore it is wise of him to exploit all available opportunities to plunder the state while there is time. In the present situation, however, the political elite seems to be fairly stable and those in power revealing themselves as embezzlers are only moved from one position to another, sometimes following a short period of quarantine. There is even a Congolese expression for this phenomenon; to be "in the garage for repair."

THE RURAL PROBLEM

While the rural sector was the focus of development interest for decades with project after project directed toward technological improvement, export crops, and the like, it has proven to be precisely that area where catastrophic results are most common.

Agriculture has historically been organized around matrilineal relations in southern Congo, and previously field labor was primarily a female task. While in the 1980s men increased their share of production it was primarily in the

sphere of newer cash crops while staples such as manioc remained female domains. The matrilineal structure requires that a woman must provide for herself
and her children since male income, above a certain minimum, belongs to his relatives and not to hers. In this period the agricultural sector including products
such as coffee, cacao, and domestic staples declined successively. Lack of technology, low and declining productivity in dense slash-and-burn areas, and the failure of market mechanisms ignited a massive exodus from the rural areas to the
two main cities where more than 50 percent of the population resided in conditions of increasing poverty. All this occurred in spite of government propaganda
for a return to the land.

The state had produced extraordinarily fine statements aimed at the solution
of the problem: the need for "concrete actions," the plan for "self-sufficiency" by
2000 in a communiqué from 1987, the formation of village-based centers for
the marketing of products, social welfare for peasants, and a slew of other reforms. Practice was very much the opposite of this. The financing of state
farms was marked by excessive stratification. In 1971 the costs for 1,700 civil
servants were higher than the income of 600,000 peasants. There were numerous attempts to encourage cooperatives. Cooperative production was not
new to the Congo and older forms of cooperation such as *dibundu, kintuari,
ekelimba, kitemo,* and *nsalasani* bear similarities to contemporary cooperatives. Cooperation of this kind was never especially popular, however, as it
consisted in submitting oneself to a common goal, one that benefitted the upper echelons of the cooperative organization. Traditional cooperation, on the
contrary, was based on a rather informalized reciprocal exchange of labor that
included payment in food and even money (*dibundu*).

The cooperative movement failed for a number of related reasons. First, the
general rural exodus led to the disintegration of rural social life. Second, the
very organization of cooperative agriculture led to accelerated accusations of
embezzlement and corruption. Third, there was a more fundamental misun-
derstanding of the message conveyed by the state in establishing a system of
credits. The peasants formed cooperatives on the understanding that they
would become points of entry of state investment in the form of credits. This
is an expression of a more general practice of clientelization that is often discussed with respect to the Kongo Kingdom as well as other hierarchical polities. The cooperatives expected to attain a position like that of lower ranked
groups in a traditional central African kingdom. But when the state referred
to "organizing the peasants according to their own interests," it rather intended quite the opposite of integration. It saw perhaps a possibility of exploiting the peasants through the system of credits, but the cooperatives in
both Pool and Kouilou could never pay back more than about 40 percent of

the credits (which is, in any case, better than the 10 percent to 20 percent by state enterprises). The peasants were intuitively aware of the segregation of the state from the popular sector and they sought a solution to their own problems by striving to link the two. Credits made no sense to them, and they did not envision their existence and future as "free" capitalist farmers, "organized according to their own interests," but instead as clients in a hierarchical society. Thus, the initial establishment of cooperatives hoping for expansion and security within the larger hierarchy melted into the discovery that the initial distributions of what in fact turned out to be U.N. gifts were not part of the establishment of anything at all.

Infrastructure and Regional Markets

One of the major contradictions of the agricultural sector was related to the incompatibility of trying to establish a larger regional or even export market with a deterioration and/or lack of infrastructure. Without electricity, running water, equipment for preserving food, and proper transport it is almost impossible to maintain a larger system of marketing. In the colonial period much of this infrastructure was controlled by the French who had organized a very productive agricultural sector, but all of that disappeared in the following years. Another impasse lay in the internal markets. Ordinary people could not afford the chicken and vegetables produced in the country even if they actually found their way to the market. Major state institutional customers such as the military did not often pay for their goods. Those with money bought imported food at the supermarkets, while the great majority of those without money bought cheaper imports from surrounding countries, often smuggled in in large quantities, from outside the CFA zone, which was artificially overvalued for years. Even local manioc had difficulty competing with state-subsidized bread produced with imported French flour. On top of this the middlemen who controlled the relations to the market often exploited the situation, which in any case was entirely ensnared in very risky credit relations. Finally, and following the general logic of the state-class system, state agencies in charge of export crops specialized in not paying peasants for their undervalued crops that then arrived on the world market at uncompetitive prices while they succeeded in skimming off a sizeable proportion of whatever income was earned.

These problems are intimately tied in with the withdrawal of the state class from the country as such, leaving the people to fend for themselves and occasionally taxing whatever wealth is eventually produced. The agricultural sector is uninteresting for such a class, however, which is far more dependent on the huge wealth that flows from oil and aid. This is a clear expression of a process of liberation, not of the people from an oppressive regime. On the contrary it is a liberation of the state from the people.

RESPONSES TO THE CRISIS AND DEGENERATION

The year 1991 witnessed increasing pressure for democratization in the Congo. This was triggered by the ruling elite's attempt in June 1990 to carry out a reduction of public-sector spending by lowering the age of retirement from fifty-five to fifty. The national union, which was composed of a number of different branches, reacted vehemently and it did not take long until it declared its determination to leave the party.

Retirement often led to personal tragedy even at fifty-five. The pension was one-third of one's salary. As there were so few jobs available, the young and unemployed in Brazzaville tended to flock around the middle-aged men with salaries. Such a man often had to feed his grown-up children, both sons and daughters, his unmarried daughters' children, and, in addition, several nephews and nieces. The pressure was intense, but he was rewarded in terms of power and authority and by being the very epicenter of a social group. At fifty-five, this group simply dissolved. When he had no money they all tended to abandon him and this accounted for the anguished fear of retirement in the Congo.

When the national union was informed about the plans to further worsen the situation, it reacted, of course, with fury to what was regarded as a deadly threat. An impressive counterproposal demonstrated how much the country would save if the cut were instead made in the various benefits accorded to the political elite. Figures were compared and the result was shocking. The union sported a long history of political struggle and resistance. It was the driving force in the opposition against President Youlou, which culminated in the Three Glorious Days of August 13–14–15 in 1963 and the new socialist government under Massamba-Débat. The union was also active around 1970, much too active for the Marxist-Leninist regime, and at the beginning of the 1970s, it was brought under the party's dominance.

After this crucial event a conflict suddenly appeared in all the ruling organizations. Brazzaville was flooded with pamphlets in the fall of 1990. Sassou's assets abroad were discussed and compared with Congo's foreign debt, the Sassou clan's penetration into various sectors of the state, the Boeing accident, the murder of president Marien Ngouabi in 1977, and so on. The Sassou clique suddenly seemed quite isolated. The one-party system was accused of bringing the country to the edge of complete disaster, and a transition to a multiparty system was demanded.

Democratization was, in the imaginary millenarianism of the moment, thought of as the key to all economic problems. Parliamentary democracy, or a multiparty system, would free the economy from the state's paralyzing grip and prevent rulers from jealously combating all initiatives beyond the confines of political power. The most important aspect of this process was to be the transformation of the central African clan system to a "modern" society. The clan structure, its hierarchies of rulers and dependents, and its ideology of "collective ownership" prevailed, as we have seen, at both the national and the local level. It was entrenched in state enterprises as well as in cooperatives. This clan structure made possible the appropriation, or embezzlement, of funds by the rulers, not least because there were no mechanisms to prevent it. This was devastating for the country since it totally thwarted economic development, creating a class of super-rich politicians whose assets were reallocated to other parts of the world, bringing on, in its wake, a general apathy among ordinary people. The NIC countries proved to the world that it was possible for Third World countries to undertake large-scale economic development. This was devastating for the Dependency School's postulate of a structural impediment to development as the nature of the relationship between North and South. Hyden's contribution (1983) to the general discussion of the African crisis had been very important since it focused on internal factors. The main mistake of the social sciences, in the 1960s and 1970s, was the underestimation of internal structural and cultural factors. The African ruling elites were supposed to act in the same way as capitalist entrepreneurs during the industrialization of the West. But the Congo's rulers were interested in their own private economies and if they could obtain money by just snatching it, so much the better. Enterprises were primarily seen as a source of cash, not as a structure that is able to generate wealth and further economic development. This type of behavior seems, however, quite understandable from their own perspective and the common mistake made by development experts and researchers is perhaps not so much that cultural factors have been neglected but that they have had no clear understanding of the structural position of the African ruling elite within the world system. If the Dependency School underestimated the importance of understanding local elite strategies, it is important to note that these strategies show remarkable similarities, indicating that there is something quite systematic in the transformation described above. There is clear evidence that a phenomenon that might best be understood in global terms is at work in the emergence of cleptocratic regimes in the same period throughout large parts of the African continent. *Global* does not mean a global mechanism but a similar articulation of globally structured opportunities and local structures.

From the mid-1970s there were important changes in the configuration of power in many African states. The takeover by military regimes and the elaboration of state-class structures occurred in a period of increasing competition between the West and the Soviet Union. The actors involved were states, expanding multinationals, and potential heads of state in Africa. The alliances established and the huge monetary transfers incurred were crucial to the changes in state structure. This amounted to the institution of military dictatorships of various official colors but similar in organization. It is in this situation that certain states became Marxist-Leninist while others allied themselves with Western powers. France, in maintaining the continuation of its "empire," was able to hold a position in between the superpowers, often cooperating with both sides. The new state classes were directly linked to massive flows of income from oil companies and from governmental aid organizations. In the above, the elevation of the Congolese state elite to a position of financial autonomy can be understood as an aspect of this global connection. It is in this way that the transformation of the Congolese state can be comprehended as more than a mere expression of the strategies of its elites. The former can only realize themselves within a global context that is historically specific.

Democracy and Civil Wars

Following the introduction of "democracy," Congo-Brazzaville experienced two devastating civil wars in the 1990s. Brazzaville, the capital, has been the main arena for both wars—the first one between November 1993 and February 1994, and the second from June 5 to October 15, 1997. This war is now over, Sassou is back in power and the idea of "free and fair elections" postponed. A simple return to the kind of system that existed before is, however, hardly possible. In a field trip to Brazzaville and Pointe-Noire, the oil center, in February–March 1998, it could be surmised that Pointe-Noire was much less affected by the war for the time being but there was a growing fear among its population that militias and bandits would continue their looting there when they ran out of money and vehicles.

What are the mechanisms of these two civil wars? Why did "democracy" open the door to violent conflict and destruction? The second question has to do with effects and consequences and with the prospects for the immediate future. The two wars differ somewhat from each other even if the general problem is the same. The latest war was more blatantly political. It was a real war between two warlords, president Pascal Lissouba and ex-president Denis Sassou Nguesso, even if ethnic militias were involved on both sides with tanks, grenade throwers, and bombers. The first war appeared as more ethnic partly because civilians took a more active part in the atrocities and partly because the political leaders did not play a very visible role. They were even criticized for withdrawing from the scene of popular action.

The introduction of "democracy" was, it would seem, caused, or at least facilitated, by a weakening of the Congolese state at the very end of the 1980s, after the fall of the Berlin Wall and the collapse of the Soviet empire. Suddenly, and quite unexpectedly for many, the pyramidal, hierarchical political system displayed tendencies to disintegration. There was a call for freedom and democracy from within at the same time as global institutional forces pressured for this kind of change. An increasingly salient disintegration and feudalization of the Congolese "nation" has been set in motion—tendencies that can be found in other parts of the subregion as well. Today this process has led to the complete demolition of the central parts of Brazzaville, to a paralysis of all social life, to starvation and misery, to the production of hundreds of thousands of refugees, and to widespread banditry.

The Point of Departure: The Former One-Party System

The state class discussed above, in many ways a clan state, a clientelistic hierarchy, was the core of the Congolese political system (Pigasse 1997:136; *La semaine africaine* 18/9, 2/10-97 on "*la classe politique*"). The liberation of the state from the people (Ekholm Friedman 1994) consisted in an alliance between the political class and the control of external sources of wealth, multinationals, aid, and the control of the military. The political hierarchy was all inclusive and relatively stable until the major global shift entailed by the collapse of the Soviet regime. The decline in external government funding and capital investment, in part, the product of the "vampire state" (Frimpong-Ansah 1991) itself led to increasing misery. Structural adjustment programs were taken out everywhere on ordinary people while state elites continued to live in absolute luxury. In the Congo the only vital sector was oil, 60 percent dominated by the French former state company, ELF. It is clear that in this kind of a structure, ELF played a crucial structural role, the major source of the wealth of the ruling elite. It is also clear that any threat to this inflow of wealth, the very life force of the clientelistic hierarchy, was likely to lead to fragmentation and political chaos.

The political structure exploded in the form of demands for democratization, demands that came from competing factions within the former hierarchy. Leveling was the beginning of conflict.

Ethnicity, Class, and Power-Sharing

Both class and ethnicity are relevant aspects of Congolese society. Class and elite alliances seemed dominant in the 1980s while ethnicity was strongly activated in the 1990s. It was evident that the class segregation of the 1980s implied cooperation among "culturally diverse" members of the political class regardless of ethnic identity, and there were few visible links between the political class and the poor.

As an expression of clientelism, ethnicity has, however, always played a crucial role in political organization. A successful politician bases his power primarily on an entourage of loyal ethnic "brothers." But he also needs alliances with other powerful politicians, his homologues. When Sassou was president at the end of the 1980s, his political network included his own ethnic group, the *mbochi*, and a great number of immediate relatives, as well as power holders from other ethnic groups and provinces. He practiced power sharing, appointed his clients ministers and directors of state enterprises, and provided them, in this manner, with access to the "common good." They were loyal and he could count on them because they owed their own power and wealth to his position.

Outside the political realm people have payed little attention to ethnicity under normal circumstances. Congo's population is divided into a number of ethnic groups, and people are well aware of their own ethnic identity as well as that of others. As intermarriage has been extensively practiced for decades, there are, however, a great number of ethnically mixed households, and thereby, ethnically mixed individuals as well. This blurring of identities was conceived as a problem during the war of 1993–1994 but it did not prevent ethnic killing.[4] There are, in other words, two kinds of ethnicity, one as a strategy at the political level for gaining access to power and wealth and the other as a collective phenomenon, a way of categorizing and identifying the "we" and the "them" in situations of conflict.

In the literature it is usually claimed that the Congo inherited from the French a multiparty system that was not altered until 1963 when the so-called socialist revolution took place. But, in fact, power sharing appeared immediately at independence. As an aspect of clientelism, it represents a fundamental principle of political organization and has accordingly been practiced ever since. After winning the election, the first president, Fulbert Youlou, invited his main political opponent to join his government. Youlou's decision was wise and certainly prevented more serious ethnic confrontations around 1960. There was an outburst of ethnic violence as early as 1959, in the wake of independence, between the *north* and the *south*. Southerners were attacked and assaulted by northerners in Poto-Poto, the northern district of Brazzaville, and people fled in hundreds to the southern parts of the town. A group of angered southerners from Bacongo retaliated in Poto-Poto and with that the open hostilities came to an end.

The ethnopolitical landscape looks very much the same today as it did in the 1960s. The opposition between the north and the south has been preserved, and recently reactivated. Within these two "super tribes," certain ethnic groups are stronger and more influential than others. Youlou was a *Lari* from the south, from Kinkala in the central Pool province. Massamba-Débat, who replaced Youlou in 1963, was also from the Pool, but he was a *BaKongo* from Boko. In 1968 a coup d'état brought the northerners under Captain Marien Ngouabi (a *kouyou*) to the center stage of power. Ngouabi was murdered in 1977, replaced at first by Yhombi from the same ethnic group (*kouyou*), and then by northerner, Sassou Nguesso (a *mbochi*). These groups, as well as the *Bembe* (from Bouenza in the south), have provided the main actors in the ethnopolitical arena during the entire postcolonial period while other groups have played more peripheral roles. Even the men in power are to a large extent the same today as in the 1960s. Lissouba, for example, was prime minister from 1963 to 1966 in the Massamba-Débat government. When I first visited Congo in 1968, these men were young and enthusiastic. Now they are old, and certainly less enthusiastic, but they are still there. The explanation is, again, the mechanism of clientelism that implies that an old man per definition has a wider political network than a young man.

The Transformation of the Political Sphere

The one-party system was dissolved in 1990, leading to a transitional government in 1991 and then to elections in 1992, which brought the south, more populous, back to power. Sassou, from the sparsely populated north, lost the presidential election by a very large percentage. The elected president, Pascal Lissouba, was from Niari province in the south, and his victory was guaranteed by an alliance between the three southern provinces of Niari, Bouenza, and Lékoumou (*Nibolek*). Lissouba was, however, not the strong man himself. He was brought in by the *Bembe*, especially the group that was later called "la bande des quatre," (the gang of four), because he was useful. He was a "professor," a "scientist," and a man of the glorious 1960s.

The new multiparty system changed the political landscape. While the former one-party system was inclusive in the sense that regional power holders were included in a unified hierarchy encompassing the entire country, "democracy" spawned fragmentation and conflict among its political leaders. The political realm was , instead, populated by an increasing number of ambitious men, each with his own political party. In 1991 there were nearly a hundred parties or political associations After the first elections of 1992, their number was, for strategic reasons, considerably reduced. But, still, a typical political party is composed of *a man and his entourage*. It is identified with its leader and presented as such—for example Clémant Mierassa's PSDC, William Otta's PAPE, André Milongo's URD-Mwinda, General Mokoko's MRC, General Ngollo's RDR, and so on.

Political leaders tried, in the same way as before, to form alliances. But when the old strategy was adapted to new circumstances, it did not end in national unity but, instead, in deadly conflict. During the five years of "democracy" there were two political blocks, *La mouvance présidentielle* (the presidential movement) and the *Opposition*. The Opposition was composed of the two allied sub-blocks, URD and FDU. URD was, in its turn, a coalition of a number of political parties, MCDDI, RDPS, UP, UPDP, PSDC, UNAPAC, and PAPE. In the same manner FDU was a coalition of PCT and a number of related parties. The *Mouvance présidentielle* was constructed in the same way.

A characteristic feature of the new political situation was that new parties were easily created, coalitions and alliances easily rerouted, and the number of politicians considerably increased. Thus, the political sphere was not only highly fragmented and unstable due to intensified competition but also substantially inflated in numbers. Another novelty was that very little political organizing took place below, or outside, the political class itself. Even if the political leaders during the one-party era lived their separate lives in comfortable exclusiveness, a single party (PCT) still penetrated both country and population through its party cells and "mass organizations." With the introduction of "democracy," politics became, paradoxically, much more of an exclusive business for politicians.

Ethnic voting is a reflex of clientelism. The only way up the hierarchy is through ethnic channels. Even if the poor in the Niari province did not exactly expect Lissouba to reward them immediately for their votes, there were no alternatives. They could not vote for another group's politician because that would be completely illogical.

The increasing number of parties and politicians may explain why there was, paradoxically, even less money, if possible, available for the Congolese people after the introduction of "democracy." The *nibolek* government was, in fact, criticized for unblushing nepotism. The *Lari*, who lost the elections of 1992 and felt excluded and deprived of resources, complained about the *Nibolek* being even more corrupt and greedy than the PCT. *They have "eaten" in all the previous governments, but they have never before been the dominant group in a government. Now it is their turn to "eat," and they do it in grandiose manner.* People in general, not only politicians, felt excluded in a way that they were not used to. The money remained in the political realm while the everyday life of ordinary citizens became increasingly precarious.

Why did the *Nibolek* government content itself with the same old distribution of wealth within its own circles while investing almost nothing on improvements for the Congolese people? When I posed this question at the beginning of 1997, a middle-aged *Lari* working for a Swedish-Norwegian aid project answered,

> It is not easy. Those who have voted for the government block must be re-warded. And politicians need a lot of money. It is expensive to live well, to send one's children to schools and universities in the West, to have the best kind of health care, to travel. They need all the money for themselves. That is why there are ministries for youth, sport, education and family, with politicians, offices, salaries and other benefits—but no activities within these sectors aimed at ben-efitting Congo's population.

Lissouba used to defend himself in international media by referring to the Congo's enormous external debt, which was generated by the former president, and also by claiming that Sassou had used up the oil money in advances of credit. This sounded quite reasonable in 1993, not least because people strove to adopt a positive attitude, but less and less so by 1996–1997. A growing pop-ular discontent made the earlier Sassou period look increasingly appealing.

Increased Competition among Politicians, the Recruitment of Militias, and the Resulting Civil Wars

The introduction of democracy dramatically altered the situation of poor young men. The intensified struggle for power among politicians suddenly created a demand for young men as militia men. They were needed in a way that was not previously the case. A new form of ethnicity emerged, groups of power holders and their young soldiers. The main opponents in 1992, Lis-souba (*Nibolek*), Kolélas (*Lari*), and Sassou (*Mbochi*), recruited their own militias—Lissouba, the *Aubevillois*, after the village Aubeville where they were trained (apparently by Israelis); Kolélas, the *Ninjas;* and Sassou, the *Cobras.* In addition, a number of private bodyguards appeared. Every man of any politi-cal importance found it necessary to have his own bodyguard. All the various militias were, of course, recruited from the power holder's own ethnic group.

None of these militias were later disarmed. Instead new groups have con-stantly been added. The *Zoulous* (*Bembe*) appeared on the scene in 1993–1994 fighting their own war against *Lari* and the *ninjas*. Lissouba later recruited the *Cocoyes* before the second war and the *Mambas* (from Niari) during the war. The "sharks" appeared in Pointe-Noire and a certain minister, Binkinkita, cre-ated his *Condors.*

In the war of 1993–1994 ethnic cleansing took place in various parts of the country. The southern parts of Brazzaville, *Bacongo* and *Makelekele*, were eth-nically cleansed of their *Nibolek* inhabitants. *Lari* were attacked and driven from the *Nibolek* provinces as well as from certain parts of the north. *Nibolek* took over the *centre-ville* of Brazzaville and seized control of the area north of the railway, *Mutabala,* which was cleansed of its *Lari* inhabitants. The three militia groups confronted each other as well as civilians, and civilians joined forces with militias in attacks on enemies. As the army was itself divided along ethnic lines, it was incapable of preventing this spiral of violence.

The minister of foreign affairs declared in an interview at the end of 1992 (*Jeune Afrique*, 2-8/4) that there was no tribalism in the Congo, "*il n'y a pas de tribalisme au Congo.*" A year later, ethnic war broke out. We are, as noted by Horowitz in his work on ethnic conflict, often surprised by the emergence of ethnic conflict due to its episodic character. It appears, suddenly, as from nowhere, "it comes and goes, suddenly shattering periods of apparent tranquility," a fact that also accounts for our defective understanding of the phenomenon (1995:13). Under normal circumstances the Congolese desire to live peacefully with one another, as we all do. Why, then, in the 1990s have they occasionally been so intent on killing each other for ethnic reasons? There are several explanations, as I see it. Clientelism in itself leads to a situation in which people easily feel excluded for ethnic reasons because they really *are* excluded for ethnic reasons. They react ethnically because they are ethnically affected. The first war had to do with the struggle for power and wealth, and ultimately for survival, a struggle between the *Nibolek* and the *Lari.* When the *Nibolek* won the elections, they gained access to the state and its wealth, and, in true democratic fashion, they kept it for themselves.

Another aspect of the phenomenon is that fantasies and rumors play an important role in the production of ethnic hatred. Rumors may be false or exaggerated, but they cannot be eliminated from reality as such, as mere fantasies. Rumors must be taken seriously as they provide a source of elaboration and an explanation of the intensity of hatred and aggression toward one another. They constitute a powerful driving force in destructive and cruel activities. During fieldwork immediately following the war I collected material on both sides that revealed that many of the atrocities in real life first appeared as fantasies concerning the acts of their enemies—as if they had first to imagine the script of a play in which they later performed as actors. One group fantasized about the other group having attacked, raped, and massacred its own people, and driven by this fantasy, inspired and angered by it, it attacked, raped, and massacred the others.

But the condition within which fantasies flourish are established by the state of conflict itself. When political leaders initiated an internal war, it became ethnic. When ethnic militias are turned against each other and against enemy civilians, a war situation is created that rapidly produces ethnic hatred.

A *Lari* had no reason to hate a *Bembe* before the war. But when his fellow *Laris*, even his close relatives, were killed by *Bembe*, he was quickly filled by hatred and feelings of revenge toward the entire category. The enemy constituted a lethal threat and had to be eliminated in order to ensure survival. And in this context the enemy is defined ethnically, by immediate association; war transforms the whole category, not just particular *Bembe* individuals, into an enemy. The conflict took on a categorical dynamic of its own reproduced by the deadly reciprocity of symmetrical schismogenesis.

After the war of 1993–1994, life never returned to normal. Armed young men have been a serious problem ever since. In 1996 there were constant attacks by bandits on civilians who were robbed and sometimes killed. These attacks included west African traders (see *La semaine africaine* 11/4 96) who have been selling their merchandise in Brazzaville for decades. They have money and are easy targets, as they are unprotected. The Lebanese, much more openly criticized (e.g., *La rue meurt* 12-18/12-96, on the "Lebanization" of the Congolese economy) for their profitable collaboration with the political class, have been much less affected due to their more effective ability to protect themselves.

An atmosphere of insecurity prevailed at the beginning of 1997. Locally people tried to solve the problem of banditry by immediately executing captured bandits. And so did the police. They took to their cars, killed a couple of "bandits," and presented the corpses proudly on TV the following day. Popular opinion was divided. Some found it reassuring that bandits were eliminated while others were concerned about the obvious arbitrariness of such actions. A human rights organization (OCDH) created a stir in this period by revealing compromising information about the conditions in the Brazzaville prison and the situation for those unfortunate foreigners who ended up in the Congo as refugees. They also criticized the police for killing presumed bandits on the spot and for torturing those who were taken in spite of the fact that torture is forbidden by law in Congo. The police answered angrily that they, after all, protected law-abiding citizens against criminals, and as for torture, how would it otherwise be possible to make people confess?

When Sassou returned to Brazzaville after eighteen months in Paris he was received with enthusiasm by his followers at Maya-Maya airport. It was obvious that he came back in order to join the political arena again. But did he really have a chance? No, said the *Nibolek*. He belonged to the past and could never win an election since the north was simply too sparsely populated to carry his election.

There are two very different versions of the civil war in 1997, which complicates the understanding of what really happened and why it happened. We know that Lissouba (or his side) attacked Sassou's headquarters in *Mpila* in northern Brazzaville on June 5. According to the Lissouba version the attack just aimed at disarming Sassou. His militia and military equipment were conceived of as a general threat, especially so, a month and a half before the upcoming presidential election, which was scheduled for July 27. The Sassou version claims that Lissouba wanted to kill Sassou because he knew that Sassou would win the election. In this version a poll was carried out by a French institute, not only one but three different polls, all of them designating Sassou as the victor, by two-thirds of the vote. So, did Lissouba attack Sassou because he feared him militarily or because he knew that Sassou had enough popular support to win the presidential election?

The Sassou version is not a very likely one. Sassou had his old supporters and he had certainly gotten some new ones, but people tend to vote ethnically in the Congo, a fact that was definitely to his disadvantage. The north was, furthermore, divided between himself and Yhombi. He probably knew that he would lose when it came to an election (cf. *Jeune Afrique* Aug.). The story of the poll, or the three polls, is probably devoid of any real substance. Stories of this type have always been very common in the Congo. It is claimed that the poll was found hidden in a drawer in the bedroom of Lissouba's mistress Munari after she fled the country. There they also found counterfeit bank notes and gas masks (!). In 1996, a similar story was told about General Mokoko. When the military entered his house, after he fled the country, they found (according to rumor) counterfeit bank notes, drugs, pornographic videos, weapons, and compromising documents, all underlining the message that he was up to serious misbehavior.

But what was Lissouba doing? He evidently misjudged the situation. Why did he underestimate Sassou's military strength? There were rumors in Brazzaville during the spring suggesting that Sassou was planning a military coup d'état. And yet the fierce resistence and counterattacks from the Sassou side evidently came as a surprise for the Lissouba. The most plausible explanation, provided by a number of my informants, including a member of his last government, is that Lissouba was out of touch with Congolese reality. He had lived abroad for years. He had no extensive political network like Sassou, and he was not really accustomed to the rules of the political game. Sassou was too cunning a political actor for old Lissouba—who prepared for an election when, in reality, a very different battle was on its way. After the final defeat a number of politicians left the country.

What we do know is that Lissouba attacked the enemy, including civilians in the northern parts of the capital, from the air, using combat helicopters imported from the Ukraine. Sassou claims not to have attacked from the air but there are quantities of statements alluding to Migs over the southern parts of

Brazzaville. Tanks and grenade throwers, the so-called Stalin organs, were utilized with alacrity by both sides. Wrecked tanks could still be observed in various parts of Brazzaville in February. The material effects of the war were massive. Official buildings, stores, and hotels in *centre-ville* and Mpila were looted
to the last rag, deserted, burned, with shell holes and smashed windows, open
to the sky and the heavy rains, some of them randomly destroyed by grenades
and others blown up on purpose, in acts of revenge. What we know for sure,
then, is that Brazzaville is in ruins.

The International and Subregional Perspective

What has happened in the Congo must of course be seen within a wider
framework. First, this war could not have taken place without outside intervention. Military equipment was bought through various channels and from
various countries. ELF helped Lissouba finance his part of the war material,
and it is claimed that it did the same for Sassou. For ELF it must have been important to be on good terms with the president, no matter who he might be
or become. Mercenaries were brought/bought in on both sides.

In his biased, pro-Sassou description of the course of events, Pigasse enu-
merates a number of factors in Sassou's favor, among them the support he obtained from other African heads of state. Here he mentions Mandela (South
Africa), dos Santos (Angola), and Bongo (of Gabon, Sassou's father-in-law)
and adds that Sassou, of course, also could count on his old friend Jacques
Chirac (1997:137–38).

From adopting a neutral attitude at the beginning of the war, France under
Chirac clearly took sides with Sassou in early September when he refused to
receive Lissouba on the latter's visit to Paris. This decision was criticized in the
French press (*Le Canard Enchaîné*, September 1997) with the ironic argument
that it could damage ELF if Lissouba survived politically. But Chirac obviously
understood, at this time, that Sassou would win the war.

France is to a large extent responsible for the present catastrophe, and this
responsibility is not of recent date. It is part of its general relationship to its
former African colonies subsequent to independence. The fact that France has
remained a "postcolonial" colonial power has, for some reason, been accepted
by the rest of the world. The strategies of the Congolese political class with respect to the country's oil resources, which left the "civil sector" completely
destitute, could not have been developed without intimate, and even secret,
cooperation with France and ELF. The French are also directly blamed for the
war in Congo, and a number of Frenchmen have been killed.

What definitively decided the war in Sassou's favor was the support he received from MPLA and dos Santos in Angola. On October 11, Angolan troops

intervened in Pointe-Noire from the Cabinda enclave (people in Pointe-Noire find this quite strange and suspect ELF of assistance in the transportation of Angolan soldiers and tanks). Lissouba had only the Angolan opposition, UNITA, on his side and this was evidently not sufficient.

Regional Destabilization and the Global Arena

What has happened in Congo-Brazzaville is part of a general destabilization process in central Africa. A great deal of attention has recently been paid to the increasing ethnic conflicts in the Great Lakes area and how these conflicts tend to spread to other parts of the subregion as the result of the formation of alliances on both sides. Uganda under Museveni evidently played a crucial role both in the return of the Tutsis in Rwanda and in the victory by Laurent Kabila in the Democratic Republic of Congo (see *New African* 1997; *Africa international* 1998). This new political bloc, or whatever we may call it, is, however, also marked by ethnic conflicts and tendencies to disintegration. The situation in the eastern parts of former Zaire is chaotic and Uganda itself has, in spite of its relative economic success, problems with rebel movements in both the north, northwest, and southwest (see the *Economist* 24-30/1-98).

Congo-Brazzaville was in various ways affected by these tendencies to destabilization as early as the early 1990s. More recently there have been internal tendencies to disintegration in the form of ethnic conflict in various provinces. In Sangha (north) there is a "liberation front" aiming at the protection of indigenous rights and the expulsion of "foreigners." There have been intrusions in the north by people from the Central African Republic, some of them fleeing from chaos and marauding soldiers/bandits (*La rue meurt* Nov. 1996) and some searching for diamonds or hunting elephants for ivory (*La semaine africaine* 12/9-96). Refugees have also entered the Congo from Cabinda where the liberation front, FLEC, opposes Angolan domination. At the beginning of January 1997, Angolan troops encroached on Congolese territory in their search for rebels (*La semaine africaine* 23/1-97).

THE PRESENT SITUATION AND PROSPECTS FOR THE FUTURE

Brazzaville is today more divided than ever, and the main conflict is again between the north and the south. In the war of 1993–1994, the quarters Moungali, Ouenze, and the Plateau de 15 ans, in the northern part of the capital, were not affected in same way as Bacongo and Makelekele where ethnic cleansing was rampant. The former areas maintained their mixed population and were even positively described by their residents as more "cosmopolitan" since no particular group could claim the land as its patrimony. In the latest war the roles were reversed. Bacongo and Makelekele were less involved in the mutual destruction while the areas in the north were severely affected by both material destruction and violent ethnic conflict. The cobras have killed and driven away *Nibolek* residents from these parts of the town and, today, it is impossible for a *Bembe* to enter this territory.

Brazzaville in 1998 was a city in total paralysis. No normal activities could be carried out. When people went to work they did so in order not to risk losing their salaries, not because there was any "real" work. There were few people circulating in the central parts of the capital. After 2 P.M. the center was almost empty. What was left, and in great numbers, were soldiers, young Congolese soldiers in every corner, and groups of Angolan soldiers driving by in military vehicles. There were still substantial numbers of Angolan troops in various parts of the south—in Brazzaville and Pointe-Noire, and in a couple of other areas where resistence was expected to flare up. The military situation was clearly not under control. Opposing militias were not easily found or disarmed.

The only actors left in the Congo were politicians and armed young men plus their women. For the rest of the Congo's population life had turned into a nightmare. They were refugees in their own country, they were starving, diseased, and dying in great numbers.

Disintegration was in evidence in all domains of the society—in *the political arena* between rival networks of politicians (who were perfectly capable of employing heavy weapons against their own civilians), in *the ethnic domain*, and in the most *local relations*, between neighbors and relatives. What was at stake here was a general destruction of the social fabric, one that seemed to be self-amplifying at the moment.

The political conflicts may have been stabilized with Sassou's return to power but this is not certain by any means. The fact that Sassou is again the president of the Congo has to do with his ability to build and maintain political networks. In this respect he is certainly, for the time being, the only man who has the potential to halt the present catastrophe. In this endeavor he needs help and support from the "international community." He is surrounded by men who eagerly await rewards for their loyalty, and this locks him into the same logic that has led to the current situation. And among those actors are powerful international conglomerates such as ELF that have provided the fuel, if not the oil, for both the vampire state and its contemporary fragments.

The ethnic conflicts are intense at the moment, especially between the north and the south. There is also a serious conflict in the north between *Mbochi* and *Kouyou*, following Sassou's massacre of his rival Yhombi's village and immediate relatives just before embarking on his war of "unification." He even had Yhombi's house blown up. This structure that groups ethnic conflicts into north and south and then into increasingly smaller subgroups embodies a potential dynamic of fragmentation, one that has been ignited by the demise of a state-class-clan system but that has also led to its partial resurrection. The massive self-destruction is a product of a crisis in the linkage of the Congo state to the world system, one that is common to the entire region. It is a crisis that expresses the articulation of transformations of the global system, that have led to the fragmentation of a specific hierarchical order in which external wealth reproduced a state class and a vast clientelistic structure to an explosive process of disintegration and internal war, the latter also fueled by external sources. And at the very bottom of this state of war are the young men who have been drugged but also armed by this vicious process, producing yet a new wave of disorder.

Every Congolese, except the very well-protected, is threatened in life and property by the young men with guns, be they ordinary bandits, militiamen, police, or members of the army. This phenomenon is, in itself, a result of a process of disintegration affecting all forms of social networks at the local level. There is very little left of authority structures as well as of trust and social solidarity.

The political leaders armed their militias for their own particular political interests. But they have not considered whether they can retrieve the weapons after the tasks are carried out. If the leaders were unified, perhaps they could put an end to this new epidemic, but given their total conflictual situation, it may be quite difficult for them regain effective control. Today's relationship between super-wealthy oil rentiers and destitute young males without a future has become a fragile new (dis)order. The latter are armed and disrespectful, and they have experienced the power that grows out of the barrel of a gun. And they, just as the elites, are also well aware of their alternatives!

NOTES

1. Marxism-Leninism was all of a sudden proclaimed by the military regime in the beginning of 1970 and it was, just as suddenly, abolished on July 4, 1990, by the Comité Central.

2. CFA (Communauté Financière Africaine). African francs were set at one-fiftieth of a French franc. Recently, they have been devalued to one-hundredth.

3. Term used to describe a state class that indiscriminately steals the wealth of the country.

4. Note here that this ethnic miscegenation is not the product of globalization as in Appadurai (1998). Intermarriage among groups that enter into conflict reflects

issues of loyalty/treachery more than issues of purity. The latter occurs in central Africa as a by-product of the former and is not a primary issue.

REFERENCES

Africa international. 1998. December/January, 310.

Amin, S., and C. Coquery-Vidrovitch, C. 1969. *Histoire économique du Congo 1880–1968.* Paris: Editions Antropos.

Appadurai, A. 1988. "Deal Certainty: Ethnic Violence within Era of Globalisation." *Public Culture* 10, no. 2:225–47.

Atipo, D. 1985. "La Politique du développement de l'élevage au Congo." In *Politiques alimentaires et structures sociales en Afrique Noire.* Edited by Frelin Haubert and Nguyen Trong Nam Tran. Paris: Harmattan.

Bertrand, H. 1975. *Le Congo: Formation sociale et mode de développement économique.* Paris: Maspéro.

Cornevin, R. 1986. "History of French Equatorial Africa until Independence." In *Africa South of the Sahara.* 16th ed. London: Europe Publications.

Desjeux, D. 1987. *Stratégies paysannes en Afrique Noire: Le Congo, essai sur la gestion de l'incertitude.* Paris: Harmattan.

Economist. 1998. 24-30/1.

Ekholm Friedman, K. 1990a. "Den politiska eliten struntar I folket." *SIDA-rapport* 3: 28–29.

———. 1990b. "Obstacles to Rural Development in Africa: The Congolese case." *Research Report 18. Programme for Social Movements and Strategies in Third World Development,* Department of Sociology, University of Lund, Sweden.

———. 1991. *Catastrophe and Creation: The Transformation of an African Culture.* London: Harwood Academic.

———. 1994. *Den magiska världsbilden: om statens frigörelse från folket I folkrepubliken Kongo.* Stockholm: Carlssons.

Frimpong-Ansah, J. H. 1991. *The Vampire Sate in Africa: The Political Economy of Decline in Ghana.* London: James Currey.

Goma-Foutou, C. 1985. "La Formation socio-économique de la République Populaire du Congo." *La Revue des Sciences Sociales* 3:3–20.

Guichaoua, A. 1989. *Destins paysans et politiques agraires en Afrique Centrale: La Liquidation du "monde paysan" congolais.* Paris: Harmattan.

Horowitz, D. 1995. *Ethnic Groups in Conflict.* Cambridge, Mass.: Harvard University Press.

Hyden, G. 1983. *No Shortcuts to Progress: African Development Management in Perspective.* London: Heinemann.

Jackson, R. H., and C. P. Rosberg. 1982. *Personal Rule in Black Africa: Prince, Autocrat, Prophet, Tyrant.* Berkeley: University of California Press.

Jeune Afrique. 1992. 4/8.

La Semaine Africaine. 1996. 11/4.

La rue meurt. 1996. 12-18/12.

Le Canard Enchaîné. 1997. 10/9.

Markowitz, I. L. 1977. *Power and Class in Africa.* Englewood Cliffs, N.J.: Prentice Hall.

————, ed. 1987. *Studies in Power and Class in Africa.* New York: Oxford University Press.

Mazrui, A. A. 1988. "Is Africa Decaying? The View from Uganda" In *Uganda Now: Between Decay and Development.* Edited by H. B. Hansen and M. Twaddle. London: James Currey.

Mouamba, C. 1985. "La Stratégie de développement auto-centré et auto-dynamique et la transition au socialisme." *La Revue des Sciences Sociales* 1:13–29.

New African. 1997. September.

Pigasse, J. P. 1997. *Congo chronique d'une guerre annoncée.* Paris: Edition-diffusion Anrf-Adiao.

Rapport annuel d'activités du PDR. 1987. Ministère du développement rural, direction de l'action coopérative, Kinkala.

Sandbrook, R. 1985. *The Politics of Africa's Economic Stagnation.* Cambridge, U.K.: Cambridge University Press.

Vennetier, P. 1963. "La Société industrielle et agricole du Niari: SIAN (Congo-Brazzaville)." *Les Cahiers d'Outre-Mer* 16.

———. 1965. "Au Congo-Brazzaville: La S.I.A.N. en 1964." *Les Cahiers d'Outre-Mer* 18.

Verschave, Francois-Xavier. 2000. *Noir Silence.* Paris: Les Arènes.

Epilogue 2002: Global Whacks and the Hazards of Hegemony

Jonathan Friedman

This volume is appearing at a time following by less than a year the writing of these chapters when global violence has taken a turn for the worse, the growth of global terrorism directed at the worlds's superpower, and the increase of violence in the Middle East and in south Asia have fed into and expressed the recent transformations of the global arena. The hostile attacks against the World Trade Center and the Pentagon shocked the nation and provoked a proliferation of reactions. Some have stressed that the world will never be the same after September 11. This is, of course, the view from within the United States, and to a lesser and rapidly declining extent in Europe. Intellectuals have rushed to assert the guilt of U.S. arrogance as the cause of these attacks by Islamic extremists. After all the United States ought to have acted the part of the *good* imperial power and it should expect the rage that has now been thrust upon it from within truly global terrorist networks with an apparently clear mission. This moralizing interpretation to the surprise attack is what we have come to expect in recent years, whether it be moral outrage against the others or demands for Western guilt. From the point of view of this collection, there is no cause for surprise, even if the acts themselves were not predicted. The assaults are part of what might be described as the hazards of hegemony, to be expected in the historical cycle of any imperial order. In one view we are undergoing a transition from a geographical system of central and peripheral zones to a system of "global cities" in which the one-time relations are compressed into urban formations where global networks of circulation and alliance become increasingly salient. Some of us might argue that this is all an expression of declining or weakening hegemony, whether of the United States in particular or of state-led regions in general, and that attempts to transform that hegemony into empire are themselves signs of weakness. Others might see the apparent political success that the current situation has enabled, that is, the emergent establishment of a global regime of political and military controls to maintain a centralizing global economy. No matter what the argument there is a commonality of focus here, one in which the configuration of global processes and political forces determine the nature of the arena within which globalization, networks of crime, commerce, and terror take shape. The contradictory dynamic of centralization and fragmentation is clearly in evidence in the post–World Trade Center political arena. The Bush administration seeks unity under Washington but the allies, excluding Britain, resist, shying away from U.S.–centered imperial politics. And throughout the world, both in political centers and peripheries, there is a seething activity of globalized networks of potential violence, not merely of terrorists, of course, but of the major trades in arms, drugs, and people, which partially feed into those political centers and peripheries. This is the world that emerges in many of the contributions to this book, a world that harbors a lethal explosiveness of its own, a far cry from the image of a world ecumene, a unified hybrid humanity looming just beyond the horizon of the nation–state system. On the contrary the current global synergy seems aimed at increasing divergence and proliferating conflict. It is surely rich in events, encounters, and entanglements and there is clearly *some* kind of future in store for us. Fukuyama's "end of history" does not seem to have lasted very long, if it ever existed at all. Indeed, history, even in his own terms, appears to be off to a flying start. And, at the same time, the announcement of a millennial globalized world is fast becoming just another *Paradise Lost.*

This may sound unbearably pessimistic to many intellectuals who have tried so very hard to imagine a brilliant future, one that in Hegelian fashion will arise as the magic effect of history itself or of some invisible hand. But it might be suggested that this position is a product of a certain prevalent and quite comfortable passivity. By confronting the nasty realities of the world we might instead discover how we might best struggle to transform the conditions that continue to generate those realities.

Index

About the Contributors

Georges Fouron is associate professor of Africana studies and of the Social Sciences Interdisciplinary Program at the State University of New York, Stony Brook. He does research in bilingual education, immigration, transnationalism, and Haiti. He is the coauthor with Nina Glick Schiller of *Georges Woke Up Laughing: Long-Distance Nationalism and the Search for Home* (2001).

Jonathan Friedman is Directeur d'études, École des hautes études en sciences sociales, Paris, and Professor of social anthropology, University of Lund, Sweden. He is the author of *Cultural Identity and Global Process* (1994), *System, Structure, and Contradiction: The Evolution of "Asiatic" Social Formations* (1998), and coeditor with Robert A. Denemark et al. of *World System History: The Social Science of Long-Term Change* (2000).

Kajsa Ekholm Friedman is professor of social anthropology at the University of Lund, Sweden. She is the author of *Catastrophe and Creation: The Transformation of an African Culture* (1992) and coauthor with Jonathan Friedman of the forthcoming *Global Anthropology* (2003).

Simone Ghezzi received a BA in political science from Università degli Studi of Milan with a thesis on the informal economy. He studied anthropology at the University of Toronto where he was a Connaught Scholarship fellow from 1996 to 2000 and received an MA in 1996 and a Ph.D in 2001 in social/cultural anthropology. He has carried out extensive fieldwork on workshops and entre-preneur-workers in Lombardy, northern Italy. He currently researches at the Dipartimento di Sociologia e Ricerca Sociale, Università di Milano-Bicocca.

Bruce Kapferer is visiting professor at the Institutt for socialantropologi at the University of Bergen, Norway and professor of anthropology at the University College London. He is coeditor with Josep R. Llobera et al. of *The Anthropology of Europe: Identity and Boundaries in Conflict* (1994) and author of *Legends of People, Myths of State: Violence, Intolerance and Political Culture in Sri Lanka and Australia* (1998) and *The Feast of the Sorcerer: Practices of Consciousness and Power* (1997).

Enzo Mingione is professor of sociology at the University of Milano-Bicocca and has previously taught at the Universities of Messina and Padua. He is among the founding editors of the *International Journal of Urban and Regional Research* and has been constantly involved with international and Italian scientific journals and research groups, as well as a consultant for the European Commission. His main fields of interest are poverty, social exclusion, informal sector, unemployment, and economic and urban sociology. He has most recently published *Fragmented Societies* (1991) and *Urban Poverty and the Underclass* (1996).

Donald M. Nonini is associate professor of anthropology at the University of North Carolina at Chapel Hill. He is the author of *British Colonial Rule and the Resistance of the Malay Peasantry, 1900–1957,* coauthor with Dorothy Holland et al. of *If This is Democracy,* and coeditor with Aihwa Ong of *Ungrounded Empires.* He is completing a book on globalization and the Chinese diaspora in Southeast Asia (*Getting through Life*) and has written numerous articles on the cultural politics and political economy of ethnicity and race in Southeast Asia and the United States.

Steve Reyna is professor of anthropology at the University of New Hampshire, Durham and visiting senior research professor at the Max Planck Institute for Social Anthropology, Germany. He is founding editor of *Anthropological Theory* and has published on topics including string-being theory, power, warfare, cultural neurohermeneutics, and Africa. His writings include *Wars without End* (1990) and *Connections: Brain, Mind and Culture in a Social Anthropology* (2002).

Steven Sampson is professor of social anthropology at the University of Lund, Sweden. He is an anthropological specialist on Eastern Europe. He is the author of *Bureaucracy and Corruption As Anthropological Problems.*

Saskia Sassen is Ralph Lewis Professor of Sociology at the University of Chicago and Centennial Visiting Professor, London School of Economics. Her most recent books are *Guests and Aliens* (1999) and *Globalization and Its Discontents* (1998). Her books have been translated into ten languages. *The Global City* and *Cities in a World Economy* have been reissued in fully updated year 2000 editions.

Nina Glick Schiller is associate professor of anthropology at the University of New Hampshire. She is coeditor with Cristina Blanc-Szanton and Linda Green Basch of *Nations Unbound: Transnational Projects, Postcolonial Predicaments, and Deterritorialized Nation-States* (1994) and *Towards a Transnational Perspective on Migration: Race, Class, Ethnicity, and Nationalism Reconsidered* (1998) and coauthor with Georges Fouron of *Georges Woke Up Laughing: Long-Distance Nationalism and the Search for Home* (2001).

Terence Turner is professor of anthropology at Cornell University, New York. He engages in research on anthropological theory, political anthropology, and human rights, and has worked among the Kayapo and Yanomami of Brazil. He is coeditor with Viviane Baeke et al. of *Kaiapo: Amazonia* (1993).

Michel Wieviorka is a professor at the Ecole des hautes études en sciences sociales in Paris, and director of the Centre d'analyse et d'intervention sociologiques (CADIS). His main books in English include *The Making of Terrorism* (1993), *The Arena of Racism* (1995), and with Alain Touraine and Francois Dubet, *The Working-Class Movement* (1987).

Unni Wikan is professor of anthropology at the University of Oslo, Norway, and has done fieldwork in Egypt, Oman, Yemen, Indonesia, Bhutan, and Norway. She is the author of *Tomorrow, God Willing: Self-Made Destinies in Cairo* (1996) and *Generous Betrayal: Politics of Culture in the New Europe* (2002).

DATE DUE

Pdcj # 321982	
der 4/16/08	